AF605844

Plantation Knowledge

Plantation Knowledge

Agricultural Colonization, Exploitation, and Exchange Since 1500

Edited by

NICHOLAS B. MILLER and
ULRIKE LINDNER

Cover credit: Wikimedia, *Un Champ de canne à sucre dans la vallée du Dallol Bosso*, 21 July 2021.

Published by State University of New York Press, Albany

Printed in the United States of America

A version of this book is made freely available in an open access edition with the support of the European Union, through a project funded by Marie Skłodowska-Curie Actions under the European Union's Horizon 2020 research and innovation programme grant agreement No. 889078.

EU GPSR Authorized Representative:
Logos Europe, 9 rue Nicolas Poussin, 17000, La Rochelle, France
contact@logoseurope.eu

For information, contact State University of New York Press, Albany, NY
www.sunypress.edu

Library of Congress Cataloging-in-Publication Data

Names: Miller, Nicholas B., editor | Lindner, Ulrike, editor
Title: Plantation knowledge: Agricultural colonization, exploitation, and exchange since 1500 / Nicholas B. Miller and Ulrike Lindner, editors.
Description: Albany : State University of New York Press, [2025] | Includes bibliographical references and index.
Identifiers: ISBN 9798855803785 (hardcover : alk. paper) | ISBN 9798855803808 (ebook)
Further information is available at the Library of Congress.

Contents

List of Illustrations ix

Acknowledgments xi

Introduction: Plantation Knowledge: Concept, History, and Research 1
Nicholas B. Miller and Ulrike Lindner

Part I: Epistemology

Chapter 1
Between Irish Plantation and the Plantation Complex: The Down Survey (1654–1658), Projecting, and the Origins of Political Arithmetic 29
Ted McCormick

Chapter 2
The *Badianus Herbal* and Forced Indigenous Labor: Art, Land, and Nahua Knowledge in Sixteenth-Century Central Mexico 57
Jennifer R. Saracino

Part II: Boundaries

Chapter 3
Sugar and Sovereignty in Hawaiʻi: John Adams Kuakini Cummins and Waimānalo Plantation, 1878–1895 87
Nicholas B. Miller

Chapter 4
Experimental Paternalism: An Owenite Plantation in Mississippi, 1820–1870 121
Claudia Roesch

Part III: Experiments

Chapter 5
Revisiting the Charduar Plantation: Local Connections, Imperial Portfolios, and the Global Pathways of Assam Rubber 145
Moritz von Brescius

Chapter 6
Sugar in Province Wellesley: Converging Streams of Plantation Knowledge in Nineteenth-Century Malaya 183
Christina Skott

Part IV: Institutionalization

Chapter 7
Cocoa and Coercion: Connected Histories of São Tomé and the Belgian Congo 217
Marta Macedo

Chapter 8
Copra and Conquest: Penal Colonies and Botanical Knowledge in the American Colonial Philippines 245
Theresa Ventura

Part V: Reform

Chapter 9
Cane Farmers Versus Sugar Factories in Post-Emancipation Era Cuba and Brazil 275
Gillian McGillivray

Chapter 10
Managing Regulation: Changes of Policy and Continuities of Practice on Indian Tea Plantations, 1901–1931 303
Rebekah McCallum

List of Contributors 329

Index 333

List of Illustrations

Figure I.1	Map of principal case studies	12
Figure 2.1	Libellus de Medicinalibus Indorum Herbis (*Badianus Herbal*)	64
Figure 2.2	Central Mexican stone symbol behind roots	73
Figure 2.3	Plants growing in swamp or pond	74
Figure 2.4	Plant grows in rocky environment	74
Figure 3.1	Royal party at Waimanalo	88
Figure 3.2	Samuel Parker, Princess Ruth Keʻelikōlani, John Adams Kuakini Cummins, 1877	91
Figure 3.3	Waimanalo Sugar Mill	97
Figure 3.4	Representative committee of delegates of the Hawaiian people to present a memorial to Hon. James H. Blount	106
Figure 5.1	Ficus elastica trees and their myriad root and stem systems	152
Figure 5.2	Selection of Ficus elastica pests	159
Figure 5.3	Charduar Caoutchouc Plantation	163
Figure 7.1	Map of agricultural concessions in the Mayombe	232
Figure 7.2	Cocoa drying trays at the Urselia plantation, Mayombe	234

Figure 7.3	Cocoa drying trays at the Vista Alegre plantation, São Tomé	234
Figure 7.4	The plantation of Auguste Jacques in Makaïa-Vuabi	235
Figure 8.1	Map of Iwahig Prison and Penal Farm, Puerto Princessa, Palawan	246
Figure 8.2	San Miguel Estate	255
Figure 8.3	San Miguel Estate, typical coconut tree	257
Figure 8.4	Before image of the San Miguel Estate	259
Figure 8.5	After image of the San Miguel Estate	260
Figure 8.6	Thong of twisted hemp used by climbers in ascending coconut trees	261
Figure 8.7	Climbing a coconut tree by means of notches in the bark preparatory to cutting down the nuts	261
Figure 9.1	Cuba's 198 sugar mills in 1917	281
Figure 9.2a–c	Selected images, Album de vistas del gran central Chaparra, 1910	284
Figure 9.3	Map of Brazil showing the three major sugar zones	288

Acknowledgments

In the first instance, the editors of this volume would like to thank all participants at an international workshop of the same name held from June 15–17, 2022, at the University of Cologne. Organized with the university's Global South Studies Center, speakers, chairs, and audience members came from across the world, including many countries comprising the contemporary Global South (Cameroon, Costa Rica, Namibia, and Kenya) and shared ideas and critical interventions. During riveting keynotes by Wendy Wolford and Richard B. Allen, perspectives on the role of knowledge at plantations past and present were exchanged across geographies, disciplines, and specialties, informing the papers discussed, revised, and now assembled for this volume. Given the remarkable vitality of this discussion, which included interventions from Marcel van der Linden, all of the chapters that follow originated at this workshop. While all contributing authors are based at institutions in North America and Europe, most draw upon extensive research stays or residences in countries of the Global South. It is earnestly hoped that Open Access publication of this volume will generate new ideas and collaborations across the world, particularly the Global South.

The editors express their deep thanks to Michael Rinella and James Peltz at SUNY Press for their sustained enthusiasm for the volume and to the two anonymous peer reviewers for their constructive and insightful feedback. Editorial assistance was provided by Antonia Schweim and Mattison Culver. Financial resources for editing this volume were graciously provided by the European Union, the University of Cologne, and the School of Liberal Arts and Sciences, Flagler College. This book is made freely available in an Open Access edition with the support of the European Union, through a project funded by Marie Skłodowska-Curie Actions under the European Union's Horizon 2020 research and innovation program grant agreement No. 889078, MIGKNOW.

Introduction

Plantation Knowledge: Concept, History, and Research

Nicholas B. Miller and Ulrike Lindner

Few institutions feature as prominently in contemporary notions of colonialism, exploitation, and racism as the modern plantation. The former slave-based and racialized plantations of the Atlantic world loom large in the public imagination, namely those of the British Caribbean and the US South from the seventeenth to nineteenth centuries. Yet, the plantation has proliferated into the Information Age and has continued to expand across the tropical zone of our planet, surviving the abolition of slavery, the collapse of European empires, and the challenge of generations of anti-capitalist thinkers.[1] Drawing on the perspectives of historical analysis, this volume examines the global spread of the plantation; the people, beings, and forms of knowledge intertwined with this process; and the elasticity and durability of the plantation as a mode of commercial agriculture.

What, exactly, is a plantation? Plantations are large-scale agricultural estates that produce select crop commodities in mass using hierarchical, frequently exploitative labor arrangements for consumption in markets beyond the immediate locality. Plants and laborers are often brought in from other regions, inducing environmental impacts and social change, and the use of natural resources, particularly soil and water, is intensive and usually unsustainable. Beyond these core elements, definitions vary through their incorporation of historical or regional particularities, whether implicitly or explicitly. That plantations are necessarily a capitalist form of production is undercut by their existence in state socialist regimes; that they are a strictly Western form of production contested by their proliferation beyond formal empire as well as after postcolonial independence; that they require slavery refuted by their flourishing after its abolition; that they depend invariably on racialized labor complicated by instances of co-ethnic operation, such as in Southeast Asia with Chinese planters and laborers; that they are distinctly modern challenged by their iterations in antiquity and the Middle Ages, particularly Roman *latifundia* and sugar cultivation in the medieval Islamic world.[2] Key to understanding the endurance of the plantation is to recognize it in its many and at times unfamiliar forms.[3]

To grasp how the plantation has spread and evolved in our modern world, this volume examines the dynamic of what it terms "plantation knowledge," or the types of expertise, experience, and information processing that have made and continue to make plantations possible. Plantation knowledge, as a term, points to the diverse forms of expertise and ways of knowing that have been historically drawn upon, exchanged, and developed at plantation sites. It cannot be merely delimited to Western or "modern" frameworks, since local knowledge, including that of Indigenous actors, was often crucial for plantation success. The conditions of these knowledge exchanges were, however, frequently asymmetric, with the rewards of plantation knowledge often redounding to foreign owners and consumers.

Plantations thus are key, if fraught, locations in the global histories of science and technology.[4] Due to the fundamentally tense relationship between land, capital, labor, and plant life at plantations, the domains of knowledge that have been historically operative on plantations are multiple, including, among others, the political, spatial, technical, natural, financial, managerial, labor, and local. These domains are porous, facilitating the global proliferation of the plantation through historical actors' cross-pollination of methods, information, and individual ambitions. Across different geographies and moments in time, attempts to apply universalized theories of cultivation often collided with on-the-ground local experience. Likewise, plantations occasioned critical encounters between different ways of knowing or doing possessed by a diverse range of actors, including visiting scientists, bonded laborers, and Indigenous residents. Foregrounding the co-constitutive dynamic of theory and practice, plantation knowledge poses a methodological contribution to the interdisciplinary field of plantation studies borne from the intersection of global and transnational history, social history, the history of science and technology, the comparative history of imperialism and colonialism, and the history of knowledge.

A considerable amount of work has studied the role of racialized labor on plantations, though interpretations vary considerably on the extent to which plantations generated new racialized hierarchies or merely reproduced preexisting ones. Influenced particularly by social histories of the British Caribbean, a long dominant account emphasized the formative role of Atlantic slave-based plantations to modern racism, which was first legally inscribed by colonial governments in view of slaveholder practices, dispositions, and ideologies and subsequently naturalized in medical, historical, and social scientific works likewise rooted in plantation experiences.[5] Such scholarship built on Edgar T. Thompson's early observation that the plantation was a "race making institution" and the judgments of mid-twentieth-century anticolonial scholars including C. L. R. James and Walter Rodney, who contended that Atlantic slavery was, in Eric Williams's terms, "economic, not racial" in its origins.[6]

A counter school of thought, most familiar today through Cedric Robinson's notion of "racial capitalism," argues that group-based labor exploitation is intrinsic to capitalism, whether based on race, religion, ethnicity, or another collective delineator.[7] De-emphasizing the novelty of exploitation practiced at plantations, Robinson deemed racialized labor hierarchy a cultural particularity of European premodernity that was merely exported to new contexts through European maritime expansion, asserting that "from its very beginnings, this European civilization, containing racial, tribal, linguistic and regional particularities, was constructed on antagonistic differences."[8] Based principally on a reading of early twentieth-century medievalists, who inaugurated interpretations of the Crusades through the dual prism of colonization and exploitation, Robinson's interpretation was simultaneously Eurocentric and Eurocritical. Taking modern capitalism as Western in its essences, Robinson did not explore the role of antagonistic differences in other cultures prior to Western colonialism.

Together with recent approaches in the global history of capitalism that move beyond Eurocentric accounts, the contributions to this volume emphasize how plantation labor hierarchies were profoundly shaped by local contexts, contingencies, and cultures across the world. Inspiration is taken from locally anchored studies of the racialization of plantation laborers, particularly by scholars including Brackette Williams and more recently Cristiana Bastos.[9]

Most of the cases discussed in this volume deal with some variant of coerced labor, whether in the US South, São Tomé, Assam, Malaya, or the Philippines. Working conditions on plantations were usually exploitative and oftentimes cruel, remaining so after the abolition of slavery, when plantations turned to alternate forms of labor coercion including contracts of indenture and debt bondage.[10] Experiences across the British Empire are emblematic of this dynamic. As early as 1839, five years after the imperial abolition of slavery, official reports were already detailing the extreme abuse of indentured Indians who had replaced enslaved Africans on sugar plantations on Mauritius.[11] After a brief suspension, Indian laborers would be recruited for sugar plantations across the globe on contracts of indenture into the early twentieth century, as planters' economic interests usually prevailed over concerns of mistreatment and exploitation. Within the historiography of plantation labor, Atlantic slavery has undeniably received the bulk of attention.[12] However, during the past few decades, scholars have increasingly recognized the variety of unfree labor situations on plantations around the world and the blurred boundaries between indenture, bonded labor, and contract labor, as well as precarious and informal labor regimes.[13]

The extent to which plantations are dependent on coerced labor must be stressed. With few exceptions, plantations drew (and draw) on coerced workers, whether as chattel slaves in the Caribbean and US South, indentured workers in various colonies of the British Empire following the abolition of slavery, or as convict laborers or contract workers in a diverse range of colonies, protectorates, and independent states.[14] Furthermore, people have been (and are) maintained as plantation laborers not only through debt bondage and labor requisitions, but, increasingly since the late twentieth century, in conditions of profound legal vulnerability at the cynical intersection between the pursuit of wage-based remittances by individual migrants, public and state opposition to mass immigration, and the enduring demand of employers for cheap labor.[15]

By emphasizing the various local contexts and cultures in which plantations were (and are) embedded, we try to eschew the notion of civilizational particularities in practices of exploitation. The chapters in this volume explore specific instances of agricultural colonization in view of the labor situations and knowledge exchanges that made them possible, shedding light on formative experiences, which structure enduring realities across sites around the world.

As a factor in global history, plantation knowledge is particularly pertinent for what has been termed the Age of New Imperialism (1870–1914), at which time most of the world's surface beyond the Americas fell under the titular sovereignty of a handful of European empires, in addition to two imperial upstarts: Japan and the United States. A geographical handbook by John Scott Keltie in 1890 is indicative of the clustering of knowledge, colonialism, and global markets in the hermeneutics of the plantation during this period, which conceived of the plantation as "a pioneering institution of European expansion."[16] Reflecting the original sense of plantation as a colony, Keltie distinguished "Colonies of Settlement"—such as Australia and Canada—from "Colonies of Exploitation"—in other words, "plantations."[17] Drawing upon the French economist and journalist Leroy Beaulieu, Keltie contended that the plantation colonies "demand a constant excess of population, as well as a certain amount of capital."[18] Writing just two years after the abolition of slavery in Brazil—which marked the formal end to slavery in the Western Hemisphere—Keltie pointed to the country's south to emphasize that tropical location was not sufficient for determining the suitability of a territory for plantations. Instead, knowledge was key:

> What are the great physical features of the colony and their distribution, and how do they help or hinder its exploitation? What is the nature of the climate? What is the distribution of temperature and rainfall in space . . . and in time? What native products are there, and how are they distributed, especially with reference to accessibility and communications, and can they be worked and brought to market at a rate that will place them in favourable competition with similar products from other parts of the world? What is the distribution and character of the soil, and for what exotic products is it adapted? The last is an all-important question . . . that of labour. . . . If the natives cannot be induced to give themselves voluntarily to systematic labour, there are evidently only two courses open if the colony is to be carried on at all: they must either be compelled to work, or labour must be imported from outside. . . . But in order that a plantation-colony may be worked effectively, white supervision is absolutely necessary.[19]

In asserting the necessity of White supervision in the operation of a plantation even after the abolition of slavery, Keltie manifested the racist assumptions undergirding the rapid expansion of European empires and European-led agricultural colonization across the late nineteenth century tropical belt. Yet, evincing Eurocentric blinders, he skipped over plantation complexes in his own time that featured non-White supervision, such as the Arab-run clove plantations of Zanzibar; the emergent sugar plantations of the Dutch East Indies; and the sugar, pepper, and gambier operations of Chinese planters in Southeast Asia.

Offering a global account of the plantation rooted in the history of knowledge, this book explores a diverse set of contexts from around the globe from the sixteenth to the twentieth centuries, covering agricultural colonization across Africa, the Americas, Asia, Europe, and Oceania. The global and temporal scope reflects the phase in which European colonization and capital drove the global spread of the plantation from the early modern period to the twentieth century. European agency was, however, not exclusive even then, presaging the contemporary proliferation of plantations amidst decolonization. Building on extensive scholarship on racialized slavery in the British Caribbean and the US South, the case studies in this volume go beyond the paradigmatic dynamic featuring European owners and African slaves, including studies of Chinese-, Hawaiian-, and African American-led iterations during the nineteenth century. By exploring a diverse range of cases, including some wherein racialized labor regimes do not seem to be applicable, this book contributes a hermeneutic reflection on the plantation through attention to its defining elements of agricultural colonization, exploitation, and knowledge exchanges.

Knowing a Plantation

Etymologically and conceptually, the term "plantation" is a product of early modern English colonial expansion into the Atlantic world. The term has an enduring connection with the process of the agricultural colonization of land. Plantation, as shown by Ted McCormick below, originally functioned as a noun and a verb, a double use that persists in French. As a verb, plantation was the act of "planting" a territory with people, analogous to the more literal early modern German phrase *Pflanzstadt*. As a noun, plantation was the territory thus planted—or in other words, a colony. It was initially used in reference to English colonization in Ireland. It was first during the eighteenth century that it gained its contemporary valence as a large landed agricultural estate and an intimate association with the racialized slavery of Africans. Up until the end of the eighteenth century, the term was used interchangeably to refer to English colonies across the Atlantic world regardless of climate or prevailing labor type, including

Ireland, Newfoundland, Nova Scotia, and New England, in addition to the Caribbean and the US South.[20] A dominant sense in reference to the racialized, slave-based agricultural estates of the Atlantic world only emerged toward the turn of the nineteenth century. However, even as late as 1890, plantation could still be used to refer to colonization, though by this time as the specific modality of plantation-based colonization (in Keltie's words, a "plantation-colony").[21]

A generic definition of the plantation materialized only in the early twentieth century, as social scientists, most prominently Edgar T. Thompson, attempted to distill the concept into an institution capable of comparative world historical analysis.[22] Before him, academic study of the plantation was situated within comparative studies of colonization and empire, wherein plantations were perceived as a distinctly European tactic for the profitable settlement of a tropical territory under European control.[23] Taking aim at what he perceived as the climatic determinism of this account, Thompson, trained in the Chicago school of sociology and a specialist of colonial Virginia, built upon Max Weber to argue that the plantation was foremost a strategy of postconquest colonization and only accidentally correlated with the tropics in the modern era.[24] As his counterexamples, he pointed to the grain estates of the early modern Baltic, for the analysis of which Karl Marx and Friedrich Engels had suggested the prism of the "second serfdom."[25] The scope of Thompson's comparative argument was expanded by Immanuel Wallerstein in his notion of the emergence of the modern capitalist world system in the sixteenth century.[26]

Combining insights from social history, world-systems theory, global history, and the history of science, Sidney W. Mintz, in 2010, offered a new take on the definition of the plantation emphasizing its conjuncture of capitalism, forced labor, land dispossession, global transfers, and—implicitly—knowledge: Plantations were "early capitalistic experiments in overseas export-oriented agriculture that used forced labor on land taken from native peoples, with capital, plants, and technology coming from Europe and Asia."[27] Through attention to the factor of knowledge, this volume proposes tightening two dimensions of Mintz's definition. First, the processes attendant to the emergence of plantations often occurred synchronously. Land dispossession often went hand in hand with the evolution of new regimes of forced, coerced, or racialized labor, reflecting how the plantation as a tactic of colonization typically resulted in a decline of subsistence farming, whether in early modern Ireland or nineteenth-century Africa.[28] Second, the range of knowledge inputs at plantations in terms of "capital, plants, and technology" was truly global in character and came from across the spectrum of colonizer and colonized, including forced labor migrants and Indigenous people.[29] This latter dynamic is essential not only in comprehending the global history of botanical knowledge but also in appreciating the extra-Western roots of the labor hierarchies and practices at specific plantations past and present.

The Stakes of Plantation Knowledge

This book stakes two claims about the relationship between plantations and the history of knowledge. First, as sites of agricultural production characterized by the exploitative interplay of land, labor, capital, and nature, plantations depend on multiple scales of knowledge exchange and knowledge extraction ranging from the augmentation of their local productive capacity to the dynamic of their global proliferation. Second, plantations have thereby historically operated as fertile sites of knowledge production, ranging from formal natural sciences such as medicine and botany, the self-serving pseudoscience of scientific racism, and as Rosenthal has recently suggested, quantitative managerial practices.[30] While plantation knowledge may have had earlier iterations, its saliency is greatest from the sixteenth century onward, continuing into the present through scientific agriculture. Beyond a primary function to produce agricultural surpluses, the plantation has thus served as a staging ground and a veritable laboratory of new techniques of agricultural cultivation, labor control, group-based classification, political rule, and carceral governance.

Within the growing interdisciplinary field of plantation studies, the aim of this book is to take knowledge as an important object of inquiry. In its emphasis on the ways knowledge is generated, produced, and negotiated in a discrete agronomic space, plantation knowledge demonstrates the situated and hybrid character of knowledge.[31] The productive impulse of plantations was made possible through the conjuncture of individuals from diverse social milieus who interacted in settings defined by gaping inequalities, including racialized hierarchies. Recent work has recognized plantations as sites for innovations in forms of exploitation (human, animal, plant, and environmental), discipline (labor order, carceral forms of rule), and media (the transmission of knowledge via planter journals, presses, botanical garden exchange).[32] Plantation knowledge thus pluralizes the sense in which plantations can be understood as sites of production, emphasizing their dynamic character across time and space. Plantations were crucial sites of knowledge production amidst the rise of a Eurocentric world system from the early modern period and became ever more institutionalized as such during this system's peak during the nineteenth and early twentieth centuries.

In its focus on the history of knowledge, this volume highlights the plantation as a socioeconomic historical formation in which diverse ways of knowing were brought into contact, negotiated, translated, and debated in a discrete social space.[33] It thereby contributes to Peter Burke and Marwa Elshakry's injunctions to embrace the historical effects of knowledges in the plural, including different orders of knowledge, communities of knowledge, or *savoir-mondes*.[34] The chapters contemplate multiple spatial layers to the circulation, exchange, extraction, or ignorance of knowledge—at local, regional, and global levels, within, across, and beyond nineteenth-century empires.

In sync with the plantation's conceptual history, the bulk of scholarly work on plantations has been pursued for American contexts prior to the abolition of slavery during the nineteenth century, particularly the US South and the Caribbean. Atlantic centrism and regional particularism have become subject to sustained critiques, particularly by Ulbe Bosma and Richard B. Allen.[35] The capitalist quality of plantations has also been the site of lively discussion, though a tension has emerged between accounts focusing on finance versus industry.[36] The former perceives the core elements of the plantation to have been forged during the long eighteenth century with the development of global capitalist markets and quantitative management. The latter, coalescing in the concept of the "second slavery," reworks Marx's notion of the "second serfdom" to emphasize a rupture in the early nineteenth century with the introduction of new technologies on quasi-industrialized plantations, particularly in the Caribbean, wherein the practice of Atlantic slavery was intensified right up to the moment of abolition.[37] Work on the nineteenth century remains vital in understanding the long-term history of the plantation given that it is when what Philip D. Curtin classically described as the "plantation complex" obtained a truly global character.[38]

The basic economic imperative of the early modern plantation—to generate profit through the intensive cultivation of cash-crops for long-distance export drawing on complex financial instruments, including joint stock companies supported by European courts and states—constituted a historically novel orientation in the human use (and abuse) of land. The recently influential concept of the Plantationocene registers this observation in a targeted critique of the Anthropocene, using the plantation as the paragon of the specifically industrial capitalist rather than essentially human transformation of nature.[39] As rendered by Wendy Wolford, the Plantationocene suggests "that large-scale, export-oriented agriculture dependent on forced labor has played a dominant role in structuring modern life since the insertion of European power in the Americas, Asia and Africa."[40] Work adopting the concept recognizes the role played by plantations in contemporary struggles over land, labor, and the environment, bringing histories of colonialism, capitalism, and ecological degradation to bear on land dispossession, global warming, and diverse forms of labor exploitation, including those involving nonhuman actors such as plants, animals, and microbes.[41] Building on these insights of the Plantationocene, this volume considers the generative and degenerative characteristics of the plantation, emphasizing its place as a space where knowledge was circulated, collected, implemented, negotiated, and contested with lasting human social, economic, political, and environmental consequences.

Plantations have increasingly been brought to bear within the vibrant field pursuing the relationship between science and empire since 1750, or "colonial science." This field has been most developed for the context of the British Empire, though extensive studies have emerged for all modern empires, including the American, French, German, Ottoman, and Japanese.[42] A major concern in this field has been the role of networking practices in the exchange of knowledge, particularly the role of maritime nodal points, botanical and natural scientific networks, and the unevenness of power relationships within these networks. Refined attention to the adjectival function of colonial science has encouraged a more nuanced approach to the relationship between scientists, colonial administration, and the local knowledge of colonized people.[43] Important work in the 1990s observed the prominence of plantations—particularly in island settings—as colonial sites of science, though tended to be quite generalizing.[44] More focused inquiry of this dynamic came with the coining of the term "plantation science" in the mid-2000s, with Prakash Kumar developing a history of indigo in the context of the British Empire that crossed methods of the history of science and intellectual history.[45] During the 2010s, several studies explored the development and circulation of scientific expertise on specific crops, particularly after 1800.[46] The function of botanical gardens as nodal points between plantations and global scientific networks has also received increasing attention.[47]

Use of the term "plantation science" has increased markedly over the past few years, flowing in two analytical streams. The first, inspired by critical theory, uses plantation science as an abstraction for concerns ranging from environmental ethics to the history of scientific racism.[48] In perhaps the most elaborate instance of this approach, Anna Lowenhaupt Tsing termed plantation science a "hegemonic, extinction-oriented practice" characterized by an extractive, domineering relationship between managers and harvesters and experts and plants.[49] The second, continuing in the influence of the history of science, is critical of the tendency to reduce plantation science to a unitary abstraction. Drawing on earlier work on imperial science, this scholarship evinces how planters on the ground often privileged practical experience over theoretical science and were dependent on the experience of individuals considered beyond the field of formal science, namely Indigenous and local actors.[50] This book follows this latter strand of interpretation, foregrounding the spectrum of knowledge actors, including Indigenous, migrant, and racialized people, as an essential factor in the operation and propagation of plantations. Moreover, the term "plantation knowledge" serves as a more appropriate characterization than "plantation science" of the primacy of practical experience over theory on plantations and in view of the diversity of knowledge forms and actors that have historically been involved with plantations.

Investigating Plantation Knowledge

To discern the diverse and changing ways in which plantations, through extraction and exploitation, have served as sites to the exchange, production, and contestation of knowledge, this book investigates plantation knowledge through ten case studies addressing different temporal, local, and global contexts (Fig. I.1). While a truly comprehensive account is beyond the scope of any single volume, each case study has been strategically selected to elucidate broad arcs in the *longue durée* global history of plantation knowledge while cognizant of the local and temporal specificities of individual plantations. Going beyond the normal regional compartmentalization of plantation studies, the chapters are organized according to the historical progression of five interconnected concepts in the evolution of knowledge systems: epistemology, boundary setting, experimentation, institutionalization, and reform. The sequencing of these five knowledge-gaining processes follows their general trajectory

Figure I.1. Map of principal case studies. *Source*: Created by the editors.

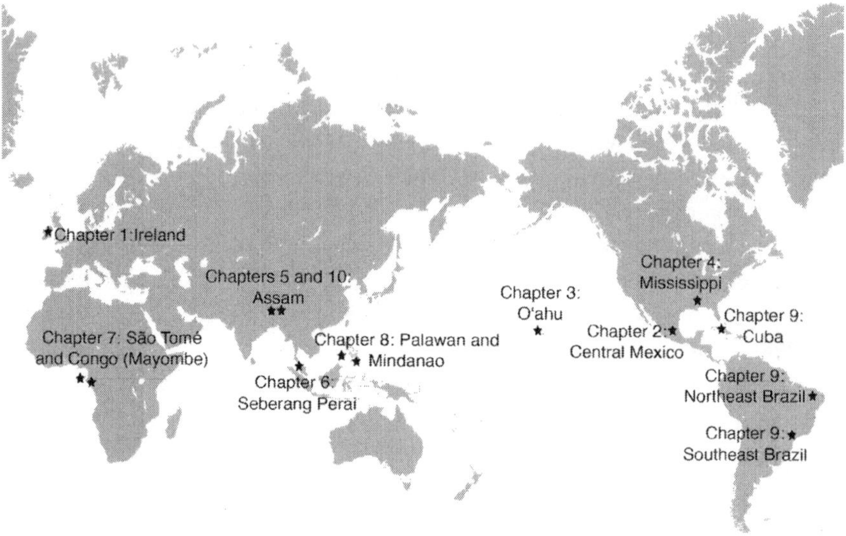

in contemporary research design while also roughly corresponding to chronological stages in the global history of the plantation since 1500.

This book may be the first to use plantation knowledge as an orienting concept, but the term has been formulated since the eighteenth century. The contributing authors' use of the concept is informed by its several evolving meanings since the eighteenth century, which mirror shifts in the concept of the plantation and changes in the circulation, collection, implementation, negotiation, and contestation of knowledge across local, international, and transnational contexts. Below, a general history of plantation knowledge since 1500 is provided, informed by this book's five key knowledge concepts, its ten constituent chapters, and key shifts in the global history of the plantation.

Epistemology

Foundational to this book's account is an epistemological reflection on the tensions between the plantation as an early modern concept and its contemporary status as an organizing device for global historical inquiry. Building on the conceptual history sketched above, Ted McCormick and Jennifer

R. Saracino reflect on the relationship between agricultural colonization and knowledge production in two early modern locations commonly left out of accounts of the plantation complex: Ireland and Mexico. Their two studies add global context to the first documented instance of "plantation knowledge" as a term in 1762 by William Bolan. For Bolan, "*Plantation* knowledge [emphasis original]" referred to the question of the "acquest of dominion, and the plantation of colonies, made by the *English* in *America*."[51] Counter to Bolan, McCormick examines plantation knowledge in the context of late seventeenth-century Ireland, emphasizing how the ends of intensified English dominion over the island were achieved through the means of innovations in information collection, including land surveys and censuses. Plantation in its early modern sense is thus understood as a political process—and as McCormick argues, a political project—which instigated developments in the realms of state and political knowledge.

Tracing a similar dynamic across the Atlantic for the sixteenth century, Saracino examines the role of knowledge production, exchange, and hybridization in the wake of the Spanish conquest of central Mexico. She draws attention to the role of Nahua actors in the production and codification of botanical knowledge under Spanish rule and the complex ways in which evolving practices of agricultural colonization built on Indigenous forms of labor control. By examining two early modern sites often considered beyond the pale of plantation studies, epistemological clarity is gained of the historical relationship of the plantation with other early modern forms of agricultural colonization.

Boundaries

During the long nineteenth century, plantation agriculture proliferated globally primarily, though not exclusively, through the expansion of Western colonial empires. Early plantations at new sites of cultivation often began prior to formal Western overrule, and the political projects invested in plantation experiments were diverse. Nicholas B. Miller and Claudia Roesch probe the boundaries of the historical identity of the plantation in relationship to colonization and racialization, thus challenging generalizations relating to the plantations of the United States and its Pacific borderlands.

Taking up the example of a Hawaiian *ali'i* (high chief) turned industrial plantation owner in the late nineteenth-century Hawaiian Kingdom, Miller underlines the participation of elite Indigenous actors in the global expansion of plantation production. Tracing the plantation career of John Adams Kuakini Cummins alongside the political upheavals experienced in Hawai'i during the final decades of the nineteenth century, including the overthrow of its Indigenous monarchy in 1893 and the annexation of the archipelago by the United States in 1898, Miller indicates the plurality of political projects active at nineteenth-century plantations, including, in this instance, a type of Indigenous sovereignty.

Roesch provides the counterpoint of a set of Mississippi plantations where attempts were made to apply an Owenite social reform model to plantation production. Originating in an attempt by the brother of the future Confederate president Jefferson Davis to practice a "reformed" version of plantation slavery, the Davis Bend plantations were site to a Union refugee camp during the Civil War followed by an experiment after the war in Black communitarian cultivation. Roesch's analysis thus engages the spectrum of efforts to moderate and later challenge plantation slavery and its attendant racialized social structure, the latter of which featured in notions of "plantation knowledge" around 1900 as knowledge of the social conditions at particular antebellum plantations.[52] Widening the boundaries of plantation research to include seemingly unconventional cases reveals the experimental and flexible character of labor organization, knowledge exchange, and production techniques practiced at plantations during the nineteenth century, challenging the common conceit of figures like Keltie around the turn of the twentieth century that plantations as an industrial means of agricultural production were inherently European.[53]

Experiments

At the frontiers of commercial globalization across the maritime tropics from the eighteenth century onward, plantations served as crucial nodal points in an emerging, globe-spanning network of scientific exchange, extraction, and experimentation along, across, and eventually beyond European empires. In 1854, plantation knowledge was used in a sense analogous to agrarian science by D. Lee in the US state of Georgia, who submitted that "plantation knowledge deserves systematic cultivation from year to year, quite as much as the plantation itself," bemoaning "the lack of experimental farms" and state investment into agrarian research in the Southern United States.[54] Lee's proposal of plantation knowledge as constitutive of a distinct branch of scientific knowledge reflected a shift from the term's secondary sense in the eighteenth century, when

Plantagenwissenschaft was used in a German novel to refer to day-to-day plantation cultivation practices on a Jamaican plantation.[55] Yet plantations in the long nineteenth century were not just sites in which formal scientific knowledge was applied or tested; they were likewise sites to the processing of knowledge, particularly through encounters and confrontations with Indigenous actors and migrant laborers.

Examining two contexts situated in the Indian Ocean circuits of the British Empire, Moritz von Brescius and Christina Skott highlight the underrecognized significance of plantations as sites of colonial science and investigate the pivotal role of intercultural knowledge exchanges, namely, the constitutive dynamic of planting experiments and local know-how. Through the example of an experimental rubber plantation funded by the British government in the Assam region of India in the late nineteenth century, Brescius emphasizes the role of intra- and interimperial knowledge exchanges and the several knowledge systems that converged at a single site of experimentation. He studies the materiality of the plantation and how factors as elemental as soil, manure, cultivar choice, and weed eradication became sites of categorized and globally exchanged knowledge.

Skott in turn explores the attempt to develop a sugar complex on the Malay peninsula following the abolition of slavery in the British Caribbean, focusing on the range of early sugar planters active in Province Wellesley, now known as Seberang Perai, an early site of British incursion opposite the island of Penang. She considers the varying success and techniques of European and Chinese sugar planters, their relation to Indigenous and labor migrant actors, and the role of global knowledge exchanges in terms of cultivars and previous experience, including those from the Caribbean. The experimental character of cultivation and management practices at plantations was consistent with their status as projects of agricultural colonization that served multiple interweaving though potentially conflicting objectives at individual, corporate, and state levels.

Institutionalization

Around the turn of the twentieth century, plantation knowledge developed into an increasingly institutionalized field of interimperial exchange and collaboration, obtaining characteristics that Burke has described as typical in the sciences as "disciplining" (from the German *Disziplinierung*).[56] A prominent example is the Institut Colonial International (ICI), an organization founded by Belgian, Dutch, and French colonial experts in Brussels in 1894, which soon included delegates from Germany, Britain, and other colonial empires. The ICI served as a nodal point for colonial and plantation knowledge, covering topics ranging from colonial law and colonial administration to plantation agriculture and labor management.[57] In *Compte-Rendu*, the ICI's in-house journal, the assembling and distribution of plantation knowledge were carried out through surveys, statistical accounts, and reports on labor, soil, and geographical conditions.[58] The question of labor supply—particularly discussions of indenture and other forms of bonded labor in the wake of the abolition of slavery—was central.[59] Less than a decade later, the International Institute of Agriculture was founded in Rome with putative aims to support the global agricultural sector and to foster knowledge in the field of agriculture, including through the establishment of a bureau of agricultural intelligence and plant diseases.[60]

Marta Macedo and Theresa Ventura investigate the dynamic of inter-imperial transfers and rearticulations of plantation knowledge during what has become termed the Age of New Imperialism (1870–1914) in Central Africa and Southeast Asia, respectively. Macedo reveals how plantation production models and practices transferred between and across empires, taking up the example of cocoa from the long-time Portuguese insular colony of São Tomé to the mainland Belgian Congo. She indicates the mobility of private actors between these contexts as well as how plantation production in both sites came under international scrutiny due to work conditions that clearly approximated plantation slavery.

Ventura embraces multiple meanings of the term "institutionalization," examining how two prison camps-cum-coconut plantations in the American colonial Philippines were established to instill plantation labor discipline in inmates and their families while generating scientific knowledge on coconuts. Through these institutionalized experiments, American scientists-cum-administrators also sought to integrate the new US colony of the Philippines within preexisting scientific networks in Southeast Asia, namely, those which converged at the Buitenzorg Botanical Gardens in the Dutch East Indies. The institutionalization of plantation knowledge during the modern height of imperial sovereignty was thus a joint product of imperial rivalry and collaboration.

Reform

World War I represented a decisive turning point in the history of plantation knowledge, wherein reform gained the limelight: The imperial map of the world was recast; the rule of empires was recognized as necessarily contingent and fragile; global governance gained the institutional framework of the League of Nations; and communist revolution became the agenda of a major new state actor, the Soviet Union. Whereas nineteenth-century abolitionism had been driven by a revulsion to the forms of bonded labor practiced on plantations—racialized slavery, then indenture—twentieth-century critiques from the labor movement emphasized the degrading character of plantation working conditions. Colonial rule, at least formally, became subject to the new ideology of mandates, wherein "colonial responsibility" and "colonial development" emerged as new keywords. Real-world conditions on plantations, however, hardly changed.[61] Prompted by the specter of communist revolution and in concert with the League of Nations, the International Labor Organization was founded in 1919 to define and establish standards of labor as well as to collect and share information about global working conditions. As the International Labor Organization gained influence over labor legislation in imperial entrepots, its attempts to intervene in the colonial spaces of plantation labor met fierce resistance from local actors.[62] Despite mounting international criticism about working conditions on plantations, governments in many tropical locations remained keen to foster plantation agriculture, given its extremely lucrative nature.

Gillian McGillivray and Rebekah McCallum indicate the spectrum of strategies adopted by planters large and small to navigate the pressures and possibilities of political reform. McGillivray, in focusing on Cuba and Brazil during the early twentieth century, complicates any clean distinction between settler and plantation colonies, describing how locations featuring a conjuncture of settler migration and plantation production witnessed an intriguing adaptation of the type of workingmen politics commonly associated with British colonies of settlement such as Canada, Australia, and New Zealand, as well as the United States. She assesses the varying strategies employed by small-scale coffee and sugar planters in Cuba and Brazil to stylize themselves as White settlers to receive distinct state benefits. By exploring the politics of a largely European-descended class of small planters in the early twentieth century, McGillivray points to how plantation knowledge was used strategically by contemporaries in the sense of vocational education, equipping plantation laborers with the practical know-how and skills needed to run their own agricultural enterprises as small planters. During congressional hearings on Hawaiian homesteading in 1920, reference was made to a Portuguese laborer in

Hawai'i who, "with his plantation knowledge gained as a laborer . . . has been a very successful homesteader and cane grower."[63] In her nuanced comparison, McGillivray underlines how small planters' appeal to racial citizenship in semicolonial Cuba was more successful than that in statist-industrialist Brazil.

McCallum, by contrast, examines the strategies employed by corporate factors in India to evade changes to practices and conditions of plantation labor. While British authorities, following the discursive turn to developmentalist empire, enacted certain reforms to ameliorate labor practices at Indian tea plantations, McCallum indicates the dubious efficacy of these reforms. She highlights the strategic cultivation of a reputation of "expertise" by these factors to lobby for self-serving policies that maintained the status quo in tea production. On the eve of decolonization, an important domain of plantation knowledge consisted of its strategic use by planters to navigate the challenges and opportunities posed by nationalism, socialism, communism, labor movements, and the rise of the interventionalist, developmentalist, and putatively welfare state.

Conclusion

Plantations, as sites to the extraction, exploitation, and engagement of knowledge, present imperative locations for continued inquiry into the interlinked histories of colonialism, capitalism, and racialization. While decentering Europe and the Atlantic in the history of the plantation, the contributions to this book remain cognizant of the formative roles of European colonization, capital expansion, and the African slave-based plantation system in driving its global spread since the early modern period. The reason for European preeminence was first and foremost easy access to capital. Yet extra-European sources of capital long existed, particularly Chinese, Arab, and Indian mercantile networks in Southeast Asia, the Pacific, and the Indian Ocean basin, enabling some non-Europeans to participate in plantation exploitation as plantation owners. Moreover, capital alone was insufficient for plantation success; Indigenous, local, and labor knowledge including access to a dependent, mostly coerced workforce were essential. Recapturing its global propagation in the wake of early modern and modern European colonization, this book emphasizes knowledge exchanges as well as attendant hierarchies and frictions.[64] Future work on plantations would do well to heed their sustaining interactions of knowledge at local, regional, and global scales, including in our multipolar present.

When assessing the historical legacies and enduring characteristics of the plantation, it is instructive to recognize its character as site to interweaving exploitation and knowledge production. Plantations were intimately interlinked with scientific institutions, most prominently the botanical gardens of imperial powers in the nineteenth century, and thus participated in the development of scientific botany. Knowledge exchanges pertaining to labor were however also pivotal, particularly in the wake of the abolition of the trans-Atlantic slave trade. Knowledge about what types of labor bondage could be profitably practiced while formally complying with abolitionist or protective legislation became an increasingly central concern during the second half of the nineteenth century, before an emerging global labor movement coincided with a steep drop in the cost of long-distance passenger transportation. The paradoxical result was the decline of formal tactics of bonded labor and the rise of informal, precarious labor arrangements that endure into the present.[65] A history of knowledge approach to plantations yields recognition of their dynamic instability as sites of material and knowledge production; their unsustainability socially, economically, and environmentally; and above all, their remarkable elasticity and durability in the contemporary world.

Notes

1. Tania Murray Li, *Land's End: Capitalist Relations on an Indigenous Frontier* (Duke University Press, 2014); Sabine Damir-Geilsdorf et al., eds., *Bonded Labour: Global and Comparative Perspectives (18th–21st Century)* (Transcript, 2016); Tania Murray Li and Pujo Semedi, eds., *Corporate Occupation in Indonesia's Oil Palm Zone* (Duke University Press, 2021); Jonathan E. Robins, *Oil Palm: A Global History* (University of North Carolina Press, 2021); Case Watkins, *Palm Oil Diaspora: Afro-Brazilian Landscapes and Economies on Bahia's Dendê Coast* (Cambridge University Press, 2021).

2. Marie Aureille, "Nostalgia for Oranges: Plantations as Development Promise in Socialist Cuba," in *Global Plantations in the Modern World: Sovereignties, Ecologies, Afterlives*, eds. Colette Le Petitcorps et al. (Palgrave Macmillan, 2023); Mohammed Bashir Salau, *Plantation Slavery in the Sokoto Caliphate: A Historical and Comparative Study* (Rochester University Press, 2018); Frederick Cooper, *Plantation Slavery on the East Coast of Africa* (Yale University Press, 1977); David

Northrup, *Indentured Labor in the Age of Imperialism, 1832–1922* (Cambridge University Press, 1995); Johnhenry Gonzales, *Maroon Nation: A History of Revolutionary Haiti* (Yale University Press, 2019), 84–128; Li, *Land's End*; Robins, *Oil Palm*; Tsugitaka Soto, *Sugar in the Social Life of Medieval Islam* (Brill, 2015), 1–32.

3. Amy Clukey and Jeremy Wells, "Introduction: Plantation Modernity," *The Global South* 10, no. 2 (2016): 1–10.

4. James Poskett, *Horizons: The Global History of Science* (Mariner, 2022).

5. Trevor Burnard, *Planters, Merchants, and Slaves: Plantation Societies in British America, 1650–1820* (University of Chicago Press, 2015).

6. Edgar T. Thompson, *The Plantation*, eds. Sidney W. Mintz and George Baca (University of South Carolina Press, 2010), 70–71; Edgar T. Thompson, "The Plantation as a Race-Making Situation," in *Sociology: A Text with Adapted Readings*, eds. Leonard Broom and Philip Selznick (Harper & Row, 1955), 506–507; Walter Rodney, *How Europe Underdeveloped Africa* (Bogle-L'Ouverture, 1972); C. L. R. James, *The Black Jacobins: Toussaint L'Overture and the San Domingo Revolution* (Secker & Warburg 1938). The first edition of Williams' text was published in 1944. Eric Williams, *Capitalism and Slavery* (University of North Carolina Press, 2014), 19. See also the collection of essays in a special edition entitled "Constructing Race," *The William and Mary Quarterly* 54, no. 1 (1997): 1–279.

7. Destin Jenkins and Justin Leroy, eds., *Histories of Racial Capitalism* (Columbia University Press, 2021).

8. Cedric Robinson, *Black Marxism: The Making of the Black Radical Tradition* (University of North Carolina Press, 2000), 10.

9. Brackette Williams, *Stains on My Name, War in My Veins: Guyana and the Politics of Cultural Struggle* (Duke University Press, 1991); Cristiana Bastos, Andrea Novoa, and Noel B. Salazar, "Mobile Labour: An Introduction," *Mobilities* 16, no. 2 (2021): 155–163.

10. Oliver Tappe and Ulrike Lindner, "Introduction: Global Variants of Bonded Labour," in *Bonded Labour*, eds. Damir-Geilsdorf, et al, 11.

11. *Report of the Committee Appointed by the Supreme Government of India to Enquire into the Abuses Alleged to Exist in Exporting from Bengal Hill Coolies and Labourers of Various Classes to Other Countries* (Calcutta, 1839).

12. Ira Berlin, *Many Thousands Gone: The First Two Centuries of Slavery in North America* (Harvard University Press, 1998); B. W. Higman, *Plantation Jamaica, 1750–1850: Capital and Control in a Colonial Economy* (University of the West Indies Press, 2005); Robin Blackburn, *The Making of New World Slavery: From the Baroque to the Modern, 1492–1800* (Verso, 1997); Michael Zeuske, *Handbuch Geschichte der Sklaverei. Eine Globalgeschichte von den Anfängen bis zur Gegenwart* (De Gruyter, 2019).

13. See for example Marcel van der Linden, *Workers of the World: Essays Toward a Global Labor History* (Brill, 2011), and Martin A. Klein, ed., *Breaking the Chains: Slavery, Bondage and Emancipation in Modern Africa and Asia* (University

of Wisconsin Press, 1993). For a case study in India, see K. Ravi Raman, *Global Capital and Peripheral Labour: The History and Political Economy of Plantation Workers in India* (Routledge, 2010).

14. Marcel van der Linden, "Dissecting Global Labour," in *On Coerced Labor: Work and Compulsion After Chattel Slavery*, eds. Marcel van der Linden and Magaly Rodríguez García (Brill, 2016).

15. See Babacar Fall and Richard L. Roberts, "Forced Labour," in *General Labour History of Africa: Workers, Employers and Governments, 20th–21st centuries*, eds. Stefano Bellucci and Andreas Eckert (James Currey, 2019), 77–118.

16. Dale Tomich, "Rethinking the Plantation: Concepts and Histories," *Review (Fernand Braudel Center)* 34, no. 1–2 (2011): 15–39.

17. John Scott Keltie, *Applied Geography: A Preliminary Sketch* (London, 1890), 16–19.

18. Keltie, *Applied Geography*, 16–19.

19. Keltie, *Applied Geography*, 16–19.

20. See, for instance, Thomas Prior, "Observations on the Trade of Ireland (1720)," in *A Collection of Tracts and Treatises Illustrative of the Natural History, Antiquities and the Political and Social State of Ireland*, vol. 2 (Dublin, 1861), 521.

21. Keltie, *Applied Geography*, 16–19.

22. Thompson, *The Plantation*.

23. Paul Leroy-Beaulieu, *De la colonisation chez les peuples modernes* (Paris, 1874), 207–290; Wilhelm Roscher and Robert Jannasch, *Kolonien, Kolonialpolitik und Auswanderung* (Leipzig, 1885), 23–32; A. G. Keller, *Colonization: A Study in the Founding of New Societies* (Ginn and Company, 1908), 9–12.

24. Thompson, *The Plantation*, 4–8.

25. Thompson, *The Plantation*, 7–8. Marx and Engels developed their notion of the second serfdom in correspondence with each other. For Engels's systematization, see Frederick Engels, *Socialism: Utopian and Scientific with the Essay on "The Mark,"* trans. Edward Aveling (International Publishers, 1969), 88–89. On the notion generally, see Johannes Nichtweiss, "The Second Serfdom and the So-Called 'Prussian Way': The Development of Capitalism in Eastern German Agricultural Institutions," trans. Gwyn Seward, *Review (Fernand Braudel Center)* 3, no. 1 (1979): 99–140; Manuela Boatcă, "Second Slavery Versus Second Serfdom: Local Labor Regimes of the Global Periphery," in *Social Theory and Regional Studies in the Global Age*, ed. Saïd Amir Arjomand (State University of New York Press, 2014), 361–388.

26. Immanuel Wallerstein, *The Modern World System, vol. 1: Capitalist Agriculture and the Origins of the European World-Economy in the Sixteenth Century* (University of California Press, 2011).

27. Sidney W. Mintz, "Introduction" to Thompson, *The Plantation*, ix.

28. See McCormick and Macedo in this volume. Also see Fall and Roberts, "Forced Labour," 77–118.

29. See Saracino in this volume. Also see, as an emblematic case, the role of African rice in plantation America. Judith A. Carney, *Black Rice: The African Origins of Rice Cultivation in the Americas* (Harvard University Press, 2001).

30. Caitlin Rosenthal, *Accounting for Slavery: Masters and Management* (Harvard University Press, 2019).

31. On situated knowledge, see Donna Haraway, "Situated Knowledges: The Science Question in Feminism and the Privilege of Partial Perspective," *Feminist Studies* 14, no. 3 (1998): 579–599; Peter Burke, *What is the History of Knowledge?* (Polity, 2015), 33. Regarding the hybrid character of knowledge, see David Bloor, *Knowledge and Social Imagery* (Routledge, 1976).

32. Le Petitcorps et al., eds., *Global Plantations in the Modern World*; Burnard, *Planters, Merchants, and Slaves*; Daniel B. Rood, *The Reinvention of Atlantic Slavery: Technology, Labor, Race, and Capitalism in the Greater Caribbean* (Oxford University Press, 2017).

33. Philipp Sarasin, "Was ist Wissensgeschichte?" *Internationales Archiv für Sozialgeschichte der deutschen Literatur* 36, no. 1 (2011): 159–172; Simone Lässig, "The History of Knowledge and the Expansion of the Historical Research Agenda," *Bulletin of the German Historical Institute* 59 (2016): 29–58; Anna Nilsson Hammar, "Theoria, Praxis, and Poiesis: Theoretical Considerations on the Circulation of Knowledge in Everyday Life," in *Circulation of Knowledge: Explorations in the History of Knowledge*, eds. Johan Östling, et al. (Nordic Academic Press, 2018).

34. Peter Burke, "Response," *Journal for the History of Knowledge* 1, no. 1 (2020): 2; Marwa Elshakry, "Beyond a Singular History of Knowledge," *Journal for the History of Knowledge* 1, no. 1 (2020): 1–4; Pilar González-Bernaldo and Liliane Hilaire-Pérez, eds., *Les savoirs-mondes: mobilités et circulation des savoirs depuis le Moyen Âge* (Presses Universitaires de Rennes, 2015).

35. Ulbe Bosma, *The World of Sugar: How the Sweet Stuff Transformed Our Politics, Health, and Environment over 2,000 Years* (Harvard University Press, 2023); Richard B. Allen, "Slaves, Convicts, Abolitionism and the Global Origins of the Post-Emancipation Indentured Labor System," *Slavery & Abolition* 35, no. 2 (2014): 339–340.

36. Rosenthal, *Accounting for Slavery*; Dale W. Tomich, *Through the Prism of Slavery: Labor, Capital, and World Economy* (Rowan & Littlefield, 2004).

37. Dale W. Tomich and Michael Zeuske, "Introduction, the Second Slavery: Mass Slavery, World-Economy, and Comparative Microhistories," *Review (Fernand Braudel Center)* 31, no. 2 (2008): 91–100.

38. Philip D. Curtin, *The Rise and the Fall of the Atlantic Plantation Complex: Essays in Atlantic History*, 2nd ed. (Cambridge University Press, 1998); Le Petitcorps et al., eds., *Global Plantations*; Kris Majapra, "Plantation Dispossessions: The Global Travel of Agricultural Racial Capitalism," in *American Capitalism: New Histories*, eds. Sven Beckert and Christine Desan (Columbia University Press, 2018).

39. Donna Haraway, "Anthropocene, Capitalocene, Plantationocene, Chthulucene: Making Kin," *Environmental Humanities* 6, no. 1 (2015): 159–165; Donna J. Haraway, *Staying with the Trouble: Making Kin in the Chthulucene* (Duke University Press, 2016).

40. Wendy Wolford, "The Plantationocene: A Lusotropical Contribution to the Theory," *Annals of the American Association of Geographers* 111, no. 6 (2021): 1622–1639.

41. Sophie Sapp Moore et al., "Plantation Legacies," *Edge Effects*, January 22, 2019, https://edgeeffects.net/plantation-legacies-plantationocene/.

42. Bernard S. Cohn, *Colonialism and Its Forms of Knowledge: The British in India* (Princeton University Press, 1995); Ulrike Lindner, "New Forms of Knowledge Exchange Between Imperial Powers: The Development of the Institut Colonial International (ICI) since the End of the 19th Century," in *Imperial Co-operation and Transfer, 1870–1930: Empires and Encounters*, eds. Volker Barth and Roland Cvetkovski (Bloomsbury Academic, 2015); Benedikt Stuchtey, ed., *Science Across the European Empires, 1800–1950* (Oxford University Press, 2005).

43. Helen Tilley, *Africa as a Living Laboratory: Empire, Development, and the Problem of Scientific Knowledge, 1870–1950* (University of Chicago Press, 2011), 5.

44. James McClellan, *Colonialism and Science: Saint Domingue and the Old Regime* (John Hopkins University Press, 1992); Richard H. Grove, *Green Imperialism: Colonial Expansion, Tropical Island Edens, and the Origins of Environmentalism* (Cambridge University Press, 1995).

45. Prakash Kumar, "Plantation Science: Improving Natural Indigo in Colonial India, 1860–1913," *British Journal for the History of Science* 40, no. 4 (2007): 537–565. See also, Rhys Isaac, *Landon Carter's Uneasy Kingdom: Revolution and Rebellion on a Virginia Plantation* (Oxford University Press, 2004), 76–77.

46. Prakash Kumar, *Indigo Plantations and Science in Colonial India* (Cambridge University Press, 2012); Michitake Aso, *Rubber and the Making of Vietnam: An Ecological History, 1897–1975* (University of North Carolina Press, 2018), 16, 60–65.

47. Dorit Brixius, "From Ethnobotany to Emancipation: Slaves, Plant Knowledge, and Gardens on Eighteenth-Century Isle de France," *History of Science* 58, no. 1 (2019): 51–75; J'Nese Williams, "Plantation Botany: Slavery and the Infrastructure of Government Science in the St. Vincent Botanic Garden, 1765–1820s," *Berichte zur Wissenschaftsgeschichte* 44, no. 2 (2021): 137–158; Dorit Brixius and Katja Kaiser, "Duplicate Networks: The Berlin Botanical Institutions as a 'Clearing House' for Colonial Plant Material, 1891–1920," *British Journal of the History of Science* 55, no. 3 (2022): 279–296; Hélène Blais, *L'Empire de la nature: une histoire des jardins botaniques coloniaux* (Champ Vallon, 2023).

48. Anna Lowenhaupt Tsing, "Arts of Inclusion, or How to Love a Mushroom," in *Why Food Matters: Critical Debates in Food Studies*, ed. Melissa Caldwell

(Bloomsbury, 2021), 311; Britt Russert, "Naturalizing Coercion: The Tuskegee Experiments and the Laboratory Life of the Plantation," in *Captivating Technology: Race, Carceral Technoscience, and Liberatory Imagination in Everyday Life*, ed. Ruha Benjamin (Duke University Press, 2019), 25–49.

49. Tsing, "Arts of Inclusion," 311.

50. Arnab Dey, *Tea Environments and Plantation Culture: Imperial Disarray in Eastern India* (Cambridge University Press, 2018), 5–12; Michael R. Dove, *The Banana Tree at the Gate: A History of Marginal Peoples and Global Markets in Borneo* (Yale University Press, 2011), 101–102.

51. William Bolan, *Coloniæ Anglicanæ Illustratæ: or, the Acquest of Dominion, and the Plantation of Colonies Made by the English in America, with the Rights of the Colonists, Examined, Stated and Illustrated* (London, 1762), 2.

52. James S. Metcalfe, "The American Slave, No. 2—The Life of the Slave," *Pearson's Magazine* (November 1900), 481; Elizabeth A. Regosin and Donald R. Shaffer, eds., *Voices of Emancipation: Understanding Slavery, the Civil War, and Reconstruction Through the U.S. Pension Bureau Files* (NYU Press, 2008), 139.

53. Keltie, *Applied Geography*, 19.

54. D. Lee, "Guano and Cotton Culture," *The Southern Cultivator* (reprinted in *Camden Weekly Journal*, January 31, 1854, 4).

55. *Die Mutter, oder das glückliche Elend: Eine Geschichte*, vol. 1 (Frankfurt, 1771), 162.

56. Burke, *History of Knowledge*, 18–20.

57. Lindner, "New Forms of Knowledge," 57–78. Florian Wagner, *Colonial Internationalism and the Governmentality of Empire, 1893–1982* (Cambridge University Press, 2022).

58. See, for instance, Institut Colonial International, *Compte Rendu de la session tenue à Berlin les 6 et 7 septembre 1897* (Brussels, 1897).

59. Benoit Daviron, "Mobilizing Labour in African Agriculture: The Role of the International Colonial Institute in the Elaboration of a Standard of Colonial Administration, 1895–1930," *Journal of Global History* 5, no. 3 (2010): 479–501.

60. Asher Hobson, *The International Institute of Agriculture: An Historical and Critical Analysis of its Organization, Activities, and Policies of Administration* (University of California Press, 1931).

61. See McCallum in this volume. See also Vernon M. Hewitt, "Empire, International Development and the Concept of Good Government," in *Empire, Development & Colonialism: The Past in the Present*, eds. Vernon M. Hewitt and Henrik Aspengren (Currey, 2009).

62. Daniel Maul, *The International Labour Organization: 100 Years of Global Social Policy* (De Gruyter, 2019).

63. US House of Representatives, *Hearings Before the Committee on the Territories, Sixty-Sixth Congress, Second Session, On the Rehabilitation and Colonization of Hawaiians* (US Government Printing Office, 1920), 65.

64. See Miller, Roesch, Skott, and McGillvray in this volume.

65. Marcel van der Linden, “San Precario: A New Inspiration for Labor Historians,” *Labor: Studies in Working-Class History* 11, no. 1 (2014): 9–21.

Part I

Epistemology

Chapter 1

Between Irish Plantation and the Plantation Complex

The Down Survey (1654–1658), Projecting, and the Origins of Political Arithmetic

Ted McCormick

As a site of commodity and knowledge production, plantation transcends the boundary between early modern and modern. As a type of place, however, it must be historicized more precisely. Scholars of modern empire, colonialism, and capitalism know plantations as distinctive, far-flung locations where more or less unfree laboring populations were settled or confined and compelled to produce a particular crop for intra-imperial circulation or global exchange: sugar, tobacco, tea, cotton, rubber, palm oil.[1] Certainly, these units of coercive production had premodern roots.[2] Yet early modern scholars are likely to think of plantation in terms of action or process rather than place. In the sixteenth and early seventeenth centuries, the word often denoted an act of planting—or, by analogy, founding—whether the thing planted was a staple, a belief, an institution, or a population and whether the site was close and familiar or distant and hostile.[3] (Thus Robert Gray's 1609 tract, *A Good Speed to Virginia*, encouraged Englishmen to "vndertake the plantation of Virginia" as a step in "the plantation of [the North American] continent" that echoed the ancient practice of "plant[ing] Colonies" and involved settlers "plant[ing] themselues" by "plant[ing] and manur[ing]" the land."[4]) As a deliberate act drafting land and people into a process of productive change, early modern plantation has been subsumed into etiologies of colonial empire and racial capitalism; these were its crucial modern legacies.[5] Reading plantation's history solely in terms of these outcomes, however, elides the shift from action and process to place. This obscures plantation's implication in multiple projects and discourses of cultural and social transformation (including civility and improvement) within and beyond Europe, simplifies its complex relationship to local agendas and histories, and smooths its crooked path to colonial and capitalist futures.[6]

Because Ireland was a site of both plantation and plantations in the sixteenth and seventeenth centuries, and because it was at once a Tudor and Stuart kingdom and an object of English colonial projecting, it can tell us much about plantation's practical and ideological complexities and mutations.[7] The period beginning with Oliver Cromwell's invasion of the country in 1649, continuing with the Restoration of the Stuart monarchy from 1660, and ending with William of Orange's victory over James II in 1692 is especially important. Having risen against Protestant domination and land hunger in 1641, Irish Catholics (both Gaelic Irish and "Old English" descendants of medieval settlers) were implicated in English minds in rebellion and in the massacre of Protestant settlers.[8] This ascription of collective bloodguilt and barbarity to the Irish legitimated Cromwell's invasion. It also testified to the failure of piecemeal, local, or regional plantation as a civilizing mechanism and solidified an English mercantile and Parliamentary commitment to the total expropriation of Catholic-owned land by means of a forced "transplantation" of Irish Catholics from Ulster, Leinster, and Munster to the Western province of Connacht.[9] A key instrument of Cromwellian and subsequent settlements—settlements designed to subjugate Ireland for good and thus *complete* the process of plantation—was a massive knowledge-making project: the Down Survey.[10]

Proposed, contested, and carried out between 1654 and 1658, the Down Survey was one of the largest state-supported scientific efforts of the seventeenth century.[11] In cartographic terms, it was not only the first systematic measurement and description of Irish land on a national scale but also "the first field-survey and *mapping* of any European country."[12] Politically and economically speaking, it helped extend and entrench Protestant dominance in Ireland for more than a century. In the shorter term, but no less consequentially, it fueled its designer and director William

Petty's subsequent articulation of "political arithmetic."[13] Retrospectively promoted to the canon of pre-Smithian economic writing, this has been described as a program of economic and demographic quantification, or "Number, Weight, and Measure."[14] Charlotte Sussman characterizes it as "the first scientific attempt to quantify the inhabitants of England."[15] As Sussman and other recent scholars of demographic thought have stressed, however, quantification here was a practical and rhetorical as well as a methodological or analytical device.[16] Political arithmetic was intended as a "New Instrument of Government" in the service of definite ends: political stability in England, English security in Ireland, and an improved political economy linking British settlements and interests on all sides of the Atlantic.[17]

The Atlantic dimension has until recently been less adequately explored, despite the emergence of the plantation complex in this same period. But Jennifer Morgan's work on Atlantic slavery pushes a cognate analysis of political arithmetic far in this direction, framing "numeracy" in this context as a process of abstraction that animated and articulated a new kind of economic calculation as constitutive of human rationality.[18] Posited as universal, and yet increasingly suppressed in printed accounts of African people and practices, numeracy in this sense underpinned and characterized a racial distinction that permitted the treatment of people who lacked a putatively natural sense of calculation, property relations, and kinship as liable to become property themselves.[19] It was during this same period that colonial legislation and imperial policies—shaped by members of political arithmetic's target audience—codified just such distinctions between Christian servants, with recognized interests distinct from their masters', and enslaved Africans, denied them.[20] In this sense, political arithmetic birthed racial capitalism.[21] This link between conceptual innovation and practical governance raises further questions about the place of seventeenth-century natural knowledge and technological ingenuity in the emergence of a property regime that rested on new racial distinctions as well as new conceptions of self- and public interest, labor, and improvement.

This connection also suggests a new way of thinking about early modern Ireland's significance for global plantation and its forms of knowledge—an historical question long construed as a matter of Ireland being either a "kingdom" or a "colony" (or both)—or of the Irish being either victims or agents of empire.[22] For in fact, neither the methodological quantification at the heart of political arithmetic nor the conception of economic rationality it discloses originated with the printed discourse of political arithmetic itself. They took shape, rather, through the multitude of earlier scientific-cum-economic-cum-political projects elaborated by Petty and many others connected with the Hartlib Circle (a network of inventors, improvers, and projectors associated with the London "intelligencer" Samuel Hartlib) during the 1630s, 1640s, and 1650s.[23] The Down Survey was the greatest of these. In and through it, quantification and contested ascriptions of economic rationality to different groups were brought to bear in competing processes and visions of plantation, including forced transplantation. By the same token, the colonial transformation of the Atlantic was an obvious if often tacit reference point for thinking about the means and ends of Irish plantation. Cromwell's Western Design and conquest of Jamaica, coinciding with the Irish survey, involved some of the same personnel as his invasion of Ireland.[24] In its character as a project, designed to produce locally transformative as well as globally transferable knowledge, the Down Survey binds the end of Renaissance plantation in Ireland to the beginnings of a kind of transformative governance, mediated by quantification, that came to characterize colonial plantations worldwide.[25]

Projects, Projecting, Projectors

Some of Britain's and Ireland's sharpest contemporary observers identified the seventeenth century as a Projecting Age.[26] Throughout the Stuart era, schemes abounded for transformations of agriculture and manufactures, trade and communications, science and education, and political and religious institutions. But while the term "project" can today be applied to almost any planned initiative with a future goal, salient features of seventeenth-century projecting—notably those associated with the Hartlib Circle—are important to grasping its importance for new thinking about plantation and its implications for plantation in practice. The most fundamental of these features was the project's promise of radical, far-reaching, long-lasting, and if necessary, violent transformation by scientific and technological means. Here the Down Survey, effected by soldiers in the wake of military conquest for the sake of systematic expropriation of the dominant landowning class, is paradigmatic. It was a technological feat designed to have massive and permanent social and political implications.

But other aspects of projecting are also pertinent to understanding the survey's origins and course and to suggesting fruitful comparisons. First, it was the work of a peculiar figure: the projector. Emerging neither from the state bureaucracy nor from existing academic or learned institutions, and ostentatiously opposed to the mysteries of established trades, the projector navigated between different parties with different stakes in the project's outcomes, intervening between existing interests and conjuring new ones into existence as he went, all the while proclaiming his own personal investment in the public good.[27] Here, too, the survey is exemplary. The work of an amateur outsider (at least from the point of view of the surveying profession), the survey counterpoised the army's claims to Irish land against the older claims of London investors, or adventurers. In Ireland, it proposed to destroy Catholic landownership, nominally in the interest of a new class of Cromwellian soldier-settler and, in a larger sense, in the service of English authority over a freshly settled, permanently pacified, and productive country. Ultimately, however, it helped create a market for Irish land from which Petty and established Protestant settlers would emerge as the biggest winners, as desperate Cromwellian soldiers sold their land debentures at a discount and Catholics stayed on the land as a labor force.[28] The result was a socioeconomic transformation premised on violent conquest but justified by a conception of public good tied to Protestant hegemony, private property, and the productive combination of intellectual innovations and material changes associated in the seventeenth and eighteenth centuries with the ideal of improvement.[29]

Second, the survey was subject to critical review from authorities and rivals at several points, necessitating the repeated justification of project and projector in the form of appeals to reason and experience, assurances of restraints on private interest, and rearticulations of both methodological soundness and ethical probity. It was this process, indeed, that transformed the Down Survey from a congeries of interpersonal communications, ephemeral proposals, and coordinated material practices into an enduring written archive not only of measurements and maps but of documents and correspondence assembled by Petty himself into histories. As is not unusual, we know the project chiefly through the apologetics it generated, secondarily through institutionally sanctioned critiques, and scarcely at all from the perspective of its ground-level targets. Third, and related, the project aimed at multiple goals, material and epistemological, open-ended and subject to strategic redefinition rather than fixed; its promises and criteria of success shifted over time, as Petty and his surveyors moved from one political and geographical context to another. Finally, for practical as well as epistemological reasons, the project involved the coordination of a wide range of actors, including soldiers, surveyors, state and army officials, London instrument makers, men of credit in Ireland's localities, and members of the Catholic population itself. Indeed, Hartlib understood this production of new relations between people, within as well as beyond the organization of the survey, to be its true novelty.[30] The process and the goals of the project were expansive and depended on aligning the activities and interests of divergent groups in new ways.

Despite the interests behind it and the transformations it promised, its character as a project makes the Down Survey harder to reduce either to a straightforward example of top-down colonial science or to a mere instrument of state policy. Rather, its history highlights the contingency of both functions and the kinds of contestation that projecting reflected in colonial contexts. On the first point, there were important differences in outlook between the survey and other Irish-focused Hartlibian scientific projects of the time, notably including Gerard and Arnold Boate's *Ireland's Natvrall History* (1652), a project with which Petty and his survey are often linked.[31] While both projects promoted knowledge of Irish land with a view to plantation and improvement, as Toby Barnard has noted, their different sources, methods, and proximate goals led them to present significantly different pictures of the Irish situation, past and present. With respect to state policy, meanwhile, a focus on the survey as a project underlines the extent to which it was at cross purposes with the signature Cromwellian policy of transplanting Irish Catholic landowners into Connacht.[32] This was so not only for narrow logistical reasons but also in terms of how the future settlement was envisioned. Here the challenges of undertaking the survey and its contents bear on the 1655 pamphlet debate over transplantation, and in a larger sense, on the problems of security, allegiance, land, and labor. Revisiting the Down Survey's prosecution as a project thus connects studies of colonial science that emphasize local contexts and contingencies with recent Irish historiography that complicates the Cromwellian nature of the Cromwellian settlement.[33] It moves past the kingdom/colony frame to the complex processes involved in producing transformative knowledge of a place—knowledge of a kind that could be replicated elsewhere.

The Down Survey as a Project

Within months of the Irish rising of 1641, the English Parliament established the basic equation that underpinned the land settlement to come.

The 1642 Adventurers' Act envisioned the rebellion as general and, hence, Irish Catholic land as systematically forfeit; adventurers who funded military reconquest would take their reward in Irish estates.[34] Events complicated this vision. Irish Catholic military and diplomatic successes after 1641, and civil war in England from 1642, delayed a full-scale invasion for the better part of a decade. When the invasion did happen in 1649, as John Cunningham has shown, Henry Ireton's concern to avoid miring the New Model Army in a protracted war produced a set of qualifications by which Irish Catholic guilt was to be graded, setting the stage by 1652 for outcomes ranging from execution for the guiltiest to transplantation into Connacht for the innocent. The accumulation of arrears owed to Cromwellian troops, finally, was also resolved with more promises of Irish land. Thus, the 1652 Act of Settlement and the 1653 Act for Satisfaction sought to reconcile adventurers' and soldiers' claims, assigning forfeit land to each in a band of ten counties stretching south-westward from Antrim to Waterford. The transplantation into Connacht, originally intended to encompass the Irish Catholic population at large, came to focus on landowners. Ulster, Leinster and Munster would become Protestant land, with a mixed laboring population; Connacht would become a carefully buffered Catholic reserve.[35]

The redistribution of lands required a survey of their extent and value. The man in charge of this Gross Survey in 1653—as also of a Civil Survey designed to help satisfy a range of other claims on Irish land—was Benjamin Worsley, who had recently had a hand in drafting the 1651 Navigation Act.[36] As Micheál Ó Siochrú and David Brown have recently described, Worsley's appointment as Surveyor-General in Ireland was the work of leading London adventurers.[37] Worsley was an increasingly heterodox Protestant, and a close associate of Robert Boyle and Samuel Hartlib, valued for his commitment to reformation and for his alchemical work and contacts in the Low Countries. In this capacity he was known to Petty, an English-born, Jesuit-educated and Dutch-trained physician, whose scientific and technological interests resembled Worsley's and endeared him to Hartlib, but whose aloofness in religious matters did not.[38] Petty had attained fame a few years earlier for the "resurrection" at Oxford of Anne Greene, a servant sentenced to death for infanticide, hanged, and collected as a cadaver for medical use while still breathing.[39] His medical reputation made, he went to Ireland in 1652 as physician to the army. As Ó Siochrú and Brown suggest, it was as an army counterweight to the adventurers that Petty pitched his project for a new survey while the Gross and Civil Surveys were still underway, in early 1654.[40]

In fact, Petty's survey absorbed much of the work of these then-ongoing surveys, as also of the Strafford survey of Connacht, undertaken in the 1630s as part of a failed scheme for plantations there. Yet while giving scant credit to these works and making no significant alteration in their basic surveying methods, Petty's survey massively surpassed them in scope and scale. In contrast to the simple boundary descriptions and valuations of the Civil Survey, Petty delivered measurements, descriptions, and classifications of soil, natural features, and improvements and maps of all forfeit lands from the parish level up. In effect, it combined the quantitative functions of a survey with the qualitative aspirations of a natural history; it professed to give not just a snapshot of where things stood but a description of nature that would speak to what had been and what might be. Paradoxically, this more thorough account would also be more quickly rendered; in contrast to the slow progress of the Gross Survey, Petty initially performed the survey in thirteen months. It ultimately covered 2.2 million plantation acres and came to be accepted by the army and the Council of Adventurers.

This outcome was not inevitable. If projects held out "lofty but tenuous prospects," as David Alff has it, the early Stuart projector was marked by deviousness, delusion, and greed, points not lost on Petty's critics in the 1650s or later.[41] Petty's *History* of the survey, composed in 1660 and incorporating extensive documentation from the previous decade, thus fashioned his character as carefully as it defended his work. Petty admitted that he had no background in surveying, no pertinent skills beyond a competence in mathematics and some artistic ability, and no relevant office.[42] He presented himself not as a skilled practitioner or expert but rather as a disinterested outsider. To the limited extent that he appealed to his own background, it was as a lover of "ingeniouse and usefull arts" and "contrivances" that might help "regulate, replant, and reduce" Ireland "to its former flourishing condition."[43] Speaking of his medical position, he claimed he "had not been landed two moneths, but observing the vast and needless exspence of medicaments," and the wastefulness of the apothecary-general, he "did forthwith . . . with the State's bare disbursement of about 120li, save them five hundred pounds per annum of their former charge . . . reduceing that afair to a state of easiness and plainess, which before was held a mistery."[44] He claimed to see similar problems in the ongoing surveys.

Petty thus presented himself as a reformer of abuses, a preventer of waste, a banisher of mysteries. He attacked his office-holding rival Worsley, however, as effectively a projector in the worst sense: self-seeking, devious, and foolish. Petty's simple improvements as a physician had quietly succeeded to the satisfaction of everyone involved. By contrast, Worsley, "frustrated as to his many severall great designes in England, hoped to improve and repaire himselfe upon a less knowing and more credulouse people. To this purpose he exchanged some dangerouse opinions in religion for others more merchantable in Ireland, and carries also some magnifieing glasses, through which he showed, *aux esprits mediocres*, his skill in severall arts."[45] A fanatic, dissimulator, and mountebank, Worsley had parlayed this vulgar "credit" into lucrative office. There, "the only true art and excellency . . . [he] expressed" was in a sort of alchemistic manipulation of appearances—"soe to frame committees of conceited, sciolous persons, intermixing some of credit and bulke amongst them, as whereby he might screene himselfe" when problems with his surveys inevitably arose.[46] There was more to this, Petty insisted, than "the pittiful effects of pride and ignorance;" Worlsey's "miscarriages" were "designes and elaborate contrivances for secret reasons of state."[47] Here, again, were mysteries to be exposed.

Despite affinities between Botero's *Della ragion di stato* (1589) and Petty's later political arithmetic, Petty used "reason of state" in his accounts of the survey to refer to behind-the-scenes politicking or plotting that placed the state's true interest in jeopardy.[48] The central novelty of his survey was its insurance against *this* reason of state and its reduction of the mysteries of state and art alike to simpler and more observable tasks. The most striking aspect of this was Petty's replacement of professional surveyors with soldiers. In part, this was a money-saving device, and in part, a recognition of the labor and security constraints of postconquest Ireland. Soldiers were, he wrote, "able to endure travaile, ill lodginge and dyett, as alsoe heats and colds;" they "could leape hedge and ditch, and could also ruffle with the severall rude persons in the country, from whome they might expect to be often crossed and opposed."[49] Petty's anticipation of violence was on the mark; eight of his surveyors were later captured and killed in the Wicklow mountains.[50] Yet while we must see the use of soldiers as a function of the political context of the work and of the Survey's embedment in the Cromwellian military regime, this was not their only significance for Petty or for plantation. Their use also represented a devaluation of the traditional surveyor's mathematical learning in favor of large-scale deployments of unlearned but fungible laborers. From the perspective of Hartlibian projecting, this substitution of simple, massed, methodical labor for abstruse learning was the innovation.

Using soldiers as surveyors depended on a new division of labor. Breaking surveying down into simple, easily learned, and repetitive tasks opened the possibility of rapidly training large numbers of men, and this underpinned Petty's promise to complete the survey quickly. An explicit point was to lower the profession of surveying to the level of a craft and craftsmanship itself to a matter of "breeding" skilled labor as needed:

> Whereas surveyors of land are commonly persons of gentile and liberall education, and their practise esteemed a mystery and intricate matter, far exceeding the most parte of mechanicall trades. . . . Petty, consideringe the vastnesse of the worke, thought of dividinge both the art of makinge instruments, as alsoe that of usinge them into many partes, vizt., one man made onely measuring chaines, vizt., a wire maker; another magneticall needles, with theire pins, vizt., a watchmaker; another turned the boxes out of wood . . . vizt., a turnor; another . . . a pipe maker; another . . . a founder; another workman, of a more versatile head and hand . . . adaptates every peece to each other.[51]

Likewise, the elementary acts of observation and measurement in the field would be left to soldiers Petty had "bred" or "made" into artists through his training and provision of purpose-built equipment: "tyme scale, protractors, and compasse-cards . . . prepared by the ablest artists of London;" "a magazine of royall paper, mouth-glew, colours, pencills . . . uniforme bookes . . . ruled and fitted" according to a standardized form; "portable tables, boxes, rulers . . . as alsoe smalle Ffrench tents . . . to enable the measurers to doe any buissnesse without home or harbour."[52] The survey was, *inter alia*, a project for producing surveyors—quickly, cheaply, and in numbers.

The use of soldiers depended, too, on a system of assessment, surveillance, and supply managed by men of credit in the localities. Controlling flows of information up and down the chain of command was crucial. The job of checking and synthesizing the work the soldiers produced, as well as determining the soldiers' pay, was reserved to a smaller cadre of "nasute and sagacious persons, such as were well skilled in all the partes, practices, and frauds, appertayning unto this worke."[53] By contrast, the simplicity of their tasks, their relative isolation, and their ignorance of the details of the distribution made the soldiers more reliable on the ground than more sagacious persons would have been; since no soldier knew where his lot would fall, only with "much art" could the soldiers "universally combine" to anyone's particular benefit.[54] Thus, a certain manufactured ignorance—manufactured by the organizational structure of the survey itself—kept the moving parts in place and facilitated the smooth running of the machine. As for himself, Petty proposed to be paid for the survey either in a lump sum or at a fixed rate per thousand acres, irrespective of quality, the better to avoid charges of self-interest corrupting the returns.[55] (Although, in the event, this is not what happened.)

From within, the survey was a byzantine operation powered at the bottom by a minimally trained, minimally informed, and tightly surveilled labor force. From without, however, the survey was a mechanism for eliminating mystery—a mechanism suggested not by deep familiarity with the trades, institutions, offices, or territories involved but, on the contrary, by standing outside and above them, in the projector's shoes. Its scope was correspondingly immodest. Besides measuring and mapping "all the forfeited lands within the three provinces" in thirteen months, "according to the naturall, artificiall, and civill bounds," the survey would furnish qualitative, essentially natural-historical assessments of each parish.[56] Petty instructed his surveyors not only to "describe the bounds of each surround you make, and the nature of the land surrounded" as profitable or unprofitable, and as arable, meadow or pasture, but further to distinguish the types of pasture ("boggy, heathy, fursy, rocky, woody, mountainouse"), note the types of bounds ("wall, ditch, hedge, river, bog-side, ridge, valley"), and note any "permanent and conspicuouse objects, as churches, castles, houses, rathes, trees, great stones, hedge corners," as well as towns, roads, rivers, harbors, havens, anchorages, sands and more.[57] Petty's books of reference for each barony were also to include indices of the names of "Irish Papists," as well as towns, crown and church lands, woods, "Castles, Wears, Mills, Ffords, Passes, Bridges, Abbies, Churches, Mines, &c."[58] More than an ad hoc instrument of Cromwellian policy, this was a project designed to produce quantitative and qualitative knowledge of Ireland for "all . . . future ends whatsoever."[59]

The Survey, the State, and the Transplantation into Connacht

In the field, Petty and his soldier-surveyors found that serving the future meant grappling with the present and the past. Operationalizing the project depended not only on networks of instrument makers and a bureaucratic hierarchy in Dublin but also on substantial assistance from local contacts throughout the country. While the books and equipment were in preparation in Dublin and London,

> care was taken to know who were the ablest in each barrony and parish to shew the true bounds and meares of every denomination, what convenient quarters and harbours there were in each, and what garrisons did everywhere lye most conveniently for theire defence, and to furnish them with guards, and with all who were men of creditt and trade in each quarter, fitt to correspond with for furnishinge mony by bills of exchange and otherwise; and, lastly, who were men of sobriety and good affection, to have an eye privately over the carriage and diligence of each surveyor in his respective undertakinge.[60]

The soldier-surveyors were quartered, provisioned, and quietly watched by these "men of creditt and trade."[61] Though there are certainly aspects of the survey that invite comparison to a "military operation," as Hugh Goodacre has termed it, the analogy deserves careful specification.[62] Rather than an officer of the Cromwellian regime, we might better think of Petty as an independent contractor—a scientific mercenary or privateer. This parallels a subsequent Cromwellian scheme to "attract Planters" to Jamaica by the forced transplantation of "Vagabonds" and "persons condemn'd" in fleets going "under the Title of Privateers."[63] While engaged in a project that would extend the power of the state, he took upon himself a considerable share of the risk and would claim an extraordinary private reward.

As such, Petty was given limited authority "for impressing persons to shew the bounds and meares . . . as alsoe guards" for the surveyors.[64] Especially important were the "mearsmen" on whom the surveyors depended for knowledge of local boundaries and Irish placenames. As he acknowledged they "must be," these men were in most instances Irish Catholic and, in at least some cases, may have been tenants or even owners of the lands being surveyed and which were ultimately to be confiscated.[65] As Petty also had cause to lament, this meant that the ongoing, judicially forced transplantation of "innocent" Catholics into Connacht—a key component of the Cromwellian settlement—directly threatened the survey by driving off its source of local knowledge. Answering Worsley's criticism of the survey's imprecise delineation of some subdivisions, Petty underlined the trouble transplantation made:

> 1st. That mearesmen could not bee found, where these omissions have been made, for any part of them.
>
> 2ndly. That mearesmen could not be found for the whole, and therefore in most cases itt was to noe purpose to meddle with any at all.
>
> 3dly. The meares of these small parcells lying . . . in common fields, were obscure and neglected, and withall never knowne but to very few persons.
>
> 4thly. The omissions are chiefly in wast places, and when the transplantation, as being most vigorously prosecuted, drove away such as might give information herein.
>
> 5thly. The want of meeresmen is rather a failer [*sic*: failure] on the States part then on mine.[66]

Securing knowledge across national and linguistic lines was a precarious business, but the survey depended on it. If transplantation got in the way, the state would have only itself to blame.

The transplantation into Connacht was not merely a logistical challenge to the survey; it was also a threat to the longer-term goal of improvement. It is thus misleading to see Petty's work from the Down Survey onward as "project[ing] into the future an Ireland emptied of its Gaelic Irish populations."[67] With the exception of a manuscript "Treatise of Ireland" written in the last year of his life, the bulk of Petty's proposals for Ireland from the Down Survey through *Political Arithmetick* (1690) and *The Political Anatomy of Ireland* (1691) favor intermarriage and systematic—in fact coerced—mixture with the English.[68] (The "Treatise" envisions removing the bulk of Ireland's population *into* Britain as a labor force and, in the context of James II's pursuit of toleration, a Catholic counterweight to Protestant numbers. This complicates analogies between Petty's Irish projects and colonial genocides elsewhere.[69]) Forced assimilation for a fluctuating mixture of political, economic, and confessional purposes was his typical goal. Additionally, it may well be that Petty formed his ideas about the management of populations, including the "impressment" of key groups (here, Irish Catholic mearsmen; later, English, Irish, and Indigenous women) through the survey. He lists a "Discourse against the Transplantation into Connaught" among his writings for 1654.[70] This does not survive, but there is no doubt that in the 1655 debate between Vincent Gookin and Col. Richard Lawrence over the transplantation, Petty took Gookin's side.[71] Irish labor was essential to English plantation, and any Irish cultural characteristics that mattered politically could be effaced through contact and mixture with a privileged English settler population—digestion, in Gookin's metaphor; transmutation, in Petty's.

The best evidence of tensions between the survey's goals and the effects of transplantation come from material the survey generated. Consider Petty's comments on soldiers' reluctance to accept lots in Tipperary: "The people of Tipperary having more universally obeyed the orders of transplantation than other countries generally had done, that countrey became soe uninhabited and wast, that it would be impossible to find mearers to doe it tolerably well. . . . It was considered that many houses and improvements were now demolished, which were, *anno* 1639, standing; and many wett grounds, heretofore pasturable, now became wholly bog."[72] These problems, and this outlook, are discernible at some points in the survey. The surveyors' description of the barony of Dunkerrin in County Kerry, for example, explains the lack of detail regarding improvements and local boundaries, "al the inhabitants being dead, transported or transplanted."[73] This should caution us against grouping together the survey and the transplantation into Connacht as functionally linked aspects of a centrally directed or ideologically coherent Cromwellian settlement, imposed on Ireland from London or Dublin. From Petty's perspective, the transplantation made surveying harder and settlement itself less attractive, compounding the devastation of war.

Reframing the Future in Terms of the Past

The biggest challenge to the notion of Ireland as a "white paper" awaiting new designs was the land itself. The experience of two surveyors, Lewis Smith and John Humphreys, is particularly revealing, for it shows not only that the bold promises and broad categories of a project might run afoul of reality but also how projects might be adapted in the face of such challenges. Tasked with assessing the quality of land, Smith and Humphreys found the rugged landscape of County Kerry a particular challenge to their understanding of profitability. Smith described the problem in a long letter of July 31, 1656, to the Lord Protector's Council for Ireland, in response to complaints about the kind of lands assigned to the army.[74] The letter expounded on the difficulty of reconciling instructions from above, and expectations forged elsewhere, with the facts on the ground. "When wee came first in the country," he wrote,

> wee viewed the place in a generall way, considering the lands to be exceeding bad, and was about not to return any part of the said countrey [as] profitable, but only arable and good pasture, though our instructions did make mention of severall kinds of pasture . . . butt yet it was soe bad, that wee intended to proceed. Butt then, coming to the more remote part . . . wee were at a loss, for the like quality that wee were about to returne unprofitable in the more habitable places was even as good as many whole denominations consisted of in the said [i.e., remote] places . . . some mens whole estates consisting of such like.[75]

Questioning former inhabitants and mearsmen, Smith and Humphreys came to "clearly see that something had been made of those places, and something might be made of them againe" if used properly; thus "wee did not judge it safe to take uppon us to cast away" so many acres "wholly for unprofitable." Indeed, being "informed that the said course plowlands formerly paid contribution or taxes . . . we could not but judge these places good for something, and resolved to make something of them."[76] Advised by Petty to stick to the instructions given, however, they found themselves in a quandary. Labeling the lands as good pasture overstated their present profitability and risked defrauding soldiers owed good land. (Since Petty was in fact paid more for returning profitable than unprofitable land, it also invited charges of corruption.) Dismissing the lands as unprofitable, on the other hand, was a waste in view of the difference that improvements might make in the future—and had made in the past. Underrepresenting this potential, or ignoring this history, might even be seen as an attempt to defraud the state. Smith and Humphreys thus conferred ("having never seen each others faces") and "lighted uppon" a solution: replacing the misleading binary of profitable/unprofitable with a tripartite classification scheme of "arable and good pasture, course pasture, and unprofitable."[77]

Just as local history conditioned present hopes for future plantation, so the effects of local improvements challenged any simple division of the land into similar parts of equal value: "Now, at the first division of plowlands, they did endeavour to make them equall in value to each other; but much of the course plowlands being bog, in process of time the inhabitants have improved some of the same, and made it fitt to bear corne; soe that in one of these great plowlands there will be as much arable now as in one of the small ones."[78] Unable therefore to "set downe any generall rule to proceed by plowlands," Smith and Humphreys instead resorted to ratio, estimating the value of an acre of "course" or "rough" plowland as a fraction of that of an acre of "good grazing land." Their solution was not a Procrustean equalization but rather a provisional attempt to better describe and more thoroughly exploit varied and changing landscapes by modifying their framework.[79]

> Now the said county being generally mountainouse, rocky, and boggy, so that all pastures came under one of these titles [implying their unprofitability], and most times they are rocky and boggy mount pastures in one and the same places, and yet there is a great deal of difference in the quality, and the same title must be given to it, though there be a great disproportion; so that we judged fitt how to value how many acres was worth one, even to distinguish betwixt course and course, to answer that clause of our instructions.[80]

Only through an evolving negotiation between the state's demands, the projector's instructions, and local facts and testimony—only if "the Act admitt of some interpretation of the word profitable and unprofitable"—could the land be represented in such a way as best to serve the goal of plantation. As Smith summed it up, "that is only barren that beares nothing, or that only unprofitable which is good for nothing."[81] It is perhaps not surprising that Petty was accused of employing drunks.[82]

On one level, Kerry confronted the surveyors with the impossibility of reducing a varied landscape to binary categories. Their response—fueled by their observations and by the attestations of "the chiefest and ablest men that lived in that place"—was to alter the categories.[83] What was initially a violation of instructions ultimately became value added, at least in Petty's self-interested assessment: "The said surveyors tooke more paines in the field, and the Dr more in the house . . . to give a just accompt of that county than was done in any other part of the whole survey."[84] Kerry challenged the surveyors to take a kind of time-lapse picture to capture a capacity for wealth now hidden by war and depopulation but recoverable with labor and time. The land's potential for improvement in the future—the basis of its value as a site of plantation in the present—became a function of its history of improvement in the past. The resulting picture was quite different from that presented in another Hartlib-sponsored project of the period: the Boate brothers' 1652 *Ireland's Natvrall History*. As Barnard has shown, the Boates's work relied heavily on Old Protestant informants driven back to England by the rising in 1641.[85] For these, the English were "introducers of all good things, in Ireland (for which that brutish nation from time to time hath rewarded them with unthankfulness, hatred, and envy, and lately with a horrible and bloody conspiracie, tending to their utter destruction)."[86] By insisting on the past profitability of seemingly waste and forfeit lands, and by cataloguing improvements that still stood or left their traces on Catholic lands, the survey told a different story. The Ireland it revealed was no white paper. Yet within a few years, that was exactly how Petty described it to restored Stuart officials in England and Ireland, as he sought patronage for the new projects that would become political arithmetic.[87]

Conclusion

Quantification was a hallmark of Restoration political arithmetic. So too was transplantation: not the transplantation of the Irish into Connacht, which Petty had opposed, but rather a novel and equally coercive "counter-transplantation" of tens of thousands of English and Irish women at a time, by means of which Petty hoped to effect a "natural and lasting union" between the two nations.[88] Proposed in manuscripts during the 1670s and 1680s and printed in *Political Arithmetick* (1690) and *Political Anatomy* (1691), this project of union depended on a mobilization not merely of numbers but of bodies, and crucially of reproductive labor. "Teeming women"—that is, young, unmarried, fertile, poor and hence disposable English women—were the key objects of Petty's signal counter-transplantation scheme.[89] These women, "imprest" into service as wives and mothers to Irish men much as soldiers and mearsmen had been pressed into mapping and measuring Irish territory, would be the active ingredient in a national "transmutation" that would remake housing, dress, language, manners, political allegiance, and economic interest—including the economic rationality of the Catholic Irish themselves.[90] In all of this, political arithmetic's gendered project of demographic governance picked up where the Down Survey, and Gookin's hopes for a union of peoples without loss of manpower, had left off.

Invoking the same assumptions about intermarriage that Protestants had long blamed for Old English degeneration since the twelfth century but reversing the terms of the mixture to make women the bearers of Englishness rather than Irishness, political arithmetic would be the culmination and the end of Irish plantation as it had been pursued since the Tudor era. But it did not stop there. In manuscript, Petty sketched ideal "colonies" for either Ireland or America, including quantitative stipulations about space, population, economic, and household arrangements, and proposed the purchase of Indigenous "girls" to serve as wives for English colonists in Virginia, thus preventing the emigration of "teeming women" from England.[91] In print, he and his contemporaries and successors extended the scope of political arithmetical calculation to urban and rural, metropolitan and colonial, free and enslaved populations across the empire. Recent analyses such as Morgan's and Sussman's make visible the Atlantic economy of variously mobilized, colonized, and enslaved reproductive labor on which such political-arithmetical projects depended.[92] Juxtaposed with the present reading of the Down Survey, they help highlight the paradoxical nature of political arithmetic's transformation from a series of projects rooted in local knowledge of land and people to a discourse of economic rationality and a mechanism of commodification.

The simultaneous naturalization and selective erasure of self-interested economic calculation, which Morgan captures as "numeracy" and discerns as the essence of political arithmetic, was a feature of projects aimed at the Irish and indeed the English poor from the early seventeenth century, if not earlier—but with a key difference.[93] Eric Ash, for example, has delineated the transformative effects early Stuart fen drainage schemes projected onto unruly land and people alike.[94] Hartlibian projects of the mid-century explicitly sought to unlock or, where the persistence of irrational or barbarous "custom" dictated, to *create* in their human objects a sense of interest consonant, in the terms of the new science, with reason and experience.[95] Such projects explicitly aimed at tying dis- or differently ordered laboring populations to the property and kinship regimes, household organization, agricultural practices, and market relations that typified southern England—or, rather, to improved versions of these. In Ireland, such projects shared some of the aspirations of Renaissance plantation, which had likewise aimed at altering kinship norms, property relations, and material culture, under the rubric of civility. Yet in the post-1641 context, the Down Survey and the settlements and projects it grounded abandoned gradual, piecemeal measures of cultural change, setting a radically abbreviated timeframe for a transformation increasingly constructed by projectors as a matter of control over the production and mobility of populations and commodities and by planters as a matter of access to land, labor, and markets. The projector might use history to make his promises plausible; he could not wait centuries for investments to mature.

Revisiting the Down Survey in light of Morgan's work on slavery and racial capitalism sharpens comparisons of plantation and its meanings in Irish and transatlantic contexts and suggests further lines of inquiry about Ireland's place in the Atlantic and about the origins of self-interested calculation as an anchor for claims or denials of autonomy and kinship. One of the striking features of projecting in England and Ireland is that it often treated this kind of rationality as an aspiration rather than assuming its unproblematic operation among the population at large. Projects justified in terms of the interests of Englishmen or Irishmen would themselves *produce* the material conditions and the knowledge that made those interests legible and calculable to the targeted groups, whether by converting fenland to arable, imposing new crops or tools on enclosed farmland or instilling in Irish Catholics a "natural" affection for English wives and children. Indeed, force (in Ireland, considerable force) might be needed to create a world in which the projector's targets could see their interests as the projector did. Yet, in England and Ireland, the expectation that self-interest *would* ultimately breed commitment to the world the projector created remained. Where labor was mobile and oversight limited, improvement depended on it. With respect to Africans, on the other hand, Morgan has shown that the imputation of numeracy was not set up as a foil to lingering custom or projected into the near future but categorically suspended or suppressed—and with it, the recognition of claims to autonomy and kinship that might have interfered with enslavement.[96] Political arithmetic's ideal plantations differed from earlier Irish plantation in being abstract spaces of production and reproduction rather than places with complex and consequential histories. The epistemic violence inherent in this abstraction and the racialized, physical, and psychic violence specific to Atlantic slavery were of new kinds and had divergent implications and effects in different places.[97] Reconnecting the Down Survey with Restoration political arithmetic and its legacies in Ireland and the wider Atlantic world nevertheless shows that the different senses of plantation at work in projects on different shores of the seventeenth-century Atlantic were historically connected even as they came to be discursively and practically opposed.

Notes

1. See Richard Drayton, "The Collaboration of Labour: Slaves, Empires, and Globalizations in the Atlantic World, c. 1600–1850," in *Globalization in World History*, ed. A. G. Hopkins (Pimlico, 2002). For more recent discussions of the "plantationocene," see e.g., Donna Haraway, "Anthropocene, Capitalocene, Plantationocene, Chthulucene: Making Kin," *Environmental Humanities* 6, no. 1 (2015): 159–165.

2. See for example Eduardo Aznar Vallejo, "The Conquests of the Canary Islands," in *Implicit Understandings: Observing, Reporting, and Reflecting on the Encounters Between Europeans and Other Peoples in the Early Modern Era*, ed. Stuart B. Schwartz (Cambridge University Press, 1994).

3. See *Oxford English Dictionary*, "plantation," https://www.oed.com/view/Entry/145169.

4. Robert Gray, *A Good Speed to Virginia* (London, 1609), sigs. B3r, B4r, C2v, C4r, D2r. All quotations here and below maintain original spelling.

5. See most recently Kris Manjapra, *Colonialism in Global Perspective* (Cambridge University Press, 2020), 71–99.

6. See David Armitage, "Literature and Empire," in *The Origins of Empire: British Overseas Enterprise to the Close of the Seventeenth Century*, eds. Nicholas Canny and William Roger Lewis (Oxford University Press, 1998). On the discourses of civility and improvement in Irish plantation specifically, see Nicholas Canny, *Making Ireland British, 1580–1650* (Oxford University Press, 2001), 165–242; David Dickson, *Old World Colony: Cork and South Munster 1630–1830* (Cork University Press, 2005), 170–214; Toby Barnard, *Improving Ireland? Projectors, Prophets, and Profiteers* (Four Courts Press, 2008).

7. For different perspectives, see Canny, *Making Ireland British*; Jane Ohlmeyer, "A Laboratory for Empire? Early Modern Ireland and English Imperialism," in *Ireland and the British Empire*, ed. Kevin Kenny (Oxford University Press, 2004); Audrey Horning, *Ireland in the Virginian Sea: Colonialism in the British Atlantic* (University of North Carolina Press, 2012); Annaleigh Margey, "Plantations, 1550–1641," in *The Cambridge History of Ireland, 1550–1730*, vol. 2, ed. Jane Ohlmeyer (Cambridge University Press, 2018); Keith Pluymers, *No Wood, No Kingdom: Political Ecology in the English Atlantic* (University of Pennsylvania

Press, 2021); Ted McCormick, *Human Empire: Mobility and Demographic Thought in the British Atlantic World, 1500–1800* (Cambridge University Press, 2022).

8. An influential early statement of this position is John Temple, *The Irish Rebellion: Or, An History of the Beginnings and First Progresse of the General Rebellion Raised Within the Kingdom of Ireland, upon the Three and Twentieth Day of October, in the Year, 1641* (London, 1646). See John Cunningham, "1641 and the Shaping of Cromwellian Ireland," in *The 1641 Depositions and the Irish Rebellion*, eds. Eamon Darcey et al. (Abingdon: Routledge, 2012).

9. On the origins and effects of the transplantation scheme, see John Cunningham, *Conquest and Land in Ireland: The Transplantation to Connacht, 1649–1680* (Boydell Press, 2011).

10. For a current overview see Micheál Ó. Siochrú and David Brown, "The Down Survey and the Cromwellian Land Settlement," in Ohlmeyer, *Cambridge History of Ireland*, 584–607.

11. All accounts of the survey draw on Petty's own accounts and collections, as, owing to the loss of original documents by fire in 1711 and firebombing in 1922, they must: William Petty, *Reflections upon Some Persons and Things in Ireland, by Letters to and from Dr. Petty* (London, 1660); Petty, *History of the Cromwellian Survey of Ireland, A.D. 1655–6, Commonly Called "The Down Survey,"* ed. Thomas Aiskew Larcom (Dublin, 1851). See also Jennifer R. Saracino's discussion of state-sponsored information collection in colonial New Spain as well as the chapters by Moritz von Brescius, Theresa Ventura, and Rebekah McCallum in this volume.

12. William J. Smyth, *Map-making, Landscapes and Memory: A Geography of Colonial and Early Modern Ireland c. 1530–1750* (Cork University Press, 2006), 167; See also Ó Siochrú and Brown, "Down Survey," 599.

13. William Petty, *Political Arithmetick* (London, 1690).

14. On Petty's stature in the history of economic thought, see for example Roger E. Backhouse, *The Penguin History of Economics* (Penguin, 2002), 67–72. On quantification in his work, compare Paul Slack, "Government and Information in Seventeenth-Century England," *Past and Present* 184, no. 1 (2004): 33–68; and Mary Poovey, "Between Political Arithmetic and Political Economy," in *Regimes of Description: In the Archive of the Eighteenth Century*, eds. John Bender and Michael Marrinan (Stanford University Press, 2005). For "Number, Weight, and Measure," see for example Petty, *Political Arithmetick*, sig. a4v.

15. Charlotte Sussman, *Peopling the World: Representing Human Mobility from Milton to Malthus* (University of Pennsylvania Press, 2020), 61.

16. See Sussman, *Peopling the World*, 54–82; Mary Poovey, *A History of the Modern Fact: Problems of Knowledge in the Sciences of Wealth and Society* (University of Chicago Press, 1998), 92–143.

17. William Petty, "The New Instrument of Government" (1682), BL Add. MS 72880, ff.60–71v.

18. Jennifer L. Morgan, *Reckoning with Slavery: Gender, Kinship, and Capitalism in the Early Black Atlantic* (Duke University Press, 2021), 4–15; see also Charlotte Sussman, "The Colonial Afterlife of Political Arithmetic: Swift, Demography, and Mobile Populations," *Cultural Critique* 56, no. 1 (2004): 96–126.

19. Sussman, *Peopling the World*, 61; Morgan, *Reckoning with Slavery*, 8.

20. On the emergent distinction between servants and enslaved people, see Jerome S. Handler and Matthew C. Reilly, "Contesting 'White Slavery' in the Caribbean: Enslaved Africans and European Indentured Servants in Seventeenth-Century Barbados," *New West Indian Guide* 91, no. 1–2 (2017): 30–55.

21. See Morgan, *Reckoning with Slavery*, 15–16, 89–109. See also the chapters by Moritz von Brescius, Marta Macedo, and Theresa Ventura in this volume.

22. Compare Nicholas Canny, "Writing Early Modern History: Ireland, Britain, and the Wider World," *Historical Journal* 46, no. 3 (2003): 723–747; Michelle O'Riordan, "Ireland 1600–1780: New Approaches," in *Palgrave Advances in Irish History*, eds. Mary McAuliffe et al. (Palgrave Macmillan, 2009), 49–83; Jane Ohlmeyer, "Introduction: Ireland in the Early Modern World," in Ohlmeyer, *Cambridge History of Ireland*, 1–19, especially 7–12.

23. See McCormick, *Human Empire*, 139–187; Abigail Swingen, *Competing Visions of Empire: Labor, Slavery, and the Origins of the British Atlantic Empire* (Yale University Press, 2015), 11–31; Vera Keller, *Knowledge and the Public Interest* (Cambridge University Press, 2015), 167–198; Carl Wennerlind, *Casualties of Credit: The English Financial Revolution, 1620–1720* (Harvard University Press, 2009), 44–79.

24. See Swingen, *Competing Visions of Empire*, 32–55; Carla Gardina Pestana, *The English Conquest of Jamaica: Oliver Cromwell's Bid for Empire* (Harvard University Press, 2017).

25. See Toby Barnard, "Last Stages of Plantation," in *Plantation Ireland: Settlement and Material Culture, c. 1550–1700*, eds. James Lyttleton and Colin Rynne (Four Courts Press, 2009).

26. Daniel Defoe, *An Essay upon Projects* (London, 1697), 1. Recent discussions of projecting include Vera Keller and Ted McCormick, "Towards a History of Projects," *Early Science and Medicine* 21, no. 5 (2016): 423–444; David Alff, *The Wreckage of Intentions: Projects in British Culture, 1660–1730* (University of Pennsylvania Press, 2017), 1–22; Frédéric Graber and Martin Giraudeau, "Définir les projets," in *Les projets: une histoire politique (XVIe–XXIe siècles)*, eds. Frédéric Graber and Martin Giraudeau (Presses des Mines, 2018).

27. On the complex and conflicted relationship between projecting, secrecy, and publicity, see Koji Yamamoto, "Reformation and the Distrust of the Projector in the Hartlib Circle," *Historical Journal* 55, no. 2 (2012): 375–397.

28. Ó Siochrú and Brown, "Down Survey," 601, 607.

29. See Paul Slack, *The Invention of Improvement: Information and Material Progress in Seventeenth-Century England* (Oxford University Press, 2015), which

however focuses on English rather than wider British, Irish, or colonial contexts; compare Toby Barnard, "The Hartlib Circle and the Cult and Culture of Improvement in Ireland," in *Samuel Hartlib and Universal Reformation: Studies in Intellectual Communication*, eds. Mark Greengrass et al. (Cambridge University Press, 1994). For other perspectives on the role of "improvement" in plantation knowledge, see Claudia Roesch's chapter as well as the chapters in the section part III in this volume.

30. See Samuel Hartlib, "Ephemerides 1655 Part 4" (13 August–31 December 1655), in *The Hartlib Papers* (hereafter HP), M. Greengrass, M. Leslie, and M. Hannon (Digital Humanities Institute: University of Sheffield, 2013), http://www.dhi.ac.uk/hartlib, 29/5/43a–58a, at 43b.

31. [Gerard and Arnold Boate], *Ireland's Natvrall History* (London, 1652); see Barnard, *Improving Ireland?*, 13–40, and Barnard, "The Hartlib Circle."

32. See Cunningham, *Conquest and Land in Ireland.*

33. On the contingency of scientific and technological projects in colonial contexts, see Jorge Cañizares-Esguerra, *Nature, Empire, and Nation: Explorations of the History of Science in the Iberian World* (Stanford University Press, 2006); Kapil Raj, *Relocating Modern Science: Circulation and the Construction of Knowledge in South Asia and Europe, 1650–1900* (Palgrave, 2007); Pluymers, *No Wood, No Kingdom*. On revisions of Cromwell's role in various aspects of the Irish settlement, see especially John Cunningham, "A Scramble for Ireland: Cromwell and the Land Settlement," and Heidi Coburn, "Cromwellian Transplantations of the Irish to the Colonies," both in *Cromwell and Ireland: New Perspectives*, eds. Martyn Bennett et al. (Liverpool University Press, 2021), 185–206 and 207–228, respectively.

34. See Karl S. Bottigheimer, *English Money and Irish Land: The 'Adventurers' in the Cromwellian Settlement of Ireland* (Oxford University Press, 1971).

35. Cunningham, *Conquest and Land in Ireland*, 11–47.

36. On Worsley, see Thomas Leng, *Benjamin Worsley (1618–1677): Trade, Interest and the Spirit in Revolutionary England* (Boydell Press, 2008).

37. Ó Siochrú and Brown, "Down Survey," 593.

38. Petty is sometimes referred to as a Puritan, apparently on the strength of his association with Hartlib. This is mistaken; later an advocate of religious toleration known to mock different styles of preaching, Petty was described as early as 1653—in contrast to the "pious" Worsley and the then-lord deputy of Ireland Charles Fleetwood—"of Gallio's belief, or temper rather." See William Rand to Samuel Hartlib, 10 January 1653, in HP 62/17/3a–4b, at 3b–4a. Gallio was Lucius Junius Gallio Annaeanus (the philosopher Seneca's brother), who dismissed Jewish charges against the apostle Paul, declaring (Acts 18:15, KJV) that "I will be no judge of such matters."

39. On the Anne Greene case, see William Petty to Samuel Hartlib, 12 December 1650, in HP 8/23/1a–2b, at 1a–1b; Laura Gowing, "Anne Greene (c. 1628–1659)," in *Oxford Dictionary of National Biography*, online edn. (Oxford University Press, 2004), https://doi-org.lib-ezproxy.concordia.ca/10.1093/ref:odnb/11413.

40. Ó Siochrú and Brown, "Down Survey," 597.

41. Alff, *Wreckage of Intentions*, 2.

42. Petty had encountered and worked with Hobbes during the latter's time in Paris in 1645–1646; Hartlib noted in 1655 that "that Treatise of his [i.e., Hobbes's] Optica is to come forth by itself Dr Petty having made the diagrams vnto it." Hartlib, Ephemerides 1655 Part 3, in HP 29/5/33b. See Lisa T. Sarasohn, "Thomas Hobbes and the Duke of Newcastle: A Study in the Mutuality of Patronage before the Establishment of the Royal Society," *Isis* 90, no. 4 (1999): 721; Quentin Skinner, "Thomas Hobbes and His Disciples in France and England," *Comparative Studies in Society and History* 8, no. 2 (1966): 153–167.

43. Petty, *History of the Cromwellian Survey*, 1.

44. Petty, *History of the Cromwellian Survey*, 1–2.

45. Petty, *History of the Cromwellian Survey*, 2. Petty elaborated on these designs in his more overtly polemical *Reflections*: "Mr. *Worsly* himself . . . traded only in flights to become suddenly rich, as by the *Universal Medicine, Making of Gold, Sowing of Salt-Peter, Universal Trade, Taking great Farms*, &c." Petty, *Reflections*, 107.

46. Petty, *History of the Cromwellian Survey*, 3.

47. Petty, *History of the Cromwellian Survey*, 3.

48. See Petty, *Reflections*, 58.

49. Petty, *History of the Cromwellian Survey*, xv.

50. See Smyth, *Map-Making, Landscapes, and Memory*, 54–55.

51. Petty, *History of the Cromwellian Survey*, xv.

52. Petty, *History of the Cromwellian Survey*, xiv, 17, 45, 83. Petty also indicated his own improvements to the tools and "practice of surveying" (but not theory); Petty, *History of the Cromwellian Survey*, 17.

53. Petty, *History of the Cromwellian Survey*, xvi–xvii.

54. Petty, *History of the Cromwellian Survey*, 20.

55. Petty, *History of the Cromwellian Survey*, 10.

56. Petty, *History of the Cromwellian Survey*, 9.

57. Petty, *History of the Cromwellian Survey*, 48.

58. Petty, *History of the Cromwellian Survey*, 38.

59. Petty, *History of the Cromwellian Survey*, xiv.

60. Petty, *History of the Cromwellian Survey*, xv.

61. Petty, *History of the Cromwellian Survey*, xv.

62. Hugh Goodacre, *The Economic Thought of William Petty: Exploring the Colonialist Roots of Economics* (Routledge, 2018), 5.

63. "A Designe for the securing of the West Indias with a Fleet in order to the weakning the Spanyards, the setling of Jamaica, and the promoting the English Interests there" (c. 1658), BL Egerton MS 2395, ff.167r–168v. On the political function of privateers, see Kris E. Lane, *Pillaging the Empire* (M.E. Sharpe, 1998), 96–129.

64. Petty, *History of the Cromwellian Survey*, 29, 35, 39.

65. Petty, *History of the Cromwellian Survey*, 20–21.

66. Petty, *History of the Cromwellian Survey*, 42, 118.

67. Nessa Cronin, "Writing the 'New Geography': Cartographic Discourse and Colonial Governmentality in William Petty's *The Political Anatomy of Ireland* (1672)," *Historical Geography* 42 (2014), 62.

68. These are examined in Ted McCormick, *William Petty and the Ambitions of Political Arithmetic* (Oxford University Press, 2009), 168–258.

69. William Petty, "A Treatise of Ireland, 1687," in British Library Additional Manuscripts (BL Add. MS) 21128, ff.52–91v, printed in *The Economic Writings of Sir William Petty*, ed. Charles Henry Hull, vol. 2 (Cambridge, 1899), 545–621. However, a manuscript proposal, entitled "Plantation" and tentatively dated to the 1670s, anticipates the 1687 scheme; see, BL Add. MS 72879, ff.112–113v. See also David Armitage, "The Political Economy of Britain and Ireland After the Glorious Revolution," in *Political Thought in Seventeenth-Century Ireland: Kingdom or Colony?* ed. Jane H. Ohlmeyer (Cambridge University Press, 2000), 229.

70. H. W. E. Petty-Fitzmaurice (Marquis of Lansdowne), ed., *The Petty Papers: Some Unpublished Writings of Sir William Petty*, 2 vols. (Constable, 1927), 2:261. Petty's nineteenth-century biographer identified him as the co-author of one or both of Vincent Gookin's printed pamphlets against the transplantation; on what evidence (besides, perhaps, Petty's list) is unclear. See Edmond Fitzmaurice, *The Life of Sir William Petty, 1623–1687* (London, 1895), 32.

71. For the debate, see Vincent Gookin, *The Great Case of Transplantation in Ireland Discussed* (London, 1655); Richard Lawrence, *The Interest of England in the Irish Transplantation, Stated* (Dublin, 1655); and Gookin, *The Author and Case of Transplanting the Irish into Connaught Vindicated, from the unjust Aspersions of Col. Richard Laurence* (London, 1655). See Patricia Coughlan, "Counter-Currents in Colonial Discourse: The Political Thought of Vincent and Daniel Gookin," in *Political Thought in Seventeenth-Century Ireland: Kingdom or Colony*, ed. Jane H. Ohlmeyer (Cambridge University Press, 2000); Sarah Barber, "Settlement, Transplantation and Expulsion: A Comparative Study of the Placement of Peoples," in *British Interventions in Early Modern Ireland*, eds. Ciaran Brady and Jane Ohlmeyer (Cambridge University Press, 2005), 280–298.

72. Petty, *History of the Cromwellian Survey*, 60.

73. Micheál Ó Siochrú et al., The Down Survey of Ireland Project (Trinity College Dublin, 2013). http://downsurvey.tcd.ie/down-survey-maps.php.

74. Reproduced in Petty, *History of the Cromwellian Survey*, 93–101.

75. Petty, *History of the Cromwellian Survey*, 94–95.

76. Petty, *History of the Cromwellian Survey*, 95.

77. Petty, *History of the Cromwellian Survey*, 96.

78. Petty, *History of the Cromwellian Survey*, 96.

79. Smith responded to the accusation that the surveyors had intended "every acre that we have soe valued must goe for one as good land as any of the rest," insisting that "it was never soe intended by us . . . wee judgeing the said values or valueing to bee the only meane between two extreames" (Petty, *History of the Cromwellian Survey*, 97)—that is, between the one extreme of claiming all potentially profitable lands as of equal value and the other of dismissing the profitability of the Kerry land in question altogether.

80. Petty, *History of the Cromwellian Survey*, 97.

81. Petty, *History of the Cromwellian Survey*, 98.

82. Petty, *History of the Cromwellian Survey*, 80.

83. Petty, *History of the Cromwellian Survey*, 97.

84. Petty, *History of the Cromwellian Survey*, 84.

85. Barnard notes the influence of Sir William Parsons, his son Richard Parsons, and Theophilus Buckworth, bishop of Dromore. See Barnard, *Improving Ireland?*, 22.

86. Boate, *Ireland's Natvrall History*, in *A Collection of Tracts and Treatises Illustrative of the Natural History, Antiquities, and the Political and Social State of Ireland, at Various Periods Prior to the Present Century* (Dublin, 1860), 1–148, at 95–96.

87. Offering his *Treatise of Taxes* to James Butler, duke of Ormond, following Ormond's appointment as lord lieutenant of Ireland in 1662, Petty wrote, "this great Person takes the great Settlement in hand, when *Ireland* is as a white paper . . . and when there is opportunity, to pass into Positive Laws whatsoever is right reason and the Law of Nature." William Petty, *A Treatise of Taxes and Contributions* (London, 1662), sig. A3r.

88. See, for instance, Petty, "About Exchanging of Women" (1674), BL Add. MS 72879, ff.71–72v, and "Of Counter-Transplanting the Irish & English" (1670s), BL Add. MS 72879, 117–118v; McCormick, *William Petty*, 168–208.

89. On "teeming women" as an economic resource, see, among many other papers, "The naturall & pecul[i]ar Interest of Ireland" (1683), BL Add. MS 72880, ff.121–151, which offers projections of Irish population growth (at f.125v and f.127v) on the predicted annual rate at which three hundred thousand or three hundred fifty thousand "teeming women" (or "teeming ffemales," f.130v) could produce children. On the contemporary significance of the term, see Margaret Pelling, "Far Too Many Women? John Graunt, the Sex Ratio, and the Cultural Determination of Number in Seventeenth-Century England," *Historical Journal* 59, no. 3 (2016): 701.

90. In "Of Counter-Transplanting the Irish and English": "1. The King has power to Impress [i.e., impress] men to serve in War. Methinks hee may doe the same to prevent war. 2. Hee can emprison & send into remote places such hee thinks may disturb the peace. 3. People who have no visible livelihood may bee disposd of [by] the magistrate." BL Add. MS 72879, f.117r.

91. See "The description of a Colony or Towneship to bee made in Ireland or America" (1680s), BL Add. MS 72867, ff.86–89, which specifies the size, population, military and economic facilities, commodity production, and household organization of the colony—including that "each Family [is] to have one Teeming maried woman, and not to consist of above 6 nor under 4 heads"—without reference to its location. On the purchase of Indigenous girls, see BL Add. MS 72880, f.127; McCormick, *William Petty*, 240.

92. Morgan, *Reckoning with Slavery*; Sussman, "The Colonial Afterlife of Political Arithmetic."

93. Morgan, *Reckoning with Slavery*, 5–6, 12–14.

94. Eric Ash, *The Draining of the Fens: Projectors, Popular Politics, and State Building in Early Modern England* (Johns Hopkins University Press, 2015).

95. McCormick, *Human Empire*, 155–156.

96. Morgan, *Reckoning with Slavery*, 110–140.

97. Morgan, *Reckoning with Slavery*, 31–54.

Chapter 2

The *Badianus Herbal* and Forced Indigenous Labor

Art, Land, and Nahua Knowledge in Sixteenth-Century Central Mexico

JENNIFER R. SARACINO

Shortly after their invasion of Indigenous lands in the Antilles and the Americas, soldiers sent at the behest of the Spanish Crown sought to exploit the economic potential of these places by implementing a forced labor system known as the *encomienda*. The basic elements of this system had their roots in Columbus's initial attempts to subjugate the people of Hispaniola (present-day Dominican Republic).[1] Later, after the invasion of Tenochtitlan, the capital of the former Aztec Empire (the heart of which was once located in what is today the historic center of Mexico City), colonists there attempted to implement a similar model. In this system, Spanish *encomenderos* could collect tribute and services from Indigenous subjects if the encomenderos promised also to provide for their spiritual welfare.[2] No history of forced labor in sixteenth-century Mexico—in what would become officially part of the viceroyalty of New Spain—would be complete without discussion of the encomienda. As part of this volume's larger aim to center knowledge production as an object of inquiry and analyze "plantations as sites for innovations in forms of exploitation, discipline, and media," this essay provides a discussion of various mechanisms and institutions implemented throughout the sixteenth century by Spanish soldiers, viceregal officials, and the Crown as these intersecting and often competing parties embarked on the task of colonization and the exploitation of land, Indigenous labor, and natural resources in New Spain.[3] Due to several factors that will be explored in this essay, the viceroyalty of New Spain never implemented a wide scale plantation complex like the model that would come to define the Caribbean and Atlantic world colonies of the following centuries. The reasons for this are numerous, ranging from the inherent difficulties of administrative control of the viceroyalty, the Crown's eventual ban against the enslavement of Indigenous people, and varying differences in the agricultural and economic profile of New Spain. In addition, as the encomienda system unfurled unevenly across the Valley of Mexico, the Spanish Crown sought to understand the botanical profile of its newly acquired territories in hopes of exporting its natural resources as part of a global, commercial network of exchange.[4] As colonial actors vied to control and regulate local labor, others focused their attention on profiting from Indigenous knowledge, particularly regarding the botanical and agricultural resources of New Spain. In short, in early colonial New Spain, numerous actors (soldiers, Nahuas, viceregal officials, and missionaries, just to name a few) had wide-ranging and competing interests that resulted in the creation of various, simultaneous approaches to land and labor exploitation, ranging from forced manual labor to economic botany projects. The colonists' and viceregal officials' attempts to subjugate the Indigenous population, appropriate their land and its resources, and harness their labor and knowledge resulted in "multiple projects and discourses of cultural and social transformation," a topic that Ted McCormick undertakes in regard to the various surveys and projects that paved the way for the plantation complex in early modern Ireland in the same chapter of this volume.[5] McCormick makes the astute point that it was precisely these knowledge-making projects that are constitutive of the action and process required to transform place, that is, specifically in this volume, the plantation complexes or agronomic spaces "where knowledge [was] circulated, collected, negotiated, contested with lasting natural, social, economic, political, and human consequences."[6]

Despite the salient differences between the encomiendas and the later plantation complexes of the Caribbean and Atlantic world, these nascent systems of colonial New Spain possessed some similarities. Both systems prioritized the extraction of labor, natural resources, and above all, knowledge in ways that were formative for how various methods of exploitation developed throughout the sixteenth century and, arguably, the remainder of the viceregal period. To develop this point, this essay focuses on the creation of the *Libellus Medicinalibus Indorus Herbis* (henceforth referred to as the *Badianus Herbal*), the first compendium of Central Mexican plant species and pharmacopeia. As a pictorial document, the *Badianus Herbal* was borne partially from its patrons' interests in economic botany, emblematizing the complex relationship between knowledge, agriculture, and colonization in sixteenth-century New Spain. The patron Francisco de Mendoza, son of the viceroy Antonio de Mendoza, sought to extract knowledge from Indigenous actors by exploiting his connection to the Colegio de Santa Cruz, a monastic institution of higher education established by Franciscan friars expressly for Indigenous nobles in 1536.[7] The Colegio was perhaps the most famous of the monastic schools for Indigenous students that the Crown established to mitigate the abuses inflicted by encomenderos on their Indigenous subjects and to prioritize their conversion. Run by Franciscan friars, the Colegio was a center of production for some of the most well-known pictorial documents of sixteenth-century Central Mexico created by Nahua artists. Thus, although circumventing the exploitative labor conditions of the encomienda, the Mendozas, via their proximity to the Colegio de Santa Cruz, could harness Indigenous knowledge for their own economic purposes, that is, to pave the way for their own monopolies on agricultural exports.

Although many scholars have interpreted the Colegio's Nahua-authored pictorial documents as emblems of artistic innovation, agency, and resistance to Spanish colonial authorities, less scholarship has focused on the connection between the exploitative labor systems established by the Spanish Crown as a direct cause for a marked shift in Indigenous artistic production of the sixteenth century. Art historian Ananda Cohen-Aponte has commented on this notable tendency in art historical writing of colonial Latin America to elide the violence, oppression, and inequality imposed by European colonists on Indigenous actors. As an alternative to long-established historiographical patterns, Cohen "see[s] a decolonial model of early modern art history as one that is keenly attentive to the hegemonic systems of power that served to naturalize the subjugation of indigenous aesthetic practices."[8] Seeking to respond to Cohen-Aponte's charge to acknowledge inherent power dynamics and systems of oppression in artistic and cultural production, this paper frames the *Badianus Herbal* within the larger context of forced labor systems implemented by the Spanish and the connection between labor and knowledge extraction.

To help rectify this historiographical tendency of overlooking how labor systems impacted Indigenous artists and their production, this essay brings together a discussion of the origins of forced labor in the Spanish Americas, the Crown's efforts to ameliorate its most egregious aspects, and the impact of these dynamics on Indigenous artistic production in sixteenth-century Mexico.

This essay investigates the relationship between the *Badianus Herbal*, a document commissioned by viceregal authorities, the fraught encomienda system and other forms of labor exploitation, and the Crown's burgeoning development of a larger state-controlled approach toward "economic botany," a practice Paula De Vos has described as the study of the botanical properties of plants to cultivate them for profit.[9] De Vos has observed that only in recent decades have scholars begun to recognize the role of local networks of knowledge production as driving engines in the establishment of imperial systems of agricultural and botanical exploitation that would go on to define the remainder of the Spanish viceregal period.[10] Likewise, less attention has been given to how these directives shaped sixteenth-century Indigenous artistic production or how Indigenous artists simultaneously negotiated their agency and creativity within the confines of these colonial projects. This essay examines how labor and agricultural systems instated by colonial authorities shaped the production of knowledge and visual culture that informed the *Badianus Herbal*, contending that the implementation of exploitative labor economies reconfigured Indigenous artistic practice. In turn, it explores how Indigenous artists destabilized the Crown's desires for botanical, labor, and economic information through their artistic agency. Through an examination of Nahua and Spanish systems of labor exploitation and their respective histories of human–landscape interaction, this paper posits that the creation of the *Badianus Herbal* marked an important early development in the Crown's embrace of state-sponsored information collection projects to form a global commercial network dependent on extraction from its newly acquired viceroyalty of New Spain.[11] An analysis of the *Badianus Herbal*'s content, as well as the circumstances of its production, reveals the tensions and slippages among ideological differences that Spanish colonial actors had in their approach toward labor, agricultural, and resource extraction and exploitation. Its content and illustrations also reveal how Indigenous contributions to colonial projects ultimately complicated the Crown's colonization of the Nahua, their lands, and their natural resources. Thorough this exposition, this paper seeks to contextualize sixteenth-century forms of coercive labor—the encomienda, the *corregimiento*, and the *repartimiento*—alongside institutions that also operated as major actors within burgeoning colonial science networks, bridging labor and knowledge production in ways that tend to be overlooked in analyses of Indigenous cultural production at monastic complexes in colonial New Spain.

The Colegio de Santa Cruz and the Creation of the *Badianus Herbal*

Throughout the initial decades after the Spanish takeover of Tenochtitlan in 1521, the Crown sought to evangelize the Indigenous population and establish a system that would help them in this endeavor.[12] The Franciscans were the chosen emissaries for this religious mission, and Pedro de Gante opened the first school for Indigenous students, the Convento de San Francisco de México, in 1527. At these Indigenous schools, friars taught students how to read and write in Latin, and they were also instructed in the mechanical arts, including skills like painting and carpentry.

The students' abilities so impressed their Franciscan instructors that not soon after, in 1534, Sebastián Ramírez de Fuenleal, bishop of Santo Domingo and president of the Second Audiencia; Juan de Zumárraga, first bishop of Mexico; and Antonio de Mendoza, the first viceroy, ordered the foundation of the Colegio de Santa Cruz in nearby Tlatelolco.[13] They established the Colegio de Santa Cruz as an institute of higher education for the continuing education of their most advanced pupils. In addition, they initially aspired to train a class of Indigenous clergymen that would assist them in their evangelization of the entire population. The educators at the Colegio implemented a three-year course of study after the model of a traditional Franciscan seminary. They taught the Latin trivium of grammar, rhetoric, and logic, and the quadrivium of arithmetic, geometry, astronomy, and music.[14] In addition, they taught reading, writing, philosophy, and Latin.[15]

Although the basic format of the curriculum seemed entirely derived from a Latin model, the friars adapted the education to fit the needs of the students and faculty. For example, when epidemics ravaged the local population in certain years, the friars incorporated studies of medicine and medical aid. These episodes in part explain the friars' keen interest in integrating the instruction of native medicine into the standard curriculum at the Colegio de Santa Cruz. After the major epidemic of 1545, the faculty created courses in Indigenous medicine.[16] It was these circumstances, along with the Crown's interest in the agricultural potential of New Spain, that led to the creation of the *Badianus Herbal.*

Nahua physician Martín de la Cruz authored the *Badianus Herbal* (the original Latin title *Libellus de Medicinalibus Indorum Herbis* loosely translates to "Little Book on Indian Medicinal Herbs"). De la Cruz served as a faculty member at the Colegio de Santa Cruz and wrote the *Badianus Herbal* in its original Nahuatl. De la Cruz trained as a physician during the precolonial period and was "of an advanced age" by 1552.[17] Juan Badiano, also a native instructor of the Colegio de Santa Cruz, translated the Nahuatl into Latin.[18] There is no definite record of who rendered the images that accompany the text.[19]

The *Badianus Herbal* as a manuscript genre has its roots in Greco-Roman classical antiquity. There is no known precedent of this genre in the Mesoamerican tradition. One of the genre's most influential iterations comes from the Greek physician Pedanius Dioscorides, who wrote his *De Materia Medica (On Medical Matters)* circa 65 CE. The oldest surviving manuscript copy of this (also known as the Anicia Codex) was completed in Constantinople circa 512 CE.[20] The original manuscript contained information on plants and their medicinal uses, including information on approximately 600 plants, 35 animal products, and 90 minerals along with their descriptions.[21] Throughout the medieval period up to the advent of the printing press, the manuscript, its derivations, and copies were translated into Arabic, Persian, Latin, and other languages, becoming the template for many vernacular editions that then influenced printed herbals in the early modern period.[22]

Other major sources for templates for *Badianus Herbal*, *Pharmacopoeia* (a book containing a list of medicinal drugs with directions for their use), or *Materia Medica*, as they are variably termed in the literature, include a printed edition of the *Liber de proprietatibus rerum* by Bartholomaeus Anglicus (first published circa 1470), the *Herbarium* of Apuleius Platonicus, and Pliny's *Natural History*.[23] The fact that both Bartholomaeus Anglicus's and Pliny's encyclopedias are cited as early print examples of *Badianus Herbal* is significant given that these two sources have also been cited as possible influences for the *Historia general de las cosas de la Nueva España* (widely known as the Florentine Codex for its present location in the Medicea Laurenziana Library in Florence), a compendium of Nahua daily customs, cultural practices, a conquest account, and natural history, also compiled within the orbit of the Colegio de Santa Cruz circa 1575–

1577.[24] In many regional traditions, including the modern-day countries of Germany, France, the Netherlands, England, and Italy, printed editions of herbals began to emerge in the second half of the sixteenth century. Thus, the creation of the *Badianus Herbal* at the Colegio de Santa Cruz in 1552 marks an important milestone and contribution to the evolution of the genre in the early modern period.

The *Badianus Herbal* is presented on European style paper in the form of a bound book.[25] The manuscript is organized into thirteen chapters according to the part of the body the plant can aid, beginning with the head and working its way through each part of the body down to the feet. The *Badianus Herbal* contains 126 pages, 8 of which are blank. It contains 185 paintings of plant images, or phytomorphs. Each page of the manuscript is marked with straight red lines delineating its margins, similarly to how a scribe might score a European illuminated manuscript (Fig. 2.1).

Each folio typically bears the illustration of one to three plant images. Each plant's Nahuatl name is transcribed above it in red ink. The plant illustration typically occupies the top half of the page and underneath is written the recipe for its use in a remedy. The accompanying description of the plant is written in Latin. The Latin text describes each plant's healing benefits as well as a recipe for its use in a medicinal compound and directions for its application. Although the *Badianus Herbal* contains primarily Central Mexican plant species and directions for their use in recipes drawing from primarily Indigenous knowledge, it was Spanish viceregal official Francisco de Mendoza who commissioned the document.

Forced Labor, Draft Labor, and Economic Botany in Sixteenth-Century Mexico

Francisco de Mendoza was the son of the first viceroy of New Spain, Antonio de Mendoza. The Mendozas were keenly interested in the economic profit to be gained from botanical knowledge and the subsequent export, trade, and transplantation of New World flora. The earliest evidence of long-distance transplantation of spices in the Spanish empire took place in the 1550s and involved the transplantation of seeds from the East Indies to New Spain and, notably, first appear in the viceroy's possession.[26] Viceroy Mendoza's interest can be traced to an expedition in 1542 when he ordered Ruy López de Villalobos to collect and send him botanic specimens from

Figure 2.1. Libellus de Medicinalibus Indorum Herbis (*Badianus Herbal*), an herbal composed in 1552 by Martín de la Cruz and translated into Latin by Juan Badiano. 1552. Folio 61r. *Source:* Instituto Nacional de Antropología e Historia, México.

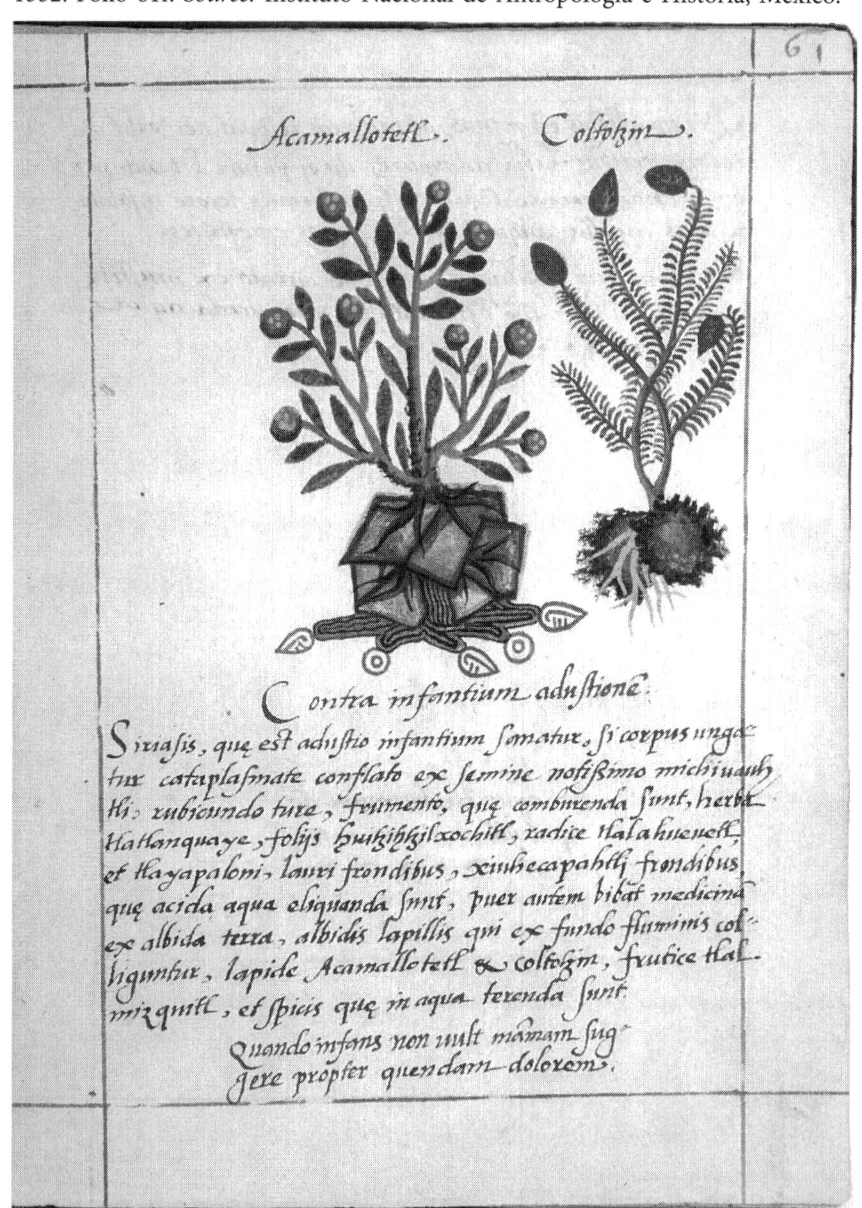

the Philippines. Although the expedition did not end well, the viceroy obtained the seeds by 1558 and likely helped his son Francisco obtain the *asiento* (monopoly rights) to cultivate the seeds.[27] This act was in keeping with the Crown's practice of granting *asientos*, exclusive rights to produce and trade in a particular commodity.[28] Through this system, the Crown could collect taxes on royal monopolies on the sale of certain goods.

Like his father, Francisco also took interest in Nahua-authored pictorial documents, and he commissioned the *Badianus Herbal* as a gift for Charles V. Not only did Antonio de Mendoza express interest in establishing control over the extraction, trade, and transplantation of New World flora, but he also enthusiastically supported the Colegio de Santa Cruz where the *Badianus Herbal* was created. Records show that the viceroy gifted the Colegio large tracts of land and livestock, and so their compliance in honoring Mendoza's commissions makes sense given his history of financially supporting the institution.[29] It is likely that both Mendozas saw in the Colegio an opportunity to harness Indigenous knowledge about the natural environment to help them make informed decisions about their *asientos*. Of note, although Antonio de Mendoza's role as viceroy was to control and mitigate the exploitation of the encomienda system, the Mendozas's financial support of the Colegio and their patronage of pictorial documents demonstrate their continued interest in the possibilities of resource extraction and commodification in New Spain. Records show that Viceroy Mendoza continued to support the institution even after he was moved to Cuzco as the viceroy of Peru. Records also demonstrate that the *Badianus* manuscript was shipped to Spain along with actual botanical specimens from the newly established viceroyalty. It was sent "as a way of encouraging the crown to support pharmaceutical cultivation and trade and to put the Mendoza family in charge of that trade."[30] Mendoza's entrepreneurial activities as well as his enthusiastic support of the Colegio reveal the close link between the exploitation of Indigenous intellectual and environmental knowledge and the expansion of economic botany under his jurisdiction.[31] The figures of Viceroy Antonio de Mendoza and Francisco as actors intimately intertwined with the *Badianus Herbal* project provide an integral link to a larger discussion of labor exploitation in sixteenth-century New Spain. Part of Viceroy de Mendoza's interest in these types of exportation projects may have been partially due to his primary charge as viceroy to curb the encomienda system, an increasing vexation to the Spanish Crown.

Encomienda and Corregimiento

After Columbus's arrival to the Antilles in 1492, he and his men established their first colonial outpost on the island of Hispaniola (present-day Dominican Republic and Haiti). Columbus left Hispaniola temporarily to return to Spain and returned in 1495 to discover that the Indigenous population had rebelled against their incipient settlement. In retaliation, Columbus enslaved many of the dissidents and sent them to Spain, inaugurating a colonial practice of enslaving Indigenous rebels as punishment. Although the Crown initially permitted the enslavement of rebels, Spanish soldiers in the Americas brutally exploited this practice, seeming to enslave any person they desired regardless of their adherence to colonial policy. However, a papal bull issued by Alexander VI on May 4, 1493, made it clear that the Spanish Crown's only and official justification for invading the Americas was the evangelization of its pagan population, and the Spanish monarchs (particularly Isabella of Castile) continually struggled to regulate the rampant enslavement of Indigenous people enacted by the colonists through a series of royal mandates.[32]

In addition to enslavement, the foundations of an exploitative, forced labor system were set in place from the inception of Columbus's establishment of the Hispaniola settlement. Columbus had petitioned the Crown to allow the colonists the use of Indigenous labor to help support the livelihood of the colony. Shortly thereafter, to regulate this system, Isabella appointed Fray Nicolás de Ovando as the royal governor, and his initial instructions formed the basis of a more structured system that would go on to become the encomienda system.[33] First, Ovando's instructions stipulated that native people be brought together in towns and live close by Spanish residents. The encomendero, or overseer, was "entrusted" with a group of indigenous persons in exchange for their forced labor—a structure that L. B. Simpson has argued was borne out of the economic system of early modern Spain. In his characterization of Spain's economy, Simpson argues that Spanish invaders customarily seized land and levied tribute on their vassals.[34] As mentioned earlier, the Crown maintained that the Spanish overseers' primary responsibility was to convert the Indigenous population to Catholicism. Thus, Ovando's rules required the Indigenous members' instruction in the tenets of Catholicism as well as a religious seminary education. In return, the Indigenous tenant was given a home for themselves and their family as well as a small plot of land for raising crops and livestock.

Deriving their authority from the royal power of the king, encomenderos could collect tribute and "personal services" from the king's subjects as long as they looked after the welfare of the Indigenous community. Overseers could compel Indigenous people to work in their service, initiating a system of *repartimiento*, or rotational draft labor.[35] These tenets were further solidified through the Laws of Burgos, a code of laws that stipulated specific ways to treat the Indigenous population, in 1512.[36] The establishment of the encomienda system emerged from colonists' efforts to adapt the existing agricultural systems of the Indigenous population and exploit the economic potential of their newly acquired territories under the guise of evangelization. Through the encomienda, colonial authorities sought to establish some kind of order to the chaotic relations between the conquistadors and the Indigenous population.

Hernán Cortés, upon his takeover of the Aztec capital of Tenochtitlan, sought to implement the encomienda system on the previously established Caribbean model in the aftermath of his victory. The Crown, however, having received reports of the havoc wreaked on the native population on Hispaniola, denied his request to implement the encomienda.[37] Cortés responded to this mandate in protest, stating that he had no intention to follow the order and that at the very least, the soldiers who assisted him in the war for Tenochtitlan should be awarded land and Indigenous service in perpetuity.[38] The encomienda system was implemented and persisted despite the Crown's written attempts to forbid the practice. Cortés and his men cited several factors for the system's continuance, including its necessity to support the economic and agricultural productivity of the colony and its sociopolitical stability.[39] Finally, in 1528, the Council of the Indies installed a regular government in the Kingdom of New Spain known as the First Audiencia. Presided over by Beltrán Nuño de Guzmán, the encomienda system reached unparalleled heights of exploitation, oppression, and rampant abuse of the Indigenous population.

Despite language specifying that the encomendero was to care for his charges, as Simpson has argued, "in the first fifty years of its existence, [it] was looked upon by its beneficiaries as a subterfuge for slavery."[40] Encomenderos fully exploited the limits of the system throughout the disastrous First Audiencia. Further complicating the politics of the Crown's incipient colonial apparatus was the presence of several mendicant orders that the Crown had sent to New Spain to assist with the evangelization and inculcation of the Indigenous population. Reports of abuse written to the Crown alleged that natives were being enslaved and that free Indigenous people were being forced to work in the mines, and the Bishop Zumárraga, a Franciscan, frequently wrote to the Crown decrying the exploitation and abuse of the native population at the hands of de Guzmán and other encomenderos.[41]

For the purposes of this volume, it serves to compare aspects of these early forced labor systems in New Spain as they arose from the outset of Spanish invasion, particularly that of the encomienda and repartimiento systems in New Spain with the later plantation system of the Caribbean and Atlantic world colonies, which were largely dependent on enslaved labor. First, plantation-based economies of the Atlantic world tended to operate as part of a larger commercial network that brought in labor and supplies to export a product or crop such as sugar, coffee, or cotton. They tended to operate at a large scale, numbering approximately fifty to several hundred enslaved laborers.[42] It is not clear from the archival record how many Indigenous people were conscripted as part of encomiendas; the numbers could range widely. However, a major difference between the encomienda and the Atlantic world plantation is that encomenderos technically had no juridical connection with land. It operated as a governmental, tribute-collecting institution.[43] Simpson argued that from its inception, although conscripted labor might have been a prominent aspect of the encomienda system in practice, it was principally designed as a grant to the right to collect tributes.[44] However, Zavala argued in his analysis that the original encomienda (in the Antilles) was a grant to the right to use labor and that tribute became a part of the system later on.[45] Although the encomienda system became a defining feature of the labor and economy of sixteenth-century Mexico, it did not persist unchallenged and, in fact, continually proved to be a controversial point of contention between encomenderos and the Crown.

The antagonistic relationship between Guzmán and Zumárraga was emblematic of an ongoing tension between the encomenderos and the mendicant friars. The Crown had installed Zumárraga as protector of the native population, and it was this role that galvanized Zumárraga to report the abuses of the Indigenous population inflicted by Guzmán and his men to the Crown. Zumárraga and other Franciscans operated monasteries where many Indigenous youths lived, and Guzmán accused the Franciscans of inciting disobedience among the Indigenous population because they would only report to and communicate with the mendicant friars. Apparently, the Spanish Crown paid little heed to Guzmán's complaints, but the tensions between the encomenderos and the friars are significant in charting the evolution of the encomienda system from the First to the Second Audiencia, which was ultimately headed by Antonio de Mendoza. Due to the copious number of reports of abuse fielded by the Crown, the Council of the Indies decided to create a new, permanent government and the Kingdom of New Spain as a viceroyalty. The council appointed Antonio de Mendoza as the president of the Audiencia. It took Antonio de Mendoza several years to arrive in New Spain, however, so in the interim, Sebastían Ramírez de Fuenleal, bishop of Santo Domingo, served on behalf of the Crown to edge back the oppressive actions of Guzmán and the other encomenderos.

One of the first steps of the Second Audiencia, headed by Fuenleal, was to wrest back control of the encomiendas granted by Guzmán during the First Audiencia and allocate them under a centralized Indigenous government controlled by the Crown, called the corregimiento.[46] The implementation of the corregimiento attempted to mediate relations between the Spanish and Indigenous populations and to integrate Indigenous leadership into the Spanish colonial political system. The establishment of the corregimiento was designed to return the authority to grant and maintain lands to the Crown. The *corregidor* was a Spanish government official with administrative and judicial powers appointed by the king and queen of Spain to serve as the king's proxy.[47] In some cases, *corregidores* might be appointed by viceroys, governors, and captains general.[48] The corregidor's main duty was the religious education of his Indigenous subjects and to mitigate the abuses of the encomenderos (such as the unregulated and illegal enslavement of Indigenous people).

Simpson has argued that the Spanish Crown's attempt to mitigate the *encomenderos'* control of Indigenous labor force was partially derived from its desire to have direct access to native labor and tribute.[49] That is, the Crown sought to eliminate the *encomendero* as the middle person, so labor and tribute could funnel directly to the Crown without the interference of an intermediary figure. In fact, as noted recently by Richard Conway, the agriculturally productive region of Xochimilco, home of the most productive region of *chinampa* agriculture, was once the largest single encomienda of central Mexico, with somewhere around 20,000 tributaries.[50] As Conway notes, after Pedro de Alvarado's death in 1541, the Crown quickly moved to escheat Xochimilco.[51] Ultimately, though, the encomienda continued to coexist alongside the newly introduced corregimiento.

Coatequitl

Because of the difficulty in eliminating the encomienda system and even regulating the corregimiento, the Crown attempted to use religious and moral obligation as an antidote. Viceroy Mendoza, in his role, was to ensure that the conversion and evangelization of the natives were the primary concerns of encomenderos and corregidores, and as part of this directive, these individuals were primarily charged with supporting the evangelization project in every way possible. This included supporting the construction of churches and the efforts of priests as well as monastic schools designed to inculcate Indigenous youths in a Western European style of humanistic education.[52]

However, although Viceroy Mendoza and the Franciscan friars sought to mitigate the abuses of the encomenderos, it does not mean that they did not seek alternatives to capitalize on Indigenous labor. As Ryan Crewe has recently discussed, the Crown, missionaries, and local Indigenous leaders in New Spain all drew on and facilitated the continuation of the Indigenous *coatequitl*, or draft labor system, well into the sixteenth century.[53] Coatequitl pertained primarily to the commoner, or *macehual* (pl. *macehualtin*) class.[54] Their duties were labor intensive and often involved grueling heavy lifting. Macehualtin were often obliged to participate in burden carrying or large-scale public work construction.

The continued use of coatequitl reveals how viceregal authorities left Indigenous systems of tenure and labor in place to optimize yields, simultaneously preserving some pre-Hispanic structures of Indigenous society. As noted by Crewe, "[t]he *coatequitl* was the linchpin of indigenous politics, for it reaffirmed the internal hierarchies of class and territoriality within the polity."[55] In a similar fashion, the coatequitl also reaffirmed the "cellular and rotational organization of the local indigenous state."[56] As Crewe's comment makes clear, there is a fundamental pre-Hispanic and Indigenous antecedent for the draft rotational labor the viceroyalty exploited in early colonial New Spain.

The distinction of Xochimilco as the former site of the largest encomienda in all of New Spain is relevant to a discussion of the *Badianus Herbal*. Both of the *Badianus Herbal*'s authors de la Cruz and Badiano hailed from the nearby village of Xochimilco, a place with a rich agricultural history where the pre-Hispanic *chinampa* floating gardens and irrigation canals still exist. In a recent landmark study of Xochimilco and its environmental history, Conway has demonstrated that the Spanish Crown largely allowed

Xochimilco's inhabitants to maintain the economic and agricultural productivity of its chinampas with little disruption until the late eighteenth century.[57] The chinampas provided great wealth for the Crown, and the Crown, in turn, left chinampa cultivation under the control of its Indigenous community members. Connecting this history to the *Badianus Herbal*, it begs the question of how the Crown's decision to leave Xochimilco under the governance of its Indigenous tenants also allowed locals to maintain precolonial Indigenous environmental and agricultural epistemologies.

By keeping pre-Hispanic patterns of land tenure intact, Indigenous inhabitants were able to continue to benefit from the chinampas' agricultural productivity. In precontact systems of Nahua land tenure, *altepetlalli*, or *calpollali*, referred to communally held lands.[58] However, Indigenous commoners, or *macehualtin*, were permitted in pre- and post-Conquest Xochimilco to work lands belonging to nobility in usufruct if they continued to cultivate the land and meet their tax obligations.[59] In early viceregal Xochimilco, Nahua officials continued to administer these land arrangements. Thus, another characteristic of Viceroy Mendoza's tenure, in addition to his early projects of economic botany, was to maintain Indigenous land holdings and systems of tenure and administration to secure tribute income and food for Mexico City. As we can see through the case studies of Xochimilco and the examples of coatequitl labor used for monastery construction and large-scale public works, the Spanish Crown and its viceregal officials found alternatives to the encomienda system and other mechanisms (often those with precolonial Indigenous antecedents) through which to draw on Indigenous labor. Additionally, at least in the case of Indigenous land tenure, preserving these structures offered an advantage to its Nahua laborers in that it granted some form of agricultural subsistence to those without proprietary rights to land.

Competing Notions of Environmental Stewardship Depicted in the *Badianus Herbal*

Economic historians and historians of medicine have recently highlighted the connection between the *Badianus Herbal* and the colonial administration's early attempts at forms of economic botany.[60] Perhaps Antonio and Francisco de Mendoza saw these types of commissions as ways to circumvent the more obvious exploitative practices of the encomienda through the means of intellectual and artistic production.

Many of the pictorial documents produced by Indigenous students at the Colegio de Santa Cruz have been historically viewed as syncretistic products of Indigenous pictographic tradition as well as Western European humanist culture and naturalistic representation. The slippages between these two graphic systems and worldviews allowed multilingual and bivisual creators and readers to interpret imagery in polysemic ways that have fascinated scholars for decades.[61] The *Badianus Herbal* has been viewed as an offshoot of the Europeans' need to learn about Indigenous medicine as prophylaxis and remedy. In addition, friars at the Colegio de Santa Cruz were keen to understand potentially pagan customs and religious rituals that may have been linked to the careful preparation of plants in various mixtures.[62] Others have analyzed how the *Badianus Herbal* exhibits characteristics of late medieval and early modern European humoral theory and Galenic medicine, analyzing the intermingling of Indigenous and European medical philosophies, theories, and epistemologies.[63]

Although the commission and creation of the *Badianus Herbal* reveal the clear influence of European botanical directives, the artistic execution of the project by its Indigenous authors also reveals competing visions of environmental stewardship between its patrons and artists. In this section, I will outline the information communicated graphically about the local flora by the *Badianus Herbal's* artists and discuss how the images convey subtle messages regarding the artists' relationship to their surroundings, revealing the fissures in the Crown's overarching designs to exploit the economic and environmental potential of its newly acquired dominions.

In the *Badianus Herbal*, the artist (or artists) of each image used small amounts of shading and contouring to indicate dimensionality. Most of the plants are rendered like flattened, two-dimensional objects. All the plants are drawn the same general size, regardless of their actual size, except for moss. The artist (or artists) chose to depict the plants as if isolated from their natural surroundings, displaying each plant's surface and root parts. Similarly, the artists' rendering of the plants varies from a more naturalistic approach to shading and contouring to a more schematized or stylized representation of the chosen specimens. At times, the plant representations recall the pre-Hispanic pictorial language that used codified forms and colors to represent ideas or objects. The thick outlines, two-dimensional patterning, and stylized representations of objects found in nature are hallmark characteristics of the early colonial style. Similarly, the symbols and pictographic conventions in certain cases also act as carriers of information that recall Central Mexican pictorial language.

In her analysis of the illustrations, Emily Emmart noted that the use of the glyphic symbol for stone (Fig. 2.2; detail of stone symbol) differed from the realistic rendering of stony ground that conveyed the plant's natural environment also present in the *Badianus*.

In Central Mexican pictorial convention, the stone symbol is drawn in the shape of an oval with three volutes on each side. Across the front of the oval are usually two or three wavy stripes. In the *Badianus Herbal*, the stone symbol always accompanied a sprouting plant. Certain identifying characteristics of individual plants, such as the root system, are rendered in a conventionalized manner that prevents proper identification. However, the artist innovated the kind of information relayed in the *Badianus Herbal* about the plant's relationship to its environment, as well as the specificity

Figure 2.2. Central Mexican stone symbol behind roots, folio 26r. *Source:* Instituto Nacional de Antropología e Historia, México.

of its environment, by incorporating pre-Hispanic pictographic symbols. For example, a root system drawn against a blue background indicated that the plant grew in an aquatic environment like a swamp or pond (Fig. 2.3), while patches of blue indicated moist soil. In some instances, a symbol at the root appears as a blue, oblong shape with lines drawn diagonally across. Small white ovals drawn at intervals around the border of the shape indicate that it is the Central Mexican symbol for water. This symbol connoted that the plant grew in swiftly flowing water (Fig. 2.4).[64] In other instances, the presence of a boulder behind the root system indicated that the plant grew in the crevices between a hard, rocky surface. With

Figure 2.3. Plants growing in swamp or pond, folio 44r. *Source:* Instituto Nacional de Antropología e Historia, México.

Figure 2.4. Plant grows in rocky environment, folio 45r. *Source:* Instituto Nacional de Antropología e Historia, México.

the incorporation of Central Mexican glyphs, the artists are innovating the *Badianus Herbal* genre by including additional information regarding that plant specimen's relationship to its surrounding environment as well as the ecological conditions necessary for its survival.

The use of native pigments and varnishes shows the artists' ability to infuse the European genre with Indigenous pictorial conventions. The continued use of Central Mexican pictorial devices to convey the ecological relationship of the plant to its environment demonstrates two important ideas about the artists in this context. First, the artists understood the desired aims of the *Badianus Herbal*, a foreign genre. Secondly, they consciously chose to employ Central Mexican pictorial language because it communicated the desired information more effectively. The artists, understanding two disparate visual traditions, manipulated the expression to convey information they understood necessary for the desired aims of the European audience.

Alejandra Rojas Silva has recently argued that the central folios of the *Badianus Herbal* suggest a symbolic connection between the mythical Mesoamerican city of Tollan and the Garden of Eden. The central folios of the manuscript differ markedly from the visual presentation of one to three plants in the other folios. In the central three folios, six plants are presented in two rows of three. There is no written description or recipe that accompanies these plants as is the custom in the other pages. Each plant is accompanied by its Nahuatl name above it in red ink, however. As Rojas Silva has noted, these are the most brilliant and vibrantly colored plant specimens in the manuscript, their colors beaming radiantly from their pages. Although there is no recipe written on these pages, some of the plants are included in a recipe just following the break in structure which notes, "[t]rees and flowers to counter the fatigue of one administering the Republic and performing public duty."[65] Rojas Silva and Patricia Granziera have discussed how flowers and gardens were linked to high-ranking nobles in Nahua society, particularly richly colored plant specimens that were likely associated with the paradisiacal origin place in Mesoamerican thought known as Tollan.[66] In Nahua cosmology, Tollan was associated with the cultural hero and elite ruler Quetzalcoatl who helped bring civilization and learning to the Nahua people. Throughout her analysis of the manuscript, Rojas Silva points out various ways in which the *Badianus* authors conflate concepts of Tollan with the Garden of Eden, in a purposeful alignment of Christological and Mesoamerican cosmological origin stories. She interprets this alignment of European and Mesoamerican tradition as a strategy to demonstrate their dual status as "civilized Christians, and as inheritors of an indigenous nobility worthy of guiding their people into a new era."[67] This idea of the authors portraying themselves as dutiful Catholics capable of synthesizing Indigenous knowledge with classical and Christian codes and formats is significant given the intended audience of the manuscript.

Just as the preservation of Indigenous systems of land tenure preserved some Indigenous patterns of social hierarchy, so might have the administrators' reliance on Indigenous botanical knowledge. As Granziera has explained, gardens and horticultural knowledge were intimately entwined with Mesoamerican cosmological beliefs.[68] In addition, gardens were highly associated with the Mexica imperial rulers. Before the arrival of the Spaniards, the *tlatoani* (rulers in Nahuatl) had constructed royal gardens in Tenochtitlan, Chapultepec, Huastepec, Ixtapalapa, el Peñon, and Tetzcoco.[69] As Granziera explains, common food crops came to the elite through tribute, thus, gardens "contained instead ornamental, aromatic, and medicine plants associated with ritual needs or those that were emblematic of high status."[70] The *Badianus Herbal*, in fact, contains a number of these types of plants including *yolloxochitl* and *cacahuaxochitl* (folio 53). These, Granziera asserts, were considered a luxury and, as such, a marker of the ruling class that reinforced social hierarchy.[71] As an analysis of the plants contained within the document reveals, the *Badianus Herbal* did not only record Indigenous recipes for native plants but also preserved aspects of pre-Hispanic Nahua social structure as well as Indigenous cosmological beliefs likely unbeknownst to its Spanish patrons.

From the patrons' point of view, the *Badianus Herbal* was intended for use by the Spanish as a guidebook for Indigenous remedies that dealt effectively with native diseases and afflictions. Because of the short period in which the *Badianus Herbal* was created, other scholars speculate that the Spanish authorities hoped to convince the king of the profit to be gained from the botanical riches of the colony.[72] The authors most likely hoped to produce work that would serve as a presentation piece and impress its recipient, the Spanish king, with its aesthetic appeal.

Knowing the intended audience is significant given the time and place in which this herbal was produced. Returning to the site of the *Badianus Herbal's* production, the Colegio de Santa Cruz, throughout its years of operation, faced monumental challenges that impeded its growth and continually threatened its existence. After the first ten years, the Franciscans had to relinquish management and left administrative duties in the hands of their students. The former pupils wrote a set of rules and elected their own rector and professors, but this system too crumbled in about twenty years.[73] As noted earlier, the epidemic of 1545 decimated some of the friars' most promising students. With the noble population almost entirely wiped out by disease, the friars made the decision to accept students of non-noble descent to boost their student population. The complex, however, deteriorated by 1550. The Colegio's most ardent supporter, the first viceroy of New Spain, Antonio de Mendoza, who had guaranteed his patronage of the school, was transferred to Peru in 1550. Finally, the decree by the Mexican Council of 1555 forbidding the ordination of native clergy negated one of the Colegio's primary reasons for existence. Up until this point, the Colegio provided a place of power, privilege, and upward social mobility for many of Mexico-Tenochtitlan's Nahua elite, a rare opportunity within an oppressive colonial system. Many of the graduates of the Colegio, for example, would go on to become instructors there. One particular alum, Antonio Valeriano, would become the *gobernador* of Mexico-Tenochtitlan.[74] Thus, the *Badianus Herbal* is a fascinating case study in how Nahua creators wielded pictorial representation, botanical and medical knowledge, and an impressive command of Christological, Classical, and Mesoamerican epistemologies to create a visual program to advance their political cause, that is, to secure funding for an institution that up to this point had provided opportunities for social upward mobility. Similarly, as other products created by Nahua authors at the Colegio de Santa Cruz, it seems that the authors of the *Badianus Herbal* wanted it to operate as a political document in which they could proclaim their rights to steward the natural environment and participate in the configuration of colonial rule in New Spain by demonstrating the need for their profound knowledge of the land and its resources.

Conclusion

The pictorial documents produced at the Colegio de Santa Cruz, prominently among them the *Badianus Herbal*, have long been lauded for their brilliant synthesis of Central Mexican and Western European modes of thought and graphic representation, epistemologies, and literary and philosophical approaches. It is also essential to recognize how they demonstrate a tension between the imperatives of the Spanish Crown and the "self-interested calculations" of individual viceregal authorities, namely the father and son Mendoza.[75] The Crown, after all, had attempted with the

Colegio to bypass the encomienda, long a contentious and exploitative establishment, by wielding the power of an alliance between the Crown, Franciscan missionaries, and their Indigenous charges. Viceregal authorities like the Mendozas, however, used their patronage of monastic institutions like the Colegio de Santa Cruz to envision new forms of agricultural and land exploitation. By collecting botanical information from Indigenous experts, they sought to secure for themselves new *asientos*, monopolistic rights to the cultivation and transplantation of desirable plant specimens. Their commission of Indigenous creators to craft the *Badianus Herbal*, in its emergence directly from entrepreneurial desires for economic gain, thus points to a conclusion similar to that in the preceding chapter, that "projects . . . would *produce* the material conditions and the knowledge that made those interests legible and calculable to the targeted groups"—the targeted group in this case being the Spanish Crown.[76]

Although not immediately evident, the creation of the *Badianus Herbal* intersected with the most notorious labor system of early post-Conquest New Spain—the encomienda—set in place essentially from the start of Spanish colonization in the Caribbean, reflecting patterns of land tenure from which the colonists' homelands came as well as the precedents of their exploits in the Antilles. Ideologically, however, the encomienda presented continual challenges to the Spanish Crown who also duly sought to prioritize the evangelization of the native population. The patronage of the first viceroy of New Spain, Antonio de Mendoza, demonstrates how viceregal authorities pursued their own exploitative desires while complying with Crown orders concerning the treatment of the Indigenous population. Encomiendas and their subsequent iterations, the corregimientos, would persist throughout the sixteenth century. There were, additionally, other mechanisms inherent to Indigenous social structure that these same Christianizing parties sought to exploit, for example, the coatequitl rotary labor system used in monastery construction. As these various situations show, colonists' approaches to exploiting the Nahua in sixteenth-century New Spain were under constant transformation and experimentation, highlighting the simultaneous, overlapping, and sometimes, conflicting ways in which various empires sought to benefit from forced Indigenous labor and resources at every segment of society.

Through the *Badianus Herbal*, a project of economic botany that exploited Nahua knowledge, Francisco might have spied an avenue through which the Crown could eventually collect taxes on royal monopolies, operating similarly to the corregimiento system in which tribute funneled directly to the Crown. The reorganization of Indigenous labor and land tenure systems in viceregal Mexico set the stage for the exploitation of Indigenous knowledge that precipitated plantation complexes in the coming centuries. The directives of his father and patron of the Colegio, Antonio de Mendoza, to record Indigenous knowledge in the format of a western European herbal might even be described as a case of epistemic violence, wherein Nahua healing knowledge about Central Mexican plants and their potential healing applications were exploited for material gain. As an analysis of some of the content of the *Badianus Herbal* evinces, however, the Indigenous authors' articulations of their own relationship to and conception of the natural environment complicate the narrative of New Spain's environmental colonization and exploitation by Spanish authorities. Indigenous creative production under colonial rule engaged a dynamic of negotiation and resistance that, at times, impeded the Crown's uncontested possession of the Nahua, their native lands, and their natural resources and exposed aspects of the relationship between environmental knowledge and Nahua social hierarchy. The viceroyalty's willingness to embrace precontact systems of labor and plant knowledge would preserve aspects of Indigenous cosmological beliefs and patterns of social hierarchy that would ultimately destabilize their plans of total cultural assimilation.

Notes

1. Lesley Byrd Simpson discusses Spanish soldiers' activities in Hispaniola and the policies that gradually evolved into the *encomienda*. Lesley Byrd Simpson, *The Encomienda in New Spain: The Beginning of Spanish Mexico* (University of California Press, 1982).

2. "Aztec" is the most commonly known term used to refer to the Indigenous population that lived in the Central Valley of Mexico at the time of Spanish conquest, but it is imprecise. The ethnic group that controlled the so-called Aztec Empire at the time of conquest was known as the Mexica who spoke the Indigenous language Nahuatl. They were one of many ethnically and linguistically diverse Indigenous groups in Mexico at the time. Nahuatl was the *lingua franca* of the Aztec Empire, thus, after Spanish conquest, the Indigenous population in central Mexico become known as the Nahua, a term I use throughout this paper.

3. From the introduction to this volume.

4. For other cases of economy botany, see the chapters by Moritz von Brescius, Christina Skott, Marta Macedo, Theresa Ventura, and Gillian McGillivray in this volume.

5. See Ted McCormick's chapter in this volume.

6. From the introduction to this volume.

7. Regarding the interaction between Indigenous and other forms of knowledge, see Moritz von Brescius's and Nicholas B. Miller's chapters in this volume.

8. Ananda Cohen-Aponte, "Decolonizing the Global Renaissance: A View from the Andes," in *The Globalization of Renaissance Art: A Critical Review*, ed. Daniel Savoy (Brill, 2017), 73.

9. As summarized by historian Paula De Vos, "Economic botany is essentially the practice of studying the botanical properties of plants that may be of use to human society and cultivating them for profit." Paula De Vos, "The Science of Spices: Empiricism and Economic Botany in the Early Spanish Empire," *Journal of World History* 17, no. 4 (2006): 400.

10. De Vos, "The Science of Spices," 400.

11. On the role of state funding for knowledge production, see the chapters by Ted McCormick, Moritz von Brescius, Theresa Ventura, and Rebekah McCallum in this volume.

12. The Indigenous population that Cortés and his men met throughout their invasion of present-day Mexico was in fact comprised of many different ethnic groups who spoke diverse languages. The Indigenous empire, widely known as the Aztec Empire, was comprised of three separate but allied groups, known as the Triple Alliance. The group that claimed Tenochtitlan as their capital called themselves the Mexica. The most widely spoken language among the Indigenous population was Nahuatl, and thus after Spanish Conquest, the Indigenous population of Central Mexico is most commonly referred to as the Nahua.

13. Elizabeth H. Boone, "The Multilingual Bivisual World of Sahagún's Mexico," in *Sahagún at 500: Essays on the Quincentenary of the Birth of Fr. Bernardino de Sahagún*, ed. John Frederick Schwaller (Academy of American Franciscan History, 2003), 141.

14. Georges Baudot, *Utopia and History in Mexico: The First Chroniclers of Mexican Civilization (1520–1569)* (University Press of Colorado, 1995), 113.

15. W. Michael Mathes, *The America's First Academic Library: Santa Cruz de Tlatelolco* (California State Library Foundation, 1985), 8.

16. Martín de la Cruz et al., eds., *Libellus De Medicinalibus Indorum Herbis: Manuscrito Azteca De 1552* (Instituto Mexicano del Seguro Social, 1964), 312.

17. Millie Gimmel, "Reading Medicine in the Codex de la Cruz Badiano," *Journal of the History of Ideas* 69, no. 2 (2008): 172.

18. Miguel León-Portilla, *Bernardino de Sahagún: First Anthropologist*, trans. Mauricio J. Mixco (University of Oklahoma Press, 2002), 123.

19. Justino Fernández, "*Las miniaturas que ilustran el códice*," in Martín de la Cruz et al., eds., *Libellus De Medicinalibus Indorum Herbis: Manuscrito Azteca De 1552* (Instituto Mexicano del Seguro Social, 1964), 104.

20. Jules Janick and Kim E. Hummer, "The 1500th Anniversary (512–2012) of the *Juliana Anicia Codex*: An Illustrated Dioscoridean Recension," *Chronica Horticulturae* 52, no. 3 (2012): 9.

21. Janick and Hummer, "Anniversary of the *Juliana Anicia Codex*," 9.

22. Janick and Hummer, "Anniversary of the *Juliana Anicia Codex*," 9.

23. Agnes Arber, *Herbals: Their Origin and Evolution; A Chapter in the History of Botany 1470–1670*, 2nd ed. (Cambridge University Press, 1953), 13–14.

24. Donald Robertson, *Mexican Manuscript Painting* (Yale University Press, 1959), 170–171.

25. Emily W. Emmart, "Commentary," in Martín de la Cruz and Juan Badiano, *The Badianus Manuscript: An Aztec Herbal of 1552*, trans. Emily W. Emmart (Johns Hopkins Press, 1940), 12.

26. De Vos, "The Science of Spices," 417.

27. De Vos, "The Science of Spices," 417.

28. De Vos, "The Science of Spices."

29. Gimmel, "Reading Medicine," 175.

30. Gimmel, "Reading Medicine," 175.

31. De Vos, "The Science of Spices," 399–427. For a biographical account of Viceroy Antonio de Mendoza, see Arthur Scott Aiton, *Antonio de Mendoza, First Viceroy of New Spain* (Duke University Press, 1927). For more on the history of the Colegio de Santa Cruz, see José María Kobayashi, *La educación como conquista: empresa franciscana en México* (El Colegio de México, 1974), and Michael Mathes, *Santa Cruz de Tlatelolco: la primera biblioteca académica de las Américas* (Secretaría de Relaciones Exteriores, 1982).

32. Simpson, *Encomienda in New Spain*, 1–2.

33. Simpson, *Encomienda in New Spain*, 9.

34. Simpson, *Encomienda in New Spain*, ix.

35. Simpson, *Encomienda in New Spain*, 10.

36. Simpson, *Encomienda in New Spain*, 31.

37. Simpson, *Encomienda in New Spain*, 58–60.

38. Simpson, *Encomienda in New Spain*, 60–61.

39. Simpson, *Encomienda in New Spain*, 60–64.

40. Simpson, *Encomienda in New Spain*, Foreword.

41. Simpson, *Encomienda in New Spain*, 73–83.

42. Philip D. Curtin, *The Rise and Fall of the Plantation Complex: Essays in Atlantic History* (Cambridge University Press, 1998), xi, 12.

43. James Lockhart, "*Encomienda* and Hacienda: The Evolution of the Great Estate in the Spanish Indies," *Hispanic American Historical Review* 49, no. 3 (1969): 412.

44. Lockhart, "*Encomienda* and Hacienda," 414, as cited in Simpson, *Encomienda in New Spain*, xiii and 8.

45. Silvio A. Zavala, "La *Encomienda* Indiana," *El trimestre económico* 2, no. 8 (1935): 425.

46. Simpson, *Encomienda in New Spain*, 85.

47. C. E. Castañeda, "The Corregidor in Spanish Colonial Administration," *Hispanic American Historical Review* 9, no. 4 (1929): 449.

48. Castañeda, "The Corregidor in Spanish Colonial Administration," 450.

49. Simpson, *Encomienda in New Spain*.

50. *Chinampa* were small artificial islands built in the pre-Columbian Valley of Mexico for agricultural purposes on freshwater lakes. Richard M. Conway, *Islands in the Lake: Environment and Ethnohistory in Xochimilco, New Spain* (Cambridge University Press, 2021), 69.

51. Conway, *Islands in the Lake*, 69.

52. Simpson, *Encomienda in New Spain*, 116–117.

53. Ryan Dominic Crewe, *The Mexican Mission: Indigenous Reconstruction and Mendicant Enterprise in New Spain, 1521–1600* (Cambridge University Press, 2019).

54. James Lockhart, *The Nahuas After the Conquest: A Social and Cultural History of the Indians of Central Mexico, Sixteenth through Eighteenth Centuries* (Stanford University Press, 1992), 96.

55. Crewe, *The Mexican Mission*, 186.

56. Crewe, *The Mexican Mission*, 186.

57. Conway, *Islands in the Lake*.

58. For an in-depth discussion of pre- and post-Conquest patterns of land tenure, see Lockhart, *The Nahuas After the Conquest*, 141–202.

59. Crewe, *The Mexican Mission*, 190. See also Lockhart, *The Nahuas After the Conquest*, 96–97.

60. De Vos, "The Science of Spices," 400.

61. Boone, "The Multilingual Bivisual World," 137–166.

62. These two reasons as possible explanations for the creation of the *Badianus Herbal* are mentioned in Debra Hassig, "Transplanted Medicine: Colonial Mexican Herbals of the Sixteenth Century," *Res: Anthropology and Aesthetics*, Spring - Autumn, no. 17–18 (1989): 30–53.

63. Hassig, "Transplanted Medicine," 30–53. Alejandra Rojas Silva, "Gardens of Origin and the Golden Age in the Mexican *Libellus de medicinalibus indorum herbis* (1552)," *Bulletin of Latin American Research*, 37, no. S1 (2018): 41–56.

64. Cruz and Badiano, *The Badianus Manuscript*, 37.

65. Rojas Silva, "Gardens of Origin," 44–45.

66. Patrizia Granziera, "Huaxtepec: The Sacred Garden of an Aztec Emperor," *Landscape Research* 30, no. 1 (2005): 93.

67. Rojas, "Gardens of Origin," 43.

68. Patrizia Granziera, "Concept of the Garden in Pre-Hispanic Mexico," *Garden History* 29, no. 2 (2001): 185–213.

69. Granziera, "Concept of the Garden," 185.

70. Granziera, "Huaxtepec," 93.

71. Granziera, "Huaxtepec," 86.

72. Emmart, "Commentary," 13.

73. Cruz and Badiano, *The Badianus Manuscript*, 220.

74. For more on Antonio Valeriano, see Barbara E. Mundy, *The Death of Aztec Tenochtitlan, the Life of Mexico City* (University of Texas Press, 2015), 190–191.

75. For Ted McCormick's use of this term, see his chapter in this volume.

76. See Ted McCormick's chapter in this volume.

Part II

Boundaries

Chapter 3

Sugar and Sovereignty in Hawai'i

John Adams Kuakini Cummins and Waimānalo Plantation, 1878–1895

Nicholas B. Miller

Despite the centrality of plantation agriculture in Hawai'i's economy for almost a century, there is only a single reference to the archipelago's plantation history in visuals that adorn (as of May 2024) the walls of the reading room of the Hawai'i State Archives in Honolulu. Reflecting its location on the grounds of 'Iolani Palace, the only former royal residence in the United States, primacy is instead granted to Hawai'i's nineteenth-century monarchy. A photograph originally titled "Royal party at Waimanalo" (Fig. 3.1) features as part of a sort of tryptic for Queen Lili'uokalani (1838–1917, reigned [r.] 1891–1893), the kingdom's final monarch, who ruled until being overthrown by a resident American-led coup d'etat in 1893.[1] Captured in the 1880s, before she would bear the golden taro leaf-lined crown of Hawai'i, "Royal party at Waimanalo" presents her seated with several other high-ranking Hawaiian women, all wearing ribboned straw hats announcing *PUAALII*, or royal flower.[2] Another sense of *Pua'ali'i* reveals, cryptically, the plantation setting of the scene—*Pua'ali'i* was also a nickname for John Adams Kuakini Cummins (1835–1913), Native Hawaiian *ali'i*, host, and founder of Waimānalo Plantation, the first industrial sugar establishment on the island of O'ahu, on which grounds the photograph was taken.[3]

Figure 3.1. "Royal party at Waimanalo," taken by Joaquin A. Gonsalves. *Source:* Hawai'i State Archives, Photographic Collection, PPWD-16-3-021. Public domain.

As staged in the Hawai'i State Archives, "Royal party at Waimanalo" testifies to Hawai'i's Indigenous sovereigns; in this chapter, it opens up new perspectives on the relationship between plantations, colonization, and the deployment of what this volume terms "plantation knowledge." The photographer, a Portuguese man named Joaquin A. Gonsalves, was himself intimately invested in these themes in ways that cut against archetypical experiences in other sugar-growing locations. He had arrived in Hawai'i less than a decade prior, in 1879, aboard a ship crammed with several hundred indentured laborers from the Portuguese island of Madeira, which would furnish, along with the archipelago of the Azores, one of the largest sources of plantation labor for Hawai'i's emerging sugar scene prior to US annexation.[4] Unlike his compatriots, Gonsalves does not seem to have ever cut cane in the field. Rather, he established a successful career in photography that included a commission as the royal photographer for Lili'uokalani's predecessor, King Kalākaua (1836–1891, r. 1874–1891), Cummins's friend and frequent guest in Waimānalo.[5]

The dozens of photographs taken by Gonsalves of Waimānalo Plantation constitute key parts of the distinct and rather unusual surviving archive on Cummins's plantation project. This archive is relatively light in terms of the administrative materials conventionally used by historians to study management, labor, technology, and agriculture on individual plantations, such as account books, labor registries, correspondence, or labor contracts.[6] It is however uncommonly dense in the breadth of visitors who left testimony of its conditions, many of whom were pursuing fields of knowledge rarely perceived in connection with plantations, including archaeology, medicine, theater, and Hawaiian oral tradition.

In its initial formulation in 1878 up to Cummins's sale of his shares in 1895, Waimānalo Plantation was a project featuring an experimental conjuncture of plantation capitalism, industrial modernity, and statist Indigenous monarchy. It was host to the first sugar train on the island of O'ahu and linked with Honolulu through a dedicated steamer line also owned by him. In 1891, the plantation produced 4,538 tons of sugar, roughly half of all that produced on O'ahu that year.[7] Unlike any other major plantation established in Hawai'i during the period, its main protagonist, Cummins, was a Native Hawaiian man who, after the overthrow of the kingdom, prominently opposed American settler overrule. In 1883, it was one of only two plantations in Hawai'i featuring majority Hawaiian ownership.[8] Prior to the contests over sovereignty during the 1890s, Cummins's goal was for profit derived from plantation-produced sugar to preserve his lavish hospitality and sociability at his estate house of Mauna Loke (Rose Mount), site to frequent feasts honoring Hawaiian ali'i and visiting foreign dignitaries.

In the first decade of operations, sugar at Waimānalo also served to patronize and perpetuate Hawaiian literary forms. The optimism and cultural horizons integral to Cummins's experiment are indicated in a set of three *mele*, or chants, composed by a still unidentified Hawaiian woman to commemorate a visit by Queen Kapi'olani, consort to reigning King Kalākaua, to Waimānalo in the mid-1880s.[9]

Ka mākou lani 'ihi nō'oe,
Puīa ke 'ala i Mauna Loke.
Ka mālamalama o ke ahi kao,
Ke kahua kolokē hone i ke anu.
Ilaila mākou 'ike i ka nani,
I ka hale wili kō helu 'ekāhi.
Nome hala 'ole mai a ka nau,
Haulani nā pana i ka mīkini.

Pipʻa ka māhu o ka moʻa ia,
Pau pono nā ʻono a ka makemake.

(Sacred, most truly majestic, you are the Chiefess
whose fragrance now precedes you to Rose Mount.
There fireworks spill their brightness
over the croquet grounds so alluringly cool.
And at Rose Mount we view the beauty
of the finest of sugar mills.
Now the grinders falter not at their grinding,
and the machine runs always at even speed.
When the steam rises, boiling-time ends.
All sweetness is concentrated there.)

Due to return to Honolulu by sea aboard Cummins's steamer, Kapiʻolani traveled the approximately four kilometers overland from Mauna Loke to Waimānalo pier in the comfort of his sugar train:

O ka noho hoʻolaʻi a ka wahine,
I ka hale aniani o ke kaʻaahi.
Aweawe ka uahi piʻo mahope,
Ka ʻowē a ka lau kō mawaho.

(The lady in the glassed-in coach
of her train need only sit and relax.
Smoke weaves and streams behind
while leaves of sugarcane rustle outside.)

This mele may strike the contemporary reader as combining rather unlikely elements in the framework of Hawaiian oral tradition, intertwining compliments to a Queen consort, celebrations of a sugar mill, references to fireworks and the game of croquet (*kolokē*), a procession aboard a sugar train, the rustling of sugarcane, and billowing clouds of cane fire. The significance of Waimānalo Plantation as a case study is precisely to address the seemingly counterintuitive character of this conjuncture for contemporary readers. In pursuing sovereign ends through industrial methods, Cummins's project of the Waimānalo Plantation is emblematic of how the plantation as a capitalist form of agriculture, sustained by the modern, rather than exclusively colonial state, transcends clear-cut cultural boundaries between the early modern and modern, and, as this chapter argues, between the colonial and the Indigenous.[10]

Emblematic of the grafting of a global plantation complex in Hawai'i during the second half of the nineteenth century, Cummins's Waimānalo Plantation was a hybrid experiment. Committed to Hawaiian national independence in the framework of a ruling constitutional monarchy headed by Hawai'i's Indigenous elite, Cummins invested in state-of-the-art industrial technology and adopted a labor regime with clearest parallels to those of Chinese-owned establishments elsewhere in the late nineteenth-century Asia-Pacific, including Hawai'i.[11] Following the overthrow of the monarchy in 1893, Cummins actively sought the restoration of Lili'uokalani, leading to his imprisonment by the American-led Republic of Hawai'i in 1895.

Figure 3.2. Samuel Parker (left), Princess Ruth Ke'elikōlani (center), John Adams Kuakini Cummins (right), 1877. *Source:* Hawai'i State Archives, Photographic Collection, PP-97-18-015. Public domain.

Through a plantation microhistory of Waimānalo, this chapter contributes to illuminating the spectrum of the projects of sovereignty that have been historically intertwined with plantations. After a discussion of Cummins's local and global contexts, the characteristics of his project are detailed in view of the surviving evidence from archival and printed sources, including his access to land and capital, his technological acquisitions, and the role of race and nationality in its labor structure and management. Details are subsequently provided on Cummins's political objectives and commitment to the Hawaiian monarchy. The chapter concludes with a comparative reflection with other cases of plantations sited in borderlands contexts, including those developed by Indigenous elites and those featuring the deployment by non-Europeans of European and American industrial machinery. As Cummins's experiment shows, some Hawaiian actors initially perceived sugar and sovereignty to be potentially reinforcing rather than antithetical.

Background

Cummins inaugurated his plantation experiment in 1878, at the centennial of Hawai'i's first sustained contact with Westerners in 1778. Rather exceptionally, legal, institutional, and labor arrangements commonly associated with direct Western rule were established under an independent government headed by an Indigenous monarch, including private, fee-simple ownership of property, a constitutional form of government, and indentured servitude.[12] The distinctive political, economic, and cultural evolution of Hawai'i during that century mediated the character of its nascent plantation complex, which was fully elaborated only during the final quarter of the nineteenth century. In lieu of slavery, a form of indentured labor emerged based on precedents in common law jurisdictions, including the colonial Caribbean and Mauritius. What especially distinguished Hawai'i was the diverse character of its laboring population during the final quarter of the nineteenth century, which featured, in addition to Hawaiian workers, indentured migrants from China, Portugal, Japan, Germany, Norway, Kiribati, and Vanuatu.[13] The participation of Europeans alongside Asians and Pacific Islanders as indentured laborers in the late Kingdom period precluded a strict racialization of status like that in the Americas, as did the diverse profile of social elites, which included Native Hawaiian governing elites and Chinese capitalists.

With claims to high status through his Hawaiian lineage and a robust inheritance from his English father, Cummins attempted to enrich himself through plantation cultivation centered not on an exploitative racialization of agricultural labor but rather on the application of industrial technology and economic collaboration with Chinese labor brokers. Characteristic of his generation of elite Hawaiians was familiarity with Western ways, particularly American and British; optimism in interacting with what they perceived as an interconnected world; and an increasingly national sense of collective identity. Counter to the dominant strand of racial and cultural chauvinism that underpinned imperial expansion in the period, Cummins saw no contradiction between the celebration of customary Hawaiian practices and the adoption of modern techniques of agricultural production, including ownership and management of a sugar plantation.[14]

To appreciate the horizons of possibility held by Cummins and his peers, it is crucial to overcome the teleology of US annexation that prevailed in twentieth-century historical accounts. Before annexation in 1898, US influence in the islands was jealously contested by France and Britain, and no foreign power exerted any direct influence on the internal affairs of the kingdom, excepting the unauthorized occupation by British officer George Paulet for five months in 1843. Cummins was a Hawaiian nationalist, sugar capitalist, and opponent of American settler imperialism.

First settled by Polynesian voyagers at least 800 years ago, a unified state across the Hawaiian Islands emerged only after Western contact through the political and strategic acumen of Kamehameha I (date of birth unclear–1819), namely his masterful adoption and adaptation of foreign military techniques, technology, and advisors. Through friendly relations with foreign traders, he imported an arsenal of guns and gunpowder. He also gained access to Western military and business knowledge by integrating European mariners into his patrimonial structure, appointing men including John Young, Issac Davis, and Francisco de Paula Marín as chiefs and arranging for their (polygamous) marriage to elite women in his orbit.[15] In so doing, Kamehameha inaugurated a cultural norm of interracial pairing which led to many elite Hawaiians having Western—and most frequently British—ancestors. Likewise, Kamehameha established a political framework for state formation defined by the mediation of Western and Hawaiian forms of knowledge.

In the three decades following Kamehameha's death in 1819, Hawai'i experienced profound cultural, economic, and demographic transformation. The impact of the arrival of the first congregationalist missionaries in the islands in 1823 was weighty though long exaggerated.[16] Rather than inaugurating a new approach to Hawaiian politics, Kamehameha's successors engaged in strategic negotiations with the missionaries along with other groups of maritime foreigners, including merchants, sailors, sandalwood traders, and later whalers.[17] Hawai'i's non-Hawaiian population during this period grew gradually and haphazardly, mainly through transiting passengers discerning local commercial or professional possibilities and deciding to try their luck. In 1850, of an island-wide population of 81,165, there were some 1,065 "foreign" men, nearly 30% of whom were married to Hawaiian women.[18] This population total reflected a catastrophic drop in the Indigenous population from at least 300,000 at the time of Cook, caused by susceptibility to newly introduced global diseases that the application of foreign medical knowledge did tragically little to arrest, as well as significant rates of labor emigration among Hawaiian men as seafarers.[19]

In an attempt to regulate interactions between Hawaiians and foreigners in ways that would be accepted by Western powers—particularly Britain, France, and the United States—the Kingdom increasingly adopted and adapted Western legal and constitutional forms during the 1840s and early 1850s.[20] Customary forms of labor obligations were abolished during this period, including the express prohibition of slavery in the Constitution of 1852. A Masters and Servants Act passed in 1850 would ultimately serve as the legal basis for indentured labor in the islands until US annexation.[21]

In 1848, a transformative alteration of Hawai'i's property regime began, known as the Great Māhele (literally, "to divide," or "to portion"). The classical land tenure system of Hawai'i had been defined by the fluctuating domains of individual ruling chiefs, who distributed lands to favorites and supporters that were cultivated by subalterns using customary, hierarchical, and collectivist notions of reciprocity.[22] Kamehameha I brought this system under the domain of a single individual ruling chief, or king. The unified government established by him and maintained by his successors yielded uncommon stability of property ownership among favored elites during the first half of the nineteenth century, as the older practice of land redistribution upon the ascent of a new ruler was terminated. However, frustration from elites who had lost from Kamehameha's conquest-era land redistributions was joined with the destabilizing new variable of property-interested foreigners, whose claims of injustice could be prosecuted through local consuls and visiting gunboats.[23] In theory, the Māhele was to settle land disputes between foreigners and Hawaiians through the introduction of allodial title, with customary, collective patterns of land use replaced by individual, alienable ownership, divided between the crown, nobility (aliʻi and *konohiki*), and commoners (*makaʻāinana*). In practice, relatively few *makaʻāinana* received titled land, and over several decades, Westerners acquired most agriculturally viable land. By 1896, fifty-seven percent of all taxable land in the archipelago was owned by Westerners.[24]

The role of marriage as a vehicle for land acquisition, however, exhibited distinctive continuities with preexisting patterns. Hawaiian elites secured considerable fee-title property through the Māhele, and after the Māhele, they were often awarded large, term-limited leases of crown agricultural lands that they profitably subleased to Chinese, Western, and Hawaiian commoner farmers. Elite marriage patterns before and after 1848 witnessed the union of customary land title (inherited by Hawaiian daughters through their chiefly fathers) with foreign capital (amassed by men of Western, Chinese, and Part-Hawaiian ancestry through shipping and business enterprises).[25]

The experiences of Cummins's parents were thus emblematic of broader historical trends. His mother, Kaumakaokane Papaliʻaiʻaina (1810–1849), was a high ranking aliʻi who was a relation of Kamehameha.[26] His father, Thomas Cummins, was an Englishman who arrived in Hawaiʻi in 1828 following an extended residence in Massachusetts, aged 26. Thomas's first employ in Hawaiʻi was for Boki (1785–1829), a powerful aliʻi who held the title of governor of the island of Oʻahu and who engaged in a wide range of business enterprises, including, in Mānoa Valley, the island's first plantation experiments in sugar and coffee with John Wilkinson, a former West Indian planter.[27] Thomas later worked in trade and retail.[28] As early as 1842, Thomas leased property in Waimānalo from Pākī, an aliʻi, and began breeding livestock including sheep, cattle, and horses.[29] During the California Gold Rush, he established a profitable enterprise in San Francisco importing Hawaiian garden agriculture.[30] He also made a series of clever property investments. Returning to Hawaiʻi in 1850, Thomas leased 970 additional acres of land from Kamehameha III, which he used to develop Waimānalo as one of the largest cattle ranches in the Kingdom.[31] By the 1870s, John Cummins's parents were the principal landholders in Waimānalo, providing the property basis for his sugar experiment.

Cummins himself grew up on the island of Oʻahu between Waimānalo and Honolulu and attended the English-medium Royal School in central Honolulu, whose student body featured young Hawaiian aliʻi—including future royals Kalākaua and Liliʻuokalani—and *haole* children from diverse social backgrounds.[32] In being of both Hawaiian and English ancestry, Cummins shared a mixed background with other high-ranking Hawaiian aliʻi who attended the school, including most prominently Emma (future Queen consort to Kamehameha IV). Despite his English-language education, memoirs of the early twentieth century suggested that his primary language was Hawaiian and that his locus of socialization was much more Hawaiian than haole.[33]

After completing his schooling, Cummins worked as a foreman on his father's ranch in Waimānalo and managed its livestock market in Honolulu. Most of the laborers employed on the ranch in Waimānalo were Hawaiian men. His business in Honolulu, however, brought him into frequent contact with the diverse commercial population of the city, including European, American, and Chinese merchants and maritime captains.[34] Cummins began playing a more active role in the management of Waimānalo Ranch in the 1870s, when he was in his thirties and his aging father in his seventies, and during which time it was converted into a plantation. He also made his first forays into the realm of politics in 1874 by being elected to the Kingdom's Legislative Assembly, representing the Koʻolau District of Oʻahu.[35] The electorate for this assembly was principally Native Hawaiian men. Cummins's background and connections prepared him well for his eventual duties as a sugar planter, trader, and entertainer of royalty and foreign dignitaries.

Throughout his life, Cummins demonstrated a self-understanding of himself as a proud Native Hawaiian aliʻi and a man open to the cultural and technological innovations of his time. Like Samuel Parker (1853–1920), a major Native Hawaiian cattle rancher on the island of Hawaiʻi, he nourished social connections with powerful senior aliʻi including Keʻelikōlani (1826–1883), over whom they reverently bore *kāhili*, feather standards symbolizing royal lineage in the Hawaiian Kingdom (Fig. 3.2). In 1861, Cummins married his first wife, Rebecca Kahalewai (1834–1902), an aliʻi from the island of Hawaiʻi. They would have six children together, residing principally in Waimānalo. A month after Rebecca's death in September 1902, he married Elizabeth Kapeka Merseberg (1877–1925) with whom he would father a son. Daughter of an aliʻi mother and a German migrant on the island of Kauaʻi, two of his second wife's brothers had previously worked as assistant manager and head luna (overseer) at Waimānalo Plantation.[36]

Cummins's plantation project was only one of dozens that germinated across Hawaiʻi in the years after 1875, when the Kingdom secured duty free access for Hawaiian sugar into the United States following aborted attempts in 1855 and 1867. A 1919 US Congressional tariff commission described this Reciprocity Treaty as a "product of political rather than economic considerations," given the insignificant size of the Hawaiian market for US exports.[37] For the Kingdom of Hawai'i, however, it was both. A market for sugar exports to California had been revealed by the American Civil War, at which time producers in Hawai'i were able to temporarily command a premium due to wartime supply chain disruptions and the disintegration of the Southern plantation slavery complex. After the war's conclusion, the acceleration of European sugar beet production and exports contributed to a decline in global sugar prices, rendering Hawaiian sugar once again uncompetitive. Duty-free entry reversed this situation, effectively subsidizing imports of Hawaiian sugar and positioning Hawai'i to satisfy growing demand in its closest potential continental market despite the vociferous objections of Louisiana sugar producers.

While the Kingdom of Hawai'i retained complete control over its internal affairs as part of this treaty, the United States would later gain

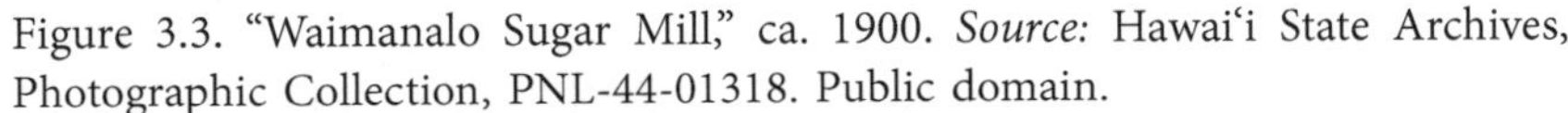
Figure 3.3. "Waimanalo Sugar Mill," ca. 1900. *Source:* Hawai'i State Archives, Photographic Collection, PNL-44-01318. Public domain.

a strategic advantage in trans-Pacific navigation through exclusive access rights to Pu'u Loa, or what is now Pearl Harbor, including the right to build a coaling and naval repair station. A large contingent of Hawaiian leaders warned that this concession risked compromising the Kingdom's sovereignty.[38] King Kalākaua, who recently ascended to the throne, however, judged that plantation-oriented economic development could provide the financial resources for the continued development of the Hawaiian state and sustain its political independence.[39] Cummins, with his combination of royalist sympathies, ali'i status, extensive land holdings, familial capital, and a business network inherited from his father, was exceptionally well poised to put Kalākaua's plantation developmentalist aspirations into action.

John Adams Kuakini Cummins's Experiment, 1878–1885

Between 1878 and 1885, Waimānalo Ranch was transformed into the most modern sugar plantation on the island of O'ahu. A company was incorporated, great profit was promised, investors were secured, a sugar mill was built, foreign laborers were indentured, a steam locomotive was acquired, rail track was laid, and a steamship line was inaugurated, all so that sugar could be grown, cut, processed, transshipped, and sold. By 1890, nearly seven thousand acres in Waimānalo Valley were under sugar cultivation. These developments were made possible through extensive knowledge networking and industrial acquisitions between Waimānalo and established nodes of sugar production and manufacturing, including British Guiana, Britain, and the United States. Local knowledge of sugar growing and labor knowledge—tactics for recruiting and disciplining laborers—were likewise important. Meanwhile, Cummins succeeded his father, Thomas, as the main proprietor at Waimānalo and perpetuated his parents' lavish hospitality of Hawaiian ali'i and foreign guests alike.[40] By the mid-1880s, Waimānalo was triply regarded as a successful sugar plantation, a point of call for visiting dignitaries, and a major venue for ali'i sociability.

While there is an absence of conventional plantation records, logs, or reports for Waimānalo before the twentieth century, its early plantation history can be recovered through vignettes provided by Cummins's many guests, newspaper reporting in both Hawaiian and English, US consular reporting, and Hawaiian government records.[41] Descriptive travel accounts of the plantation between 1879 and 1885 were provided by the German naturalist Otto Finsch, the American medical student L. Vernon Briggs, the globe-trotting German-American Shakespearean actor Daniel E. Bandmann, and the Irish-American judge D. J. Toohy.[42] Incidents in the history of the plantation, including laborer contracting and disputes, acquisitions of equipment and land, annual company meetings, and the exhibition and sale of sugar were reported in Honolulu's lively multilingual press, as were the frequent visits of King Kalākaua, who came to Waimānalo with foreign dignitaries at least three times in 1883 alone.[43] The plantation's purchase of machinery from the British firm Mirrless, Tait, and Watson rather than an American producer attracted the ire of the US minister resident in 1879, and the plantation's use of contract labor was documented by the Kingdom's Board of Immigration.[44] The surviving evidence permits insights into the original formation of the plantation and its commercial, labor, managerial, technological, and logistical characteristics.

Initial experiments with sugar in Waimānalo were conducted by Hawaiian and Chinese small planters, including a Hawaiian man named Waieleele, who subleased four acres of land from Waimānalo Ranch during the 1870s.[45] Waieleele possibly received sugar cane seeds in 1877 from Cummins, who reportedly bought some that year from the West Maui Sugar Association in Olowalu, Maui, which had been cofounded by King Kamehameha V (1830–1872, r. 1863–1872) in 1869.[46] Soon after the incorporation of the Waimanalo Sugar Company in mid-1878, two stalks of Waieleele's sugar cane were exhibited at the Honolulu office of the Cummins's business partner Alexander Joy Cartwright (1820–1892). Inspecting the cane samples, writers from the *Hawaiian Gazette* claimed they had grown an astounding ten feet in five months, satisfying "anyone that the growth is a wonderful one," promising a "yield not less than from six to seven tons of sugar per acre." The article was a promotional piece for investors and circulated widely, being republished in an agricultural weekly based in Florida by October 1878.[47] While Waieleele's stalks proved that sugar cane could flourish in Waimānalo, small grower cultivation would ultimately be replaced by a corporate plantation.

In an informal interview in 1906, Cummins claimed to have first perceived the potential for a sugar plantation in Waimānalo in 1877, judging there to be sufficient water supply.[48] He carried out this project with his father Thomas and two American businessmen who had settled in Hawai'i amidst the California Gold Rush (1849–1850): Franklin Seaver Pratt (1829–1894) and the aforementioned Cartwright, of fame in the history of sports for developing the rules of modern baseball. Past studies on

Waimānalo plantation have argued in turn for the primacy of Cummins, his father Thomas, and Cartwright.[49] While the idea of the sugar plantation was probably John Cummins's, he lacked any formal role in the initial incorporation of the Waimanalo Sugar Company, possibly because he and his partners judged that capital would be easier to obtain from Euro-American sources with more experienced—and all-White—leadership.

At the inaugural meeting of stockholders on April 30, 1878, Thomas was elected president, Cartwright secretary, and Pratt treasurer.[50] Obituaries written upon his death in 1885, aged 83, suggested that Thomas founded the sugar plantation with Cartwright and Pratt.[51] The *Gazette* however noted that he had soon turned the business over to his son due to his declining health.[52] He had sold his entire interests in the company along with some fee title property in Waimānalo to Cummins in September 1882.[53] As common in family enterprises, ownership may have just taken time to reflect management—the property had been described as "John Cummins' Ranch" as early as 1872.[54] The generational gap prevailing between the four men should be kept in mind. In 1878, Thomas was 76, Cartwright 68, Pratt 59, and John Cummins 42. In any case, Cummins replaced his father as president of the company in the early 1880s, possibly as early as 1881 and certainly by 1883, and there is clear evidence that he directed day-to-day operations by early 1881.[55]

Cartwright and Pratt were important collaborators in the initial formation of the plantation, interlinking Waimānalo with international commercial, knowledge, and even fertilizer networks. Cartwright had worked as the Hawai'i-based broker for a British insurance firm since the 1850s, and Pratt served as an agent for the Phoenix Guano Islands Company in Micronesia in the 1860s and 1870s.[56] Both were founding investors in Waimānalo Sugar and served on its board throughout the 1880s.[57] Local connections, including those reflecting the multiracial character of nineteenth-century Hawai'i's political and commercial elite, were also essential. Pratt was connected with Cummins socially through his marriage to the ali'i Elizabeth Keka'aniau La'anui (1834–1928), another of his former peers at the Royal School. Cartwright had a long working relationship with Cummins's friend Chuck Afong, the wealthiest Chinese merchant in the Kingdom of Hawai'i and owner of the Pepe'ekeo Plantation on the island of Hawai'i.[58] While the collaboration with Cartwright and Pratt seems to have begun with Thomas, Cartwright maintained an active correspondence with Cummins between 1880 and 1881 on matters related to the plantation, emphasizing the importance of economy.[59] Drawing on his father's business partners and his own successful sugar-producing friends like Chuck Afong, Cummins had access to intermediaries active in sugar production in Hawai'i and across the globe.

The conversion of the Waimānalo Ranch lands to intensive sugar cultivation occurred in two distinct phases. The first phase between 1878 and 1882 featured a combination of subleased and direct cultivation and capital-intensive outlays for industrial production and transportation, including a sugar mill, a sugar train, and steamships. The second phase, beginning in 1882 and running into the 1890s, saw a shift toward direct cultivation and the use of state-of-the-art mechanization, the pursuit of property consolidation, and a mainly Chinese workforce, obtained through collaboration with Chinese labor brokers. During this phase, Cummins consolidated his position as the premier landowner in Waimānalo, inheriting his father's estate and purchasing lands held by small competitors such as Myron J. Rose, an American settler who had attempted to grow sugar on lands he probably acquired through his Hawaiian wife, Mary Rose Kekalo.[60] By 1885, the core elements of the plantation were in place that would be retained until the plantation's recapitalization in 1920, except for laborer nationality.

At no phase under Cummins's management could a steady racialized labor order be said to prevail at Waimānalo. In part, this was because what Bastos terms the "color of labor" was in a state of flux across the archipelago.[61] As late as 1873, 79% of the plantation laborers in the islands were classified as Native Hawaiians, the rest consisting almost entirely of Chinese men.[62] As sugar boomed after 1875, the laboring population grew considerably more diverse as the Kingdom embarked on an unusual government-led labor migration program based on binding contracts of indenture. This policy married populationist imperatives for the Kingdom's future with the urgent necessity among planters for additional laborers to work the cane fields. The target origin countries catered to the loyalties, preferences, and imperatives of several constituencies in the island polity, including Hawaiians who desired migrants from other islands in the Pacific, Euro-Americans who sought a larger White population, and planters who perceived Chinese migrants as an ideal fit for their needs. Crucially, White settler and planter objectives in this matrix did not overlap and were in relation to continued Chinese migration antagonistic. Between 1882 and 1884, a total of 17,262 indentured migrants arrived in Hawai'i. The majority (50.6 percent) were Europeans, of which 88.2 percent were Portuguese and 11.8% German.[63] The migrants from this three-year period comprised more than one-fifth of the total population of the archipelago in 1884. The conditions of these contracts, which bound migrants to labor at a plantation assigned by the Board of Immigration from 3 to 5 years, drew immediate ire from European governments, particularly political parties aligned with the labor movement, and occasioned polemics in the United States and Europe about "White slavery" in the islands. The Kingdom signed a labor treaty with Japan soon after, and Japanese laborers would predominate on Hawaiian plantations during the 1890s. The decisive effect of the surge of European and Chinese indentured laborers on Hawaiian plantations during the early 1880s was to transform commercial agriculture in Hawai'i from a space of labor predominated by Native Hawaiians to that of a multinational and multiracial worker population.

While of too short a duration to amount to a racialized labor structure, the plantation's first phase of 1878–1882 seems to have been characterized by an ethnically segmented supervisory structure, wherein Chinese and Micronesian laborers did field work, and Hawaiians served as overseers, teamsters, and mill workers.[64] In September 1878, *Ka Nupepa Kuokoa* described a dispute at the new plantation between a Hawaiian *luna* (overseer) named Akana Kalauki and a group of Chinese laborers, some of whom had recently moved to Hawai'i from California.[65] The dispute suggests an attempt at employing Chinese laborers either through indentured modalities or as directly contracted day laborers. Additionally, Cummins had engaged in the early phase of the sponsored immigration program between 1878 and 1881, wherein 12,436 indentured migrants arrived in Hawai'i from China, along with 1,730 from the South Pacific.[66] On May 29, 1878, several men recruited by the Kingdom's Board of Immigration from the Micronesian island of Tabiteuea (then referred to as Drummonds, and now part of Kiribati) signed contracts of indenture to "labor for Mr. Cummins and his copartners in the Waimanalo Sugar Co. as a plantation laborer at Waimanalo, Oahu" for a period of three years.[67] In 1881, L. Vernon Briggs, a young American medical student contracted by the Hawaiian government to administer smallpox vaccines in Waimānalo, reported that fieldwork was principally conducted by Micronesians, with millwork and teaming done mainly by Hawaiians, though he may have overestimated the presence of Micronesians given that they were the primary population he vaccinated, besides Cummins and his family.[68] In 1882, Cummins reported a total workforce of 116, of whom 91 were Chinese, 10 were Hawaiian, 3 were Portuguese, and 12 were "other," presumably South Sea Islander.[69]

In his division of labor, Cummins may have been drawing upon an incipient racialization of labor that perceived Hawaiians as best suited for teamster work with other nationalities, including Chinese, more effective in the field. Yet, the diversity of opinion expressed in surveys conducted by the Bureau of Immigration throughout the 1880s on planters' "preferred nationalities" for different types of plantation labor underline the fluctuating and unsteady character of labor racialization in Hawaiʻi.[70] Cummins might also have been catering to the occupational preferences of local Hawaiians who preferred these positions, as they were better paid.

After 1882, Cummins eschewed indenture in favor of contracting Chinese day laborers, a practice he would retain until selling his majority share in the plantation in 1894. Representing an alternative to racialized plantation hierarchies such as in the Caribbean, this model was based on the co-ethnic character of labor and supervision. Plantations contracted laborers already based in Hawaiʻi individually or through Chinese intermediaries rather than through the Board of Immigration.[71] Such laborers had either worked off their initial contract of indenture with another employer or had financed their transportation to Hawaiʻi using family and kin networks or through Chinese labor brokers in a bonded labor arrangement termed the "credit-ticket system."[72] Besides personal distaste for the contract labor system, it is likely that Cummins was relying on preexisting forms of labor recruitment in Waimānalo valley. Already in 1879, Otto Finsch, a German ethnographer who visited Waimānalo as part of an archaeological research trip across the Pacific, noted the presence of about twenty "small houses and worker accommodation for Chinese" workers and that on the plantation, "one sees more Chinese than natives."[73] In July 1882, the *Pacific Commercial Advertiser* announced the landing of 234 Chinese laborers in Honolulu, all of whom were "engaged for Chinese plantations, no less than 130 of them being for one employer at Waimanalo."[74] The employer in Waimānalo was likely a Chinese sublessee, perhaps Tai Lee.[75]

While Cummins's use of Chinese labor brokers differed considerably from American and Caribbean plantation models, it approximated those employed throughout Southeast Asia during the nineteenth century.[76] It likewise represented a continued engagement with the plantation knowledge commanded by Chinese planters, which had been instrumental in the early phase of sugar production in the islands.[77] Cummins was a close friend to Chuck Afong, the premier Chinese capitalist of the islands, and entertained him frequently at Waimānalo.[78] An additional continuity, as noted previously in the case of Waieleele, was Cummins's practice of subleased agricultural cultivation. Plots at the ranch had been subleased to Hawaiian and Chinese small growers for the cultivation of taro and rice since the 1850s, and Cummins at first encouraged these producers to shift to sugar in the 1870s.[79] Purchases from Chinese sugar growers remained significant throughout the 1880s, with up to 1,200 acres planted, including 800 by a man named Tai Lee.[80] The total workforce reported by Cummins between 1887 and 1890 ranged between 337 and 367 of which the proportion of Chinese laborers varied from 91.8 to 95.8 percent.[81] Whether Cummins changed the basis of calculating "his" workers to include those employed by Chinese sublessees or greatly increased his workforce between 1882 and 1887 is unclear; however, it was specified that no laborers were "under contract" in 1890.[82] After 1882, Waimānalo under Cummins's leadership was unusual in foregoing a labor supply brokered by the Kingdom's Board of Immigration. However, its labor practices closely resembled those employed by the biggest Chinese sugar planters of the time in Hawaiʻi, including Chuck Afong, Luke Aseu, and Goo Tet Chin Akina.[83]

The scale of industrial investments made in Waimānalo was striking; by 1882, it featured a working sugar mill, was linked to Honolulu by telephone and steamer, and was the first plantation on Oʻahu to have a working sugar train.[84] On August 12, 1878, Pratt received delivery of a steamship named the *Waimanalo* built in San Francisco capable of carrying about 400 kegs of sugar.[85] Cummins soon purchased it and used it to transport sugar from various producers on the Windward side of Oʻahu. He acquired a second steamer in 1884.[86] Construction of the sugar mill began in January 1880, with Cummins described as its superintendent. B. M. Withard, a sugar boiler with previous experience in British Guiana, was hired to supervise its initial operations.[87] An order was placed for a locomotive in May 1880 that began operations by May 1881.[88] That year, Briggs reported the mill to have a productive capacity of eleven tons, with 1,200 acres of cane under cultivation.[89] The locomotive, named the *Thomas Cummins*, brought freshly cut cane from the fields to the mill and. After the cane was crushed, its juice strained, boiled, cooled, passed through a centrifuge, and the resulting sugar bagged, the train continued to Waimānalo pier for the transshipment of the freshly produced sugar to Honolulu.[90] It was joined by a second train, the *Puaalii*, in 1883, later renamed the *Olomana*. In 1881, about half a mile of portable track was employed, but by 1886, nine miles of track had been laid using English and German steel.[91] While the machinery for the mill had been purchased from the British firm Mirrless, Tait and Watson in 1879, the steamers and locomotives were ordered from American producers, including the

Baldwin Locomotive Works, the largest US producer of trains during the second half of the nineteenth century.[92]

To a certain extent, Cummins's spirit of hospitality extended to his laborers.[93] His behavior resembled far more the patriarchal European factory owner than the typical absentee sugar planter. In 1883, he oversaw the construction of a recreational building housing a reading room and a gathering space "intended for the use of the plantation laborers," which was decorated by Max Kohn, a recently arrived designer from San Francisco.[94] Flanked by several portraits of Hawaiian royals and ali'i, the rooms accommodated several canaries and "a large automatic organ" and were adorned with "Chinese and Japanese fans, easels, and parasols."[95] A plantation band, "its members all being laborers," had also been formed, intended to provide relief from "the usual tediousness and monotony of plantation life."[96] A contributor to the *Pacific Commercial Advertiser* judged the plantation's recreational center to be "probably the best of its kind, if not the only one, on any plantation in the Kingdom."[97] While we lack any testimony of what laborers thought about Cummins's management, visitors remarked on the abstention from indentured labor contracts, meaning that laborers were "free to come and go as they please, without having recourse to a court of law to hold them to their engagements."[98]

By 1885, Cummins's experiment to pursue sovereign ends through plantations had born fruit. That February, he reported to the *Pacific Commercial Advertiser* that the plantation was due to "turn out some 8,000 tons of sugar" and that his son Thomas Pua'ali'i (1869–1926), who had just been in Japan for seven months, would soon set out to Europe, where he would pursue his "decided taste for mechanics" which he had "always shown."[99] It was an optimistic time. The traveling thespian Daniel E. Bandmann would herald him as one of "nature's gentlemen" and a modern, humanitarian industrialist: "Some of us went with our host to inspect the sugar-mills, and I was very much impressed with what I saw: the machinery was of the most perfect kind: every modern method had been introduced, with the result of minimizing toil and securing satisfactory results."[100] Californian judge D. J. Toohy, who also visited that year, emphasized instead the scale of human labor operating on the plantation: "Hundreds of laborers were at work cutting down the cane, while other hundreds were engaged in trimming off the tops and broad leaves, and piling the naked stalks in bundles ready for transportation to the extensive steam-power mill on one end of the grounds."[101] In just seven years, Waimānalo had made the shift from cattle to sugar and in so doing secured a platform for Cummins to pursue a return to politics.

From Royalist Politician to Anticolonial Activist, 1885–1895

Buoyed by the financial resources of a successful and profitable plantation, Cummins reached a position of great public prominence around 1890. He had long participated in elite Hawaiian circles of sociability, hosting Queen Emma in Waimānalo in 1875 and 1877, serving as marshal of the funeral for her mother Fanny Kekelaokalani in 1880, and participating in a regatta with Kalākaua in 1883, his steamship festooned with ribbons.[102] Following his father's death in 1885, he was one of the wealthiest ali'i in the islands. His stature peaked between 1887 and 1892, during which time he held high political office, including a brief stint as the Kingdom's minister of foreign affairs in 1891. A disastrous sugar harvest in 1892, followed by the overthrow of the Hawaiian monarchy on January 17, 1893, however, resulted in the undoing of Cummins's plantation experiment. Dismayed by the fall of Hawai'i's sovereign, which was immediately perceived by Native Hawaiians as an assault on Hawaiian national sovereignty, Cummins devoted his attention to Lili'uokalani's restoration (Fig. 3.4), heading an appeal to Washington, DC, in late 1894.[103] Soon after returning to Hawai'i,

Figure 3.4. "Representative committee of delegates of the Hawaiian people to present a memorial to Hon. James H. Blount, praying for the restoration of the monarchy under Queen Liliuokalani." John Adams Kuakini Cummins (seated, center, with very long mutton chops); Joseph Nāwahī (immediately to his right); John E. Bush (immediately to his left). *Source:* Library of Congress, Prints and Photographs Division, cph 3b42806. Public domain.

he was arrested in early 1895 on charges of treason against the recently established Republic of Hawai'i for allowing opponents of the regime to amass an arsenal at Waimānalo for an attempted counterrevolution. Within the space of five years, Cummins had traced an arc from proplantation royalist politician to imprisoned anticolonial activist.

Cummins's plantation experiment in Waimānalo began early in the reign of Kalākaua, his childhood friend. During his Royal Process in April 1874, Kalākaua and his wife Kapi'olani "were received in splendid style by Mr. [J. A.] Cummins and his numerous tenantry, who cheered heartily and where many of the ancient customs in receiving the high chiefs were revived."[104] A twenty-one-gun salute was issued, children from the local school sang three songs, people presented *ho'okupu* (offerings), "and the assembled people bowed to the ground in ancient style."[105] Cummins had been elected to represent the district of Ko'olau, O'ahu, at the Kingdom's legislature prior to Kalākaua's ascent, and during the first year of his reign, he enthusiastically endorsed the new King's signature populationist policy, *Ho'oulu Lāhui*, which he rendered as "the great work of re-peopling Hawaii for the Hawaiians."[106] This concept would later be used to justify the contract labor migration scheme discussed earlier.[107] Amidst the sugar boom of the mid-1870s, Cummins left elected office to build up his plantation.

Cummins only returned to politics in 1887, after Kalākaua faced a major political crisis. For about a decade prior, Kalākaua had pursued an increasingly nationalistic politics featuring the growing presence of Native Hawaiians in elected and appointed office, a revival of Hawaiian cultural traditions banned during the missionary ascendancy of his forebearers, and an attempt to establish anticolonial alliances with Japan and Samoa.[108] That this strategy coincided with an active promotion of the plantation economy, including demographically transformative rates of indentured labor immigration that resulted in Hawaiians no longer being the majority of the population by 1887, is the defining paradox of Kalākaua's reign. Cultural and racial anxieties among White residents were further inflamed by accusations of the King's practice of cronyism and influence peddling along with the prominence of controversial adventurers in his cabinets, especially Walter Murray Gibson. Fearing a coup, Kalākaua dismissed his existing ministers and granted what is known in the scholarship as the Bayonet Constitution of July 6, 1887, which considerably limited the royal prerogative and the franchise, though left the basic structure of the constitutional monarchy in place.[109] Untainted by any association with the despised Gibson, Kalākaua turned to Cummins as a trusted friend who would also be satisfactory to White militants, promptly appointing Cummins to the Kingdom's Board of Immigration.[110]

Between 1887 and 1893, Cummins was perceived as a compromise (or compromised) political figure: a royalist who was also committed to Hawai'i's bourgeoning plantation complex. As a firm supporter of the monarchy and the plantation economy, Cummins fit the agenda of the royalist National Reform Party like a glove. As part of its ticket, Cummins was elected to consecutive sessions of the House of Nobles in 1890 and 1892. Between these elections, he was appointed as commissioner of the Hawaiian exhibit at the Exposition Universelle of 1889 in Paris and briefly served as Kalākaua's final minister of foreign affairs, from September 9, 1890, to January 29, 1891, when Lili'uokalani succeeded her brother to the throne.[111]

During this six-year period, the three political parties in the Kingdom considered nominating Cummins for office. Besides the royalist National Reform Party, who enthusiastically supported Kalākaua and Lili'uokalani, there was the antimonarchist, *haole*-dominated Reform Party, which endorsed the Bayonet Constitution, as well as the National Liberal Party, the smallest of the three, which embraced interracial workingmen's politics and was led by Hawaiian radicals including John E. Bush and Robert Wilcox who were critical of the plantation economy. In 1888, the nominating committee of the Reform Party judged Cummins too much of a royalist. In his favor was that he was "rich in worldly goods and well known in every part of the country."[112] Against him was the unpredictability of his stance in the event of a contest between "the people and prerogative"—the people here meaning the reshaped electorate of the 1887 constitution, which granted most *haole* men suffrage, regardless of citizenship.[113] Conversely, for backers of the National Liberal Party in 1892, Cummins was compromised by his plantation experiment. Support for "sugar baron J.A. Cummins" back in 1874 may have been understandable, an editorialist noted, given that "no influx [of Asian migrants] threatened to overwhelm us, and drive the native race to the sea and the foreigner to other lands. But now, with his well-known sugar interests, and his entire dependence upon . . . enemies of free labor, his candidacy becomes an insult to labor, and a threat to liberty."[114] Cummins epitomized a royalist position asserting an alignment between the growing plantation economy and the endurance of the Hawaiian monarchy, one that was increasingly challenged by White settlers seeking to establish Anglo-Saxon political supremacy and Native Hawaiian radicals critical of plantation capitalism and its attendant rates of labor migration.

Two crises would undermine Cummins's status as ali'i politician and sugar industrialist between 1892 and 1893. First, after about fifteen years of intensive cane growing, the soils of Waimānalo had been exhausted. Yields at Waimānalo for 1892 were less than a quarter of what they had been during the bumper crop of 1891 and would not recover for a decade. Losses for the year were compounded by the default of many of the Chinese sublessees, further diminishing what had still been an important source of cane for the mill.[115] Second, the overthrow of the Hawaiian monarchy in January 1893 fundamentally transformed the archipelago's political landscape. Not only was Cummins out of office but the new provisional government was dominated by White Americans desiring swift annexation to the United States. The partisan politics of the late Kingdom were immediately transformed, as royalists and Hawaiian radicals alike came to see the reinstatement of Lili'uokalani as not just the restoration of a Hawaiian sovereign but of Hawaiian national sovereignty itself.[116]

Within two months, in March 1893, Cummins cofounded the Hui Aloha 'Aina, or Hawaiian Patriotic League, a prominent Hawaiian nationalist organization that protested the overthrow of the monarchy and later opposed US annexation.[117] His wife, Rebecca, joined Cummins in his activism, serving as vice president of the Hui Aloha 'Āina o nā Wāhine, the women's equivalent.[118]

Amidst the political turbulence of 1893, Cummins sold more of his shares to William G. Irwin, a close associate of the German-American sugar entrepreneur Claus Spreckels.[119] Irwin, born in England though raised in Hawai'i, opposed the overthrow of the monarchy for mainly pragmatic reasons, fearing that annexation by the United States would imperil the labor supply in view of the Chinese Exclusion Act.[120] Cummins had first sold some of his shares to Irwin in 1885, though remained majority owner and president of the company. In 1893, he accepted Irwin's appointment of G. C. Chalmers as manager in his place.[121] After returning from Washington DC, where he appealed for Lili'uokalani's restoration amidst the partisan politics of late 1890s America, Cummins decided to sell additional shares in Waimānalo Plantation in November 1894.[122] The purchasing syndicate comprised Robert Robson Hind, an English sugar planter in Kohala, Island of Hawai'i; Robert Paterson Rithet, a Scottish-Canadian merchant based in Victoria, British Columbia; and J. E. Miller of the California Fertilizer

Company.[123] Cummins retained minority shares of the sugar company, ownership of fee-simple land, and his estate house.

In January 1895, Cummins was arrested on charges of treason following the unsuccessful counterrevolutionary action of Wilcox, alleged to have been stockpiling munitions in Waimānalo.[124] He pled guilty before a military commission consisting mainly of newcomers to the islands and was sentenced to five years' hard labor and a fine of $5,000.[125] Shocked by the sentence, Cummins subsequently protested that he had not taken an active part in amassing an arsenal but merely permitted one of his houseguests, the royalist American Maj. W. T. Seward, to do so. Due to his age, his sentence was commuted after about a month to just the fine, which he paid by mortgaging one of his Honolulu properties.[126] Cummins protested the case for the rest of his life.[127] More immediately, several months after being released from jail, he expressed discontent with the plantation's new management, asking that he be returned as manager or his son-in-law appointed in his place.[128] Irwin dismissed the idea as "insane," judging Cummins as ungrateful despite saving him from "financial ruin."[129] To keep him in line, Irwin instructed his assistant Walter Le Montais Giffard to threaten to withhold the five hundred dollar check paid to Cummins monthly, dismissing this payment as Cummins's "allowance," though it was given as compensation for the company's use of his land lease.[130] At this point, it was clear that Cummins had lost any effective control of the plantation. He sold additional shares in the company in 1896 and moved to Honolulu, from where he managed his other properties and lived a quiet life outside public scrutiny until his death in 1913.[131] The plantation would endure until 1947, though a good part of its lands were absorbed by the US military in 1917 to develop what is now Bellows Air Force Station.

Conclusion

An enduring contention in scholarship on plantations is their status as a frontier tactic of colonization, associated since the early modern period with European expansion and facilitated through the deployment of European and Asian knowledge. Thompson began his classical definition of the plantation by describing it as "an incident in the conquest, settlement, and exploitation, politically and commercially, of an invaded country."[132] Sidney Mintz later defined the plantation as a set of "early capitalistic experiments in export-oriented tropical agriculture that used forced labor on land taken from native peoples, with capital, plants, and technology coming from Europe and Asia."[133]

As this chapter has shown, attention to the role of Indigenous elites in the propagation of plantations in borderland contexts complicates parameters of conquest and dispossession in these accounts.[134] To adapt Mintz's definition of the plantation, Cummins's project at Waimānalo was a capitalistic experiment in export-oriented tropical agriculture that used migrant labor on land retained in Hawaiian hands, "with capital, plants, and technology coming from Europe and Asia" deployed toward anticolonial ends.[135] It might seem exceptional that an industrial sugar plantation was established, promoted, and administered by a Hawaiian ali'i, but it is indicative of the full spectrum of political projects—including those counter to colonialism and imperialism—that have been invested in plantations at distinct conjunctures across time and space.

Across US borderlands, a parallel can be drawn an ocean and a century away with the case of James Vann (c. 1762–1809), a Cherokee leader and plantation owner in late eighteenth- and early nineteenth-century Appalachia. Born to a White trader and a Cherokee mother, Vann developed a plantation in what is today Northern Georgia using the labor of enslaved Africans. His surviving residence, the subject of several impressive public history projects, was long regarded as the finest plantation house in the region and a monument to Cherokee sovereignty.[136] Like Cummins, Vann gained privileged access to Western business practices and knowledge through his English father while possessing social affinities that hewed decisively to his Indigenous mother's community. While the plantations run by Cummins and Vann differed in terms of the crops raised and the labor modality used, they were both early capitalist experiments in labor-intensive export agriculture featuring international exchanges of plantation knowledge mediated by Indigenous elites on their own land. For Cummins and Vann alike, projects of Indigenous-national sovereignty and elite prosperity through plantations were situationally reinforcing and pursued with countercolonial ambitions in mind.[137]

Extending the comparison to the late nineteenth-century Asia Pacific, Cummins's contemporaries reveal how individuals around the world were adapting the plantation and its forms of knowledge to pursue self-enrichment and to preserve status in their rapidly changing present. Cummins's collaboration with Hawaiian and Chinese sublessees, the latter of whom provided him with rent, cane, and labor, parallels the experiences of Chinese actors in new plantation sites in nineteenth-century Southeast

Asia such as the Malay peninsula, whether under direct British rule in Province Wellesley or self-governing Johor.[138] Another common point is the interest by Asian entrepreneurs in the latest industrial techniques of production, including railroads, steam-powered mills, and steamer ships from Malaya to Japanese-occupied Taiwan.[139] In the Western-dominated global economy of the late nineteenth and early twentieth centuries, these acquisitions could only be sourced from industrial nodes in North America and Europe. This would change in the twentieth century, when local control over land and national industrial production became two hallmark aspirations of anticolonial independence movements. Yet postcolonial national sovereignty altered little to the economic logic of the capitalist plantation, which has endured and thrived into the present with a wider global reach than ever before.[140] To understand the continued proliferation of plantations across our contemporary world, cases like Cummins's remind us that capitalist experiments can sustain a wide spectrum of political projects, including those opposed to colonialism and imperialism.

Notes

1. Elsewhere in the room, one may admire a portrait of Liliʻuokalani regnant along with a photographic reproduction of a ribbon for her educational society, which featured the crown of Hawaiʻi floating above the word *aloha*. Tom Coffman, *Nation Within: The History of the American Occupation of Hawaiʻi* (Duke University Press, 2016).

2. The women in the front row are Princess Kaiulani, Princess Liliʻuokalani (designated heir to her brother King Kalākaua), Queen Kapiʻolani (consort to reigning King Kalākaua), and Princess Poʻomaikelani.

3. "Waimanalo Plantation and Mill," *Daily Bulletin*, January 6, 1886, 3.

4. Cristiana Bastos, "Portuguese in the Cane: The Racialization of Labour in Hawaiian Plantations," in *Changing Societies: Legacies and Challenges, vol. 1, Ambiguous Inclusions: Inside Out, Inside In*, eds. Sofia Aboim, Paulo Granjo, and Alice Ramos (Imprensa de Ciências Sociais, 2018), 65–96.

5. Joan Abramson, *Photographers of Old Hawaii* (Island Heritage, 1976), 75–76.

6. Caitlin Rosenthal, *Accounting for Slavery: Masters and Management* (Harvard University Press, 2018), 1–7.

7. C. Bolte, "Sugar Crops of the Hawaiian Plantations, 1891 to 1900," in *The Hawaiian Annual for 1901*, ed. Thomas G. Thrum (Black & Auld, 1900), 46.

8. The other majority Hawaiian-owned plantation was the Reciprocity Sugar Company in West Maui. There was a total of fifty-six registered sugar companies

in the Kingdom of Hawaiʻi in 1883. American capital represented about two-thirds of the total. Two plantations and a separate "planting interest" featured majority Chinese ownership, including Pepeʻekeo Plantation on the Island of Hawaiʻi, one of top ten plantations in terms of value and owned by John Cummins's friend, Chuck Afong. "Ownership of Hawaiian Sugar Plantations," *The Planters' Monthly* 2, no. 8 (1883): 171.

9. The *mele* were first published in 1886; authorship remains undetermined (Mrs. A. L. K). "He Inoa Nuʻa Hulu No Ka Mōʻīwahine Kapiʻolani," *Ka Nupepa Kuokoa*, December 25, 1886, 6. The most extensive study on the *mele* is Kīhei de Silva, "Aia i Waimānalo Kō Nuʻa Hulu: An Essay," 2017, http://www.hikaalani.website/uploads/3/4/9/7/34977599/waimanalo_for_hweb.pdf. I rely mainly on the classic English translation offered by Pukui/Korn, though integrate corrections were made by Silva. See *The Echo of Our Song: Chants & Poems of the Hawaiians*, trans. and eds. Mary Kawena Pukui and Alfons L. Korn (University Press of Hawaiʻi, 1973), 156–164.

10. See Ted McCormick's chapter in this volume.

11. Nicholas B. Miller, "Plantation Colonialism in Late Nineteenth-Century Hawaiʻi: The Case of Chinese Sugar Planters," in *Global Plantations in the Modern World Sovereignties, Ecologies, Afterlives*, eds. Colette Le Petitcorps et al. (Palgrave Macmillan, 2023), 177–213. Also see Christina Skott's chapter in this volume.

12. Sally Engel Merry, *Colonizing Hawaiʻi: The Cultural Power of Law* (Princeton University Press, 2000), 35–62.

13. Nicholas B. Miller, "Trading Sovereignty and Labour: The Consular Network of Nineteenth-Century Hawaiʻi," *International History Review* 42, no. 2 (2020): 261–262, 271.

14. Riánna M. Williams, "John Adams Cummins: Prince of Entertainers," *Hawaiian Journal of History* 30 (1996): 153–168.

15. Patrick V. Kirch and Marshall Sahlins, *Anahulu: The Anthropology of History in the Kingdom of Hawaii* (University of Chicago Press, 1992), 37–45. Ralph S. Kuykendall, *The Hawaiian Kingdom, vol. 1, 1778–1854* (University of Hawaiʻi Press, 1938), 34–35.

16. Noelani Arista, *The Kingdom and the Republic: Sovereign Hawaiʻi and the Early United States* (University of Pennsylvania Press, 2019), 117.

17. Arista, *Kingdom and Republic*, 18–51.

18. "Census of the Hawaiian Islands, Taken January 1850," *The Polynesian*, May 4, 1850, 2.

19. Seth Archer, *Sharks upon the Land: Colonialism, Indigenous Health, and Culture in Hawaiʻi, 1778–1855* (Cambridge University Press, 2018).

20. J. Susan Corley, *Leveraging Sovereignty: Kauikeaouli's Global Strategy for the Hawaiian Nation, 1825–1854* (University of Hawaiʻi Press, 2022). J. Kēhaulani Kauanui, *Paradoxes of Hawaiian Sovereignty: Land, Sex, and the Colonial Politics of State Nationalism* (Duke University Press, 2018), 9–10.

21. Miller, "Plantation Colonialism," 183.

22. Kirch and Sahlins, *Anahulu*, 45.

23. Kirch and Sahlins, *Anahulu*, 45.

24. Theodore Morgan, *Hawaii: A Century of Economic Change, 1778–1876* (Harvard University Press, 1948), 139.

25. Davianna Pōmaikaʻi McGregor, "Constructed Images of Native Hawaiian Women," in *Asian/Pacific Islander American Women: A Historical Anthology*, eds. Shirley Hune and Gail M. Nomura (New York University Press, 2003), 32.

26. "Mookuauhau Alii, Na Iwikuamoo o Hawaii Nei, Mai Kahiko Mai, Ko John Adam Cummins Ma [. . .]," *Ka Makaainana*, October 19, 1896, in Edith Kawelohea McKinzie, *Hawaiian Genealogies, Extracted from Hawaiian Language Newspapers* (University of Hawaiʻi Press, 1983), 1:76–77.

27. Kuykendall, *Hawaiian Kingdom*, 1:172; Noenoe K. Silva, *Aloha Betrayed: Native Hawaiian Resistance to American Colonialism* (Duke University Press, 2004), 34; Gregory Rosenthal, *Beyond Hawaiʻi: Native Labor in the Pacific World* (University of California Press, 2018), 168.

28. "In Memoriam—Thomas Cummins," *Hawaiian Gazette*, April 22, 1885, 3.

29. Williams, "John Adams Cummins," 154.

30. "In Memoriam—Thomas Cummins," 3.

31. Williams, "John Adams Cummins," 154.

32. Originally meaning "foreigner," the Hawaiian term *haole* came to refer mainly to people of European ancestry over the nineteenth century. In contemporary Hawaiʻi, it remains a primary category of ethnoracial identification analogous to White.

33. James W. Girvin, *The Cummins Case: A Reminiscence of 1895* (Mercantile Printing, 1905), 7.

34. Girvin, *Cummins Case*, 8.

35. Girvin, *Cummins Case*, 8.

36. Bureau of Immigration of the Kingdom of Hawaiʻi, *Report of the President of the Bureau of Immigration to the Legislature of 1892* (Honolulu, 1892), 4–22.

37. US Tariff Commission, *Reciprocity and Commercial Treatises* (US Government Printing Office, 1919), 24–25.

38. Girvin, *Cummins Case*, 9.

39. Rosenthal, *Beyond Hawaiʻi*, 187–189.

40. "Waimanalo Plantation and Mill," *Daily Bulletin*, January 6, 1886, 3; "Hawaiian Sugar Plantation History, No. 17—Waimanalo, Island of Oahu," *Honolulu Star-Bulletin*, June 22, 1935, 9.

41. Annual reports seem to have been produced for the plantation from the time of its incorporation, but the earliest edition held by the Hamilton Library of the University of Hawaiʻi is from 1910.

42. Otto Finsch, "Bericht über die Insel Oahu," *Zeitschrift für Ethnologie* 11 (1879): 325–377; L. Vernon Briggs, *Experiences of a Medical Student in Honolulu, and on the Island of Oahu, 1881* (David D. Nickerson, 1926); Daniel E. Bandmann,

An Actor's Tour, or Seventy Thousand Miles with Shakespeare (Boston, 1885), 290–298; "A Delightful Interview with Hon. D. J. Toohy Regarding His Tour of the Islands," *Pacific Commercial Advertiser*, August 24, 1885, 3.

43. *Pacific Commercial Advertiser*, March 14, 1881, 2; April 28, 1883, 5; November 24, 1883, 5.

44. Comley to Evarts, Honolulu, June 9, 1879, *Papers Relating to the Foreign Relations of the United States* (Washington, DC, 1879), 542–543. Hawaii State Archives, Interior Department, Miscellaneous Files, Box 151, January–March 1878, Labor Contracts for Teu Tow, Mawaii, Tarnee Our, Te Baboo, and Ma Nua.

45. Jason W. Girvin, "Waimanalo," *Pacific Commercial Advertiser*, October 12, 1906, 8.

46. Girvin, "Waimanalo," 8. Makee v. Dominis, 3 Haw. 579 (1874).

47. *The Florida Agriculturalist*, October 30, 1878, 4.

48. Girvin, "Waimanalo," 8.

49. Jesse C. Condé and Gerald M. Best, *Sugar Trains: Narrow Gauge Rails of Hawaii* (Glenwood Publishers, 1973), 364; Harland, Bartholomew, and Associates, *A General Plan for Waimanalo Valley, Island of Oahu* (Commissioner of Public Lands, 1959), 13–14; Jay Martin, *Live All You Can: Alexander Joy Cartwright and the Invention of Modern Baseball* (Columbia University Press, 2009), 95.

50. *Pacific Commercial Advertiser*, May 11, 1878, 3.

51. "a ma ke ano Hui me Kakalaika [Cartwright] a me F.S. Pratt ua hoalaia ae la he hui mahi ko malaila," "Make o Mr. Thomas A. Cummins," *Ka Nupepa Kuokoa*, April 25, 1885, 2. Also see *Daily Bulletin*, April 20, 1885, 3.

52. "In Memoriam—Thomas Cummins," 3.

53. *Evening Bulletin*, October 4, 1882, 2.

54. *Pacific Commercial Advertiser*, December 7, 1872, 3.

55. *Pacific Commercial Advertiser*, July 28, 1880, 3; February 12, 1881, 2; July 21, 1883, 5.

56. Martin, *Live All You Can*, 95.

57. Martin, *Live All You Can*, 95; *Pacific Commercial Advertiser*, May 11, 1878, 3; *Pacific Commercial Advertiser*, July 21, 1883, 5; *Evening Bulletin*, August 7, 1884, 3.

58. Miller, "Plantation Colonialism," 187–189, 195; Hawaii State Archives, M-36 Cartwright, Box 3, Papers 1877–1883, May 14, 1878.

59. Hawaii State Archives, M-36 Cartwright, Box 3, Papers 1877–1883, July 29, 1879, and Box 6, folder January 24, 1880–November 15, 1881. Martin, *Live All You Can*, 96.

60. *Pacific Commercial Advertiser*, November 3, 1883, 5.

61. Cristiana Bastos, *The Colour of Labor*, ERC Advanced Grant project no. 695573, 2016–2023.

62. Miller, "Plantation Colonialism," 185. Edward D. Beechert, *Working in Hawaii: A Labor History* (University of Hawaiʻi Press, 1985), 60.

63. Additionally, 48.4% were Chinese, and 1% were from the South Pacific. Robert C. Schmitt, *Historical Statistics of Hawaii* (University Press of Hawaii, 1977), 97.

64. Briggs, *Experiences of a Medical Student*, 32.

65. "Hooweliweli ia," *Ka Nupepa Kuokoa*, September 28, 1878, 3; *Pacific Commercial Advertiser*, September 28, 1878, 3.

66. Miller, "Trading Sovereignty and Labour," 261–262, 271.

67. Hawaii State Archives, Interior Department, Miscellaneous Files, Box 151, January–March 1878, Labor Contracts for Teu Tow, Mawaii, Tarnee Our, Te Baboo, and Ma Nua.

68. Briggs, *Experiences of a Medical Student*, 31–37, 225–226.

69. Attorney General of the Kingdom of Hawai'i, *Biennial Report of the Attorney General to the Legislative Assembly of 1882* (Honolulu, 1882), 17.

70. "Report of CN Spencer, Inspector General of Immigrants," *Pacific Commercial Advertiser*, October 13, 1887, 2. Board of Immigration of the Kingdom of Hawai'i, *Hoike a ka Peresidena o ka Papa Hoopae Limahana i ka Ahaolelo Kau Kanawai o 1888* (Honolulu, 1888), 16.

71. Beechert, *Working in Hawaii*, 65; Clarence E. Glick, *Sojourners and Settlers: Chinese Migrants in Hawaii* (University of Hawai'i Press, 1980), 42–46.

72. Adam McKeown, "Conceptualizing Chinese Diasporas, 1842 to 1949," *Journal of Asian Studies* 58, no. 2 (1999): 317–321.

73. Finsch, "Bericht über die Insel Oahu," 327–329.

74. *Pacific Commercial Advertiser*, July 15, 1882, 2.

75. John Wesley Coulter and Chee-kwon Chun, "Chinese Rice Farmers in Hawaii," *University of Hawaii Bulletin* 16, no. 5 (1937): 167.

76. See Christina Skott's chapter in this volume for more on this point.

77. Miller, "Plantation Colonialism."

78. Miller, "Plantation Colonialism."

79. Harland et al., *General Plan for Waimanalo*, 14.

80. Tin-Yuke Char and Wai Jane Char, *Chinese Historic Sites and Pioneer Families of Rural Oahu* (University of Hawai'i Press, 1988), 35; Harland et al., *General Plan for Waimanalo*, 14.

81. *Planters Monthly* 6 (1887): 499; Board of Immigration of the Kingdom of Hawai'i, *Report of the President of the Board of Immigration to the Legislative Assembly of 1888* (Honolulu, 1888), 13–14; Board of Immigration of the Kingdom of Hawai'i, *Biennial Report of the President of the Board of Immigration to the Legislature of 1890* (Honolulu, 1890).

82. *Biennial Report of the President of the Board of Immigration to the Legislature of 1890*.

83. Miller, "Plantation Colonialism," 185, 198–200.

84. *Daily Bulletin*, March 13, 1882, 2.

85. *Hawaiian Gazette*, August 14, 1878, 5.

86. *Pacific Commercial Advertiser*, August 27, 1884, 2.
87. *Pacific Commercial Advertiser*, September 4, 1880, 3.
88. Condé and Best, *Sugar Trains*, 364.
89. Briggs, *Experiences of a Medical Student*, 30.
90. "A Delightful Interview with Hon. D. J. Toohy," 3; "Waimanalo Plantation and Mill," *Daily Bulletin*, January 6, 1886, 3.
91. "Waimanalo Plantation and Mill," *Daily Bulletin*, January 6, 1886, 3.
92. Robert A. Ramsay, "Sugar Plantation Railroads in Hawaii," *The Railway and Locomotive Historical Society Bulletin*, 114 (1966), 16; Condé and Best, *Sugar Trains*, 364.
93. Williams, "John Adams Cummins," 154.
94. "At Waimanalo," *Pacific Commercial Advertiser*, August 16, 1883, 3; "The Evils of Painting, and Their Remedy," *Daily Bulletin*, February 23, 1883, 1.
95. "At Waimanalo," *Pacific Commercial Advertiser*.
96. "At Waimanalo," *Pacific Commercial Advertiser*, 3.
97. "At Waimanalo," *Pacific Commercial Advertiser*, 3.
98. "Waimanalo Plantation and Mill," *Daily Bulletin*, January 6, 1886, 3.
99. *Pacific Commercial Advertiser*, February 12, 1885, 3.
100. Bandmann, *An Actor's Tour*, 291–294.
101. "A Delightful Interview with Hon. D. J. Toohy," 3.
102. *Pacific Commercial Advertiser*, August 25, 1877, 3; Saturday *Press*, October 2, 1880, 3; October 9, 1880, 3; *Daily Bulletin*, February 23, 1883, 2.
103. Williams, "John Adams Cummins," 162; Girvin, *Cummins Case*, 13–14.
104. *Pacific Commercial Advertiser*, April 5, 1874, 3.
105. *Pacific Commercial Advertiser*, April 5, 1874, 3.
106. "Hooulu Lahui," *Pacific Commercial Advertiser*, November 14, 1874, 2; Tiffany Lani Ing, *Reclaiming Kalākaua: Nineteenth-Century Perspectives of a Hawaiian Sovereign* (University of Hawai'i Press, 2019), 99; Robert Lydecker, *Roster Legislatures of Hawaii, 1841–1918* (Hawaiian Gazette, 1918), 132; Jonathan Kay Kamakawiwo'ole Osorio, *Dismembering Lāhui: A History of the Hawaiian Nation to 1887* (University of Hawai'i Press, 2002), 250–260.
107. "Hooulu Lahui," 2; Miller, "Trading Sovereignty and Labour," 261–262, 267–268.
108. Lorenz Gonschor, *A Power in the World: The Hawaiian Kingdom in Oceania* (University of Hawai'i Press, 2019), 64–111.
109. Osorio, *Dismembering Lāhui*, 192–249; Tom Coffman, *Nation Within: The History of the American Occupation of Hawai'i*, revised edition (Duke University Press, 2016), 75, 80–83.
110. Hawaii State Archives, Privy Council, Series 421, Vol. 14T, Letterbook, 1881–1892, 239.
111. Lydecker, "Roster Legislatures," 178, 182. Daniel Logan, *A History of the Hawaiian Islands, Their Resources and People* (Lewis Publishing, 1907), 194.

112. “Hooulu Lahui,” 2.

113. *Daily Bulletin*, August 23, 1887, 1, 9; Pennie Moblo, “Leprosy, Politics, and the Rise of Hawai‘i’s Reform Party,” *Journal of Pacific History* 34, no. 1 (1999), 75–77.

114. *Ka Leo o ka Lahui*, February 1, 1892, 6.

115. “Receiver’s Sale on Foreclosure,” *Daily Bulletin*, June 9, 1892, 2.

116. Coffman, *Nation Within*, 104–115, 132, 161–162; Girvin, *Cummins Case*, 13.

117. Silva, *Aloha Betrayed*, 131. “Halawai Nui a Na Makaainana o Hawaii Nei,” *Hawaii Holomua*, July 3, 1894, 2.

118. Silva, *Aloha Betrayed*, 130–133.

119. *Daily Bulletin*, September 22, 1893, 3.

120. Colin Newbury, *Patrons, Clients, and Empire: Chieftaincy and Over-rule in Asia, Africa, and the Pacific* (Oxford University Press, 2003), 209–210.

121. “Hawaiian Sugar Plantation Corporations,” in *The Hawaiian Annual for 1894*, ed. Thomas G. Thrum (Honolulu, 1893), 41.

122. Williams, “John Adams Cummins,” 162; Girvin, *Cummins Case*, 13–14.

123. “Hawaiian Sugar Corporations and Plantations,” in *Hawaiian Almanac and Annual for 1890*, ed. Thomas G. Thrum (Honolulu, 1889), 28; *Hawaiian Star*, November 14, 1894, 3.

124. Williams, “John Adams Cummins,” 163–164; Girvin, *Cummins Case*, 15–21.

125. Williams, “John Adams Cummins,” 163–164.

126. Williams, “John Adams Cummins,” 164; Girvin, *Cummins Case*, 122.

127. Girvin, *Cummins Case*, 6.

128. University of Hawai‘i at Mānoa Library, Hawaiian and Pacific Collections, Giffard Papers, Box 2, File 12, Irwin to Giffard, May 30, 1895.

129. University of Hawai‘i at Mānoa Library, Hawaiian and Pacific Collections, Giffard Papers, Box 2, File 12, Irwin to Giffard, June 24, 1895.

130. University of Hawai‘i at Mānoa Library, Hawaiian and Pacific Collections, Giffard Papers, Box 2, File 12, Irwin to Giffard, June 24, 1895.

131. Williams, “John Adams Cummins,” 165. Logan, *A History of the Hawaiian Islands*, 193.

132. Edgar T. Thompson, *The Plantation* [1932], eds. Sidney W. Mintz and George Baca (University of South Carolina Press, 2010), 15.

133. Sidney W. Mintz, “Introduction,” in Thompson, *The Plantation*, ix.

134. On the production of plantation knowledge in frontier regions, see the chapters by Theresa Ventura, Marta Macedo, Moritz von Brescius, and Gillian McGillivray in this volume.

135. Mintz, “Introduction,” in Thompson, *The Plantation*, ix.

136. Tiya Miles, *The House on Diamond Hill: A Cherokee Plantation Story* (University of North Carolina Press, 2010).

137. Kauanui, *Paradoxes of Hawaiian Sovereignty*, 7–8.

138. See Christina Skott's chapter in this volume. See also Nicholas B. Miller, "Family Resemblance? Colonialism, Sovereignty, and the Global Royal Family in Nineteenth-Century Hawaiʻi and Johor," in *Global Royal Families: Cultures of Transnational Monarchy in the Nineteenth and Twentieth Centuries*, eds. Robert Aldrich et al. (Oxford University Press, 2024).

139. See Christina Skott's chapter in this volume. Chih-Ming Ka, *Japanese Colonialism in Taiwan: Land Tenure, Development, and Dependency, 1895–1945* (Westview, 1995); Jack F. Williams, "Sugar: The Sweetener in Taiwan's Development," in *China's Island Frontier: Studies in the Historical Geography of Taiwan*, ed. Ronald G. Knapp (University of Hawaiʻi Press, 1980).

140. Tania Murray Li, *Land's End: Capitalist Relations on an Indigenous Frontier* (Duke University Press, 2014); Tania Murray Li and Pujo Semedi, eds., *Plantation Life: Corporate Occupation in Indonesia's Oil Palm Zone* (Duke University Press, 2021); Case Watkins, *Palm Oil Diaspora: Afro-Brazilian Landscapes and Economies on Bahia's Dendê Coast* (Cambridge University Press, 2021); Jonathan E. Robins, *Oil Palm: A Global History* (University of North Carolina Press, 2021).

Chapter 4

Experimental Paternalism

An Owenite Plantation in Mississippi, 1820–1870

Claudia Roesch

In June 1825, Southern plantation owner Joseph Emory Davis allegedly met British social reformer Robert Owen during a stagecoach ride from Pittsburgh to Buffalo.[1] Davis, the older brother of future Confederate President Jefferson Davis, had recently taken over his father's cotton plantation at Davis Bend, a peninsula in the Mississippi River, thereby becoming the owner of fifty slaves.[2] Owen was the manager of one of the largest textile mills in the world, New Lanark in Scotland, where he had established a holistic system to provide housing, schooling, leisure, and nutrition for two thousand five hundred workers to curb crime, child labor, and alcoholism. In his attempts to fight poverty and vice among his workers, Owen developed a new "social system" of cooperative labor to increase the education and happiness of his workers while at the same time increasing profits. This included designing a parallelogram village, wherein one thousand five hundred inhabitants would live, work in agriculture and manufacture, attend school, trade with neighboring communities, and share the profits derived from the mill.[3] In 1826, he bought the settlement of New Harmony, Indiana, to test out his village scheme and from 1825 to 1829 traveled throughout the Americas to promote his social system among New World elites. During this journey, Owen is said to have used the nine-hour stagecoach ride to Buffalo to convince Davis that his system of labor organization could work profitably on a plantation as well.

While doubts exist whether this stagecoach conversation actually took place, it is clear that Davis visited Owen at New Harmony, Indiana, in July 1826, where he likely also met abolitionist Frances Wright.[4] Wright and Davis sought to implement the Owenite system of labor organization in a plantation setting. While Wright had the intention to eventually manumit the enslaved workers after educating them, Davis, according to his biographer Janet Sharp Hermann, had no intention of abolishing slavery altogether but rather was exploring how to practice it in a more humane way.[5] In 1999, Hermann took a more critical view of Davis, arguing that he was actually seeking a way to run a more profitable plantation based on the newest insights of science and labor management.[6] Davis's experiments would continue up to the American Civil War, and two years after its close, in 1867, he sold his plantations to his formerly enslaved accountant Benjamin T. Montgomery.

Together with his sons Isaiah Montgomery and William Thornton Montgomery, Benjamin T. Montgomery continued the communitarian experiments on the peninsula until the end of Reconstruction in 1877. The refugee camp set up on Davis Bend by the Freedmen's Bureau during the Civil War is often mentioned in studies on African-American wartime experiences.[7] Mound Bayou, the Montgomery's second settlement, has also received some interest by historians and sociologists for being a hub of Black civil rights activism from the late nineteenth century onward.[8] Its founder Isaiah Montgomery, Benjamin T. Montgomery's son, became the first African American to be elected to the Mississippi State Assembly in 1890.[9] Through access to education and property, the Montgomery family managed to establish itself as an African American middle-class family and statewide political force.

Previous studies on the connection between Owenism and the plantations of Davis Bend have either been characterized by a rather uncritical stance toward the racial dynamics of the antebellum era or have paid insufficient attention to the specific workings of Owenite community organization.[10] Recently, scholars in management studies have taken up Davis Bend as a case study to trace "the genealogical link between Montgomery and management history," linking the region not only to Owenism but to textile factories in Lowell, Massachusetts, as well.[11] While that scholarship focuses on the transfer of management concepts from one industry to another, this chapter approaches the Davis Bend plantations from a history of knowledge perspective. It investigates experiments with plantation labor management that were inspired by Owenite social reform, making it possible for plantations that developed under racial capitalism to be maintained as sites of production even after the end of slavery.[12]

American scholarship has mainly studied Owen from the perspective of Utopianism, considering his intentional communities in tandem with religious settlements.[13] In this scholarship, Owen is often represented as a failed utopian whose views were incompatible with the ideals of the American founding fathers since he rejected organized religion and private property.[14] This line of argumentation, however, neglects the broad curiosity in Owen's schemes held by a broad range of American actors, including Washington elites, factory owners, abolitionists and, in the case of Davis, plantation owners. Meanwhile, the British history of ideas has extensively debated whether early socialists like Owen, Charles Fourier, and Claude-Henri de Saint Simon were more experimental and practically minded than Karl Marx and Friedrich Engels gave them credit.[15] Recent German-language scholarship takes the aspirations of intentional settlements seriously, approaching early socialist intentional communities as "laboratories of modernity" and sites of experimentation in community organization.[16] Building on this research trajectory, this chapter examines the Davis Bend plantations as sites of knowledge production and experimentation in the Owenite mode of labor organization. First, a short overview is provided of the principles of plantation management operative during Joseph Davis's ownership of the Davis Bend plantations. Afterward, the experiments of the Freedmen's Bureau during the Civil War are discussed, centering on the years 1866 to 1868, when detailed correspondence between Davis and Montgomery illuminates how Montgomery as a new plantation owner experimented in organizing a profitable plantation.[17]

Testifying to the cross-pollination of ideas between plantations and factories, Davis Bend is an important case study in the reception of Owenite labor management.[18] At Davis Bend, factory-inspired social reforms were placed within the very distinctive socioeconomic setting of slave-based economy, thus turning the Davis Bend plantations into sites of knowledge production in labor organization. During the experiments, Davis, the Freedmen's Bureau, and Montgomery produced different forms of knowledge about labor organization since all of them strived to find a new way of running a profitable cotton plantation without slave labor, work gangs, and violence, while at the same time trying to maintain control over their workforce. This chapter argues that labor organization at Davis Bend upheld the structure of the large-scale plantation that resembled a factory system and was dependent on the benevolence of the paternalistic owner-manager even after abolition of slavery.[19] It shows that the similarities between the Owenite factory and the Davis Bend plantations go beyond management styles and the experimental character of community organization. They also included a preference for large-scale on-site production as compared to small-scale family farming, home production, or piece work.

Hurricane and Brierfield Plantations Under the Management of Joseph E. Davis, 1828–1861

Two years after visiting New Harmony in 1826, Joseph E. Davis began implementing some aspects of the Owenite system on his plantations. He provided housing, a hospital, a blacksmith workshop, and a shop where enslaved workers could trade their homegrown vegetables for consumer goods. He gave land to his younger brother Jefferson Davis, who cleared it to establish the neighboring plantation Brierfield. Jefferson Davis later left Brierfield for Joseph to manage while he was running for political office in Washington, DC. On Hurricane and Brierfield, Davis extended to enslaved workers limited freedoms based on the Owenite system that other enslaved persons in the US South did not hold. For example, he permitted his enslaved workers to learn how to read and write as well as had them trained in mechanics, mathematics, and artisanal skills. In 1902, Isaiah Montgomery, who had been born into slavery on the Hurricane Plantation in 1847, told the *Boston Evening Transcript*: "We just barely had an idea of what slave life was. The conditions on our place were better than most. The overseers had only a partial power."[20] Later in the interview, he described the working conditions on the plantations, including how two "squats" of enslaved workers competed against each other. Hermann has likened Davis's use of competitions and small gifts to increase worker motivation to the function of the performance meters at Owen's factory in New Lanark.[21]

According to Isaiah Montgomery, Davis would not allow overseers to punish enslaved workers without his permission.[22] Instead, he organized a plantation-wide court system modeled after Owen's arrangement in New Lanark, wherein enslaved workers could only be corporally punished after they had been sentenced by a jury of their peers. In this way, he avoided some of the brutality characterizing the slave economy of the antebellum

US South. Davis also insisted on calling enslaved workers by their actual names, prohibited the sexual exploitation of enslaved women, did not use dogs to chase refugees, and granted enslaved workers a home in old age, rather than sale.[23] Nevertheless, the coercive nature of their employment meant that the plantation was far from being a "true village of voluntary co-operation."[24]

Benjamin T. Montgomery, Isaiah Montgomery's father, was, despite being enslaved, the plantation's manager, overseeing accounting, the plantation's steam engine-powered cotton gin, and its elaborate levee system.[25] Born in Loudon County, Virginia in 1819, Benjamin T. Montgomery had received an above average education before being sold to Davis in 1836. His skills included reading and writing as well as mathematics, mechanics, and civil engineering.[26] At Davis Bend, he was also allowed to run the plantation shop, which earned him enough income to buy his wife's freedom in 1843, though he remained enslaved himself until the Civil War.[27] Additionally, his engineering knowledge made Hurricane and Brierfield two of the most successful plantations in Mississippi. Prone to flooding, the plantations relied on civil engineering projects such as levees, canals, and irrigation ditches to control water saturation. Davis also saw to the education of some of his enslaved workers in natural sciences and engineering, equipping them with the mechanical skills necessary to run and repair the plantation's steam powered cotton gin, and thus increasing its productivity.[28] Like the plantation's court system and use of performance incentives, this practice was also copied from Owen. In drawing upon Owen's plan at New Lanark, Davis gained an edge over his competitors.

Davis Bend in the Aftermath of the American Civil War, 1865–1866

Joseph E. Davis abandoned his lands at Davis Bend at the outbreak of the American Civil War (1861–1865) and spent the war years in Alabama. As the Union Army advanced along the Mississippi River in 1862, enslaved workers escaped the sites of their bondage, looting plantations along the way. Between 1863 and 1865, the Union Army requisitioned the Davis Bend plantations, establishing Brierfield as a so-called contraband camp, where the Union army gathered and housed Black refugees. Approximately ten thousand formerly enslaved people found refuge there.[29] According to a White missionary agent who visited in 1864, the conditions were abominable, with children under the age of twelve sleeping in an open cattle shed and sharing a few blankets between them.[30] Ira Berlin et al. argue that the main problem at the refugee camps was the absence of able-bodied adult men, as most of them had left the camps to fight for the Union army or to work in military-related jobs. Only women, children, and disabled or sick men remained, often having nothing but the clothes on their backs and dependent on army rations for survival.[31] At the end of the war, amnesty laws endorsed by President Andrew Johnson returned most property confiscated by the Union army to their former Southern owners, except for plantations that had belonged to Confederate leaders. Given this policy, officials were unsure what to do with Hurricane and Brierfield, since Joseph's brother, Jefferson Davis, had been the president of the Confederacy. While Joseph was adamant that he had been their exclusive owner, his initial petitions fell on deaf ears.[32]

In May 1865, the newly founded Freedmen's Bureau became responsible for managing the Davis Bend plantations. It would oversee the harvests of 1865 and 1866. During this time, the assistant commissioner for the Freedmen's Bureau in Mississippi, Colonel Samuel Thomas, proposed to turn the Davis Bend plantations into an experimental project in African American self-management.[33] A similar experiment had been conducted on Robert E. Lee's former plantation in Arlington, Virginia. Contemporary Northern commentators thought a particularly fitting form of historical justice was for the plantations formerly owned by prominent Confederate leaders to now be run by their liberated, formerly enslaved workers.[34] Since Jefferson Davis was particularly scorned by Northern commentators, Davis Bend served as an ideal site for an experiment in Black self-management.[35] Conjointly, as Berlin has indicated, the approach reflected shifts in Northern opinion from benevolence to the formerly enslaved to demands for their self-sufficiency.[36]

In his letters of 1865 to Washington, Colonel Thomas proposed an independent Black community on Davis Bend, using land that "had belonged to noted rebels who have abandoned the land in Fall of 1862."[37] Thomas reported that a colony of freedmen had already established itself there in the past year with already promising results, "living in good houses, making and enforcing its own local laws, managing its own affairs, separate and apart from the white citizens of the state."[38] If the land was returned to its prewar owners, Thomas argued, the colony would have to be abandoned, since he assumed White landowners in Mississippi would be unwilling to sell or rent land to the formerly enslaved. The colony would permit the Black farmers to support themselves financially and thus eliminate the need for federal support, since as a community they would be able to bear the cost of educating their children and taking care of their old, sick, and disabled: "If the land be set apart for the purpose I ask it, a pauper colony of several hundred old and infirm negros can be located here who will be supported by the colored people who receive the land. The colony will bind themselves to take charge of one thousand destitutes unable to work."[39]

Thomas clearly stated his intention to establish a segregated, self-sufficient Black community that, by producing and selling cotton and other crops on the capitalist market, could raise enough money to take care of their own. His plan originated in a petition by twenty freedmen on Davis Bend (among them Benjamin T. Montgomery) who presented themselves as "industrious good farmers" looking for a site for their colony and advised to contact Thomas.[40] They sought two thousand acres of flood-protected land and were ready to pay rent to the federal government "to make such an experiment a success." The federal government thus would not only save money on welfare spending but even make a return.[41]

Thomas's own petition in 1865 explained how the community should be arranged: "It is not proposed that these men shall work the plantation as a whole, but will divide it so as to suit the means of each person giving each, however, an opportunity to cultivate what land his means will justify."[42] Core to the experiment was the abolition of work gangs and overseers. Instead, "companies or partnerships" mostly consisting of family units would manage small plots of land. The community leaders would buy the necessary supplies for cultivation, sell the resulting crops on the market, and share all profits among the members. The leaders would additionally provide schooling for children and health care for the sick and disabled. Eventually, this model was put into practice. As in an Owenite parallelogram village, the community conducted trade with outsiders as a single whole, but in contrast to Owenism, community members had to pay rent to the landowner, which at first was the federal government and, later, the Montgomery family.

In his report for the fourth quarter of 1865, Thomas wrote that the "experiment has been a grand success."[43] During the harvest season that year, a total of 181 "companies," consisting of 1,300 adults and 450 children had produced 1,736 bales of cotton; 12,000 bushels of corn; and a large quantity of market vegetables (including watermelons and potatoes), together worth a total of $397,000. Deducting expenses for stock and supplies as well as refunds to the Freedmen's Bureau for the initial cost of food rations, the community made a collective profit of $159,000 in 1865.[44] Crucially, they did not have to pay rent to the federal government that year. By comparison, a neighboring plantation farmed by "transient people" on a wage labor basis had only produced 234 bales of cotton with a net profit of $44,429.80. According to Thomas, wages for the supervisors of Black laborers constituted a large part of that plantation's expenses. At Davis Bend, community-based plantation management thus seemed to be a more productive and profitable form of cotton farming than that based on supervised wage labor. Despite this apparent success, Thomas was pessimistic that the experiment could be replicated since he had to return four of the plantations on Davis Bend to their previous owners and could only retain Hurricane and Brierfield on the provision that rent would be charged.[45]

The Continued Experiment and the Sale to Montgomery, 1866–1867

In 1866, ownership of Hurricane and Brierfield reverted to their antebellum owner, Joseph E. Davis. Rather than return to Davis Bend, however, he ultimately placed the lands under the management of his longtime Black plantation manager Benjamin T. Montgomery, who sought to continue the spirit of experimentation with modalities of plantation cultivation. In continuing dialogue with Davis, Montgomery adopted the basic elements of Owenite teaching in his focus on rationality, justice, and community organization. At the same time, he adjusted the concept of cooperative ownership into a system of land leases he deemed fair in the circumstances. Davis Bend was typical of community experiments within the Owenite model in this regard, which tended to adjust theory according to local specificities.[46]

During the ownership dispute between Joseph E. Davis and the Freedmen's Bureau in 1865 and 1866, Montgomery became an unofficial spokesperson for Black freedmen on Davis Bend. Montgomery and his sons had gained their freedom when they fled to Ohio in the midst of the Civil War in June 1863, finding work in Cincinnati as dock workers. They returned to Davis Bend in 1865 to open three convenience stores on the peninsula. The Union Army's occupation of Mississippi provided most of the newly freed persons in the refugee camp their first opportunity to work for wages; Montgomery's store stocked consumer goods for them to spend these wages.[47] The Montgomery family prospered from the store, permitting them to live comfortably and educate their children.[48]

After working together to successfully establish the model community at Davis Bend in 1865, an initial flashpoint between Thomas and four Black leaders including Benjamin T. Montgomery was the matter of commission fees due for use of the steam-powered cotton gin at Hurricane. Montgomery decried charges set by the Freedmen's Bureau as excessive, while Thomas accused Montgomery of illegally selling alcohol in his stores.[49] In this conflict, Montgomery called on the support of former plantation owner Joseph E. Davis on his behalf. Davis soon petitioned President Andrew Johnson to reinstate his family's ownership of Hurricane and Brierfield, emphasizing that he had owned the deeds to the properties personally, rather than his infamous brother.[50] Davis's claim was successful, and in October 1866, he requested that the Freedmen's Bureau turn management of the two plantations over to Montgomery by January 1, 1867.[51]

Since Black families were not yet allowed to buy property in Mississippi, Davis and Montgomery initially described their arrangement officially as a three-year lease, stipulating that the land would be returned to Davis's heirs if Montgomery could not meet the contractual interest payment.[52] This was just a pretense. The two signed a sales agreement on November 15, 1886, that agreed to turn ownership of the plantations over to Montgomery on January 1, 1867, or as soon as Black people were allowed to own property in Mississippi, which occurred in March 1867. Since Montgomery did not hold sufficient capital to pay the $300,000 to purchase the plantation outright, the sales contract featured installment payments of $18,000 annually, with an interest rate of five percent if paid in gold or seven percent if paid in paper money.[53] An ultimately decisive clause stipulated that the property would revert to Davis if an installment payment was not made on time. This came to pass almost twenty years later, after Jefferson Davis inherited the properties. Joseph E. Davis died just a few years after the contract was signed, in 1870. In his will, he assigned his grandchildren as inheritors of the installment payments. This provision was contested by his younger brother, who demanded that he be assigned as their recipient, claiming that the property had been owned collectively as a family before the war. Jefferson Davis would press his case for nearly a decade until the Mississippi Supreme Court ruled in his favor in 1879, about two years after federal troops withdrew from the South.[54] When Montgomery's sons fell behind on the installment payments due to a decline in cotton prices in 1886, he enforced the terms of the sales contract and expelled them from Hurricane and Brierfield. Forced to move, the Montgomery family and their community went first to the neighboring Ursino Plantation before moving to Mound Bayou in 1887, about 130 miles north of Davis Bend.

After starting to buy Hurricane and Brierfield on installment, Montgomery continued to inform Joseph E. Davis of their development. According to Rosen, Davis and Montgomery had envisioned Davis Bend to be "a monument to freedman industry and co-operation. It was to become the latest iteration of utopia, modeled of course, on Davis's interpretation of Owenite cooperative principles."[55] With his experience as an enslaved plantation manager and spokesperson for the community, Montgomery had, in Hermann's words, become one of the "undisputed leaders of the black community . . . with a cooperative spirit that would have done credit to Robert Owen."[56]

The lease agreement of 1866 stipulated that Hurricane and Brierfield were to be run as communalist projects. Rosen argues that Montgomery sought "to organize a community composed exclusively of colored people, to occupy and cultivate said plantation, and invit[e] the cooperation of such as are recommended by honesty, industry, sobriety, and intelligence in the enterprise."[57] The lease explicitly stated that Montgomery's objective was to organize a community of African Americans in a cooperative system, with community members selected by Montgomery according to the moral standards set by Davis. At variance with the prominence of sobriety in Owenite ideals, Montgomery paid community members "twenty five to thirty dollars' worth whiskey per day" and hired day laborers at twenty dollars' worth of whiskey for helping with levee repairs, noting that this was necessary since he was short on cash.[58]

Montgomery was faced with the problem of a shortage of labor, since many recently freed Black people found plantation work to be abhorrent and sought independence off the former plantations.[59] Hermann surmised that the only workers who remained were either old or content with Davis's arrangements prior to the outbreak of the Civil War.[60] Less than a year after taking over management, Montgomery placed an advertisement in the Vicksburg newspapers, seeking Black workers for a community "such are recommended by honesty, industry, sobriety and intelligence," quoting the explicit terms of the lease agreement between Davis and him.[61] The advertisement promised that in return for their rent payments and a levy of fifty cents per acre to pay for levee repair and a school for Black children, workers would have full ownership of the crops they raised and be able to choose members of a governing council. It was also warned members could be expelled for drunkenness.[62]

In his correspondence with Davis in 1866, Montgomery expressed his plans to rent out parcels of land to producers, as practiced in the ongoing experiment by the Freedmen's Bureau, rather than sharecropping, wherein lessees paid rents in kind (that is, crops) to landowners. He explained, "now if renting does not conflict with the laws of the state we would prefer it to share as it would give less trouble to collector."[63] The latter justification was merely a pretense, as Montgomery made clear in December 1867 when comparing his plantations to those of his sharecropping-practicing neighbors. According to Montgomery, the neighboring Lovell Brothers controlled virtually all the cotton produced by their sharecroppers, most of whom were already in debt due to the cost of the supplies they furnished.[64] Instead, he conducted himself "with a willingness to do as near right as the teachings of reason, justice and experience dictates" to find a fair system of renting out parcels that would benefit workers and increase productivity for all.[65]

Due to the experimental character of Montgomery's endeavor, the outcome for the model colony was far from certain. Montgomery however was hopeful that "although we have a tight time of it in common with almost everybody else I am inclined to think the community system will work after becoming properly systematized, which will require time."[66] The statistics of the cotton harvest proved him right. In November 1867, Hurricane and Brierfield shipped 241 bales of cotton despite severe floods and insect infestation. His sharecropping-practicing neighbors, the Lovells, produced only 129, and the other two plantations on Davis Bend, managed by White absentee owners, bore only 190 and 24 bales.[67] It must be noted that this total of 584 bales for 1867 was less than a third of that produced in 1865 in which year all six plantations were under military-endorsed Black self-management.

Transportation and Crop Experimentations as Communal Problems, 1867–1870

Even after agreeing to purchase Brierfield and Hurricane on installment, Montgomery continued to write weekly reports to Joseph Davis about the progress of the plantation experiment. The correspondence reveals insights into the everyday affairs of the plantation, including matters of cotton harvests and tax payments, the spread of diseases among community members, flood prevention, and the difficulties in organizing transportation and collective levee repairs, including small catastrophes such as crayfish undermining a levee.[68] Montgomery dutifully recorded the number of renters and the amount of rent collected. He also diligently reported cases of illness, including the names of those afflicted with cholera and the course of their symptoms to either recovery or death. According to Gates, Burke, and Humphreys, these practices of record keeping were typical of nineteenth-century business management operations, requiring skills "in reading, writing, math and social interactions."[69] Montgomery and Davis knew the names of the renters and their relatives, indicating the personal character of the relationship they maintained with them.

Montgomery's letter of August 8, 1867, provides a good overview of the problems he faced as a new plantation owner: "We are still troubled with some cases of cholera; have had one death since I last wrote you. The case of the victim was not reported in time to render the aid that might otherwise have been given. The Gin will be held subject to order as advised. The worms are here on many [parts] of this and other plantations on the Bend in pretty large force."[70] The letter went on to report how Montgomery employed the children to catch worms, paying them twenty cents per cup, and that the renters had planted turnips as a food staple since it was too late to plant anything else for the season. Farmers who had leased parcels of the plantation were expected to collaborate as a community in planting food staples and fixing problems such as pests or flooding.

Montgomery's correspondence reveals that, despite the communitarian aspirations of the experiment, he was the person who made the ultimate decisions. In June 1867, he went so far as to suggest that once the community organization was fully incorporated, he planned to exclude any community member "who may leave to work elsewhere when their services are needed here either in their own associate or neighbors' field. Any one persuaded off shall be required to stay away. No objection to their working for any other community when their services are not needed at home."[71] Around this time, Montgomery had grown frustrated from attempts by labor agents to lure away his lessees. Montgomery went on to note that labor agents were only successful "among the unstable minded" among his renters. As common with projectors and managers of intentional communities from Owen to Davis, Montgomery was not free from a patronizing attitude toward his workers-cum-community members.[72]

Montgomery held expectations of mutual support of his lessees, who were to chip in with community work to help their own community and their neighbors. Flood protection on the Mississippi banks was communal work, and those who did not want to take part in the community should leave. Correspondence between Montgomery and Davis suggests that these expectations were communicated verbally. Few of the renters would have been literate, and no written lease agreements are known to have existed. Highlighting the importance of flood protection, Montgomery carefully recorded the water levels of the Mississippi River in his letters. The Davis Bend plantations were situated in an environmentally precarious area and were hit each spring by floods lasting from late February until mid-May. In the spring of 1867, Montgomery sent weekly reports to Davis about the rising tides. He noted on March 21 that, on the neighboring Woods Plantation, the tide was one foot higher than at Hurricane, assuming that this was "caused probably by the cutoff, which I am told is enlarging rapidly and all boats except the—[Packer] are passing through it both up and down."[73]

The cutoff was a canal begun by the neighboring plantation owners before the Civil War that turned Davis Bend into an island, providing a twenty-mile shortcut for the other plantations but placing Hurricane and Brierfield in a disadvantageous position.[74] It was completed by Union troops during the Civil War. On May 6, 1867, Montgomery reported that despite receding waters, the two steamboats that served as the primary means of communication and transportation for Davis Bend were able to pass through the cutoff thus bypassing Hurricane and Brierfield.[75] The isolation of the plantations from the steamships would have had severe consequences, since their Black communities relied on the steamboats for mail courier, goods shipment, and the transport of their cotton to sales agents in Vicksburg.[76] After the change in steamship routing in 1867, Hurricane, Brierfield, and their community members became dependent on the landings provided by the Woods Plantation.[77]

The move of the steamship landing site to Woods Plantation meant that community members at Hurricane and Brierfield now had to convey goods and produce several miles away by horse or mule-drawn carriage, leading the plantations' draft animals to take on a new prominence.[78] In her diary from 1872, Montgomery's daughter Mary Virginia mentioned riding horses or taking a horse-drawn carriage to commute between the plantations almost every day.[79] Before the Civil War, the Davis Brothers were racing aficionados, keeping an average of thirty racehorses on their plantations according to the local tax records. By contrast, in 1870, the Montgomery family kept 10 horses and 23 mules. Besides these numbers, lessees often had one mule or horse for riding and transportation.[80]

It was difficult to obtain feeding supplies for all these draft animals. On May 6, 1867, Montgomery reported, "I have heard of the death of one mule since I last wrote you. Very much of the stock is in a lean condition. They have been fed on young cotton wood branches, cane + [moss] with a limited quantity of corn, oat + hay."[81] By the end of 1867, Montgomery had bought four new mules and decided his lessees should grow their own animal feed. He asked Davis for his opinion, noting that "[i]n one of the Vicksburg papers I noticed that the planting of Early Northern Corn is recommended. I should like to learn your view of the proposition as well as the character of the corn."[82] Davis's answer is unknown, though he probably recommended some other type of corn, since Montgomery wrote back a week later thanking Davis for his "advice respecting the different characters of corn."[83] Montgomery continued to seek the best grain options. On January 23, 1868, he wrote to Davis, "[w]e are planting potatoes as for early use, have grown some oats, and having noticed that barley is recommended by some authors as good food for horses, I would be thankful for your opinion of it and how it is likely to grow here if planted?"[84] He continued that if Davis's opinion of barley were favorable, he would import the seed from Louisville or St. Louis, since nobody was growing barley in the vicinity of New Orleans. This anecdote indicates two elements of Montgomery's knowledge practices. First, he was actively pursuing the most efficient way to use the land, the most nutritious way to feed his farm animals, and the best way to obtain the necessary seeds. Second, it shows that Montgomery tapped into diverse sources of knowledge to inform his decisions, including newspapers and farming periodicals, in addition to Davis for his opinion.

Montgomery, in the Owenite spirit, embraced the scale of research and experimentation required to run a rational, and as he and Davis saw it, fair and communal plantation. Montgomery even used the term "experiment" explicitly: "As sowing [barley] now would be a mere experiment I deem it prudent to pospone [*sic*] until better prepared and plant instead such as we know more about."[85] Beyond experiments in crop type and his documentation of flooding, Montgomery continued the experiment of a communitarian plantation. The mode was ultimately paternalist—renters were responsible for farming their own lands and paying plantation-wide dues for community purposes. Montgomery, as patriarchal leader, thought it his role to ultimately make the big decisions after conferring with Davis, including questions relating to the plantation's transportation logistics and crop choice. While renters had some degree of independence, the large-scale plantation continued to be the preferred mode of production and labor organization under Montgomery's leadership.

Conclusion

Between 1820 and 1870, the plantations at Davis Bend, Mississippi, were site to a range of experiments ranging from early socialist cooperative economy to Black self-management. At first, from the late 1820s, plantation owner Joseph E. Davis attempted to run a more profitable slave labor–based plantation through the incorporation of elements of Owenite factory management. After the outbreak of the Civil War, the experiment changed to alternatives to slavery, and in the aftermath of the war, to alternatives to sharecropping. In the end, Davis, Colonel Samuel Thomas, and Benjamin T. Montgomery developed a communitarian system in which free farmers would lease plots of land from the plantation and collectively bear the costs for levee maintenance and a local school for Black children. As this system matured during early Reconstruction, the formerly enslaved plantation manager turned Black community leader Montgomery and his family adopted a paternalist style of organization, taking care of the supply, transportation, and sale of commodities. Common to all phases of the management experiments at Davis Bend was that each upheld the "plantation" as the preferred form of labor organization. All attempts at restructuring labor and translating knowledge about factory work organization sought to maintain the large-scale industrial-like production mode for cotton production in the US South.

Comparing Davis Bend to the famous example of the Owenite factory community in New Lanark, Scotland, one can see at both sites how experiments in social structure were undertaken as a response to traditional forms of coercive work organization that had become subject to mounting critique as inhumane by the early nineteenth century. The results were not democratically organized unions, but rather, central administration by a benevolent, paternalist leader. Additionally, these leaders cherished the experimental character of the communities at the theoretical and practical levels. In considering day-to-day questions through information exchange and scientific methods including experimentation and observation, the factory and the plantation became important sites of knowledge production.

The correspondence of Montgomery reveals the everyday problems faced by a Black plantation owner during the Reconstruction era (1865–1877) in terms of knowledge, management, and politics. His detailed descriptions of flood damage and draft animals reveal the practical challenges of running a plantation. Further, Montgomery presented himself as the rational and experienced community leader, challenging a prominent contention in contemporary political discourse wherein many White commentators questioned whether Black men were capable of self-organization. Montgomery's scope of maneuver, however, was constricted, in ways that paralleled most freed people of the era. While legally free, he was financially indebted to Davis and relied on Davis's advice and legal protection. Antebellum power structures defined Montgomery's room for agency as a communitarian plantation owner, and Davis's influence was essential for the preservation of the plantation experiment.

The experiments at Davis Bend ended soon after the end of Reconstruction in 1877, due not to bad management or because its labor system was unfeasible but rather by falling cotton prices and the ruling by the Mississippi Supreme Court to pass the lands over to former Confederate president Jefferson Davis in 1879. Unsurprisingly, the younger Davis refused to show the Montgomery family the same benevolence as his brother when they were unable to make the lease payment for the year. This reveals the contingent character of these plantation experiments on a mode of production that in the US South had been the paradigmatic instance of racial capitalism. Other factors were however important. While the connection with Jefferson Davis would be part of its undoing, it is also what made the wartime and subsequent phases of the experiment possible. The military had refused to return the plantation back to the ownership of its prewar White owners because of the family's prominence, similar to the case of Robert E. Lee and Arlington Estate, his plantation in northern Virginia, which ultimately became Arlington National Cemetery. Beyond wartime punishment, the embrace of individual initiative by the Freedmen's Bureau and the business sense of Montgomery was also pivotal. However, it could be said that the experiments at Davis Bend did not end in 1879 but rather changed scene. Montgomery's sons moved the community north to Mound Bayou, where they established the most successful Owenite cooperative village in the Americas. It would be the only Owenite-inspired community in the hemisphere to last into the twentieth century.

Notes

1. I would like to express my gratitude to Lara Raabe and Tobias Schweitzer for helping me transcribe the Montgomery letters, to the German Historical Institute Washington for generously sponsoring the archival research for this project, to Nicholas B. Miller and Ulrike Lindner for their careful editing of this chapter, and the anonymous reviewers for their positive feedback. Janet Sharp Hermann, *The Pursuit of a Dream* (University of Mississippi Press, 1999), 4; Carol A. Kolmerten, *Women in Utopia: The Ideology of Gender in the American Owenite Communities* (Indiana University Press, 1990), 61.

2. This plantation was known as Hurricane. Joseph Davis subsequently established another plantation at Davis Bend named Brierfield. Janet Sharp Hermann, *Joseph E. Davis: Pioneer Patriarch* (University Press of Mississippi, 1990), 41.

3. Chris Jennings, *Paradise Now: The Story of American Utopianism* (Random House, 2016), 111.

4. Janet Sharp Hermann cites the diary of Owen's travel companion Donald MacDonald as the origin of the stagecoach anecdote, which has appeared in several monographs on Owenism. In the diary, MacDonald mentioned that he and Owen shared a stagecoach with a Mr. Davis on June 24, 1825, but did not relate any information on conversations taking place during the ride. Joel Nathan Rosen wrote that while he was not able to verify the anecdote, he was able to place Owen and Davis in New Harmony at the Fourth of July celebrations of 1826; see Joel Nathan Rosen, *From New Lanark to Mound Bayou: Owenism in the Mississippi Delta* (Carolina Academic Press, 2011), xxi; see also Caroline Dale Snedeker, *The Diaries of Donald MacDonald* (Indiana Historical Society, 1942), 299.

5. Hermann, *Pursuit of a Dream*, 12, 40. Hermann first wrote a biographical study of Joseph Davis in 1990 (Hermann, *Joseph E. Davis*) aimed at a general audience before publishing an academic study of the Davis Bend plantations in 1999. According to Hermann, Davis made Frances Wright's acquaintance through the Marquis de Lafayette in 1825. Hermann also claims that Wright introduced Davis to Owen's *A New View on Society*, 4 vols. (London, 1813), convincing him that it was applicable to slavery as well. According to MacDonald's diary, Lafayette met the traveling party in Buffalo in June 1825. See Hermann, *Joseph E. Davis*, 5, 39–40; Snedeker, *Diaries of Donald MacDonald*, 300.

6. Hermann, *Pursuit of a Dream*, 5.

7. James A. Marten, *Civil War America: Voices from the Home Front* (ABC-CLIO, 2003), 215; Armstead L. Robinson, *Bitter Fruits of Bondage: The Demise of Slavery and the Collapse of the Confederacy, 1861–1865* (University of Virginia Press, 2005), 144; Amy Murrell Taylor, *Embattled Freedom: Journeys through the Civil War's Slave Refugee Camps* (University of North Carolina Press, 2018), 211–218.

8. See for instance August Meier, "Booker T. Washington and the Town of Mound Bayou," *Phylon* 15, no. 4 (1954): 396–401.

9. Rosen, *New Lanark to Mound Bayou*, 11–12.

10. Hermann, *Joseph E. Davis*; Hermann, *Pursuit of a Dream*; Rosen, *New Lanark to Mound Bayou*. See also Thavolia Glymph, "The Second Middle Passage: The Transition from Slavery to Freedom at Davis Bend, Mississippi" (PhD diss., Purdue University, 1994).

11. Nicole Jones et al., "The First Documents of Emancipated African American Management: The Letters of Benjamin Montgomery (1865–1870)," *Journal of Management History* 18, no. 2 (2012): 47; see also Sandra Gates et al., "The Hidden History of Benjamin Montgomery: Slave, Manager and Accountant," *Accounting History* 27, no. 1 (2022): 24–40.

12. Even though the scholarship often uses the name Davis Bend only for the plantations owned by the Davis brothers, there were in fact six plantations on Davis Bend: Hurricane and Brierfield, which belonged to the Davises; Ursino, which Montgomery bought in 1870; Palmyra; Quitman; and Woods Plantation. For other discussions of management knowledge in this volume, see the chapters by Marta Macedo, Theresa Ventura, Gillian McGillivray, and Rebekah McCallum.

13. See for instance Arthur Bestor, *Backwoods Utopias: The Sectarian Origins and the Owenite Phase of Communitarian Socialism in America, 1663–1829* (University of Pennsylvania Press, 1950); Donald E. Pitzer, ed., *America's Communal Utopias* (University of North Carolina Press, 1997); Jennings, *Paradise Now*, 100.

14. J. F. C. Harrison, *Robert Owen and the Owenites in Britain and America: Quest for the New Moral World* (Charles Scribner's Sons, 1969), 55.

15. Gregory Claeys, "Non-Marxian Socialism 1815–1914," in *The Cambridge History of Nineteenth Century Political Thought*, eds. Gareth Stedman Jones and Gregory Claeys (Cambridge University Press, 2011), 524–525.

16. For instance, Anne Kwaschik investigates Fourierian settlements in Algeria as sites of experimentation in social science and colonial knowledge production, see Anne Kwaschik, "Gesellschaftswissen als Zukunftshandeln: Soziale Epistemologie, genossenschaftliche Lebensformen und kommunale Praxis im frühen 19. Jahrhundert," *Francia: Forschungen zur westeuropäischen Geschichte* 44 (2017): 190, 210. Hannah Ahlheim recently argued that Owen intended to design communities in the same way that engineers designed machines; see Hannah Ahlheim, "Ex Machina: Die Gestaltung der Utopie in der Arbeitswelt des britischen Frühsozialisten Robert Owen," *Historische Zeitschrift* 311, no. 1 (2020): 44.

17. The main source material for this chapter is the correspondence between Montgomery and Davis in the years 1866 to 1868. Approximately one-third of this correspondence has been digitized by the University of Mississippi Civil War Project; see "eGrove Civil War Collection," University of Mississippi, accessed April 25, 2022, https://egrove.olemiss.edu/civ_war/. Other sources include contemporary newspaper reports, the correspondence of the Freedmen's Bureau at the US National Archives (NARA), and the diary of Montgomery's daughter Mary Virginia from 1872 detailing the everyday life on the plantation, as well as an

interview given by Montgomery's son Isaiah in 1902 at the Library of Congress Manuscript Collection (MSS40857).

18. For the debate on exchanges between factory and plantation management, see Dale Tomich, "The Second Slavery and World Capitalism: A Perspective for Historical Inquiry," *International Review of Social History* 63, no. 3 (2018): 477–501; Barbara Hahn, *Technology in the Industrial Revolution* (Cambridge University Press, 2020), 186; Caitlin Rosenthal, *Accounting for Slavery: Masters and Management* (Harvard University Press, 2018), 63–64; Caitlin Rosenthal, "Slavery's Scientific Management: Masters and Managers," in *Slavery's Capitalism: A New History of America's Capitalist Development*, eds. Sven Beckert and Seth Rockman (University of Pennsylvania Press, 2016).

19. For a critique of Owen's paternalism, see E. P. Thompson, *The Making of the English Working Class* (Pantheon Books, 1963), 781. For a conceptualization of Davis's leadership style as paternalistic leadership, see Mario Hayek et al., "Ending the Denial of Slavery in Management History: Paternalistic Leadership of Joseph Emory Davis," *Journal of Management History* 16, no. 3 (2010): 367–379; see also Jones et al., "Letters of Benjamin Montgomery," 50.

20. Quoted after Gladys Byram Shepperd, *The Montgomery Saga: From Slavery to Black Power* (unpublished manuscript, 1971), 210, in "Benjamin T. Montgomery Family Papers," 1872–1938, MSS40857, Library of Congress, Manuscript Division, Washington, DC (hereafter cited as Benjamin T. Montgomery Family Papers).

21. Hermann, *Pursuit of a Dream*, 33–34.

22. Hermann, *Pursuit of a Dream*, 33–34.

23. Hermann, *Pursuit of a Dream*, 34.

24. Hermann, *Pursuit of a Dream*, 34.

25. According to Hermann and Rosen, Davis's family were frontier farmers from Georgia. The oldest son, Joseph E. Davis, received little education. See Hermann, *Joseph E. Davis*, 5, 10; Rosen, *New Lanark to Mound Bayou*, 77.

26. Rosen, *New Lanark to Mound Bayou*, 96; Hermann, *Pursuit of a Dream*, 18. For the importance of Montgomery's education in fostering a close relationship with Davis, see Gates et al., "Hidden History," 33.

27. Rosen cites Glymph, "The Second Middle Passage," for this argument; see Rosen, *New Lanark to Mound Bayou*, 98.

28. Hermann, *Pursuit of a Dream*, 32–34.

29. Taylor, *Embattled Freedom*, 211.

30. Marten, *Civil War America*, 215.

31. Ira Berlin et al., *Slaves No More! Three Essays on Emancipation and the Civil War* (Cambridge University Press, 1992), 100, 102–104.

32. Taylor, *Embattled Freedom*, 218.

33. Steven Hahn et al., eds., *Freedom: A Documentary History of Emancipation 1861–1867, Series 3, vol. 1 Land & Labor 1865* (University of North Carolina Press, 2008), 403.

34. On Lee's plantation, see Marten, *Civil War America*, 210; Berlin, *Slaves No More*, 132. Missionary chaplain James A. Hawley's reported in a letter to Freedmen's Bureau Assistant Commissioner Samuel Thomas about visitors to a Fourth of July party in 1865 singing songs demanding that Jefferson Davis be hung, see Report from Chaplain James A. Hawley to Colonel Samuel Thomas, July 4, 1865, in Hahn et al., *Freedom*, 124.

35. For the Northerner's determination to punish treason among Southern leaders, see Berlin et al., *Slaves No More*, 95.

36. Berlin et al., *Slaves No More*, 123.

37. Letter by Colonel Samuel Thomas to General Oliver Otis Howard, September 19, 1865, in Hahn et al., *Freedom*, 433–434.

38. Hahn et al., *Freedom*, 434.

39. Letter by Colonel Samuel Thomas to General Oliver Otis Howard, September 19, 1865, in Hahn et al., *Freedom*, 434. This argument in favor of Black self-management was raised for instance in a contemporary newspaper article in the *New York Times* as well; see N. N., "The Lease of Plantations to Negroes," *New York Times*, December 2, 1866, 1.

40. Letter by John W. Young to Colonel Samuel Thomas, August 7, 1865, in Hahn et al., *Freedom*, 701.

41. Letter by John W. Young to Colonel Samuel Thomas, August 7, 1865, in Hahn et al., *Freedom*, 702.

42. Letter by John W. Young to Colonel Samuel Thomas, August 7, 1865, in Hahn et al., *Freedom*, 702.

43. Report by Colonel Samuel Thomas to General Oliver Otis Howard, January 10, 1866, in Hahn et al., *Freedom*, 742.

44. Report by Colonel Samuel Thomas to General Oliver Otis Howard, January 10, 1866, in Hahn et al., *Freedom*, 742.

45. Report by Colonel Samuel Thomas to General Oliver Otis Howard, January 10, 1866, in Hahn et al., *Freedom*, 742.

46. For a more in-depth discussion of the elements of Owenite social theory that Davis and Montgomery adopted, see Jones et al., "Letters of Benjamin Montgomery," 50.

47. For the first opportunities of refugees to earn their own wages, see Marten, *Civil War America*, 215.

48. In her diary, Mary Virginia Montgomery relates how she began attending Oberlin College in 1873; see Mary Virginia Montgomery, Diary 1872, transcribed by Gladys Shepperd, in "Benjamin T. Montgomery Family Papers," 135, 158. For more information on the store as a source of income for the Montgomery family, see Jones et al., "Letters of Benjamin Montgomery," 52.

49. Hermann, *Pursuit of a Dream*, 67–72; Jones et al., "Letters of Benjamin Montgomery," 55–56.

50. Hermann, *Pursuit of a Dream*, 76.

51. Joseph E. Davis, Letter to the Freedmen's Bureau, December 28, 1866, in NARA Records of the Assistant Commissioner for the State of Mississippi Bureau of Refugees, Freedmen, and Abandoned Lands 1865–1869 (M826), Role 13.

52. Rosen, *New Lanark to Mound Bayou*, 106.

53. The historiography differs on how to assess the sale price. Sharp judged the price fair compared to the prewar value of the two plantations, whereas Rosen and others think that Davis overcharged Montgomery since cotton prices were plummeting. See Hermann, *Pursuit of a Dream*, 109–110, Rosen; *New Lanark to Mound Bayou*, 109; Hayek et al., "Ending the Denial of Slavery," 372; Glymph, "The Second Middle Passage," 228.

54. N. N., "A Tale of Two Brothers," *New York Times*, June 21, 1879, 4.

55. Rosen, *New Lanark to Mound Bayou*, 109.

56. Hermann, *Pursuit of a Dream*, 100.

57. Rosen, *New Lanark to Mound Bayou*, 106, cited from Steve Williamson, "Portrait of a Black Town: Mound Bayou—Past, Present and Future," *The Voice* (Mound Bayou) 4, no. 8 (1971): 5.

58. Benjamin T. Montgomery, Letter to Joseph E. Davis, March 28, 1867, in Joseph E. Davis Collection (MUM00101), Department of Archives and Special Collections, J. D. Williams Library, University of Mississippi (hereafter cited as MUM00101).

59. Hermann, *Pursuit of a Dream*, 111; see also Benjamin T. Montgomery, Letter to Joseph E. Davis, May 6, 1867, in MUM00101.

60. Hermann, *Pursuit of a Dream*, 144. For the idea to establish social security for Black communities to take care of their own women, children, old, and disabled members in a self-sufficient manner, see Berlin, *Slaves No More*, 95.

61. Hermann, *Pursuit of a Dream*, 112.

62. Hermann, *Pursuit of a Dream*, 112.

63. Benjamin T. Montgomery, Letter to Joseph E. Davis, October 7, 1866, in MUM00101.

64. Benjamin T. Montgomery, Letter to Joseph E. Davis, December 19, 1867, in MUM00101.

65. Benjamin T. Montgomery, Letter to Joseph E. Davis, December 19, 1867, in MUM00101.

66. Benjamin T. Montgomery, Letter to Joseph E. Davis, November 14, 1867, in MUM00101.

67. Benjamin T. Montgomery, Letter to Joseph E. Davis, November 14, 1867, in MUM00101.

68. On the impacts of ecological precarity, see also the chapters by Gillian McGillivray, Rebekah McCallum, Christina Skott, and Moritz von Brescius in this volume.

69. Gates et al., "Hidden History," 29. Similar instances of record keeping are discussed in the chapters by Moritz von Brescius, Christina Skott, Marta Macedo, Theresa Ventura, and Rebekah McCallum in this volume.

70. Benjamin T. Montgomery, Letter to Joseph E. Davis, August 8, 1867, in MUM00101.

71. Benjamin T. Montgomery, Letter to Joseph E. Davis, June 13, 1867, in MUM00101.

72. Benjamin T. Montgomery, Letter to Joseph E. Davis, June 13, 1867, in MUM00101. For a critique of Montgomery's paternalism and his copy of Davis's Owen-inspired techniques, see Rosen, *New Lanark to Mound Bayou*, 105.

73. Benjamin T. Montgomery, Letter to Joseph E. Davis, March 21, 1867, in MUM00101.

74. Nowadays it is called Davis Island; see Hermann, *Pursuit of a Dream*, 119.

75. Hermann, *Pursuit of a Dream*, 119.

76. Hermann, *Pursuit of a Dream*, 120.

77. Hermann, *Pursuit of a Dream*, 119–120.

78. Hermann, *Pursuit of a Dream*, 119, 148.

79. See for example, Mary Virginia Montgomery, Diary 1872, in "Benjamin T. Montgomery Family Papers," 85.

80. Hermann, *Pursuit of a Dream*, 181–182.

81. Benjamin T. Montgomery, Letter to Joseph E. Davis, May 6, 1867, in MUM00101.

82. Benjamin T. Montgomery, Letter to Joseph E. Davis, December 30, 1867, in MUM00101.

83. Benjamin T. Montgomery, Letter to Joseph E. Davis, January 6, 1868, in MUM00101.

84. Benjamin T. Montgomery, Letter to Joseph E. Davis, January 23, 1868, in MUM00101.

85. Benjamin T. Montgomery, Letter to Joseph E. Davis, February 11, 1868, in MUM00101.

Part III

Experiments

Chapter 5

Revisiting the Charduar Plantation

Local Connections, Imperial Portfolios, and the Global Pathways of Assam Rubber

Moritz von Brescius

Cash Crop Portfolios and the Rubber Plantation Revolution

In 1911, the world's leading rubber journal published an article on "Rubber Planting in the East."[1] This article reflected on the legacy of the British Empire's first government-sponsored rubber plantation in Asia, which, at the time of publication, was struggling for survival. In the few short years since the turn of the twentieth century, the epicenter of plantation rubber had shifted from South Asia to Southeast Asia and, in the process, from endemic rubber trees to the cultivation of the acclimatized *Hevea brasiliensis* species from Brazil. One of the Indian plantations sidelined by these changes—and eventually abandoned and forgotten—was Charduar, which was established by colonial administrators and scientific foresters eighteen miles north of the Brahmaputra River in northeastern India in 1873. The 1911 article reminded readers of Charduar's illustrious history as the first plantation of its kind: "Perhaps the most widely advertised rubber plantation ever formed has been that of the Indian government at Charduar . . . the details presented in the annual [forestry] reports . . . found their way in one shape or another into many thousands of newspaper publications, often losing entirely their original form and meaning. It was made to appear often that the Indian government had become exceedingly large producers of rubber."[2] The article explained that the plantation—begun nearly four decades earlier in the Assamese borderlands, at the foot of the Himalayas—had not been "formed for commercial purposes, but mainly for scientific study, though of recent years some shipments of rubber well prepared have brought good prices." According to the article, the multipurpose rubber project at Charduar had captured the imagination of planters, officials, newspapers and rubber consumers, manufacturers, and commodity brokers—both near and far. Its history was being told and twisted in "many thousands" of tales of imperial ingenuity, foresight, frustration, renewed hope, and temporary triumph.[3] While the article emphasized the importance of Charduar as a pioneering venture (indeed, as one of the first large rubber plantations in the world), it failed to note that the plantation had also functioned as a significant distributive institution—a clearing house for planting expertise and materials. Similarly, recent literature on Assam rubber, while excellent in its treatment of the history of "wild" rubber extraction, has also overlooked Charduar's momentous local and global entanglements. As a result, existing histories have, for the most part, treated the government plantation in Assam as an oddity—a mere footnote in the longer history of the trans-frontier rubber trade—and its failure, therefore, as a foregone conclusion.[4]

What is missing, both in articles at the time and the historiography in recent years, is a deeper understanding of the intentions and impacts of the government venture at Charduar beyond profit making. I argue that Charduar is best understood as a living laboratory of plantation capitalism that was never intended to operate in isolation. On the contrary, the estate was dedicated to making knowledge and agronomic resources such as seeds and codified planting techniques available to British officials, economic botanists, investors, and planters around the world. The plantation was thus not an independent entity in an Assamese backwater but was conceived and functioned as part of a much larger imperial vision of commodity production. I seek to bring these local and global entanglements squarely into view. Charduar provided a virtual blueprint for *Ficus elastica* production that, its proponents thought, could be exported for general applicability in the tropics and beyond.

Charduar did indeed originate new plants and agronomic practices that would inform the expansion of rubber "commodity frontiers" in other parts of India, the British Empire, and ultimately, all tropical regions the world over.[5] In this respect, the government plantation resembled imperial botanical gardens. These, too, were created to experiment, exhibit, educate, and disseminate cash crops in a transcontinental network of aligned institutions. A critical examination of the pioneering Assam rubber field can thus help bridge the gap between the numerous studies of botanical gardens as knowledge hubs, on the one hand, and commercial estates on the other. The existing historiographical bifurcation tends to overlook the significant overlap between the two. Charduar was a hybrid form that vividly illustrates the intersections between state-sponsored science and instruction, commodity colonialism, and private enterprise.[6] I examine the Assam government field from this particular angle, as a quasi-agricultural experiment station and global hub of knowledge dissemination. Taking Charduar's role seriously requires a significant shift in perspective, since the literature on global rubber plantations in general remains heavily focused on the Southeast Asian planting boom in the early twentieth century.[7]

Another reason why Charduar has escaped more thorough attention is that it was almost entirely devoted to propagating what became (in retrospect) a failed plantation species. The vast historiography of the post-1900 Southeast Asian rubber boom has dwelled exclusively on the transplanted *Hevea brasiliensis* tree from the Amazon, which came to completely dominate the world's natural rubber supplies by the 1910s. In contrast, the Assam government field bet, in a sense, on the wrong species, and its once-prominent history faded into the background. This development was scarcely imaginable in the late nineteenth century, at which time the managers at Charduar were promoting the region's indigenous rubber species, *Ficus elastica*, on a global scale. Even as late as the early 20th century, *Ficus elastica* was cultivated for its latex on all five continents. During this period of hope for this species, the government plantation functioned as a training hub for state officials, Indigenous rubber growers, recruited "coolie" workers, and agronomic specialists. The Indian Viceroy and other dignitaries visited Charduar and paid homage to its self-proclaimed civilizing mission amidst supposedly wild jungle tracts and "savage tribes." Leading foresters and insect and pest specialists were invited to document and treat major pest outbreaks. Their findings were widely published and read, contributing to rapid advancements at the time in the field of colonial entomology. Charduar was thus the epicenter of very diverse forms of knowledge transfers, mobilities, and migrations—human and biological, intellectual, and ideological. Its novel insights, plant materials, and protocols were, from the start, intended to be used elsewhere.[8] The continuous circulations that underpinned the plantation's operations were thus not the result of reform or rationalization but had been envisioned by its original founders and managers as an essential feature of the estate's function.[9] Its purpose and legacy were never limited to Assam's rubber frontier, which experienced a boom period between circa 1860 and 1912.[10] On the contrary, the materials and knowledge the site produced soon reached other shores and extractive operations, informing—and misinforming—subsequent ventures of resource imperialism.

Given the large investments of land and labor required for jungle clearing and planting, such tropical estates were, in a sense, highly immobile, grounded assets. Over time, the government field in Assam developed heavy infrastructures such as roads, housing complexes, nurseries, wells, and especially the planted trees, which in the case of Charduar developed extensive root systems that were impossible to transplant. However, certain elements of all plantations must be mobile. They are inherently artificial creations and are sustained by factors outside themselves, including knowledge, labor, seeds, and capital. By focusing here on issues of knowledge transfers and material exchanges, the following analysis proposes a new understanding of the logics and spatiotemporal limits of ostensibly local plantation cultures. While plantation concepts and designs circulated widely across political and ecological boundaries, this chapter also revisits the inherent tensions between the local and the global, that is, how implementation was adapted and improvised due to local factors and how these experiences could generate new knowledge that in turn circulated and again had to be recalibrated elsewhere. What follows, then, suggests the need to move beyond a simplified understanding of circulation.

Finally, this chapter uses Charduar as a lens to consider how empires managed uncertainty and risk. How did the British Empire go about creating a highly planned and organized plantation system for a "wild" resource (coveted by domestic industries) at a time when knowledge of the best ways to grow latex-producing plants was extremely limited? By the 1870s, dozens of rubber species were known and still more were being discovered.[11] The global extent of British overseas possessions facilitated the pursuit of an "inventory science" of different rubber plants, including their identification and mapping.[12] The cataloging made possible the development of what I call an "imperial portfolio" of potentially profitable plants that were used in the development phase of a territory or to attain a specific product. Like private entrepreneurs and merchants who diversify their commercial activities and investments with a broad portfolio to hedge against risk, so too did empires diversify the number of agricultural projects and plant species they bet on. Thus, British scientists and state institutions, such as the botanical gardens at Kew, Calcutta, Singapore, Peradeniya, or Lagos, pursued the cultivation and tested the viability of many different rubber species all at once, knowing that some might fail. The notion of the imperial portfolio as a heuristic shifts our focus to a global perspective, from which we can see that the process of cross-regional agricultural competition (and the winners and losers it produced) was normal and normalized within the British Empire. As a strategic agro-economic measure, the imperial portfolio was encouraged and, at least to some extent, coordinated by the directors of Kew Gardens, who consciously pursued a global vision of plant hunting and experimentation.[13] The imperial portfolio thus required a certain degree of metropolitan oversight and intentionality to function. Leading British economic botanists in London encouraged capitalist and scientific investment in the belief that the diversity of projects provided a kind of insurance against future rubber famines. But this system also relied on the initiative of agents at the margins of empire, including in Assam, where the rubber plantation revolution began in the early 1870s. The testing of a wide crop portfolio in different regions soon created a multipolar framework of plant competition.[14] At a time of great uncertainty within Western empires about which rubber species would prove to be the quickest yielding, most adaptable and profitable, the victorious variety could be declared only after a long period of experimentation and numerous attempts at acclimatization and propagation.[15] Charduar was the British Empire's central hub for experimenting and promoting the tree called *borgāch* ("big tree") by the indigenous Assamese, which European botanists had taxonomized as *Ficus elastica* in 1810.

The sheer size and geographical diversity of the British Empire was thus the condition that made possible the testing of different latex-yielding species on different continents, altitudes, and soil types. Nevertheless, within this global matrix, Assam offered a uniquely generalizable environment, as it lacked extremes. Assam was defined by what it was not: it was not a hot, burning plain, and it was not a dry, parched tropical environment. It was much less characterized by settled agriculture and established patterns of land rights than by the land use system of swidden agriculture. But it did have abundant vegetation and plenty of rainfall, given the annual monsoon cycle and recurring floods. Since the aim was to generate techniques and knowledge that could be used elsewhere, Assam's generalizable environment was critical. The region thus emerged after the 1840s as a particularly dynamic area for experimentation with various plantation crops, including teak, cinchona, tea, or caoutchouc, whose operation also required novel forms of labor recruitment, control, and agronomic experimentation. Moreover, Assam allowed foresters and speculators to test a particularly diverse crop portfolio because the highland frontier region had different ecological niches and was less constrained by the antiquity of its agrarian system, settled peasant populations, and the established nature of crop production than other Indian regions. Here, the colonial state and its forestry department (founded in 1874) created a massive forest enclosure and instituted zoning programs to provide, among other things, favorable land grants to private planters.[16] There were, in other words, important ecological and social factors that made this frontier region especially valuable for experimentation with so many different crops from the British imperial portfolio.

The government plantation at Charduar always had one overarching aim: to help secure future supplies of tropical rubber within British-controlled territories—a desire that drove other imperial rubber initiatives in the same period. These government interventions marked a turning point in the commodity's history.[17] They helped transform rubber from a wild species to a systematically cultivated plantation crop. Crucially, the state was initially the only driver in the process.[18] The trial cultivation of rubber was considered too costly and unpredictable for private planters. While some imperial officials hoped that Charduar could serve as a bridge to attract private capital into the industry (as had been the case with Assam tea), others maintained that the colonial government should always remain involved in rubber cultivation under direct state control.[19] An expanding regional patchwork of rubber plantations modeled on Charduar was supposed to save Assam's wild rubber tracts, which faced the specter of exhaustion from frenzied overexploitation.[20] Ultimately, however, after decades of exuberant interest and experimentation, the estate was abandoned in the early years of World War I.

Looking into the demise of a plantation (and its legacies) can be as instructive as examining its creation. This chapter explores the rise and fall of Charduar, from its role, first as a central hub of knowledge and materials and later as a commercial enterprise, to its abrupt abandonment just a few years later. Although it was a groundbreaking experimental site for systematic propagation, Charduar became the victim of the profound shifts in the global economics and geography of rubber plantations. The superior yield rate of other latex-yielding plants, cultivated elsewhere in the British Empire as part of its imperial portfolio, portended its demise. In particular, the booming plantations of Southeast Asia showed the virtues of the Brazilian tree *Hevea brasiliensis*, which yielded a purer product and had far superior planting rates, production times, and fewer silvicultural problems than the Assamese species that had confounded foresters for decades.[21] Only a grounded global history can recover both diachronic developments taking place in Assam and explain how these were, in turn, profoundly shaped by synchronous processes that were seemingly unconnected to Charduar, even if that estate came to feel the full impact of forces that had gathered momentum thousands of miles away.

The analysis will proceed in several interlocking steps. I first trace various intellectual and material transfers that emanated out of Charduar, as it became the nucleus for highly ambitious, if often fraught, transplantation and cultivation schemes of *Ficus elastica* between the 1870s and early 1900s. The chapter then turns to the plantation's myriad regional connections and constraints. It explores official visions of how the site would initiate a fundamental transformation of rubber production in northeast India. This objective again mobilized external collaboration with metropolitan resource institutes and rubber manufacturing firms such as Siemens that I analyze as an instance of plantation research and development. The chapter concludes by tracing the shifts in worldwide rubber production that portended Charduar's sudden decline amidst the outbreak of the Great War, signaling the closure of one possible path for rubber plantations in the twentieth-century world.

Charduar's Global Entanglements

Charduar's initial appeal among European agronomists lay in its pioneering nature. Up until the early 1870s, next to nothing was known by foresters and private planters about the systematic propagation of any rubber tree species, even as new botanical discoveries continually extended the list of possible latex-yielding plants. By contrast, highland communities in Assam had long since planted *Ficus elastica* (Fig. 5.1) close to their villages as a shade-giving and ornamental tree, though never, it seems, as a potential export commodity.[22] They were accustomed to tapping the bark of the tree to extract the latex used to produce various everyday objects such as torches, balls, and impregnated vessels.[23] Some of the seeds for starting the Charduar plantation were procured from local "tribal" communities.[24] Additionally, the choice for where to locate the plantation was informed

Figure 5.1. *Ficus elastica* trees and their myriad root and stem systems, depicted with South Asian laborers at the entrance to the Royal Botanical Gardens, Peradeniya, Ceylon (Sri Lanka). Photograph by William Louis Henry Skeen, 1881–1882, albumen print. *Source:* © Royal Collection Enterprises Limited 2024 | Royal Collection Trust. Used with permission.

by the testimonies of Indigenous rubber collectors, who disclosed where the trees that yielded supreme latex grew abundantly.[25] The officials' dependence on such non-European know-how and provisions decenters the view of the Charduar enterprise as resulting purely from imperial ingenuity, agency, and material networks. Yet, once plantation operations were securely under way, few further references in the imperial archive were made to "native" cultivation practices. By then, agronomic breakthroughs at Charduar were trumpeted through the channels of imperial correspondence and print culture.

While imperial foresters had initially sought to tap into rich vernacular knowledge about *Ficus elastica*, they assumed that most intricacies of plantation production would have to be learned from scratch through trial and error. The colonial government was confident that their large outlay would eventually pay off. Rubber was then an exclusively tropical material on whose "infinite" applications North American and European industries and manufacturers increasingly relied as the nineteenth century progressed.[26] Some of the principal officials involved in Charduar's establishment believed that the natural rubber reserves of Mexico and especially the Amazon were becoming gradually exhausted, even though Brazil then supplied the vast majority of tropical rubber.[27] Charduar was a scheme of artificial cultivation intended to preempt a possible rubber famine that was not yet materially felt.

The broad circulation of the first plantation report in 1874 shows that disseminating data was intrinsic to the project from the beginning. The report was forwarded by the chief commissioner of Assam "to such of the forest officers in Madras, Bombay, North-Western Provinces, Punjab, Oudh, Central Provinces, British Burma, Mysore and Coorg, Ajmere, Hyderabad, as take an interest in the subject."[28] The report's data was also well received. As a botanist at the Royal Botanic Gardens at Kew near London noted, "[t]hese experiments and facts are most interesting and of the greatest value to those interested in the cultivation of the Ficus elastica as a rubber-producing tree."[29] As a global hub of economic botany, Kew Gardens regularly included the newest insights from Charduar in its various publication series, thus multiplying the Assam plantation's outreach. The government field assumed over time, however, additional instrumentalities of instruction, display, and dissemination. Its reputation as a place for vital research helps explain why the colonial authorities continued, after multiple reevaluations in the 1890s, to support the future extensions and operations of the estate—even in the face of questionable financial returns.[30]

By then, it was not only agronomic protocols and statistics that Charduar produced. When an emerging class of rubber experts and planters began to form their own infrastructure and forums of exchange, including sections at world fairs like the Exposition Universelle in Paris in 1878, the staff at Charduar participated by sending rubber samples—to promote *Ficus elastica*—together with a series of "specimens of woods and other forest products" from northeast India to the French capital.[31] Assamese "raw materials" and "forest products," including sample produce of *Ficus* rubber, equally found their way into the collections of the Museum of Economic Botany at Kew and the Botanical Museum and Botanical Laboratory for Product Research in Hamburg.[32]

The longtime conservator of forests in Assam, Gustav Mann (1836–1916), a German-born, Kew-educated horticulturist who became a naturalized British subject in India in 1871, also became an active agent in the transcontinental exchange of information and seeds. Mann had been instrumental in launching Charduar in 1873 in cooperation with other imperial foresters and officials, especially the conservator of forests in Bengal, Wilhelm Schlich, and the commissioner of Assam, Colonel Henry Hopkinson.[33] Mann remained formally in charge of the plantation until his retirement from colonial service in 1891. But the day-to-day running of Charduar was managed by a succession of foresters including W. R. Fisher. British planters, agronomists, officials, investors, and manufacturers could seek Mann's advice on rubber from his Assam station at any time.[34] It was also Mann who was requested by the Government of India to dispatch, in 1890, fifty kilograms of *Ficus elastica* seeds to the governor of British-ruled Lagos. Accompanying the seeds, Mann provided the governor with a long account "of the mode of culture pursued in Assam," describing the most recent practices adopted in the Charduar plantation down to the minutest detail.[35] The seeds and cultivation advice traveled, in a sense, in the opposite direction to Mann, who had, decades earlier, himself traveled in West Africa during a bioprospecting mission between 1859 and 1863, during which he identified several African rubber species.[36] The episode adds a human dimension to the global transfer and acclimation of useful plants in the nineteenth century, since personal itineraries like Mann's mattered and indeed shaped the vectors through which such botanical globalization took place.

Charduar's rubber expertise was further disseminated through print channels throughout the British Empire and in the metropolis of London. Sir Alfred Moloney, Governor of Lagos from 1886 to 1890, informed the Secretary of State for the Colonies, Lord Knutsford, after receiving "three packets of seed of the *Ficus elastica*" and Mann's extensive report, that the "information supplied is of such general interest and value that I have ventured to issue it *in extenso* as a circular, of which I would ask your Lordship to allow the Director of the Royal Gardens, Kew, to have some copies."[37] Moloney also confirmed that the seeds received in Lagos had been "treated in accordance with the method employed in Assam in the cultivation of this rubber tree," revealing how locally devised practices of plantation economies could be made to travel to other continents thanks to written instructions and the authority accorded to their author.[38]

The entire West African acclimation scheme was driven by the hope that the *Ficus elastica* species could "replace the wholesale disappearance of the rubber tree indigenous to that country—viz, the *Funtumia elastica*."[39] However, in contrast to Mann's great efforts to develop a systematic body of knowledge about *Ficus* cultivation in Assam, other correspondence stated that "little or no skill is required" to cultivate the tree, reflecting the hope "that it will soon establish itself in this Colony and the neighbouring States."[40] Data and local expertise were clearly lost in translation and transfer, pointing to the mere chimera of a frictionless diffusion.[41] *Ficus* seedlings were subsequently "distributed in the colony, where the tree soon made itself a home."[42] Yet the imperial ambitions around transplantation went even further. Lagos was supposed to be only the starting point for much wider planting schemes of the Assam rubber tree. Seedlings raised by the Botanical Station at Lagos were to lead, it was hoped, to the official and private adoption of the species in other parts of the African continent. In 1897, for instance, "*Ficus* was introduced into Egypt," as "efforts are being made to establish plantations of this tree," while "the Indian Forest Department has been glad to supply seed to the authorities for this purpose."[43] The colonial official and explorer Ernest A. Floyer, who then acted as director of plantations, state railways and telegraphs of Egypt and who was responsible for the introduction of many economic plants, informed Kew Gardens in 1897 that besides growing *Ficus elastica* from seed, he had also put out "some 50,000 cuttings," of which ninety-seven percent were thriving.[44] Yet this was only the beginning of a much larger operation, since he claimed Egypt will "need millions of trees"—especially since he asserted that the "trees here yield more freely than those of the Chardwar experiment."[45]

As attention at Charduar turned from *Ficus elastica* rubber as an object of governance and expertise to a notable industrial commodity, the plantation and the tree species "held together an extensive imperial network" of officials, foresters, botanists, travelers, private planters, journalists, illustrators, seed merchants, and vernacular advertisements.[46] Charduar's keepers not only noted down their experiments in meticulous detail but also published regular reports that helped justify the costly trial operations. The authors made use of numeric data to communicate the often perplexing nature, irregular growth, and yield patterns of the Indian rubber tree and to render it comparable with other species.[47] Visual representations and detailed descriptions of the work in the nurseries, the tapping knives used, the shapes in which the tree barks were cut, and so on, allowed rubber investors and planters to become virtual witnesses of this pioneering enterprise. What could not be personally observed in remote Assam could thus be studied thousands of miles away—and Charduar's results critiqued and compared with alternative *Ficus* and other rubber species' trials and temporal calculations.[48] Indeed, one of the main challenges of *Ficus elastica* was the extremely long gestation period between planting and harvesting, which could take up to fifty years. The Charduar staff (and soon numerous imitators in various empires and continents) attempted to halve nature's clock and alter the tree's natural growth patterns as an epiphyte by planting the seeds directly on the ground, but with limited success. The biological rhythms still made *Ficus elastica*—even when made tappable after eighteen to twenty-five years—vastly inferior to the quickly yielding *Hevea* trees that offered a return on investment after four to seven years.

Knowing the economic outcome of a project that had "still not turned a profit thirty years" after its foundation has led historians to brush aside Charduar's overall importance.[49] Historian Bodhisattva Kar, for example, in a pathbreaking article on Assam's wild rubber trade, avoided writing about "the dull destiny of the government plantations," which economically proffered only "unsatisfactory results."[50] However, a purely economic view of the colonial state's rubber programs in Assam obscures the rich history of anticipation and long-term investment in an experimental, knowledge-generating endeavor that contemporaries took very seriously. Indeed, the discussion of "failed" projects—an evaluation that can only be made with hindsight—can illuminate much about the logic of imperial resource management, and perhaps more than conventional stories of success and expansion.[51]

What we know is that Charduar's reports and manuals remained in circulation for decades and soon also entered into intra- and interimperial circuits of exchange. With the Dutch East Indies becoming an important site of the global rubber economy by the early twentieth century, Dutch officials and planters closely followed developments in Assam, translating planting treatises, comparing outcomes, and eventually offering potent critiques of Charduar's calculations.[52] To be sure, by no means were all propagation projects directly guided or inspired by the Assam venture—but that *Ficus elastica* continued to be seen as a promising plantation crop for so long was undoubtedly linked to the vocal presence that Charduar maintained among transimperial groups of planters and governments as the most famous rubber plantation "ever formed," at least before the 1910s.[53] In the 1890s, rubber plantations of *Hevea brasiliensis*, *Manihot glaziovii* (Ceara rubber), *Castilla elastica*, *Funtumia elastica*, and *Ficus elastica* were increasingly established in equatorial regions by various states and private investors, although it was not yet clear which of these rubber plants would produce the best yields in different climates, soils, and altitudes. In the early 1900s, for-profit schemes to cultivate *Ficus* rubber were simultaneously pursued in Cuba, Karachi, Ceylon, the Belgian Congo, French Indochina, West Africa, Nigeria, Australia, the Philippines, British New Guinea and Papua, in the Seychelles, California (US), and Singapore—where "the Chinese" were especially keen, Henry N. Ridley noted, to secure supplies from this particular species.[54] *Ficus elastica* also entered the planting regimes of the German colonial empire in Africa, where it was raised in tropical research stations and planted by African farmers.[55] Even Brazil, which had been the world's center of natural rubber production until the early twentieth century, acclimated and cultivated *Ficus elastica* "in an attempt at reverse plant transfer."[56] Indeed, for a long time, the tree was considered a true rival to all other rubber plantation crops.

The ultimate global triumph of *Hevea brasiliensis* was unforeseen into the early twentieth century. In 1911, William Wicherley wrote of the Assamese tree in his authoritative work *The Whole Art of Rubber-Growing*: "Lately large areas in Borneo have been planted with it, and the Dutch greatly favour it as against the Hevea, which they find capricious and uncertain in behaviour. The Ficus elastica grows rapidly, and yields a high-class rubber, the percentage of pure caoutchouc in its latex being nearly 87 per cent."[57] Driven by the seemingly encouraging results at Charduar and elsewhere, the species thus experienced a global window of opportunity. Its cultivation was contemplated even on European soil by gardeners and officials from the Botanic Gardens in Palermo, Sicily, as well as in various regions of Spain and France.[58] The reason for such acclimation schemes within Europe was that *Ficus elastica* was known to thrive in a variety of climates and topographies—from the hot and humid jungles of northeastern India to the drier plains and even the cold mountain regions up to five thousand feet, the flora and climates of which were compared with the temperate plant life of Europe. Besides Assam, *Ficus elastica* was also endogenous to Nepal, Burma, Bhutan, Myanmar, Yunnan in China, and parts of Southeast Asia, including Indonesia and Malaysia. Hence, an Italian agricultural book of 1903 echoed the wishful thinking of the time when it recommended that "[b]y making incisions in the roots and trunk of this plant, one can collect, as in India and Java, the latex and [thus] begin among us, in the extreme Mezzogiorno [southern Italy and Sicily], an industry, which promises to become more and more gigantic."[59]

Yet, while *Ficus* may have thrived beyond its "native" habitats, the unresolved question was whether the tree would yield any rubber in such diverse localities as the Bengal Delta, Italy's southern rim, Florida, or the Andalusian plains. As a series of botched attempts would reveal, the regions where the plant could live were not congruent with where conditions encouraged a profitable amount of rubber. This reveals a particular imaginary of Charduar's proponents that assumed locally proven cultivating techniques could be easily transported and applied elsewhere—a phantasm that the different soil, climatic, and social conditions in other regions often frustrated. Instead, the way in which *Ficus elastica* plantations manifested themselves locally across tropical and nontropical zones, and how they mutated and adapted to diverse localities, demonstrated how cultivating practices had to be kept elastic in the context of plantation production.

Contrary to the hopes of its founders and keepers, Charduar also became a much frequented site for the agronomic and entomological study of pests and diseases. The invasion of natural enemies of rubber trees forced this new branch of enquiry and experimentation onto plantation staff and required outside cooperation. But decades after the plantation had been launched, little was known among European foresters and officials about the natural enemies of the Indian rubber tree. At a moment when its global distribution and cultivation as a promising plantation crop was actively propagated, the Assam plantation suffered from several separate emergencies, turning it into a living laboratory for the study of pests. By the mid-1890s, it had become clear that in the plantation nurseries, "[t]he young plants are often attacked by insects which must be got rid of at once either with tobacco water or phenyl."[60] While this danger to the young plants could be contained, a more substantial attack occurred in October 1905, when a larva of the true silk-worm moth "completely defoliated several compartments" of the plantation.[61]

Consequently, in April 1906, one of British India's most eminent entomologists, E. P. Stebbing from the Indian Forest Service, left the imperial Forestry School at Dehra Dun to pay a visit to the government estate, "during which some observations were recorded on the life history of the rubber defoliating pest Gunda sikkima and notes recorded on a number of other pests of the F. elastica."[62] Stebbing was chosen because of his widely recognized fieldwork on *The Insect World* and his earlier publications on insect attacks on different rubber species.[63] At Charduar, he was supposed to observe in particular "the blocks where the tapping of the trees for rubber was in progress."[64] Once there, however, he was forced to widen his pest enquiries to include all spaces of the plantation complex, so widely were rubber-pests detected during his fortnight stay. Stebbing published the pioneering results from Charduar in a comprehensive work on *Indian Forest*

Insects of Economic Importance in 1914. He was certain that his book would "prove of value to planters and those interested in commercial concerns connected with the growth for profit of rubber," since many of the insects were clearly not confined to the Indian subcontinent (Fig. 5.2).[65]

As Stebbing's richly illustrated oeuvre evinced, the cultivated rubber trees suffered from different natural enemies at all stages of plant life, from their fragile beginnings in nurseries to the planted-out lines of young rubber trees to older trunks being tapped for rubber in whose fresh wounds certain pests laid their eggs. Such insights into the pests of a promising latex-yielding species were intended to be disseminated and used elsewhere. Within a few years, Stebbing's work on *Ficus elastica*–attacking insects had influenced numerous entomological treatises, including in the United States, where Henry Ford and others attempted to cultivate *Ficus elastica* as part of a program of domestic, "temperate" rubber production in the 1920s.[66] For instance, W. Dwight Pierce, an entomologist of the US Department of Agriculture, extensively reported on Stebbing's findings from Charduar in his widely circulated *Manual of Dangerous Insects Likely to Be Introduced in the United States Through Importations*.[67] Such works often included Stebbing's original illustrations of *Ficus* pests, which allowed easier identification and thus added to the practical value of the work in the hands of private planters and agronomic practitioners.

Figure 5.2. Selection of *Ficus elastica* pests at Charduar. *Source:* E. P. Stebbing, *Indian Forest Insects of Economic Importance* (Eyre & Spottiswoode, 1914), 339, 366, 67, 362, 259, 100, 256 (from left to right). Public domain.

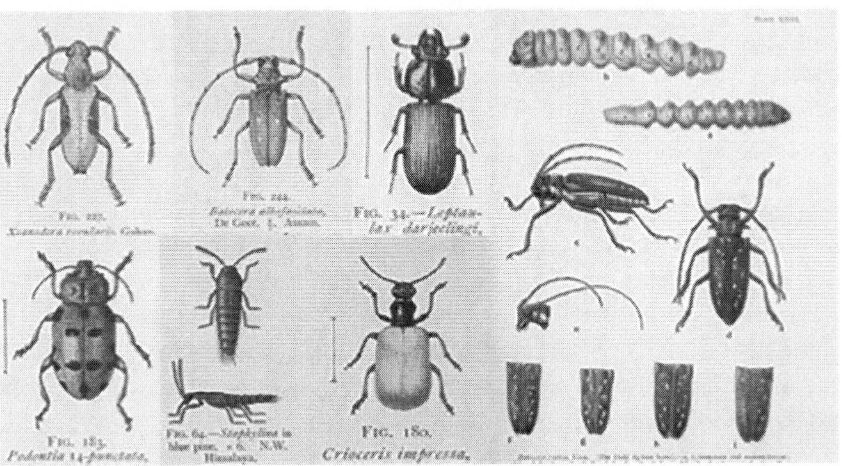

Charduar was thus linked to an explosion of knowledge from the 1880s to the 1920s, when the problems of plant parasites and diseases and the insects that carried them became a major concern for tropical investors and cultivators. The rise of colonial entomology required other kinds of specialization, scientists working in laboratories with proper equipment and disseminating their findings in specialized research journals, to make this knowledge authoritative and mobile to serve other colonial economies. In a sense, there had existed a palpable naivete about the nineteenth-century project of the tropics, with the assumption that if planters and foresters got rid of the jungle and brought in cultivation and suitable crops, most speculative schemes would succeed almost effortlessly. This story quickly turned sour on many fronts, and insects were part of that disillusionment. As the imperial foresters of Assam, involved in rubber, tea, sal, and other monocrop schemes, discovered, tropical agriculture was an extremely difficult and complicated enterprise to pursue profitably. It was not just the soil, it was not just the labor, it was not just the market, it was the nature of insect life and the diseases that attacked the crops that required a deeper understanding of highly complex and fragile plantation systems.

As I have shown, after its foundation in 1873, the Charduar plantation quickly became the central reference point for *Ficus elastica* cultivation within and well beyond the British Empire. Even if the divergent environmental and social conditions in specific sites often required adaptation from the agronomic and labor protocols developed and exported from Assam, the experimental government site was nonetheless constantly used as the benchmark for systematic raising and tapping of *Ficus* rubber. It was here that numerous bark-cutting systems and tapping rhythms were developed and refined over decades. Moreover, since plantations often create their own ecosystems and entomological challenges, the government estate was also ground zero for wide-ranging studies of the cash crop's pests and insects, including how to eliminate them. While the trial-and-error approach for domesticating the obstinate *Ficus* tree in a plantation setting required huge official outlays and never turned Charduar into a source of revenue for the administration, scholars so far have missed its raison d'être as a site of groundbreaking experimentation and useful knowledge production. Its extensive costs were for a long time accepted by the colonial state as an investment in the future in which officials imagined the imperial need to secure a permanent supply of the indispensable raw material from within the empire.

Ficus elastica and the Politics of the Local

The value of the Charduar rubber plantation, the first by the British Empire in Asia, was more than just pecuniary; it embodied a new ecological and extractive vision of how long-term experimental science by plant pragmatists could develop alternative systems for rubber cultivation at a resource frontier perceived to be in decline due to unchecked extraction. Charduar's distributive functions therefore require serious study also from a local and regional perspective. In addition to the gated government plantations in Assam, there were simultaneous initiatives to restock the increasingly exhausted wild rubber reserves in India's northeast, for which the estate played a key role. What had been put into practice in West Africa several years earlier by planting *Ficus elastica* on a large scale was now also proposed for Assamese forests and "tribal" territories. In 1906, Major Cole, superintendent of the Lushai Hills (annexed in 1890), for instance, sought, "with apparently every prospect of success, to introduce the cultivation of *ficus elastica* into his district."[68] Officials believed that the overtapping of wild rubber reserves over the past decades resulted in "very few trees" surviving. The colonial state had long since noticed that the "trees of ficus elastica are [there] in the same exhausted condition as those in Assam Proper, perhaps more so, since the Lushais make it their business to come in the cold weather from their own country, where there is less rubber now, in search of it to the Cachar forests."[69]

Since the mid-nineteenth century, colonial officials in Assam sought in vain to come up with appropriate measures and laws "to put a stop to this raiding of the rubber forest" across various frontier districts.[70] They also started to prepare forest nurseries. Among the chosen areas was the Lakhimpur division, where rubber seedlings were to be planted out in the government forest reserves. The latter had "to a large extent, become denuded of this tree by bad treatment in the past," so that the "natural reproduction of *Ficus Elastica* continues to be unsatisfactory."[71] It was a destructive spiral: The more wild trees were tapped to death, the less chance *Ficus elastica* trees had to establish themselves in the jungle, as other species took up the space and light the trees needed to thrive. In the early 1900s, thousands of raised young *Ficus* seedlings were therefore introduced on earth mounds in forests, fifty feet apart as at Charduar, either "in convenient blanks or by the sides of paths."[72]

For the purpose of reinvigorating the rubber supplies in their own territory, a handful of representatives of the Lushais were "sent to Charduar for a practical course of instruction and are now teaching the Lushais" back home amidst their ranks.[73] Charduar's purported success at cultivating the endemic tree meant that entire highland communities were viewed as possible planters. This was not a case of "compulsory cooperation," as the recruited Lushais participated willingly in the imperial program, even if frictions later arose.[74] Supplied with seeds and instructions from Charduar, the imperial officials stipulated that villagers and chiefs were "entitled to the produce of the trees owned by them, the Government only claiming the royalty of Rs. 17 per maund [1 maund equaling 37 kg], or whatever rate may be in force for the time being."[75] These provisions reflected the fact that, almost from its inception in the late 1820s, the wild rubber trade was entirely in the hands of a group of powerful Indian merchant capitalists, the Marwaris (locally called *kayas*), who directly purchased rubber from the hill "tribes" at their shops (*golas*) and controlled its export trade via the Brahmaputra river to Calcutta.[76] In the wake of World War I, it was at least reported that in "the Lushai Hills 25,418 planted rubber trees" were still "in existence."[77] While the scheme fell short of its overambitious promise to provide rubber from hundreds of thousands of newly planted trees, it was long-lasting and drew the Lushai people into the imperial circuits of planting knowledge and seed exchanges. In the longer history of rubber cultivation, this was a striking arrangement that questions established narratives. After all, Indigenous smallholders, who came to produce up to fifty percent of the world's natural rubber supplies before the outbreak of World War II, are usually seen as the unwanted competition of European plantation economies in the tropics. They were therefore frequently subjected to various forms of state discrimination to undermine their production.[78]

The Lushai scheme adds another layer to the complexities of the British imperial presence at the Assamese borderland. It shows how the interactions between the colonial state and Indigenous communities unfolded on a large spectrum of possible and at times contradictory relationships. Certain communities were, as in this case, perceived as allies, trained "instruments," and useful producers of an industrial commodity that imperial Britain craved. At the same time, Indigenous Assamese were also perceived as indispensable but undisciplined and obstreperous plantation "coolies," including at Charduar. Finally, Indigenous rubber tappers and collectors were seen as potential enemies of British conservation schemes of jungle tracts and their natural rubber stocks—and were denounced, policed, and punished for "illegally" tapping *Ficus* trees in protected forests or for plundering government plantations such as Charduar.[79]

The government rubber field was indeed a highly symbolic space of the colonial reordering of nature according to capitalist interests.[80] It was a charged site of imperial ingenuity and ecological engineering at the frontier of wild jungle tracts and supposed "savage tribes." For this reason, several high-ranking officials, including the viceroy of India, Lord Curzon, visited the Charduar plantation, as part of the state-making program of itinerant governance.[81] In 1901, Curzon also personally planted a *Ficus elastica* tree as a token of colonial transformation and progress in this frontier region, later regarded as "a worthy memorial of the Viceregal visit."[82] The act of putting out a young rubber seedling reflected how high imperial officials believed in a prosperous future of rubber production in northeast India, with the growing plant symbolizing the lasting commitment of the state to its strategic propagation under the protective umbrella of empire. Charduar's perfectly parallel structure of lines of cleared forest and artificially planted rubber trees, as depicted on a contemporary map, stood in stark visual contrast to the jungle and swirling natural course of the nearby Mansiri River, evoking a striking juxtaposition of geometrical and wild forms—the colonial aesthetic of the plantation itself (Fig. 5.3).

Figure 5.3. "Charduar Caoutchouc Plantation, Block No. 1, scale 8 inches = 1 mile," surveyed by W. E. D'Arcy in 1877–1878, depicting "cleared lines" and "planted lines." *Source: Progress Report of Forest Administration in Assam for the Year 1877–1878* (Assam Secretariat Press, 1877). Public domain.

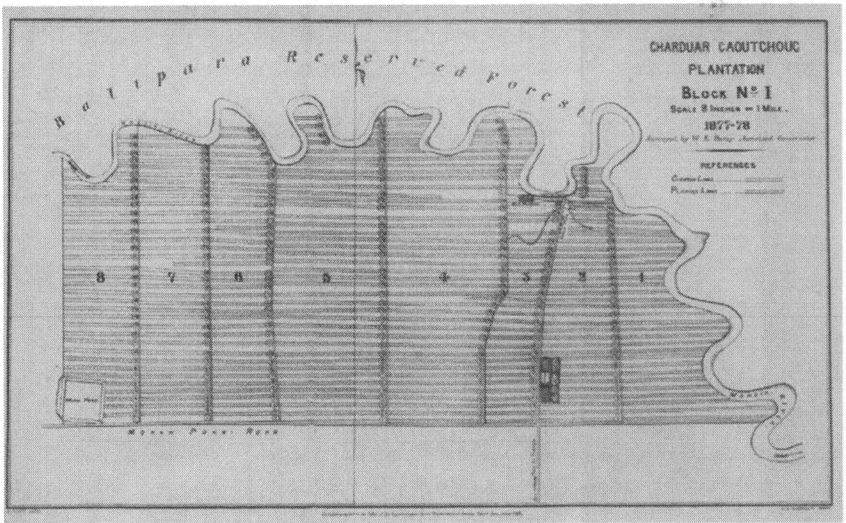

While the colonial civilizing mission assumed that foresters would transform "wild" jungles into orderly "gardens," it is important to understand the longstanding Indigenous relationships with *Ficus elastica* trees. The Assamese forests presented revered landscapes, and the majestic rubber tree had its place in Indigenous cosmologies. Assamese communities had for centuries planted the tree for protection, as a shade giver, for its beautiful foliage, and to perform religious rites under it.[83] The tree grew naturally scattered across ten thousand square miles in the region, mostly as a solitary tree, or in small groups of two or three that usually dominated the surrounding jungle. The arrival of systematic, densely planted *Ficus elastica* plantations in the form of grid-locked lines disrupted these sacred forests. It also alienated the Assamese from their lands through government enclosures, with their own practices of forest use and shifting agriculture labeled barbaric, destructive, and shortsighted by foresters and officials. Crucially, "[p]rotection was always, of course, also the language that masked acts of expropriation."[84]

But Assamese highland communities were not only the silent, passive victims of the expansion of British rule, forest enclosures, and government plantations that were located within the Inner Line (established in 1873) and, thus, in areas under British jurisdiction.[85] The example of the "Aka tribe" traditionally living north of the Charduar estate is particularly instructive in this regard. As colonial officials knew by the 1870s, "[r]ubber is the chief source of wealth of the Akas."[86] Administrators dated the conflictive "political relations of the Akas with the British" to the year 1868, when "the Akas first became alive to the fact that they possessed a valuable and marketable commodity in the form of rubber. It is really to the rubber question (i.e., whether the Akas [have] the right, which they claim to have, to cut rubber down)" in specified areas that a great deal of debate and violence on both sides must be attributed.[87] From the Akas' perspective, the Charduar plantation symbolized the loss of access to their forest and its valuable products, which were an important source of income.[88] Both sides were aware that Charduar sought to change the social ecology by alienating the Akas from their land and that the government rubber estates were intended to make the British Empire independent of wild rubber supplies, such as those the Akas used to procure money, provisions, and manufactured products from the Assam plains. The Akas therefore attacked a village and a forestry office in Assam in 1884, taking two officials as hostages and through such "disturbances" forcing the Charduar plantation to halt activities for several months.[89] This violent incident was avenged by a punitive British military expedition.[90] The expedition to the Akas was, however, also used to initiate new rubber planting experiments in areas beyond the limits of British control. Its members set young *Ficus elastica* plants into the forks of trees whose growth was to be observed and recorded later. Science and violence on the frontier thus became inseparable, and the sphere of plantation experiments (literally) branched out.[91]

Yet, for other groups, the incremental expansion of the Charduar plantation also opened opportunities for employment and income.[92] While Charduar was a site of subjugation under foreign and strict temporal and manual regimes, it was also an estate where hired Indigenous people learned new planting and cultivating techniques, skills that were transferable to silvicultural schemes in their home territories. Rubber tapping on the estate was also less dangerous than wild rubber extraction in the forest from the huge *Ficus* trees that often reached a height of 100 to 120 feet.[93] As a government report noted, "[i]t is only necessary to see the tree to appreciate the fearful risk encountered by the gum gatherers, who by no means confine their operations to the base, but climb up as high as the roots extend and higher along the horizontal branches, chopping with their *dhaus* [knives] at intervals of every few inches, the cuts answering as well for their foothold as for the sap to exude them"—a risky operation that cost numerous anonymous latex collectors their lives.[94]

Finally, Charduar was a place of extraction for several ethnic groups. While the foresters employed several watchmen to control the estate, as it grew to thirty thousand trees, their tight oversight became impossible and opened the door to illegal operations. Hence, in 1893, a forester acknowledged that the estate "is rendered tolerably safe against everything but illicit tapping."[95] This formulation tantalizingly left open whether rubber was illegally removed by the contractually hired plantation staff or outside intruders, or both. In either case, it showed how Assamese and distantly recruited plantation "coolies" (including Mikir, Garo, and Nepalese tappers) saw Charduar as a site of disruption and marginalization as well as an opportunity for personal gain.[96] Since the government strictly recruited only male laborers onto the plantation, given the backbreaking work of jungle clearing and tapping it required, and paid Nepalese and other groups more than the supposedly indolent and ineffective Assamese, the plantation reified gendered divisions of labor and reflected racist views of different groups.[97] However, since labor shortages perennially threatened to shut down plantation operations, and with the workforce fully conscious of their indispensable labor, Charduar saw various acts of worker resistance, including successful strikes against poor working and health conditions, which at times led to increases in the meagre wages of 7–8 annas a day for tappers.[98]

As more *Ficus elastica* rubber schemes emerged out of the government plantation by the late nineteenth century (including in Burma, Bengal, and Madras), they increasingly included private capital and European planters as well. Similar to the way the Assam tea gardens had received considerable state support through the provision of infrastructure and affordable land, so was Assam's Chief Commissioner in 1897 "anxious to encourage private enterprise in rubber planting." He therefore gave "a lease of land on favorable terms for this purpose."[99] To promote private rubber planters, colonial officials "relaxed" existing rules for land grants.[100] Charduar's plant life thus spread out and started to influence the cultivation choices on other Assam estates. As a rubber journal noted approvingly in 1900, "the tea-planters lately have begun to grow Ficus elastica on their waste lands, seeing a possible source of extra income from the rubber-tree."[101] It was widely held that "[i]n this adventure they should receive every encouragement."[102] Since the "Assam rubber industry" was seen as being "well worth fostering," the surplus saplings from the Charduar nurseries were to be distributed free of charge to private planters—a policy supported from the top, by the Inspector General of Forests, Berthold Ribbentrop.[103] The site was, in other words, envisioned as a kind of mother plantation that would have numerous progenies across the wild Assam forests and private estates. Charduar's most ardent promoters in the imperial bureaucracy, like W. R. Fisher, considered it as nothing less than the revolutionary nucleus for a profound transformation of Assam rubber production, as the tree was to be cultivated within small but growing islands of order amidst the perceived chaos of the unmanageable wild rubber trade of the region.[104]

Plantation Research and Development

There existed also much less enthusiastic voices about Charduar in the bureaucracy, but for surprisingly long, the hopes of imperial officials dominated the decision making of the state.[105] For the latter, controlled plantation production promised to solve, once and for all, the long-standing issue of the inferior quality of wild Assam rubber, which often contained a number of added impurities such as bark, wood, and stones that depressed world market prices for the "brand."[106] The reason was that Indigenous gatherers were harvesting in the forests (outside state supervision) the largest quantities by far. The tappers then sold on the produce by weight mostly to Marwari merchants, the unchallenged intermediary traders and, in doing so, sought to increase profits by adding adulterations of up to thirty-five percent.

To improve the preparation of the plantation product, Charduar's outside connections became again significant. They entailed new kinds of expert exchanges with British metropolitan scientists and rubber manufacturers that informed the commercial operations on the government field. In the early years of the twentieth century, the plantation regularly expanded, sometimes considerably, and in 1899, serious experiments were begun in tapping and selling rubber.[107] It is striking to note, however, that, at least initially, there was little market interest and low enthusiasm among the British public and manufacturers for the government-grown rubber.[108] When the Assam Forest Department "sold in London the first produce of the Charduar Rubber Plantation @ Rs 2-8-6 per lb.," it resulted in a meagre profit of only Rs 1-2-6 per pound, after the transport costs from Tezpur and the agent's and sale expenses were deducted.[109] In other words, empire rubber did not land with a bang. However, the next year marked an upward trend, as some 4,280 pounds of Charduar produce were sold in England at the profitable price of three shillings and seven pence per pound. As was noted with growing pride: "The agents through whom the sale was effected, reported that it was the finest rubber ever sent from Assam; and that, if it could be delivered in larger quantities and with regularity, it would realise a price still nearer to the rate paid for fine Para rubber" from Brazil.[110] The old dream that Assam rubber could be equal to, if not superior to, the world-market dominating *Hevea* rubber had not yet vanished.[111]

To improve the processing of the plantation's product, Charduar's external links again became important. They involved a new kind of exchange of expertise with scientists and rubber manufacturers in the British metropole, which informed the government's commercial operations. To this end, various samples of Charduar rubber were sent to the Imperial Institute in London from 1897. This government-sponsored resource institute, whose Scientific and Technical Department (including numerous laboratories) was led by the Professor of Chemistry Wyndham R. Dunstan, was tasked with testing out various natural resins, dyestuffs, food crops, and any other natural products that could be grown, extracted, and sold for profit.[112] Dunstan was expected to attend to the scientific analysis of the Charduar rubber, to make suggestions for its enhancement and to communicate his findings to brokers and manufacturers who would in turn provide their own feedback to Charduar. This presented an entangled system of commodity production on tropical estates with direct feedback loops from metropolitan producers and manufacturers that I call "Plantation R & D." The first Charduar samples were tested in 1899 but considered as the result of a "defective operation."[113] Consequently, upon receiving Dunstan's suggestions for optimized methods, a second sample was provided in 1900.[114] This was unanimously judged to be of "a very much better appearance than the first."[115]

While the consulted rubber manufacturer in London found the second Charduar sample of good quality and "free from foreign admixture," it was nonetheless considered too soft for the manufacture of insulated wires.[116] Electrical purposes required hard rubber. In consequence, the suggestion was made to mix the Charduar product with superior Para rubber for "the manufacture of soft rubber articles."[117] To increase the number of expert verdicts, the Inspector General of Forests, Berthold Ribbentrop, also directly enlisted the service of one of the world's leading producers of cable and other electrical devices: Messrs Siemens Brothers, the well-known manufacturing electricians. This scheme built on an established collaboration with Siemens Brothers, whose laboratories had tested many profitable gums and resins for British institutions, including Kew Gardens.[118] The company was not only asked for an industrial assessment of samples (their verdict remains unknown) but also informed about the total amount of the same quality rubber being shipped to Britain that year: around four tons. Dunstan, in turn, offered to coordinate these multiple evaluations of the commodity "and, if desired, to accept for the Forest Department the highest tender for the consignment."[119]

No efforts were spared to help the self-grown rubber enter British industrial production. The cooperation of Charduar with the Imperial Institute continued for years. Improved production methods meant that by 1905, Charduar rubber could "be used for the manufacture of ebonite," or hard rubber, thus greatly widening the range of possible applications.[120] Such schemes allow us to shift the analytical lens from the sites of resource extraction to the strategic expansion of a different kind of "commodity frontier": rubber's *frontier of industrial applicability*. The cooperation of the Indian foresters with metropolitan specialists, resource institutes, and commercial producers demonstrates how even remotely stationed agents deeply immersed in local forest production and management thought consistently about both ends of global commodity chains.[121] Scientific foresters were not backwoodsmen with a parochial view of the political economy of colonial forests, but producers of industrial commodities, albeit with an urge to maintain an equilibrium between patterns of extraction and necessary conservation and, if needed, strategic "artificial reproduction."[122]

Conclusion

The 1911 article in the *India Rubber World* on the Charduar plantation with which this chapter opened already alluded to the estate's uncertain future. Even though the plantation at the time contained thirty thousand raised trees distributed across 2,700 acres, these trees were exclusively of the *Ficus elastica* variety, said to be "now less favored for planting" than the South American *Hevea* tree.[123] The editors recognized already that the estate was at a crossroads, and its existence threatened. Over the next few years, *Ficus elastica* would experience a sudden fall from grace as a global plantation crop. As John Carruthers, a government botanist in British Malaya, noted in 1909: "Four years ago the question of the relative advantages of planting *Hevea braziliensis* (Para rubber), or *Ficus elastica* (Rambong), was considered an open one, and the fact that the latter was a native tree and grows freely in Malaya induced some to prefer it to the Brazilian plant."[124] In his eulogy to the species, under the heading "The Passing of *Ficus Elastica*," Carruthers gave several reasons for the eclipse.[125] Above all, the planters' decision to supplant *Ficus* in Malaya and elsewhere with its Brazilian competitor was due to the greater regularity of resource extraction from *Hevea* trees—their much greater uniformity of growth that allowed their more routine, mechanical tapping. This aligned *Hevea* much more closely with the work of a "plantation machine."[126] Carruthers stressed that *Hevea*'s triumph was underpinned by its greater potential for standardizing and mechanizing resource extraction:

> There are various difficulties attending the treatment of *Ficus* in regard to pruning it or allowing it to form its aerial roots unchecked, in relation to tapping and preventing of entrance of boring insects and fungi into the wounds, also the direction and shape of the branches and stems make the collection of latex no easy matter. . . . The symmetrical stem of the Para, the

> facilities for running the latex into the single cup at the base of the tree, regularity of its growth and its reaction to a wound, have especially commended this tree to the rubber grower.[127]

The same account described the strategic destruction of cultivated *Ficus* species to make room for the higher-yielding and more profitable *Hevea* type in British Malaya.[128] The integration and dis-integration of *Ficus* regimes on rubber plantations shows, in other words, the enormous capacity of modern agronomic systems to acclimatize new species around the world if there was a perceived commercial demand. Moreover, it sheds light on the capacity of these systems to quickly correct earlier decisions and realign global planting with changing industrial demands. This restructuring was "in principle irreversible: This is the essence of transformation, in contrast to mere change. When transformations occur, the processes of change are condensed and accelerated, new actors appear, and the winners and losers become easier to tell apart."[129]

When Malayan and Indonesian planters ripped out established *Ficus elastica* to replace with *Hevea*, the changed global context could no longer be ignored; the world came crashing down on the Charduar plantation, which had to abandon its previous goals and visions. These events showed how quickly and unexpectedly seemingly thriving plantations could end, even amidst optimistic—even euphoric—evaluations. The strategy of specialization was always high risk, high gain. After 1908, repeated government efforts to sell the Charduar estate to private planters failed. Less than a decade later, operations came to a near halt: No more extensions were made after 1916, and an elaborately devised rotation system for scientific and commercial tapping was entirely discarded. Toward the final years of World War I, it was calculated that the continued "low price of Assam rubber [made] tapping prohibitive except with free labour."[130] This led the British officials to take desperate steps. For several years, the once carefully guarded government estate, with its myriad temporal and spatial logics of neat compartments as distinct laboratories of *Ficus* cultivation, was now opened up to uncontrolled tapping by outsiders. "Forest villagers" were allowed to extract latex from any part of the plantation, unchecked, unpaid, and undocumented. The former system of precisely recording every step of plantation operations collapsed.

The most painstaking and coordinated efforts to turn Assam rubber into a plantation crop thus stumbled and faltered. Nevertheless, the idea of liberating the British Empire from the need to import external resources exercised its influence for decades to come and partly explains the vast expansion of *Hevea* plantations in Southeast Asia after the turn of the twentieth century. Meanwhile, colonial servants, foresters, and private planters in Assam had little time to react to the sudden and profound changes in the global rubber industry. As demand for *Ficus elastica* rubber on the world market dried up, plantations and wild harvesting of *Ficus* ceased, while the trees, now untouched by axes or tapping knives, continued to grow. The records of colonial administrations and private firms that invested in Assam rubber fell silent.[131] Additionally, several attempts since the late nineteenth century to acclimate and grow *Hevea* in India's northeastern frontier proved of little significance, even if some government-owned *Hevea* plantations existed in neighboring Burma by the early twentieth century, and a large private *Hevea* industry was established in southern India after 1900, particularly in Kerala.[132]

By 1919, among the concerned government circles involved with Charduar, it had become "a matter for consideration whether further expenditure on this plantation is justifiable for it appears that there is practically no demand now for rubber obtained from the Ficus elastica and even when a sale is effected the price is so low that it does not cover the cost of tapping."[133] This was an astonishing twist of fate. After decades of enormous government investment in the experimental estate, no private buyers signaled any interest, and thus officials conceded that "the question of *abandoning* the plantation will be taken up."[134] As a contemporary explained Charduar's predicament: "The extensive plantations of Pará rubber in the East . . . have sealed its doom as a commercial proposition."[135] This point needs stressing: The enormously successful *Hevea* plantations in Southeast Asia were also the result of British imperial efforts to propagate rubber. The coexistence of competing rubber schemes within the empire followed an old recipe: It was part of maintaining what I call an imperial portfolio of potentially profitable plants. Various species were part of systematic cultivation experiments, with the new rubber estates in Southeast Asia eventually proving *Hevea* to be the superior crop, marginalizing every other species in the process. It had taken the European botanists and planters more than a century to establish a definitive global hierarchy of rubber plants. Once this hierarchy had been achieved, the "inferior" varietals fell by the wayside.

After World War I, land-hungry tea gardeners fixed their prying eyes on the Charduar plantation. In 1929, a forestry report contained a brief panegyric that seemed to capture its erasure. It merely recorded that "[t]he extensive ficus elastica rubber plantation of 2,500 acres . . . put out at great labour and expense by the department have been disforested, the demand for this type of rubber having gone out."[136] There is some irony in the timing of the plantation's abandonment. Occurring almost exactly half a century after operations had begun, it was at precisely the time when its trees reached their full maturity and when the output, according to its founding fathers, would reach its triumphant climax. The long gestation period of *Ficus* rubber was out of sync with the shorter production times of other species, condemning Charduar to be a relic of past futures of the global rubber industry. While it was a possible future in ruins, this "failure" demonstrated the profitability of the British approach of insuring against future scarcity by investing in an imperial resource portfolio.

Notes

1. "Rubber Planting in the East," *India Rubber World* 43, no. 4 (1911): 124.
2. "Rubber Planting in the East," 124.
3. "Rubber Planting in the East," 124.
4. Bodhisattva Kar, "Historia Elastica: A Note on the Rubber Hunt in the North-Eastern Frontier of British India," *Indian Historical Review* 36, no. 1 (2009): 131–150; Aparajita Majumdar, "The Colonial State and Resource Frontiers: Tracing the Politics of Appropriating Rubber in the Northeastern Frontier of British India, 1810–84," *Indian Historical Review* 43, no. 1 (2016): 25–41; Tara Acharya, "Elusive Frontier: The Failure of a Rubber Plantation in Colonial Assam," *Political & Economic Weekly* 58, no. 37 (2023): 22–25. Exceptions are Arupjyoti Saikia, "Forests in Assam: Merchant Trade to Imperial Economy," in *Forests and Ecological History of Assam, 1826–2000* (Oxford University Press, 2011); and Aparajita Majumdar, " 'Objects' of Appropriations: Locating Material Efficacies of Rubber in the Northeastern Resource Frontier of British India, 1810–1906," in *Objects and Frontiers in Modern Asia: Between the Mekong and the Indus*, eds. Lipokmar Dzüvichü and Manjeet Baruah (Routledge, 2019), 43–67.
5. The concept of "commodity frontiers" highlights the mutual dependence between nature and societies and underscores how capitalism has expanded through a succession of frontiers that transformed socio-ecological landscapes. It was recently revisited by Sven Beckert et al., "Commodity Frontiers and the Transformation of the Global Countryside: A Research Agenda," *Journal of Global History* 16, no. 3 (2021): 435–450.
6. Kew-centric is Lucile H. Brockway, *Science and Colonial Expansion: The Role of the British Royal Botanic Gardens* (Yale University Press, 1979); see also Donal P. McCracken, *Gardens of Empire: Botanical Institutions of the Victorian British Empire* (Leicester University Press, 1997); Richard Drayton, *Nature's*

Government: Science, Imperial Britain, and the 'Improvement' of the World (Yale University Press, 2000). For an important reassessment of the Calcutta Botanic Gardens, see Marine Bellégo, *Enraciner l'empire. Une autre histoire du jardin botanique de Calcutta (1860–1910)* (Muséum national d'histoire naturelle, 2021).

7. J. H. Drabble, *Rubber in Malaya, 1876–1922: The Genesis of the Industry* (Oxford University Press, 1973); Phin Keong Voon, *Western Rubber Planting Enterprise in Southeast Asia, 1876–1921* (Penerbit Universiti Malaya, 1976). On the massive expansion of plantation production, see Stephen L. Harp, *A World History of Rubber: Empire, Industry, and the Everyday* (Wiley, 2016), 20.

8. See also Pamela H. Smith, "Science on the Move: Recent Trends in the History of Early Modern Science," *Renaissance Quarterly* 62, no. 2 (2009): 345–375.

9. I draw on excellent conceptual reflections on the mobility of museological collections in Victorian Britain as developed in Felix Driver, Mark Nesbitt, and Caroline Cornish, "Introduction: Mobilising and Re-Mobilising Museum Collections," in *Mobile Museums: Collections in Circulation*, eds. Felix Driver et al. (UCL Press, 2021), 1–20.

10. Kar, "Historia Elastica"; Saikia, *Forests*; Majumdar, "Resource Frontiers."

11. Emma Reisz, "Knowledge and Political Economy in the Rubber Trade of the British Empire, c.1800–c.1930" (PhD diss., Cambridge University, 2004).

12. Suzanne Zeller, *Inventing Canada: Early Victorian Science and the Idea of a Transcontinental Nation* (McGill-Queen's University Press, 2009), 4.

13. David Arnold, *The Tropics and the Traveling Gaze: India, Landscape, and Science, 1800–1856* (University of Washington Press, 2006); David Arnold, "Plant Capitalism and Company Science: The Indian Career of Nathaniel Wallich," *Modern Asian Studies* 42, no. 5 (2008): 899–928.

14. On the simultaneous testing of various rubber species in the French Empire, see Michitake Aso, *Rubber and the Making of Vietnam: An Ecological History, 1897–1975* (University of North Carolina Press, 2018).

15. On the political significance of ignorance, see Robert Proctor and Londa L. Schiebinger, eds., *Agnotology: The Making and Unmaking of Ignorance* (Stanford University Press, 2008).

16. Andrew B. Liu, *Tea War: A History of Capitalism in China and India* (Yale University Press, 2020); Maan Barua, *Plantation Worlds* (Duke University Press, 2024).

17. Colin Barlow, *The Natural Rubber Industry: Its Development, Technology, and Economy in Malaysia* (Oxford University Press, 1978); Warren Dean, *Brazil and the Struggle for Rubber: A Study in Environmental History* (Cambridge University Press, 1987); John Tully, *The Devil's Milk: A Social History of Rubber* (Monthly Review, 2011).

18. Friedrich Lenger, *Der Preis der Welt: eine Globalgeschichte des Kapitalismus* (C. H. Beck, 2023); Sven Beckert, *Capitalism: A Global History* (Penguin, 2025).

19. On Assam tea, see Jayeeta Sharma, *Empire's Garden: Assam and the Making of India* (Duke University Press, 2011).

20. For the establishment of Charduar amidst other imperial efforts to conserve overworked forests through the Assam Forestry Department, see Saikia, *Forests*, 172–176.

21. On *Ficus elastica*'s enigmatic nature, see Majumdar, " 'Objects' of Appropriations."

22. William Griffith, *Journals of Travels in Assam, Burma, Bootan, Afghanistan and the Neighbouring Countries* (Calcutta, 1847), 192.

23. George Watt, *A Dictionary of the Economic Products of India* (London, 1890), 4:345.

24. Saikia, *Forests*, 217; Majumdar, " 'Objects' of Appropriations."

25. Gustav Mann, *Progress Report of Forest Administration in Assam for the Year 1874–75* (Shillong, 1875), 35.

26. John Loadman, *Tears of the Tree: The Story of Rubber – A Modern Marvel* (Oxford University Press, 2005).

27. Gustav Mann to Joseph Hooker, from Debrooghur, Upper Assam, October 26, 1870, Library and Archives at Royal Botanic Gardens, Kew [RBGK], Directors' Correspondence [DC], 153/513.

28. C. J. Lyall, Under Secretary to the Government of India, to the Chief Commissioner of Assam, Simla, June 23, 1875, Assam State Archives [ASA], File no-43/51, "Experimental Rubber Plantation in Kamrup, 1873."

29. John R. Jackson, "India Forest Administration," *The Journal of Forestry and Estates Management* 1, no. 4 (1877): 239.

30. Berthold Ribbentrop, *Review of Forest Administration in British India, 1895–96* (Calcutta, 1897), 59.

31. Dietrich Brandis, "Introduction," in *Catalogue of Specimens of Timber, Bamboos, Canes and other Forest Produce from the Government Forests in the Provinces under the Government of India . . . Sent to the Paris Exhibition of 1878* (Calcutta, 1878), 3.

32. Max Lierau, *Das Botanische Museum und Bot. Laboratorium für Waarenkunde zu Hamburg* (Cassel, 1888), 9.

33. See ASA, File no-43/51, "Experimental Rubber Plantation in Kamrup, 1873."

34. James Collins publicly encouraged such information exchange in 1872. James Collins, *Report on the Caoutchouc of Commerce* (London, 1872), 47.

35. "Assam Rubber for West Africa," *Bulletin of Miscellaneous Information (Royal Gardens, Kew)* 52 (April 1891): 97; Gustav Mann, "Brief Account of How Rubber Trees (Ficus Elastica) are Grown in Assam," *Bulletin of Miscellaneous Information (Royal Gardens, Kew)* 52 (April 1891): 100.

36. Mann had then been in the service of Kew Gardens, the Royal Navy, and the Foreign Office; see Moritz von Brescius, *German Science in the Age of Empire: Enterprise, Opportunity and the Schlagintweit Brothers* (Cambridge University Press, 2019), 83.

37. "Assam Rubber for West Africa," 98.

38. Martin Dusinberre and Mariko Iijima, "Editorial. Transplantation: Sugar and Imperial Practice in Japan's Pacific," *Historische Anthropologie* 27, no. 3 (2019): 330; Helen Tilley, *Africa as a Living Laboratory: Empire, Development, and the Problem of Scientific Knowledge, 1870–1950* (University of Chicago Press, 2011), 10.

39. William Wicherley, *The Whole Art of Rubber-Growing* (West Strand, 1911), 89.

40. Alvan Millson, "Circular," Colonial Secretary's Office, Lagos, September 30, 1890, in "Assam Rubber for West Africa," 98.

41. Important critical reflections on "circulation" have recently been offered by Stuart Alexander Rockefeller, "Flow," *Current Anthropology* 52, no. 4 (2011): 557–578; Stefanie Gänger, "Circulation: Reflections on Circularity, Entity, and Liquidity in the Language of Global History," *Journal of Global History* 12, no. 3 (2017): 303–318; Kapil Raj, "Networks of Knowledge, or Spaces of Circulation? The Birth of British Cartography in Colonial South Asia in the Late Eighteenth Century," *Global Intellectual History* 2, no. 1 (2017): 49–66.

42. Wicherley, *Rubber-Growing*, 89.

43. Wicherley, *Rubber-Growing*, 91; Berthold Ribbentrop, *Review of Forest Administration in British India, 1896–97* (Calcutta, 1898), 60. However, this scheme proved troublesome; see letter from Ernest Ayscoghe Floyer to the Royal Botanic Gardens, Kew, Cairo, September 13, 1898, RBGK, DC, 179/339.

44. "Assam Rubber in Egypt," *Bulletin of Miscellaneous Information (Royal Gardens, Kew)*, Additional Series, VIII. III. - Rubber (1906): 169–170. The first experiments with *Ficus* cuttings at Charduar were undertaken in 1875.

45. "Assam Rubber in Egypt," 169–170.

46. Daniel Morris, "Cantor Lectures on the Plants Yielding Commercial India-Rubber," *Journal of the Society for Arts* 46, no. 2384 (1898): 745–760. On the comparative value of Assam rubber, see the various "Memoranda" of the United States Rubber Company, 1892, Baker Business Library, Harvard University, U.S. Rubber Company, 1876–1900, V. 1–3, Mss 63, U58. Also see various rubber notifications in Assamese in the *Assam Gazette*, November 1, 1884, 614–616.

47. Majumdar, "'Objects' of Appropriations."

48. A. H. Berkhout, "De Gouvernements caoutchouc-aanplantingen in Britsch-Indië," *De Indische Gids: Tijdschrift voor Nederlandsch-Indië* 26, no. 1 (1904): 707–720.

49. Reisz, "Knowledge and Political Economy," 225.

50. Kar, "Historia Elastica," 141.

51. For other examples of "failure," see also Christina Skott's, Marta Macedo's, and Theresa Ventura's chapters in this volume.

52. For example, "Iets Over De Aanplanting Van Caoutchouc-Boomen in Britsch Indië" ["On the Planting of Caoutchouc Trees in British India"], *Tijdschrift voor nijverheid en landbouw in Nederlandsch-Indië* 21 (1877): 182–194.

53. "Rubber Planting in the East," 124.

54. Camille Spire and André Spire, *Le Caoutchouc en Indo-Chine: étude botanique industrielle et commerciale* (A. Challamel, 1906), 207–210. The first *Ficus elastica* plantation in French Indochina dated from 1882, established at Thuduc (Thủ Đức). The planting protocols developed at Charduar were translated and published in French colonial journals, see for example, "Rapport sur la culture des Ficus elastica en Assam," *Revue des Cultures Coloniales* 12, no. 118 (1903): 84–88. On West African schemes, see Félix Faure to Sir David Prain, from Gabon, August 20, 1910, RBGK, DC, 185/416. For the Philippines, see the letter from Cornelius Robert Blair Pickford to Daniel Morris, from Cebu, July 9, 1891, DC, 165/312–313. On Californian experiments, see J. L. Sanford to George Nicholson, from San Francisco, August 13, 1887, DC, 199/401–402. For Singapore, see Henry N. Ridley to Sir William Thiselton-Dyer, January 2, 1900, DC, 166/696, and Letter from Ridley to Thiselton-Dyer, Singapore, March 8, 1904, DC, 168/102–104. On the Seychelles and Southern Nigeria, see Imperial Institute, *Colonial Reports—Miscellaneous*, No 82, IV, *Rubber, Gutta Percha* (London, 1912), 263–434, 339–341, and a global survey of *Ficus elastica*, in John H. Holland, "The Useful Plants of Nigeria, Part IV," *Bulletin of Miscellaneous Information (Royal Gardens, Kew)*, Additional Series IX (1922): 623–625.

55. A. Zimmermann, "Kultur und Kautschukgewinnung von Ficus-Arten," *Der Tropenpflanzer* 22, no. 21 (1905): 321–350.

56. William Beinart and Lotte Hughes, *Environment and Empire* (Oxford University Press, 2007), 238.

57. Wicherley, *Rubber-Growing*, 86.

58. John A. Stevenson, *Foreign Plant Diseases: A Manual of Economic Plant Diseases Which are New to or Not Widely Distributed in the United States* (US Government Printing Office, 1926), 76–77; Italo Giglioli, "Camphrier et Ficus à caoutchouc en Italie," *Journal d'Agriculture Tropicale* 35 (May 31, 1904): 152–153; see also Italo Gigliolo, *Malessere agrario ed alimentare in Italia* (Imprimerie E. Della Torre, 1903), 325–326.

59. Italo Giglioli, "Di Alcune Vere Questioni Meridionali," *Rivista d'Italia. Lettere, Scienza ed Arte* 6, no. 2 (1903): 59. See also E. M. Coventry, *Ficus Elastica: Its Natural Growth and Artificial Propagation* (Calcutta Superintendent Government Printing India, 1906); Majumdar, " 'Objects' of Appropriations."

60. D. P. Copeland, "Rubber Plantations at Charduar in Assam," National Archives of India, Delhi [NAI], Inspector General of Forests, February 1896, Proceedings no. 1–2, 7.

61. E. P. Stebbing, *A Manual of Elementary Forest Zoology for India* (Calcutta Superintendent Government Printing India, 1908), 122.

62. "Charduar Rubber Plantation Pests," *Annual Report of the Board of Scientific Advice for India, 1906–07* (Calcutta Superintendent Government Printing India, 1908), 102.

63. E. P. Stebbing, *The Insect World in an Indian Forest, and How to Study It* (Indian Forest Service, 1903), 11.

64. Edward Percy Stebbing, *Indian Forest Insects of Economic Importance – Coleoptera* (Eyre & Spottiswoode, 1914), 439.

65. Stebbing, *Indian Forest Insects of Economic Importance*, vi.

66. Mark R. Finlay, *Growing American Rubber: Strategic Plants and the Politics of National Security* (Rutgers University Press, 2009).

67. W. Dwight Pierce, *A Manual of Dangerous Insects Likely to Be Introduced in the United States Through Importations* (US Government Printing Office, 1917), 100–105.

68. *Report on the Administration of Eastern Bengal and Assam, 1906–1907* (Shillong Secretariat Press, 1908), 44. See also Kyle Jackson, *The Mizo Discovery of the British Raj: Empire and Religion in Northeast India, 1890–1920* (Cambridge University Press, 2023), 63.

69. Mann, *Progress Report of Forest Administration in Assam for the Year 1874–75*, 17.

70. "India-Rubber in British-India," *India Rubber World*, July 10, 1895, 285.

71. M. Hill, *Progress Report of Forest Administration in the Province of Eastern Bengal and Assam for the Year 1907–1908* (Eastern Bengal and Assam Secretariat Printing Office, 1908), 9.

72. A. V. Monro, *Progress Report of Forest Administration in the Province of Eastern Bengal and Assam for the Year 1909–1910* (Eastern Bengal and Assam Secretariat Printing Office, 1910), 7.

73. *Report on the Administration of Eastern Bengal and Assam, 1906–1907*, 44.

74. For Mann's discussion of the role of compulsory cooperation in imperialism, see Michael Mann, *The Sources of Social Power* (Cambridge University Press, 1986), 1:130–178. Compare with John Gallagher and Ronald Robinson, "The Imperialism of Free Trade," *Economic History Review* 6, no. 1 (1953): 1–15. On the scheme's voluntarism but also Indigenous critiques of exploitation, see Joy K. L. Pachuau and Willem van Schendel, *The Camera as Witness: A Social History of Mizoram, Northeast India* (Cambridge University Press, 2015), 174–175.

75. M. Hill, *Progress Report of Forest Administration in the Province of Eastern Bengal and Assam for the Year 1908–1909* (Eastern Bengal and Assam Secretariat Printing Office, 1909), 10.

76. The first recorded sale of Assam rubber to Britain via Calcutta was in 1828; see "Observations on Caoutchouc, communicated in a letter from Dr. Royle to Dr. H. H. Spry, London, 12th July, 1837," *Transactions of the Agricultural and Horticultural Society of India*, 6 (1839): 27–29. *Report on the Administration of the Province of Assam for the Years 1874–75 and 1875–76* (Shillong, 1877), 14. Also, masterfully, Kar, "Historia Elastica."

77. A. W. Blunt and F. H. Todd, *Progress Report of Forest Administration in the Province of Assam for the Year 1919–1920* (Shillong Secretariat Printing, 1920), 11.

78. "Memorandum: Labour and European Supervision," National Archives, Kew, AVIA 12/4, Rubber Study Group, December 1944, 4–5. On the enormous

resilience and efficiency of Indigenous smallholders, see Peter Bauer, *The Rubber Industry: A Study in Competition and Monopoly* (Longmans, Green, 1948).

79. E. S. Carr, *Progress Report of Forest Administration in the Province of Assam for the Year 1902–1903* (Shillong Assam Secretariat Printing Office, 1903), 6.

80. See also Theresa Ventura's chapter in this volume.

81. See Kristopher Radford, "Curzon's Cruise: The Pomp and Circumstances of Indian Indirect Rule of the Persian Gulf," *International History Review* 35, no. 4 (2013): 884–904. See also Bérénice Guyot-Réchard, "Tour Diaries and Itinerant Governance in the Eastern Himalayas, 1909–1962," *Historical Journal* 60, no. 4 (2017): 1023–1046.

82. R. N. G., "The Charduar Rubber Plantation: Enterprise of the Assam Government," *Englishman's Overland Mail*, March 31, 1904, 17.

83. Philip Richard Thornhagh Gurdon, *The Khasis* (David Nutt, 1907), 34, 116. Gurdon was superintendent of ethnography in Assam.

84. Kalyanakrishnan Sivaramakrishnan, "Ethics of Nature in Indian Environmental History: A Review Article," *Modern Asian Studies* 49, no. 4 (2015): 1295.

85. The Inner Line Regulation of 1873 marked the boundary between the "administered" and "unadministered" areas of Assam and sought to cordon off various hill tracts from the plains, not least in an attempt to reduce border frictions caused by the steady expansion of British tea gardens and the conflict-ridden wild rubber trade.

86. Major Macgregor, "Notes on Akas and Akaland," *Proceedings of the Asiatic Society of Bengal*, 17, no. 3 (1885), 205.

87. Macgregor, "Notes on Akas and Akaland," 199.

88. Besides violent acts of resistance, the Akas also submitted petitions to the colonial government to protest loss of lands; see "Claims of Kopas Chor Aka Chief to Certain Lands," NAI, Foreign Department, Political A, Progrs. June 1874, no. 223/228, "Translation of a Petition from Midhi Aka Raja, Paru Raja, and Other Five Aka Rajas, to the Deputy Commissioner of Durrung."

89. D. P. Copeland, "Rubber Plantation at Charduar in Assam," NAI, Inspector General of Forest, Working Plans, 1896, Proceedings Nos 1–2, 46.

90. R. G. Woodthorpe, "The Aka Expedition," *Journal of the United Service Institution of India* 18, no. 77 (1889): 432.

91. Berthold Ribbentrop, "Observations and Suggestions Recorded by the Inspector General of Forests to the Government of India in Connection with his Inspection of the Charduar Rubber Plantation in the Darrang district," ASA, Revenue A, 1897, no. 164–165.

92. While tappers received between six and eight annas a day, the cleaning of the rubber was arranged for separately at one anna a seer (weight unit). In 1875, the establishment had also included one Mohurrir on Rs. (rupees) 14 per mensem, for nine months, one Mohurrir on Rs. per mensem 20 for two months, and one Watcher on Rs. 7 per mensem for nine and one-half months.

93. Coventry, *Ficus Elastica*, 2.

94. Charles Brownlow quoted in Watt, *Economic Products of India*, VI, 349.

95. "The Charduar Rubber Plantations in Assam," *Indian Forester* 19, no. 9 (1893): 347.

96. E. G. Chester, "The Tapping of Rubber Trees in the Charduar Rubber Plantation, Assam, 1899," *Indian Forester* 36, no. 5 (1900): 175–179.

97. *Progress Report of Forest Administration in Assam for the Year 1876–77* (Shillong, 1877), 22; Sharma, *Empire's Garden*.

98. On strikes, see *Report on the Administration of Eastern Bengal and Assam, 1906–1907* (Eastern Bengal and Assam Secretariat Press, 1908), 44. On improved salaries and housing conditions, see A. V. Monro and H. Carter, *Progress Report of Forest Administration in the Province of Eastern Bengal and Assam for the Year 1910–1911* (East Bengal and Assam Secretariat Press, 1911), 9, and *Report on the Administration of the Province of Assam for the Year 1878–1879* (Shillong, 1880), 87. For another example of insubordination and resistance, see Gillian McGillivray's chapter in this volume.

99. As noted by Campbell in "Forest Administration Reports for 1896–97 for Assam, Central Provinces and Ajmere," *Indian Forester* 24, no. 6 (1898): 211.

100. See "Waste Land Applied for by Mr. M. Chamney for Cultivation of India Rubber Trees, Darrang," ASA, File No 111, Land Revenue Department, Commissioner's Office, 1898.

101. "The Rubber Industry in India," *India Rubber and Gutta Percha and Electrical Trades Journal: A Record of the Caoutchouc, Gutta Percha, Asbestos, and Allied Industries* 20, no. 2 (1900): 234. This included some of the biggest tea producers at the time, including the Assam Company and the Jorehaut Tea Company; H. A. Antrobus, *A History of the Assam Company 1839–1953* (T. and A. Constable, 1957), 188.

102. "The Rubber Industry in India," 234.

103. "India Rubber," *Homeward Mail from India, China and the East*, July 30, 1900, 1020. See also Berthold Ribbentrop, *Forestry in British India* (Calcutta Office of the Superintendent of Government Printing India, 1900), 199–200.

104. W. R. Fisher, "Cultivation of India-Rubber," *Nature* 1113, no. 43 (1891): 390-391.

105. Most derogatory was the one-time assessment of *Ficus* government plantations by the Chief Commissioner of Assam in 1882 that "work of this kind should be looked on as a toy, to occupy the leisure hours of officers." See "Resolution on the Assam Forest Report for 1880–81," *Assam Gazette*, January 21, 1882, 66.

106. "The Production of India-Rubber in British India," *Board of Trade Journal* 18, no. 105 (1895): 415–417.

107. However, earlier experimental samples of Charduar rubber had already been tested and assessed by the reporter on economic products to the government of India.

108. "Tapping was first begun on a considerable scale in 1899, and the receipts under this head in 1903 amounted to Rs. 13,700;" B. C. Allen, *Assam District Gazetteers, Vol. 5, Darrang* (Pioneer Press, 1905), 149.

109. "Sale of Rubber from the Charduar Plantation in Assam," *Indian Forester* 25, no. 11 (1899): 440. Monetary value is expressed as rupee-anna-paisa; one anna is 1/16 of a rupee and one paisa is 1/64 of a rupee.

110. "Rubber Production in Assam," *Indian Engineering* 29 (January 19, 1901): 42.

111. See also Morris, "Cantor Lectures."

112. "Notice: The Scientific and Technical Departments of the Imperial Institute," *Agricultural Bulletin of the Straits and Federated Malay States* 1, no. 4 (1902), i–ii.

113. Wyndham R. Dunstan, "Report on a Second Sample of Rubber (Ficus elastica) from the Charduar Plantation, Assam," *Imperial Institute, Indian Section. Annual Report for the Year 1899–1900* (Majesty's Stationery Office, 1900), December 8, 1899, 36–37.

114. Dunstan, "Quarterly Report by the Director of the Scientific Department on Enquiries conducted for the Government of India," January 17, 1900; Dunstan, "Report on a Second Sample of Rubber," 29–30.

115. Dunstan, "Report on a Second Sample of Rubber," 29–30.

116. Dunstan, "Report on a Second Sample of Rubber," 36.

117. Dunstan, "Report on a Second Sample of Rubber," 36.

118. See A. Straube, of Siemens Bros & Co, Ltd, to the Royal Gardens, Kew, 19 October 1898, "An Analysis of Sun-Dried Balata Latex," reprinted in J. Ferguson, *All About Rubber and Gutta-Prcha*, 3rd ed. (Colombo, 1899), ccxix–ccxx.

119. Dunstan, "Report on a Sample of Rubber, February 7, 1899," Imperial Institute, Indian Section, Extracts from the Annual Reports, 1898–99, Appendix N, 149.

120. "Ficus Elastica Rubber from the Charduar Plantations, Assam (1905)," in *Selected Reports from the Scientific and Technical Department*, No. 82, IV: Rubber and Gutta Percha, part of *Accounts ad Papers, Colonies and British Possessions*, LIX, ed. Wyndham R. Dunstan (n.p., 1912–1913), 338.

121. Foresters like Brandis also discussed quality requirements directly with rubber "manufacturers in London." G. T. Pearson, "The Preparation of India-Rubber in Assam," May 1872, reprinted in ASA, 43/51, "Experimental Rubber Plantation in Kamrup, 1873," no 6.

122. Henry E. Lowood, "The Calculating Forester: Quantification, Cameral Science, and the Emergence of Scientific Forestry Management in Germany," in *The Quantifying Spirit in the Eighteenth Century*, eds. Tore Frangsmyr et al. (University of California Press, 1991), 315–342; Ravi S. Rajan, *Modernizing Nature: Forestry and Imperial Eco-Development, 1800–1950* (Clarendon Press, 2006).

123. "Rubber Planting in the East," 124.

124. J. B. Carruthers, "Report of the Director of Agriculture for the Year 1908," *Agricultural Bulletin of the Straits and Federated Malay States* 8, no. 9 (1909): 400.

125. Carruthers, "Report of the Director," 400.

126. Moritz von Brescius and Christof Dejung, "The Plantation Gaze: Imperial Careering and Agronomic Knowledge between Europe and the Tropics," *Comparativ* 31, nos. 5/6 (2021): 572–590.

127. Carruthers, "Report of the Director," 401.

128. Carruthers, "Report of the Director," 401.

129. Jürgen Osterhammel, "Geschichtskolumne: Große Transformationen," *Merkur* 65, no. 7 (2011): 627.

130. A. W. Blunt and W. F. L. Tottenham, *Progress Report of Forest Administration in the Province of Assam for the Year 1917–18* (Assam Secretariat Printing Office, 1918), 10.

131. Indicative of the larger shift is that the prominent Assam Valley Rubber Company, Ltd., incorporated in 1897, at the height of rubber exports, was dissolved before 1916. See National Archives, Kew, Trade and Commerce, BT 31/7279/51502, 1897–1916. For collapsing Assam rubber exports, see Department of Statistics, *India, Rubber Statistics, 1919, Statements Relating to Area, Production, Stocks, Exports and Imports of Rubber in India in the year 1919* (Office of the Superintendent of Government Printing India, 1921), National Library, Kolkata, G.P.338.17498 65 (54).

132. Voon Phin Keong, "The Rubber Industry of Burma, 1876–1964," *Journal of Southeast Asian Studies*, 4, no. 2 (1973): 216–228; "Rubber Planting in the East," 124.

133. Blunt and Todd, *Progress Report of Forest Administration in the Province of Assam for the Year 1918–19*, 10.

134. "Resolution on the Report of Forest Administration in Assam for the Year 1918–19," in Blunt and Todd, *Progress Report of Forest Administration in the Province of Assam, 1918–19*, 2.

135. Robert Scott Troup, *The Silviculture of Indian Trees* (Clarendon Press, 1921), 865.

136. F. H. Cavendish, *Quinquennial Review of Forest Administration in the Province of Assam for the Period 1924–1925 to 1928–29 with the Progress Report of Forest Administration for 1928–29* (Assam Government Press, 1929), 4.

Chapter 6

Sugar in Province Wellesley

Converging Streams of Plantation Knowledge in Nineteenth-Century Malaya

Christina Skott

In the 1880s a British visitor to the west coast of the Malay Peninsula found reason to marvel at the views opening up before him:

> The labyrinth of jungles abandoned to snakes and tigers and of waters infested with murderous pirates has been cleansed and reclaimed for industry and order. Well-made roads, better far than most country roads in England, extend from end to end of the province of 170 square miles. Almost the entire area is under cultivation, whether in sugar, rice, tapioca, coffee or cocoanuts, and there are numerous large sugar-mills with machinery of the most recent kind. It seems almost incredible that at the beginning of the century this wealthy and prosperous district was part mangrove swamp, part impenetrable jungle.[1]

The rapid transformation of the so-called Province Wellesley, a strip of land opposite the British settlement on Penang Island, in several ways signaled the start of British expansion on the Malay Peninsula. The English East India Company had founded a trading post on Penang in 1786, but its existence was initially dependent on the volatile relationship with the Sultanate of Kedah on the mainland. It was then mostly for strategic and security reasons that the British acquired land on the mainland in 1800. It took several decades before the area attracted attention as a potential site for colonial agriculture, but the early 1840s saw a sudden interest among Europeans for investment in sugar cultivation, and within a few years several sugar plantations were established. Although other crops, most importantly tapioca, were cultivated in the Province, the focus on sugar continued until the end of the century. But the fortunes of the Province's European plantation owners fluctuated wildly; after a shaky but promising start, the 1880s were a time of crisis. In the 1890s production was at an all-time high, but in the new century, production declined sharply, and by 1913 sugar had been replaced by other crops, mainly rubber.

Sugar cultivation in Province Wellesley thus came to an end as abruptly as it had taken off. Both processes were propelled by events on a global and imperial stage; it was no coincidence that the sudden British interest in investment here took place a decade after the abolition of slavery in the British Empire in 1833. In the West Indies, this led to, among other things, a fall in production and profits, which meant that West Indian planters as well as investors began to look elsewhere. Some planters moved to the East-Indies, Mauritius and India in particular, taking their experience and expertise with them. In India, sugar cultivation was encouraged by the colonial government, and new fields were swiftly established in distant locations.[2] But production in India was hampered by differential import duties, and logistical problems further contributed to a sharp decline in sugar production in the 1840s, so some planters looked to move further onward. The investors who would rush in to acquire land in Province Wellesley, as well as the men who arrived to manage sugar plantations, became crucial actors in processes that drove the global circulation of plantation knowledge.

This chapter aims to see the case of Province Wellesley in Asian and regional contexts. Historians concerned with sugar production in Asia have until recently focused on the emergence of industrial production in Java, India, and the "Sugarlandia" of the Philippines. The mid-nineteenth century saw sugar become a major commodity in Java. By the end of the century, the island had become a globally important site for scientific research and the modernization of processing technology. In several ways, Java also led the way for developments in Province Wellesley.[3] In regional studies of Southeast Asia, however, developments in Malaya have been mentioned only in passing, although among local historians the Province has long attracted attention as Malaya's first destination for indentured labor from India. Within economic history, a recent study has examined Penang Sugar Company as an example of a plantation model where estates were run remotely by "absentee owners."[4] As this chapter aims to show, the rise and eventual demise of Province Wellesley's sugar plantations provide a number of further prisms through which the many facets of plantation knowledge can be observed and reexamined, within global, regional, and in particular, local contexts.

Against global and regional backdrops, and by focusing on the cultivation of cane rather than the processing and manufacturing of sugar, the main aim of this chapter is to highlight the unique local circumstances that enabled and shaped the production of sugar, in particular the dependence on Chinese labor and agricultural experience and skills. It was the profits made by immigrant Chinese agriculturalists growing sugar in the province that drew European attention to the site's potential for large-scale sugar plantations. Having secured ownership of land, Europeans initially became totally dependent on Chinese labor and agricultural knowledge to run plantations and would themselves pay little attention to growing techniques.

Europeans instead focused on the processes of milling and manufacturing sugar, whereby a unique dichotomy was created, a labor division along ethnic lines: Field work was in the hands of largely independent groups of Chinese, whereas Europeans oversaw Indian workers engaged in the milling and manufacturing of sugar.[5] The factory workers had arrived as indentured laborers from the Indian subcontinent, which meant that European plantation owners in Province Wellesley became dependent not only on the volatile changes in migration policies set by the colonial government but on global movements of labor as well. The case of Province Wellesley then illustrates the workings of interactions between the global and the local in determining the success or failure of plantation agriculture.

A New Sugar Colony

In the eighteenth century, British official presence in Southeast Asia had been limited to a trading post in Bencoolen (Benkulu) on the east coast of Sumatra. On the Malay Peninsula, British privateers, so-called country-traders, had operated for a long time, especially along the west coast. One of these was Francis Light, whose campaign for the English East India Company to become established in the region led to the opening of an official trading post on Penang Island in 1786.[6]

The new British trading post quickly attracted new inhabitants: local Malays from the mainland and groups of Chinese, some of whom had arrived in the region generations ago, as well as smaller numbers of Indians and Burmese. Enthusiastic reports compiled by officials in Penang claimed that the lush tropical forest that covered the island was an indication of the fertility of the soil, and extensive forest clearing took place to enable cultivation. As experienced tree cutters, the Malays were commissioned to clear the jungle, Chinese workers were used to prepare the ground, and small-scale agriculture quickly took off with padi and other food stuff. The first commercial crop on Penang Island was pepper, grown by Chinese and European aspiring planters, but pepper was soon replaced by spice trees. This was due to a serendipitous series of global events: As a result of Britain's short occupation of the so-called Spice Islands in the 1790s, thousands of nutmeg and clove seedlings were shipped to Penang.[7]

Cultivation of nutmeg had until then been confined to the Banda islands, tightly guarded by the Dutch who had occupied these small islands since the early seventeenth century. There was therefore little knowledge in Penang about how to grow the nutmeg tree in a commercially viable way, but after years of disappointment and experimentation, nutmeg cultivation took off, and the 1840s were a time of "nutmeg mania," not only in Penang but also in Singapore, which since its founding in 1819 had taken off as the main British trading post in Southeast Asia. Together with Malacca, acquired from the Dutch through treaty, Penang and Singapore formed one administrative unit—the Straits Settlements.

When the eyes of European planters in Penang eventually turned to the mainland, the area had already been ceded to the British for decades. In 1800 the East India Company signed a treaty with the Sultan of Kedah for the lease in perpetuity of a rectangular area from the Kedah River in the north to the border with Perak state in the south, at an annual payment of $10,000. The area, from 1827 referred to as Province Wellesley, was 21 kilometers (13 miles) at its widest and 52 kilometers (32.5 miles) at its longest.[8] In the north, Malay fishermen and woodcutters had long been growing rice and coconuts, whereas the southern parts of the Province were marshy and covered in mangrove.[9] It was here, on a swampy island called Batu Kawan, that groups of Chinese in the 1820s began to grow sugar with commercial success noticed by Europeans in Penang.

Sugar cane had been grown by local Malays for centuries and traded in the form of jaggery and black sugar and syrup.[10] The arrival of Chinese sugar cultivators to the area had, however, started from southern Thailand, where groups of Teochew from Fukien province in south China had moved during the latter half of the eighteenth century.[11] Fukien was a region well known for its sugar production, and so these immigrants possessed the necessary skills and knowledge for growing and processing sugar.

The rise of Penang as an entrepot attracted many of these Teochew, organized around *kongsis*, clan societies, and it was Chinese labor that enabled the establishment of the first European-owned sugar estate on Penang Island in 1838.[12] This was owned and set up by the Brown family—Penang merchants turned planters. The Browns were keen to introduce modern manufacturing techniques, but this ended in disappointment, as "encyclopaedias and elementary works on chemistry were ransacked in vain. The sugar *would* not granulate."[13] It was clear that professional help was needed, and it was at this point that a trickle of European planters from Mauritius were invited to visit Penang.

Attention was now increasingly turned toward the mainland and Chinese sugar cultivators in Batu Kawan in particular. Visiting the Province in the early 1830s, T. J. Newbold noted that a wide range of foodstuff, such as cattle, poultry, and rice, were produced here, arguing that the Province had several advantages over Penang Island for commercial agriculture. Importantly, Newbold also noted the large profits made by the Chinese, who exported their sugar to China.[14] The *Pinang Gazette* reported that Chinese sugar planters "carried away a competent future to their native country, attesting that the employment was lucrative in a high degree."[15]

European interest in the agricultural prospects of Province Wellesley was greatly boosted by the official James Low, who in his 1836 publication *A Dissertation on the Soil and Agriculture of the British Settlement of Penang* gave a detailed account of the Province's soil conditions, pointing out the fertility of the alluvial soil here, especially in comparison to Singapore where two sugar plantations were opened up at this time. An inspection by the governor of Penang confirmed that that "the richness of the soil and the mildness of climate," meant that "no spot could be better selected for agricultural purposes."[16]

Apart from the perceived advantages of topography, soil conditions, and climate, a clear attraction in Province Wellesley was the land situation. Initially, new land was given out at yearly rents, but this was revoked, and land was consequently sold at five to ten rupees per acre, equal to the usual colonial rates of ten shillings per acre.[17] This was a clear advantage compared to the other Straits Settlements, as Malacca at this time still had a complicated system of land rent, and in Singapore no decision had yet been taken regarding land title.

There was, however, a view that sugar production would not be profitable unless the rates of duty on sugar from the Straits Settlements were lowered in relation to rates applied in India. A public meeting by prospective European planters was held in Penang in 1841, but a petition sent to Calcutta was at first rejected. Another petition made to Parliament resulted in a preferential duty being granted to the Straits Settlements. This provided a "sudden impetus" for the cultivation of sugar in Province Wellesley.[18] Behind this impetus were two distinct groups of investors: merchants and traders from Penang with little or no agricultural experience and experienced planters from other sugar growing regions, primarily Mauritius, India, and the West Indies, attracted by the prospects of opening up new sugar fields on virgin land.

Having applied for eight hundred *orlongs* of land,[19] Nathaniel Bacon opened the first European sugar estate in 1840, followed by the Frenchman Joseph Donadieu from Mauritius. By the end of 1841 eighteen requests for 12,800 orlongs of land had been made, and Singapore newspapers could report that "parties in the Mauritius and elsewhere are preparing to embark in a speculation." Within twelve months, eight new European estates sprang up, partly on newly cleared land, partly by Europeans buying up padi land, and work began on extensive networks of canals.[20] In 1845, twenty applications for land were made, and the year 1847 saw fifty-five applications for 27,500 acres.[21]

But the initial enthusiasm waned after a few promising years. In 1848, a general financial crisis hit India, where in the 1830s attempts had been made to introduce West Indian methods of sugar manufacture. These projects failed within a decade, and planters who had not much earlier moved from the West Indies to India now moved on.[22] Among them was Leonard Wray, who started out as a planter in Barbados but had moved to the new sugar fields in India in the early 1840s. After a few years in India, Wray moved on to Province Wellesley where he published a volume entitled *The Practical Sugar Planter* in 1848, which for decades would inform and advise prospective sugar planters throughout the British imperial world.[23]

The late 1840s saw a few years of uncertainty, with European estates changing hands, sometimes selling at a price less than the cost of the machinery. The 1850s looked brighter, and there was a new influx of experienced planters, such as the Frenchman Leopold Chasseriau, who named his estate Malakoff after a French victory in the Crimean war.[24]

European estates were now larger and concentrated in fewer hands, and there were a few substantial plantations owned by wealthy Chinese, backed by Penang merchants. In the late 1840s, there were fourteen European estates, some up to five hundred acres each, but in 1858 this number had gone down to eleven.[25] As before, a smattering of Chinese smallholders also grew sugar cane, in addition to food crops.

The 1850s were also a time when the Province came to the attention of investors in Britain, and a number of plantations were bought by British capitalists who never visited their plantations. The most prominent of these was Edward Horsman, of Baring & Co. in London, who was able to buy six of the best European estates and owned a quarter of the total of 4,340 hectares of cultivated land in 1858. Horsman's estates, registered as a joint stock company in 1876 as Penang Sugar Estates, struggled financially and, after bankruptcy in 1874, were taken over by his wealthy brother-in-law Sir John William Ramsden.[26]

In the last years of the 1850s approximately four thousand tons of sugar were produced annually and exported to Britain as well as China, in addition to approximately two hundred thousand gallons of rum, which were sold to India and Burma.[27] The Province's population also grew rapidly, to reach 67,000 in 1858, and police stations, canals, and roads were constructed at a rapid pace.[28] By the 1860s European domination became apparent, as four-fifths of the sugar grown in the Province came from European plantations. Although production costs on Chinese estates were low, it became increasingly difficult to compete on a scene where substantial capital was needed to invest in the new machinery necessary for profitable sugar manufacture. This meant that Chinese-owned estates of all sizes sold their canes to Europeans for processing.[29]

The early 1860s saw another crisis for all planters, this time brought on by drought, but in the later part of the decade, cultivated areas grew again through clearing of mangrove forest, for both rice and sugar cane.[30] However, during the last decades of the century, expansion of European sugar plantations was not possible. The best land, situated in the north, was still used for padi and other food crops and in the possession of Malay and Chinese smallholders, "who would not sell up."[31] It was also clear that sugar cultivation could not expand further inland due to transportation costs.

Production of sugar in the Province increased in 1883 and 1884, after which the general world depression hit.[32] In this, the Province shared experiences with Java, where sugar producers were thrown into deep crisis at this time. A more localized factor was labor shortages, a problem that worsened in the 1880s, and parts of the Province were reported as "reverting to jungle from want of labourers to cultivate the soil."[33] Chinese planters found new opportunities further south, in the Krian district in the state of Perak, encouraged by British officials who, following the so-called Pangkor Treaty in 1874, implemented policies to develop agriculture in Perak.[34]

By the early 1890s the situation for Province Wellesley's European sugar growers again looked more positive. In 1891 some of the European estates made a profit, at least partly due to the introduction of new technology. The years 1892–1896 turned out to be record years, with 15,600 acres under sugar and 35,700 tons exported, an amount twice the amount exported from Jamaica.[35]

Labor Divisions

The issues that, to the greatest extent, determined the viability of sugar cultivation in Province Wellesley were local and regional rather than global: dependency on local skills and knowledge, as well as overall access to labor. Although laborers from Java constituted part of the workforce, especially in the tapioca industry, the three ethnic groups from which European sugar planters mainly would draw labor were the local Malays, immigrant Chinese, and indentured workers from the Indian subcontinent.

The Malays formed the native ethnic group of the Malay Peninsula. On the west coast Malays were padi cultivators, but they were also seen by Europeans as experts on tree felling and cutting. On Penang Island, the Malays had been instrumental in the initial clearing of forest, and this seems to have been the case in Province Wellesley as well. Malays were also employed as workers on the Alma Estate, the only European-owned plantation growing tapioca only, but overall the local Malays were reluctant to leave their village economy, choosing to remain as growers of padi and versatile food crops.[36] European plantation owners dismissed Malays as plantation workers, mainly employing them for "building sheds" and other less-skilled tasks. This reflected long held views among Europeans in Southeast Asia—that immigrant Chinese were more industrious and hardworking than the Indigenous Malay.

Immigrants from southern China had been present in the region for generations, and in the eighteenth and early nineteenth centuries almost all commercial crops grown in the Malay Peninsula, mainly pepper and gambier, were produced by Chinese agriculturalists.[37] This was well known to prospective European sugar planters, who from the start argued for the use of free labor in Southeast Asia. Contrary to slaves, it was argued, Chinese would not need supervision. A widely held prejudice that Chinese alone had the physical strength and stamina needed in a tropical climate was also aired: A Chinese laborer, it was claimed, "works away like a piece of machinery, apparently without effort and without fatigue."[38]

Another persistent view of the Chinese was that "few labourers in the world can equal them, when working on the account, but on regular wages are most complete eye-servants."[39]

In Province Wellesley, this was the reason for the use of the so-called *rumah kechil* system. This meant that European estates were divided into sections (typically of fifteen to two hundred fifty hectares) and let out to Chinese contractors who were responsible for clearing the land and then grow and harvest the canes and transport them to the mills. The contracts stipulated fixed prices, but owners usually paid an advance, used to buy implements and erect buildings for accommodation.[40] This meant that European planters in the Province initially became entirely dependent on Chinese labor, provided by groups who had already grown sugar in the Province as well as the constant influx of new migrants, so-called *sinkeh*. Whereas the system initially was mutually beneficial, as some of the new European plantation owners had no experience at all of cane cultivation, it gradually became clear that the traditional methods used in the rumah kechil system were ineffective and outdated; in the 1860s the yields per acre was the same as it had been on Chinese plantations in Batu Kawan in the 1830s.[41]

Whereas cultivation was at least partly contracted out to Chinese groups throughout the century, European estate owners became increasingly dependent on indentured Indian labor to work the fields. This had not always been the case; initially, Indian laborers mostly worked in mills and factories, supervised by Europeans, whereas the Chinese until the 1860s had "monopoly of field work."[42] Although this labor division became more blurred over time as increasing numbers of Indians were assigned to the fields, the ethnic separation remained, in work and outside.

The unreliable supply of Indian workers would be problematic for plantation owners throughout the period, but the problems were caused by the Europeans themselves, as ill treatment and miserable living conditions led to high instances of sickness and mortality rates.

Small numbers of laborers from southern India had crossed the Bay of Bengal for decades, but the supply of labor from south India became increasingly regulated by official policies. The system of indenture had been introduced in 1867, a year that marked the transfer of the Straits Settlements from the government of India to the Colonial Office. Laborers from India arrived in their thousands, but the import of indentured labor was abruptly prohibited in 1870s, only to be resumed a few years later.

In the early 1880s the labor situation remained uncertain, and petitions were made by European planters for the authorities to stabilize migration policies.[43] The Indian Immigration Ordinance passed by the Straits Settlements government in 1884 secured access to labor for European planters, but abuse of Indian laborers continued to be an issue that attracted the attention of government and the general public alike. Despite hospitals being built on various European estates, death rates were at times as high as twenty percent. This was at least partly because many of these new arrivals were not used to heavy manual work; officials acknowledged that most of them had been weavers in India, and "never had a changkol in their hands before."[44]

Another problem was the high instances of desertions, something that worsened in the 1890s, as new plantations opening up elsewhere in Malaya secured higher wages; many also wanted to move on to the fast-expanding tobacco plantations in Sumatra.[45]

Growing Sugar: The Circulation of Knowledge

Province Wellesley's natural advantages for sugar cultivation seemed obvious to commentators: the assumed richness of the soil, with a topography that meant the area was intersected by rivers and streams that facilitated transport, as well as the "salubrity" of climate. The most important advantage for sugar production, it was agreed, was that firewood used in the processing of canes was available cheaply and in abundance.[46]

Although parts of Province Wellesley were already cultivated, by Malays mostly growing padi in the north and Chinese growing sugar and other crops in the south, much of the land sold to Europeans had to be cleared. Although the cutting down of trees was done by Malays, the rumah kechil contract included preparation of the land for cultivation. In the 1840s, Wray gave a detailed description of how this was done "for the information of the sugar planters and others in the Straits."[47] After the cutting, clearing, and digging, roots and stumps were burned twice, after which the ashes were spread, manure applied, and the soil was again turned by hoe digging (*changkoling*) before planting could begin.[48]

Although Chinese growing padi used the plough, changkoling by hand remained the main method in cane cultivation in Province Wellesley. This was different from Java, where Chinese sugar planters around Batavia ploughed their sugar fields to save labor on weeding.[49] There were attempts to move away from the labor intensive and uneconomical hoeing, but ploughing using buffaloes caused great difficulties, as newly cleared land contained roots and stumps, and the soil was wet and swampy. Wray described how after a couple of days' rain "the plough buffaloes very often could not move a step without sinking up to their bellies into the soil."[50]

Wray therefore suggested that elephants could be used for ploughing in the Province. This was not new, as elephants caught in the jungle and tamed were widely used as draft animals on the Malay Peninsula, and Low had a decade earlier elaborated in great detail on the prices and sizes of elephants available.[51] In Singapore, Wray himself had observed a ploughing elephant called Raja at work on one of the two sugar plantations there, having "repeatedly walked up and down the furrow with him, and been delighted with his performance." Wray especially recommended small elephants and explained the technicalities of the procedure: "One man holds the plough, and another (the keeper) walks beside the animal, and directs him in this duty. The docile little creature obeys every word that is said to him, and (although, no doubt, sorely tempted) will plough all day between the cane rows, without plucking a single cane."[52]

There is no evidence that elephants would have been used for ploughing in the Province, but the labor-intensive methods of working the soil remained an issue of concern. Wray firmly believed that a "small auxiliary locomotive engine" could be used in for ploughing in the Straits. Providing a drawing of a ploughing "locomotive steam engine and its assistant," he suggested that the engine could be placed on boats along two parallel canals, working the plough with the help of chains and ropes, so that the plough is drawn "backwards and forwards between the two canals."[53] Inspired by experiments in Demerara, a steam plough was indeed tried out on a tapioca plantation in the Province. Although it "worked for some time," it was not seen as viable due to the softness of the ground, and workers eventually returned to the hoe.[54]

The economic use of labor was also an issue in planting canes, which was done around the year, as harvesting had to be spread out due to scarcity of labor and, at least initially, a shortage of sufficient milling capacity.[55] This was different from Java, where sugar was cultivated in rotation with padi. Planting practices also differed from those in Java, as the Chinese in the Province did not use the ratoon method, whereby canes were left to shoot, but new canes were planted after each harvest.[56]

The issue of manuring, that is, whether to use fertilizers, is a theme that meanders through the history of sugar planting in Province Wellesley. In their earliest observations of Chinese cultivation of pepper and spices in Singapore and Penang, Europeans had commented on the heavy use of fertilizers. This was possible as the Chinese "never let anything be wasted which can serve as manure": pig manure mixed with burnt earth, human waste, "urine from coolie lines," as well as traditional fertilizers such as "prawn-dust," fish refuse and blood, and carcasses of animals.[57] A fertilizer used by Malay and Chinese was bat guano (*tai klawa*) transported from limestone caves in Kedah and the island of Langkawi.[58] When European eyes first turned to the profits made by the Chinese in Batu Kawan, it was reported that this was partly due to the versatile range of manure applied.[59] These local fertilizers, especially fish residue and bat guano, were used on European plantations throughout the period.[60]

But it was not only fertilizers that determined the success of cultivation. Varieties of cane were tried and changed, reflecting the ways in which local knowledge and expertise interacted with emerging global exchanges of botanical knowledge. The first European attempts to grow sugar on Penang Island had made use of an imported variety, the so-called Otaheite, obtained from Mauritius but originally brought to the West Indies from Tahiti in the 1790s. Otaheite became widely used in the West Indies as it was thicker and stronger than other varieties and so was more resistant to wind damage.

On the early estates on Penang Island, Otaheite cane was said to grow with "uncommon luxuriance," and the failure of sugar here was ultimately caused by lack of knowledge about processing.[61] Otaheite cane (locally named *tebu telor*) was also first used on European estates in the Province but "did not pay to manufacture into sugar."[62] Planters then turned to local varieties, as the extraordinary size of local canes caught the attention "of those who had seen the comparatively dwarfish plants of India."[63] Writing in 1836, Low listed six cane varieties already grown in the Province, identified by their Malay names.[64] The Chinese on Batu Kawan had grown the largest of the local varieties, *tebu kapor*, also named Selangor cane.[65]

As it happened, the late 1840s were a time of a new intense interest in agriculture in Singapore, driven by the authorities' decision to sell land leases in perpetuity. Experiments with various canes imported from China, Java, and Manila were carried out. All of these, however, failed in favor of indigenous canes, *tebu liat* and *tebu kapor*.[66] It is possible that it was this experimentation that led to the Otaheite variety being replaced by Selangor cane on the European estates in Province Wellesley in the later 1840s.[67]

One crucial factor that continued to steer the choice of cane variety was the presence of disease. In the 1860s, many sugar estates in the Province suffered badly from disease, at least partly a result of several years of drought early in the decade. In 1865, canes suffered from larvae of an insect, and a few years later a new disease was reported, causing "withering of the points of the leaves." This prompted further interest in other traditional local varieties. Writing in 1865, the British official John Cameron listed six varieties of *Tubboo* pointing out that "the only indigenous plant, or those which were early introduced by the Malays themselves, have come into anything like extensive or remunerative production."[68]

Following the difficulties of the early 1860s, the Province's planters began to undertake experimentation in search for more resistant varieties. Java cane and varieties from the West Indies were tried, unsuccessfully.[69] Striped Bourbon was imported from Mauritius in 1866, and this variety proved to be resistant to the disease that had done so much damage and had the additional advantage of maturing more quickly. By the 1880s, the Striped Bourbon had replaced the Selangor cane as the main variety in the Province.[70]

In the 1880s and 1890s experimental nurseries were set up on European plantations, where new varieties were tried out, among them a range of Jamaican canes. In 1886 thirty varieties of sugar were sent from Mauritius, but new attention was also again turned to regional varieties: Planters traveled to Borneo and other islands in the hope of obtaining hardier local plants, as it had been seen in India that local Asian varieties resisted vermin better than imported.[71] This quest for new and hardier cane varieties was largely propelled by a need to counter the Province's weather and climate.

Ecology, Climate, and Weather

The ecological impact of monoculture on soils and, consequently, productivity of the land only gradually entered the consciousness of the Province's European planters.[72] In Singapore, pepper grown in conjunction with gambier had been commercially cultivated by groups of Chinese before the establishment of a British trading post. Pepper was also the first commercial crop in Penang, grown by Chinese and Europeans, but pepper had a severe impact on the soil, and this was at least partly why Penang's planters so eagerly turned to nutmeg, as one cycle of pepper planting (approximately twelve years) came to an end by the turn of the nineteenth century. Nutmeg plants did not exhaust the soil in the same way, although this was not immediately apparent, as soil conditions varied across the island.[73]

There was thus no overall experience among Europeans of how local soils reacted to monoculture on a large scale. In Province Wellesley it soon became clear not only that also here soils varied considerably but that local cultivation already had had an impact. Wray contrasted Chinese and Malay ways of using the land. The Chinese chose more fertile soils, following the principle that it was more profitable to cultivate a smaller area more intensely and therefore paid more attention to hoeing and draining. In comparison, the Malays were seen as representing a haphazard and short-sighted attitude, taking little care in preparing the ground and quickly moving on to new land if the harvest was unsatisfactory. Naturally, for Wray, the Chinese system was the only way forward: Soil looked after will continue to produce "ad infinitum." It was the Europeans' task to "apply our own labour and skill in the furtherance of nature's operations."[74]

The rubber boom taking off in the new century would cause widespread and much discussed environmental damage, but the impact of sugar was observed much earlier.[75] The practice of clean weeding was not indigenous, but brought from China, and this would cause concern, as some officials saw this not compatible with the soil conditions of the region.[76] Despite these warnings, European planters in the Province supported the Chinese method of clean weeding, which tellingly displayed ideas of orderliness and efficiency, which characterized imperial thinking of the day. As it turned out, the British in Malaya later insisted on clean weeding after this had been abandoned on European plantations elsewhere in Southeast Asia.[77]

Soil erosion was also the issue when Wray criticized the Chinese practice of using cane trash as fuel in the processing of sugar, as he argued that returning trash to the soil would ensure "constant fertility."[78] As in Penang, the Province's Chinese independent smallholders were particularly targeted, as surveys carried out by officials revealed that a great deal of land was occupied and cultivated by Chinese who had not taken out title, which not only deprived the authorities of income but also exhausted the soil by intensive cultivation, as it was easier for the planter to move on to another location.[79]

Soil erosion was ultimately one of the reasons planters in the Province made conscious attempts to move away from monoculture. Other local commercial crops, such as coconuts, areca nuts, nipa, and nutmeg had throughout the century been grown on a substantial proportion of available land.[80] Of the alternative crops, tapioca was grown on a larger scale on land less suitable for sugar, and the interest in tapioca grew in the 1890s. In Malacca, tapioca was the main crop, but it was well known that tapioca exhausted the soil to a greater extent than sugar; after three crops, the land had to be allowed to "revert to jungle for 20 or 30 years" before it could be profitably cultivated.[81] Double planting with sugar and tapioca was successful on some estates, such as Golden Grove, but issues of soil exhaustion remained, although experiments of planting exhausted land with cassava (*ubi kayu*) showed good promise.[82]

Apart from the soil exhaustion on cultivated land, the depletion of surrounding forests became a pressing problem in the last decades of the century. Initially, the access to forests and mangrove needed as firewood was seen as an advantage, but the continued use of traditional methods for boiling sugar had a severe impact on wood supplies.[83] Wood shortages were sorely felt in the later decades and led to steep price increases, and this also meant that smaller estates not yet mechanized to use steam power for processing simply had to abandon sugar and turn to indigenous crops such as coconuts, tapioca, or indigo.[84]

Local newspapers often commented on shortages of firewood but also increasingly on the actual ecological impact of the unrestricted cutting down of forests. The "great and very unusual degree of sickness" (dysentery and cholera) among the plantation workers, was now blamed on the "cutting down of large quantities of timber in the vicinity."[85] Trees were consequently planted along newly constructed public roads, nurseries for trees were attached to police stations and other public works, and in the early 1880s it was suggested that that abandoned land should be planted with timber trees to minimize the ecological impact on agriculture.[86] However, official reports as well as correspondence between the Province and Europe make it clear that it was not soil conditions but climate and weather that caused the greatest concerns.

It was initially thought that the mainland had a better climate than Penang Island, and the weather situation was indeed slightly different. Sugar required periods of lower rainfall, and this was normally the case in the Province. But rainfall and weather generally turned out to be unpredictable. Despite the relative evenness in rainfall, droughts did occur, and it was these climactic events and their impact on sugar and other crops that would be observed and reported.[87]

In the early years of the 1840s, drought occurred two years in a row, with the *Pinang Gazette* providing weekly updates. It emerged that sugar plantations in the Province suffered less from droughts than nutmeg plantations, whereas padi had not been substantially affected.[88] The early 1860s saw several years of reoccurring droughts, causing disease in canes.[89] On Penang Island several of the nutmeg estates in the interior were abandoned at this time, and from the Province it was reported sugar plantations "suffered severely from the long, and most unusual drought."[90] In the two following years sugar planters again reported losses due to drought, although the situation improved and cane recovered at the end of 1865.[91]

It was noted, however, that Province Wellesley fared better than Malacca, where British agricultural initiatives were even harder hit by these climate events. There, heavy rain caused attacks by locusts, while drought led to rice shortages and famine, and in 1863, murrain killed most of the cattle.[92] This localized impact of weather and climate was not lost on Malacca's European planters, already struggling with unresolved land issues, and in the end, colonial agriculture in Malacca would largely be unsuccessful in the nineteenth century.

The years 1876–1878 saw the worst modern occurrence of the weather phenomenon now referred to as El Niño. Every part of the world experienced some form of impact: Hawai'i, the Philippines, southern Africa, and northeast Africa saw extensive drought, whereas India and China were hardest hit, with millions dying from hunger.[93] With regard to Southeast Asia, historians have suggested that, overall, El Niño events had a lesser impact.

Still, it can be asked whether Province Wellesley and areas around it were spared the more severe impact of the weather of the "Victorian holocaust" seen elsewhere. In the late 1870s, it was reported from Perak state, south of Province Wellesley, that floods, droughts, insects, rats, and blights caused bad harvests for several successive years, and murrain among the draught cattle had a severe impact on the preparation of land.[94] From the Province, plantation managers wrote that "this matter of the weather" was becoming serious, but no major disasters in cane crops were reported. [95] It also seems that these severe El Niño years caused migration from the east coast of the Malay Peninsula and Borneo to Province Wellesley in particular, indicating that conditions were more favorable here.[96]

It has been suggested that the low profits presented by the Penang Sugar Estates in the 1880s were caused by drought, but there were also excessive rains during this time, causing damage to padi, and various forms of cattle disease reported throughout the decades were blamed on the weather.[97] In neighboring Perak, the spread of cholera due to extreme weather events was experienced almost annually.[98] It seems, then, that for the east coast of the Malay Peninsula, the El Niño of 1878–1879 did not have the profound impact felt on a global scale but also that weather events continued to be a constant concern.

Province Wellesley and Colonial Science

Observations on climate and weather had been made and reported from Penang and Malacca since the early nineteenth century, but these had mainly focused on wind and temperature.[99] During the latter half of the century, reports from Province Wellesley became increasingly concerned with rainfall and droughts and a standing point in official annual reports as well as in correspondence between plantation managers in the Province and company directors in London. As it was increasingly realized that weather had a direct impact on sugar production and profits made, calls were made for setting up weather stations in the Straits Settlements to enhance meteorological knowledge and counter the impact of extreme weather. The establishment of a meteorological observatory in Singapore in the 1840s brought in a more systematic collection of weather observation from around the Straits Settlements, including Province Wellesley.[100]

Scientific interest in meteorology in the Straits Settlements would form an important contribution to global and imperial meteorological science, but this was not the only area where the Province became part of increasingly thickening scientific networks. The search for disease-resistant canes occupied planters in situ and absentee estate owners in the last decades of the century. There was not only communication with disease control networks set up within the British empire but knowledge as well as actual specimens were increasingly obtained from Java, where scientific experiments with local and regional varieties were carried out on a large scale, supported by colonial authorities.

In the 1890s several of the European estates in Province Wellesley also experimented with new alternative crops, some being sent from Kew Gardens to be tried out. Havana tobacco failed as it was believed that the soil was too poor. Coffee was tried for many years with some success, although there were serious doubts about its profitability. Bowstring hemp sent from Mauritius was "not practical," as the processing had to be done in situ. Similar problems were encountered with ramie, known to exhaust the soil, but seen as suitable for "worn out sugar land."[101]

The cultivation of sugar cane was impacted by advances within agricultural chemistry, initiated in the 1840s by the German scientist Justus von Liebig, who had argued that soil exhaustion could be avoided by using manufactured, chemical fertilizers. The end of the century saw the global distribution of chemical fertilizers taking off, partly prompted by the new and very profitable trade in Peruvian guano.[102]

In the Province the situation was different from Java, where fertilizers had not been needed to the same extent, as sugar was often grown in rotation with rice.[103] From the 1870s onward discussions about fertilizers intensified in the Straits Settlements. Experiments whereby bat guano was mixed with other organic substances were carried out, and local fertilizers were analyzed for their chemical properties. There was, however, no consensus on whether "home manure" was to be preferred over the expensive imported fertilizers.[104]

By the 1890s chemical fertilizers in the form of slag and ammonia were increasingly imported from Britain. The fertilizer considered the strongest and preferred if financially viable was Peruvian guano (which by now quickly could be ordered by telegram), but the logistics of finding suitable transportation was often difficult, and freights costs were high. Uncertainties around deliveries meant that trusted fertilizers, such as bat guano and fish refuse, provided by the Chinese were still used on European plantations by the beginning of twentieth century.[105]

One area where the impact of new scientific and technological advances had the most profound impact on production and profits was the technology related to machinery for milling and manufacturing of raw sugar. Milling, the initial process whereby the juice was extracted, was initially dependent on traditional Chinese techniques, where mills consisted of simple vertical wooden or stone rollers, turned by cattle.[106] Although these local methods were initially said to be "superior to Hindustan," they were elaborate, labor intense, and increasingly seen by Europeans as inefficient, particularly in comparison to the increasingly mechanized sugar manufacturing in the West Indies.[107]

The initial period of sugar plantation in Province Wellesley would coincide with a period of great innovation in processing techniques that followed the abolition of slavery in the West Indies. Crucial here was the steam-powered mill fitted with iron or steel crushers, which had first been used in Cuba in the 1790s and had become common in the West Indies by mid-century.[108] In Java, there had been attempts to modernize processing techniques during the British occupation, and steam engines were used along with traditional mills worked by cattle by the mid-1820s.[109] In India, a rush to introduce steam-driven mills in the 1820s also constituted a vulnerability, as much of the machinery was found to be unsuitable, and it became extremely difficult to repair broken machines due to long and difficult transportation up rivers.[110]

In the coastal Straits Settlements transport was not as problematic. However, when two sugar plantations were opened up in Singapore in the 1830s, Chinese methods with a water-driven mill were still used. One of the entrepreneurs, Joseph Balestier, invested and borrowed money to invest in steam engines, but by 1848 he was bankrupt, and the estate had to close.[111] On Penang, the initial attempts at growing sugar had used iron machinery also driven by water.[112] The first steam engines seem to have been imported to Penang not long after, as it was reported in 1844 that the third steam-driven mill had been ordered from England, and in Penang rice mills powered by steam were commonplace in mid-century.[113]

In Province Wellesley, steam-powered sugar mills seem to have been used from the start of European enterprise, as newspapers reported that a third steam engine for milling had been ordered from England already in 1844.[114] This initial push to employ steam was probably driven by the first generation of planters, Frenchmen having arrived from Mauritius, such as Chasseriau, who bought his machinery from France.[115] Writing in 1848, Wray could report that all European estates have "excellent steam-engines." He also outlined further visions for the use of steam power in the fast-progressing cane fields of Province Wellesley, as he suggested that the versatility of steam was not fully utilized in places such as Demerara. Steam could, for example, be used for transport, with "waggons" going at slow speed, but also for pumping water, sawing up timber, and draining.[116] Although there is no evidence that steam power was used in these operations until the very end of the century, the early 1870s saw some of the

Chinese-owned estates beginning to replace the old buffalo-driven mills with steam engines, and by the 1880s, all European-owned plantations were said to be employing steam machinery "of the highest order."[117]

Although the modern steam mills were always pointed out by visitors, some of the novelties attracting attention were related to the manufacturing of raw sugar rather than the milling process. Here, the Province joined the global sugar revolution, nineteenth-century developments whereby sugar manufacturing developed into an industrial project. The most drastic applications of new scientific methods took place within cleansing and reducing processes, whereby the sugar juice was turned into raw sugar.[118]

The most revolutionary invention was the vacuum pan, which replaced the open boiling pan to enable lower boiling temperatures and crucially reduced consumption of fuel.[119] Invented in the 1820s, the vacuum pan spread swiftly, particularly in Asia, and was used globally within a decade. By 1847 one-third of sugar exported from India, Java, and Mauritius was produced using vacuum pans.[120] From Province Wellesley, Wray reported in 1848 that one vacuum pan was in operation, and by 1874, vacuum pans were said to be "extensively adopted" in the Province, in line with development in the rest of Asia's sugar-producing regions.[121]

The reducing process was mechanized further with vacuum pans operating with a centrifuge, invented in the 1840s, in which sugar was spun to separate the molasses.[122] The first sugar-producing areas to adopt these new technologies were Cuba and the Caribbean, but centrifuges were also used in the Philippines, driven by British capitalist interests there.[123] It seems that European estates in Province Wellesley were at the forefront of this new technology; already in 1857 two estates operated "centrifugal machines" imported from Belgium, and in the mid-1860s, centrifuges were said to be commonly used in the Province.[124]

The surge in sugar production in Province Wellesley in the 1890s can to a large extent be explained through the increasing investment in new and ever improved machinery and new technologies, especially on the bigger estates owned by the Penang Sugar Company.[125] It has been suggested that Malaya gained the upper hand in the race for modern technology in comparison to Mauritius and the Philippines due to the fact that both suffered from lack of new capital investment at the end of the century.[126] To this could be added local issues driving the need for labor-saving machinery in the Province: the volatility of access to manual labor, partly caused by frequently changing official migration policies regarding indentured labor.

Conclusion

The viability of sugar production was, ultimately, dependent on the skills, cost, and availability of labor, and this chapter has considered the uniqueness of Province Wellesley and Malaya in this respect. While in Britain extensive parliamentary debates on labor costs contrasted the East and West Indies, ultimately leading to the abolition of slavery, slave labor was never considered in Malaya. Instead, European estate owners were able to rely on different ethnic groups and initially opted for the contract model, where the cultivation process was farmed out to groups of Chinese operating in a strict hierarchical order. As the century wore on, European owners and planters became wholly dependent on indentured labor from India. This means that although nominally free labor was used, varying forms of dependency were always at play. Still, the speed with which sugar cultivation took off here in the 1840s was a direct consequence of the abolition of slavery in the British Empire, here seen through the prism of knowledge transfer.

The immediate effect of the decline in sugar production in the West Indies following abolition was the establishment of large sugar estates in remote parts of India. The sudden collapse of sugar projects in India in the early 1840s became a driver for initial investments of capital and knowledge in this remote spot on the fringes of empire. The career of the sugar planter Wray provides a full illustration of this global circulation of knowledge. Able to compare the West Indies, India, and Province Wellesley, Wray produced the detailed and instructive *Practical Sugar Planter*, a book that quickly became a cornerstone of agricultural literature in the British Empire.

Toward the end of the century, Province Wellesley's sugar plantations were gradually but surely incorporated into a global sugar economy where competition was propelled by increasingly mechanized processing methods. Within the study of plantations, this global industrialization of sugar has contributed to the concept itself, having been increasingly seen as homogenous, enveloped in earlier conceptions of coerced labor and Indigenous peasantry.[127] The story of sugar cultivation in Province Wellesley serves to challenge this concept on several fronts. European attraction to the Province's potential for sugar cane cultivation was largely driven by observations of the profits made by Chinese cultivators already operating there, and later European-owned plantations were entirely dependent on agricultural knowledge and work carried out independently by groups of

Chinese workers. Although the fortunes of European plantation owners fluctuated due to changes in colonial policies, local factors such as lack of agricultural knowledge, unpredictable climate, and the reliance on Chinese experience and skills were decisive throughout the period.

Some of the unique characteristics of Province Wellesley were also at play in the eventual demise of sugar cultivation. After the record years of production in the mid-1890s, rapid decline set in around 1905. By 1913 only twelve hectares were under sugar in Province Wellesley, estates put up for sale attracted no buyers, and the last European sugar factory on the Malay Peninsula closed in 1914.[128]

There was a range of reasons for this abrupt fall. In the 1890s the labor situation overall became more difficult and largely unresolved. After prolonged criticism of the system of indenture locally and in India, indenture in the Straits Settlements was eventually abolished altogether in 1910.[129] Migration from China increased overall, but the supply of laborers was unpredictable due to global events such as the outbreak of the bubonic plague in the 1890s, and newcomers were better paid on the new sugar areas in Perak.[130] Global and regional competition within the sugar industry also became increasingly fierce. Propelled by government support and ambitious schemes of modernization sugar production in Java, the "Oriental Cuba," quadrupled between 1899 and 1907. Most importantly, subsidized beet from Europe began to flood the market. Already in 1900, half of the world's sugar originated from beet production in northern Europe.[131]

The demise of sugar cultivation in the province was also a direct consequence of the acceleration of British expansion in the Peninsula. There had long been strong British interests in the state of Perak, situated to the south of Province Wellesley, where large new tin deposits had been found in the late 1840s. Increasing British intervention had resulted in the so-called Pangkor Treaty of 1874, whereby a British Resident was installed in Perak, eventually leading up to its annexation and the creation of the Malay Federated States in 1895. Whereas expansion into this part of the Malay Peninsula has usually seen as propelled by "politics of tin," some officials at the time considered agricultural policies a priority. As it became clear that there was no further land suitable for sugar in Province Wellesley, European as well as Chinese planters turned their eyes to the south, to the Krian area of Perak, where virgin land waited for investment. However, of the more than twenty sugar plantations eventually set up in Krian, only one was European owned. Sugar cultivation in Perak was now steered by Chinese capital, whereas European planters found a new focus growing coffee in Perak's highlands.[132]

One reason for European reluctance to invest in sugar in Perak was the rather abrupt change in government policies toward sugar as a colonial crop. As British presence in the Peninsula became increasingly formalized, the authorities had to acknowledge that a growing population had to be fed to avoid famine. It was therefore decided to promote the expansion of padi to replace sugar, leading to an irrigation scheme that enabled rice cultivation in Krian, completed in 1906 at high cost.[133]

The story of the swift and rather dramatic introduction of rubber in Malaya is well known and was entirely a result of experiments and acclimatization processes that had been conducted on a global scale and, most importantly, in the botanic gardens of Singapore.[134] The Penang Sugar Company planted its first rubber trees in the mid-1890s and was able to start sales by 1903. By 1905, all major sugar plantations in Province Wellesley had been planted with rubber trees, which also meant one last return to a local crop, as coconut was widely planted as a catch-crop for rubber, the new imperial commodity.[135]

Notes

1. *Saturday Review*, June 26, 1886, 894.

2. See Shahid Amin, *Sugarcane and Sugar in Gorakhpur: An Inquiry into Peasant Production for Capitalist Enterprise in Colonial India* (Oxford University Press, 1984).

3. Ulbe Bosma, *The Sugar Plantation in India and Indonesia: Industrial production, 1770–2010*, 2nd ed. (Cambridge University Press, 2016). On Java, also see Jock H. Galloway, *The Cane Sugar Industry: An Historical Geography from its Origins to 1914* (Cambridge University Press, 1989); G. R. Knight, "From Plantation to Padi-Field: The Origins of the Nineteenth Century Transformation of Java's Sugar Industry," *Modern Asian Studies* 14, no. 2 (1980), 177–204; G. R. Knight, *Sugar, Steam and Steel: The Industrial Project in Colonial* Java, 1830–1885 (University of Adelaide Press, 2014).

4. Sunil S. Amrith, *Crossing the Bay of Bengal: The Furies of Nature and the Fortunes of Migrants* (Harvard University Press, 2013); David Chanderbali, *Indian Indenture in the Straits Settlements, 1872–1910* (Peepal Tree, 2008); Lynn Hollen Lees, "International Management in a Free-Standing Company: The Penang Sugar Estates, Ltd., and the Malayan Sugar Industry, 1851–1914," *Business History Review* 81, no. 1 (2007): 27–57; Kernial Singh Sandhu, *Indians in Malaya* (Cambridge University Press, 1969).

5. See also Nicholas B. Miller's chapter in this volume.

6. See, for example, L. A. Mills, "British Malaya 1824–67," *Journal of the Malaysian Branch of the Royal Asiatic Society* 33, no. 3 (1960): 36–59; Marcus

Langdon, *Penang: The Fourth Presidency of India 1805–1830. Volume 1: Ships, Men and Mansions* (Areca Books, 2013), 5–9.

7. See Christina Skott, "'A Ruinous Infatuation': Nutmeg Cultivation in Early Penang," *Journal of Southeast Asian Studies*, 53, no. 4 (2022): 672–673.

8. See "Treaty with Quedah," in T. J. Newbold, *Political and Statistical Account of the British Settlements in the Straits of Malacca*, vol. 1 (London, 1839), 456–459. The governor of Penang, George Leith, named the province after his friend the Duke (Richard) of Wellesley, governor general of India. See John Thomson, *The Straits of Malacca, Indo-China and China, or Ten Years' Travels, Adventures and Residence Abroad* (London, 1857), 2.

9. The migration from China to Thailand took place during the reign of Thai ruler Phraya Taksin, who was half-Teochew. In 1820, the population of Province Wellesley was 6,000 people, but due to an influx of refugees from Kedah, the population had risen to 47,000 in 1836 of whom 2,000 were Chinese. See Langdon, *Penang*, 10, 222; James Low, "An Account of the Origins and Progress of the British Colonies in the Straits of Malacca," *Journal of the Indian Archipelago and Eastern Asia* 4 (1850): 378; Newbold, *Political and Statistical Account*, 105.

10. James Low, *A Dissertation on the Soil and Agriculture of the British Settlement of Penang, or Prince of Wales Island, in the Straits of Malacca, including Province Wellesley on the Malayan Peninsula* (Singapore Free Press Office, 1836), 49–50; Newbold, *Political and Statistical Account*, 105. It is likely that sugar grass originated in New Guinea, where it was domesticated and traveled to Southeast Asia via Austronesian migration. See Galloway, *Cane Sugar Industry*, 11–18; Peter Griggs, *Global Industry, Local Innovation: The History of Cane Sugar Production in Australia, 1820–1995* (Peter Lang, 2011), 15–17.

11. D. J. M. Tate, *The RGA History of the Plantation Industry in the Malay Peninsula* (Oxford University Press, 1996), 106.

12. The estate was later managed by Europeans, with machinery ordered from Calcutta and expertise provided by visiting planters form Mauritius and Bengal. *Pinang Gazette*, September 4, 1841; *Singapore Free Press*, October 7, 1841.

13. Tate, *RGA History*, 116.

14. Newbold, *Political and Statistical Account*, 100–107.

15. Quoted in Tate, *RGA History*, 108.

16. Low, *A Dissertation on the Soil*, 90; *Pinang Gazette*, December 9, 1843, quoted in *Singapore Free Press*, December 21, 1843.

17. Thomas Braddell, *Singapore and the Straits Settlements Described* (Penang, 1858).

18. The petitioners consisted of fifty-one Europeans, seventy-three Chinese, forty-one Chulias (Indians), seventeen Arabs and Malays, and one Parsee, reflecting the diversity of the planter community at this time. Turnbull, *Straits Settlements*, 144. Singapore was still excluded from this preferential duty, as it was

thought that Singapore mostly acted as an entrepot for sugar from China, Java, and Manila. See James C. Jackson, *Planters and Speculators: Chinese and European Agricultural Enterprise in Malaya, 1786–1921* (University of Malaya Press, 1968), 134; Noel Deerr, *The History of Sugar* (Chapman and Hall, 1950), 2:438; Mills, "British Malaya," 220.

19. 1 orlong = 1.3 acres. Jackson, *Planters and Speculators*, 139.

20. The refugees from Kedah were able to return by the early 1840s and were willing to sell their land to Europeans. But this was problematic, as the land had a multitude of owners, and it became very difficult for Europeans to acquire land in the northern parts of the Province. J. R. Logan, "Journal of an Excursion from Singapúr to Malacca and Pínang," *Journal of the Royal Geographical Society of London* 16 (1846): 321–322; Jackson, *Planters and Speculators*, 141.

21. This also meant that price for land changing hands quickly surged, by November 1845 land sold for three times the price as at the beginning of the year. *Pinang Gazette*, January 3, 1846.

22. This was due to a combination of factors, some of which were local, such as the rising *gur* prices within India.

23. Bosma, *Sugar Plantation in India and Indonesia*, 79.

24. The neighboring Alma Estate was named after another victory won by the British and French.

25. Leonard Wray, *The Practical Sugar Planter, A Complete Account of the Cultivation and Manufacture of the Sugar-Cane* (London, 1848), 125.

26. Due to the absentee ownership, Penang Sugar Company is important as generating sources, in the form of correspondence between Province Wellesley, directors in Penang, and London. The Penang Sugar Company has been examined in detail by Lynn Hollen Lees. See Lynn Hollen Lees, *Planting Empire, Cultivating Subjects: British Malaya, 1786–1941* (Cambridge University Press, 2017); Lees, "International Management in a Free-Standing Company."

27. Though not the focus of this chapter, it is worth noting that large quantities of rum would be produced in the Province throughout the period.

28. The large majority of inhabitants were still the padi-growing Malays in the north. Turnbull, *Straits Settlements*, 14.

29. Tate, *RGA History*, 118; Lees, "International Management in a Free-Standing Company," 33; Constance Mary Turnbull, *A History of Modern Singapore, 1819–2005* (National University of Singapore Press, 2009), 63.

30. "Report for 1865–66," in *Annual Reports of the Straits Settlements, 1855–1941*, ed. Robert L. Jarman (Archive Editions, 1998), 1:709.

31. John Cameron, *Our Tropical Possessions in Malayan India* (London, 1865), 343–344.

32. See Jackson, *Planters and Speculators*, fig. 27.

33. Jackson, *Planters and Speculators*, 152.

34. Tate, *RGA History*, 120–124.

35. Jackson, *Planters and Speculators*, table 12, 154. The southern boundary of the Province had been extended in the Pangkor Treaty of 1874 to the Trans-Krian.

36. David Chanderbali, *Indian Indenture in the Straits Settlements, 1872–1910* (Peepal Tree, 2008), 60–63; G. W. Earl, *Topography and Itinerary of Province Wellesley* (Penang, 1861); Alma Estate (RCMS 103/8/10), Cambridge University Library.

37. See Barbara Watson Andaya and Leonard Y. Andaya, *A History of Malaysia* (Palgrave, 2001), 139–140.

38. Bosma, *Sugar Plantation in India and Indonesia*, 47–48; Wray, *Practical Sugar Planter*, 113; *Report from the Select Committee on Sugar and Coffee Planting 1847–1848*, vol. IV (supplement 1), 9, quoted in Bosma, *Sugar Plantation in India and Indonesia*, 79.

39. F. L. Baumgarten, "Agriculture in Malacca," *Journal of the Indian Archipelago and Eastern Asia* 3 (1849): 14.

40. Wray, *Practical Sugar Planter*, 126–127; *Singapore Free Press*, March 5, 1846.

41. Tate, *RGA History*, 119.

42. *Pinang Gazette*, March 8, 1856.

43. See, for example, a protest from Province Wellesley against the decision to restrict contracts for indentured workers to one year from the earlier five years. "Petition Against the Proposed Amendments to 'The Labour Contracts Ordinance,' 1882," in *Proceedings of the Legislative Council of the Straits Settlements, 1882* (Singapore, 1882), 433.

44. *Straits Settlements Government Gazette*, 1879, quoted in Jackson, *Planters and Speculators*, 151. For abuse of Indian workers, see Chanderbali, *Indian Indenture in the Straits Settlements*, 143–161; "Report by the Principal Medical Officer, Straits Settlements, regarding the state of the Hospital, &c, at Batu Kawan Estate," in *Proceedings of the Legislative Council of the Straits Settlements, 1879* (Singapore, 1879), cccxxxix; Jarman, "Annual Report for 1879," *Annual Reports of the Straits Settlements*, 2:279.

45. Jarman, Annual Report for 1888," *Annual Reports of the Straits Settlements*, 3:359.

46. Arnold Wright and H. A. Cartwright, *Twentieth Century Impressions of British Malaya: Its History, People, Commerce, Industries, and Resources*, abridged ed. (Lloyd's Greater Britain Publishing, 1908), 369; T. M. Ward, "Contribution to the Medical Topography of Prince of Wales Island, or Pulo Pinang," in T. M. Ward and J. P. Grant, *Official Papers on the Medical Statistics and Topography of Malacca and Prince of Wales Island and on the Prevailing Diseases of the Tenasserim Coast* (Penang, 1830), 50–51.

47. Wray, *Practical Sugar Planter*, 41.

48. Jackson, *Planters and Speculators*, 130–131.

49. George Richardson Porter, *The Nature and Properties of the Sugar Cane: With Practical Directions for the Improvement of Its Culture, and the Manufacture of Its Products*, 2nd ed. (London, 1843), 238; Galloway, *Cane Sugar Industry*, 205.

50. Wray, *Practical Sugar Planter*, 116, 130.

51. Low, *Dissertation on the Soil and Agriculture*, 14–15.

52. Wray, *Practical Sugar Planter*, 131, 136.

53. Wray, *Practical Sugar Planter*, 115.

54. Jarman, "Report for 1881," *Annual Reports of the Straits Settlements*, 2:535.

55. Low, *Dissertation on the Soil and Agriculture*, 51.

56. Jackson, *Planters and Speculators*, 131.

57. Logan, "Journal of an Excursion," 305; Henry N. Ridley, *Spices* (Macmillan, 1912), 119–120; Dr [John] Lumsdaine, "Cultivation of Nutmegs and Cloves in Bencoolen," *Journal of the Indian Archipelago and Eastern Asia* 5 (1851): 80; also see Anthony Reid, *A History of Southeast Asia: Critical Crossroads* (Wiley Blackwell, 2015), 194.

58. Jarman, "Report for 1865–1866," *Annual Reports of the Straits Settlements*, 1:709.

59. J. Balestier, "View of the State of Agriculture in the British Possessions in the Straits of Malacca," *Journal of the Indian Archipelago and Eastern Asia* 2 (1848): 142.

60. Jarman, "Report for 1860–1861," *Annual Reports of the Straits Settlements*, 270; Cameron, *Our Tropical Possessions*, 1:341.

61. Wray, *Practical Sugar Planter*, 151; Bosma, *Sugar Plantation in India and Indonesia*, 69.

62. J. M. Vermont, "List of Sugar-Canes Known in Province Wellesley, Straits Settlements," in "Annual Report for 1881," Jarman, *Annual Reports of the Straits Settlements*, Appendix 2, 536–538; Jackson, *Planters and Speculators*, 144.

63. *Singapore Free Press*, October 7, 1841.

64. Low, *Dissertation on the Soil and Agriculture*, 50–51. The issue of identifying cane varieties in Province Wellesley is complicated, as a multitude of Malay names were listed throughout the century. There is also confusion around the term "China cane," which could refer to varieties imported from China and local varieties grown by Chinese.

65. Jackson, *Planters and Speculators*, 130. It seems that this variety was the Chinese sugar cane sent to and tried out in the botanic garden in Calcutta in 1797. See Adrian P. Thomas, "The Establishment of Calcutta Botanic Garden: Plant Transfer, Science and the East India Company, 1786–1806," *Journal of the Royal Asiatic Society* 16, no. 2 (2006): 173.

66. J. T. Thomson, "General Report on the Residency of Singapore, Drawn Up Principally with a View of Illustrating its Agricultural Statistics," *Journal of the Indian Archipelago*, 4 (1850): 139; Timothy P. Barnard, *Nature's Colony: Empire,*

Nation and Environment in the Singapore Botanic Gardens (National University of Singapore Press, 2016), 22.

67. Wray, *Practical Sugar Planter*, 14–15.

68. Cameron, *Our Tropical Possessions*, 340–341.

69. E. M. Underdown to Sir John Ramsden, July 24, 1878. DPEN/301, Malaya Estate records, Pennington-Ramsden family of Muncaster Castle, Muncaster, Cumbria County Council Archives (hereafter Cumbria).

70. Tate, *RGA History*, 128.

71. W. E. M. Cantley and N. Dennys, "Notes on Economic Plants. Straits Settlements," *Journal of the Straits Branch of the Royal Asiatic Society* 18 (1886): 311; J. Turner to J. M. Arnold, August 11, 1898. Penang Sugar Estates Company, Letters and Papers, vol. XXIV, COLL MISC 0373, London School of Economics, London (hereafter LSE). Also see Bosma, *Sugar Plantation in India and Indonesia*, 157.

72. For other instances of ecological precarity, see also the chapters by Gillian McGillivray, Rebekah McCallum, Claudia Roesch, and Moritz von Brescius in this volume.

73. See Skott, " 'A Ruinous Infatuation.' "

74. Wray, *Practical Sugar Planter*, 41–42, 55.

75. Jeyamalar Kathirithamby-Wells, *Nature and Nation: Forests and Development in Peninsular Malaysia* (NIAS Press, 2005), 150.

76. Ridley, *Spices*, 116.

77. Corey Ross, *Ecology and Power in the Age of Empire: Europe and the Transformation of the Tropical World* (Oxford University Press, 2017), 115–116.

78. Wray, *Practical Sugar Planter*, 137–138.

79. Jarman, "Report for 1858–1859," *Annual Reports of the Straits Settlements*, 1:171.

80. With 10,700 acres under cultivation on European estates, only 4,500 were planted with sugar cane; see Jackson, *Planters and Speculators*.

81. "Paper Laid Before the Legislative Council by Command of His Excellency the Governor," *Proceedings of the Legislative Council of the Straits Settlements, 1882* (Singapore, 1882), 324; Jarman, "Report for 1881," *Annual Reports of the Straits Settlements*, 2:547.

82. Earl, *Topography and Itinerary of Province Wellesley*, 11.

83. Earl, *Topography and Itinerary of Province Wellesley*, 12; Knight, "From Plantation to Padi-Field," 177.

84. *Annual Report, Federated Malay States*, 1903, 13.

85. "Penang and Province Wellesley," *Straits Times*, May 13, 1865.

86. Orfeur Cavenagh, *Reminiscences of an Indian Official* (London, 1884), 179–180; Jarman, "Report for 1863–1864," *Annual Reports of the Straits Settlements*, 1:423–424. Planted trees, however, often disappeared as the coolies broke them to "obtain sticks to beat their bullocks with." Jarman, "Report for 1865–1866,"

Annual Reports of the Straits Settlements, 1:709. Also see "Paper Laid before the Legislative Council," 324; Jarman, "Report for 1881," *Annual Reports of the Straits Settlements*, 2:547–548.

87. The west coast of the Peninsula is overall less affected by the monsoon than the east coast.

88. *Pinang Gazette*, February 10, 1844.

89. Turnbull, *Straits Settlements*, 145.

90. Jarman, "Report for 1863–1864," *Annual Reports of the Straits Settlements*, 1:495.

91. Jarman, "Report for 1864–1865," *Annual Reports of the Straits Settlements*, 1:604; Report for 1865–1866, Jarman, *Annual Reports of the Straits Settlements*, 1:709.

92. Jarman, "Report for 1863–1864," *Annual Reports of the Straits Settlements*, 1:395; Report for 1864–1865, Jarman, *Annual Reports of the Straits Settlements*, 1:605; Jarman, "Report for 1865–1866," *Annual Reports of the Straits Settlements*, 1:710.

93. Gregory T. Cushman, *Guano and the Opening of the Pacific World: A Global Ecological History* (Cambridge University Press, 2013), 71; Mike Davis, *Late Victorian Holocausts: El Niño Famines and the Making of the Third World* (Verso, 2017).

94. Council Minutes, Perak, November 3, 1879, quoted in J. R. Wilkinson, *Papers on Malay Subjects*, ed. P. L. Burns (Oxford University Press, 1971), 206.

95. "Penang Sugar Estates Company Limited, Report to Be Presented to the Shareholders," March 1878; L. Ray to Sir John Ramsden, May 20, 1878, Cumbria.

96. Emily Sadka, *The Protected Malay States, 1874–1895* (University of Malaya Press, 1968), 328. See also Han Knapen, "Epidemics, Droughts and Other Uncertainties on Southeast Borneo During the Eighteenth and Nineteenth Centuries," in *Paper Landscapes: Explorations in the Environmental History of Indonesia*, ed. Peter Boomgaard et al. (KITLV Press, 1997), esp. 140.

97. Lees, "International Management in a Free-Standing Company," 43; Jarman, "Report for 1881," *Annual Reports of the Straits Settlements*, 2:532–533.

98. Kathirithamby-Wells, *Nature and Nation*, 6.

99. See, for example J. T. Thomson, "General Report on the Residency of Singapore, Drawn Up Principally with a View of Illustrating its Agricultural Statistics," *Journal of the Indian Archipelago and Eastern Asia* 3 (1849): 625–626. Also see Fiona Williamson, "El Niño and the Human–Environment Nexus: Drought and Vulnerability in Singapore, 1877–1911," in *Droughts, Floods, and Global Climatic Anomalies in the Indian Ocean World*, ed. Philip Gooding (Palgrave Macmillan, 2022), 231–258, where it is argued that in Singapore the drought of 1877 was more severe but had less impact than the later drought of 1902.

100. See Fiona Williamson, "Weathering the Empire: Meteorological Research in the Early British Straits Settlements," *British Journal for the History of Science*

48, no. 3 (2015): 475–492; M. A. Skinner, "Straits Meteorology," *Journal of the Straits Branch of the Royal Asiatic Society* 12 (1883): 245–255.

101. See, for example, J. M. Arnold to John Turner, September 17 and 29, 1897, LSE. Also for ramie, processing was a problem, as this had to be "treated on the spot." J. M. Arnold to J. Turner, January 7, 1898, LSE.

102. Edward D. Melillo, "The First Green Revolution: Debt Peonage and the Making of Nitrogen Fertilizer Trade, 1840–1930," *American Historical Review* 117, no. 4 (2012): 1028–1060; Cushman, *Guano and the Opening of the Pacific World*; Jimmy M. Skaggs, *The Guano Rush: Entrepreneurs and American Overseas Expansion* (Macmillan, 1994); Richard Drayton, *Nature's Government: Science, Imperial Britain, and the "Improvement" of the World* (Yale University Press, 2000), 195.

103. However, when chemical fertilizers initially were used, controversies arose around the impact of sulphate and ammonia on rice. Suzanne Moon, "Empirical Knowledge, Scientific Authority, and Native Development: The Controversy over Sugar/Rice Ecology in the Netherlands East Indies, 1905–1914," *Environment and History* 10, no. 1 (2004): 59–81.

104. Lumsdaine, "Cultivation of Nutmegs," 79–80; J. Turner to J. M. Arnold, October 15, 1897, LSE.

105. J. Turner to J. M. Arnold, 19 May 1898, LSE; *A Statement of Fields Cut during the Fortnight Ending 1st April 1899*, LSE.

106. Jackson, *Planters and Speculators*, 132. This had originally been copied from the Spanish and Portuguese and is said to have been introduced to China by the Jesuits. Sucheta Mazumdar, *Sugar and Society in China: Peasants, Technology and World Market* (Harvard University Press, 1998), 152–153, 157.

107. Low, *Dissertation on the Soil and Agriculture*, 51.

108. Jennifer Tann, "Steam and Sugar: The Diffusion of the Stationary Steam Engine to the Caribbean Sugar Industry, 1770–1840," *History of Technology* 19 (1997): 63–84.

109. Knight, "From Plantation to Padi-Field," 182.

110. Galloway, *Cane Sugar Industry*, 135–141; Knight, *Sugar, Steam, and Steel*, 14; *Report from the Select Committee on Sugar and Coffee Planting*, 1847–48, quoted in Bosma, *Sugar Plantation in India and Indonesia*, 79.

111. Balestier, "View of the State of Agriculture"; Jackson, *Planters and Speculators*, 134–137.

112. *Singapore Free Press*, October 7, 1841.

113. See, for example, an advertisement in *Pinang Gazette and Singapore Chronicle*, September 19, 1863.

114. *Pinang Gazette*, January 6, 1844.

115. *Singapore Free Press*, October 20, 1846; Tate, *RGA History*, 110.

116. Wray, *Practical Sugar Planter*, 117–118, 125, 120.

117. Jarman, "Report for 1871," *Annual Reports of the Straits Settlements*, 2:118; but also see Jackson, *Planters and Speculators*, 133; "Five Years Sojourn in Province Wellesley," *The Field*, July 3, 1880.

118. The final process of turning raw sugar into white sugar was still done in refineries located in Europe.

119. See for example Knight, *Sugar, Steam and Steel*, 16–17. See also Gillian McGillivray's chapter in this volume.

120. Richard Allen, "The Slender, Sweet Thread: Sugar, Capital and Dependency in Mauritius, 1860–1936," *Journal of Imperial and Commonwealth History* 16, no. 2 (1988): 177–200. Deerr, *History of Sugar*, 2:561–562. As sugar production in India saw a sudden decline in the 1840s, vacuum pans there disappeared.

121. Peter Soames, *A Treatise on the Manufacture of Sugar from the Sugar Cane* (London, 1872), 59. Also see Cavenagh, *Reminiscences of an Indian Official*, 279–280.

122. See Deerr, *History of Sugar*, 2:573–577.

123. Filomeno V. Aguilar, *Clash of Spirits: The History of Power and Sugar Planter Hegemony on a Visayan Island* (University of Hawai'i Press, 1998).

124. *Pinang Gazette*, March 1, 1856.

125. Tate, *RGA History*, 119; Lynn Hollen Lees, "International Management in a Free-Standing Company: The Penang Sugar Estates, Ltd., and the Malayan Sugar Industry, 1851–1914," *Business History Review* 81, no. 1 (2007): 43.

126. Knight, *Sugar, Steam and Steel*, 26–27.

127. Ulbe Bosma et al., "Sugarlandia Revisited: Sugar and Colonialism in Asia and the Americas, 1800 to 1940, an Introduction," in *Sugarlandia Revisited: Sugar and Colonialism in Asia and the Americas, 1800–1940*, eds. Ulbe Bosma et al. (Berghahn Books, 2007), 9–12. But see Knight, *Sugar, Steam and Steel*, 4.

128. Tate, *RGA History*, 85–86.

129. Chanderbali, *Indian Indenture in the Straits Settlements*, 198–199. Existing contracts would run until 1913.

130. Jarman, "Report for 1894," *Annual Reports of the Straits Settlements*, 4:191. For the introduction of the so-called Kangani system, see Sandhu, *Indians in Malaya*, 88–90.

131. Knight, *Sugar, Steam and Steel*, 30; Jackson, *Planters and Speculators*, 172; Galloway, *Cane Sugar Industry*, 215–216.

132. Between 1877 and 1888, twenty new Chinese sugar estates had been set up in Krian. Jackson, *Planters and Speculators*, 154–160; Sadka, *Protected Malay States*, 346; Tate, *RGA History*, 120–126.

133. Jackson, *Planters and Speculators*, 170–171; "A Report on the Rice Supply of the Colony and Native States, Straits Settlements," in *Proceedings of the Legislative Council of the Straits Settlements, 1893* (Singapore, 1893), 18.

134. J. H. Drabble, *Rubber in Malaya, 1876–1922: The Genesis of the Industry* (Oxford University Press, 1973), 14–47; Barnard, *Nature's Colony*; Ross, *Ecology and Power*, 99–135; Andaya and Andaya, *History of Malaysia*, 217–218.

135. Jackson, *Planters and Speculators*, 169, 173.

Part IV

Institutionalization

Chapter 7

Cocoa and Coercion

Connected Histories of São Tomé and the Belgian Congo

Marta Macedo

In February 1911 the baron Charles de T'Serclaes de Wommersom addressed the young men present at the Catholic Circle of Louvain, encouraging them "to live, to move, to get out of this narrow Belgium," in other words, to embrace the colonial crusade.[1] T'Serclaes' lecture, a crude piece of propaganda in the broader campaign to portray the Congo as a land of opportunity for audacious White settlers, had the virtue of relying on firsthand knowledge, as he was just returning from a journey to Africa. Accompanied by lieutenant Auguste Jacques, he claimed to have meticulously surveyed the entire Mayombe over three and a half months and to have assessed the local agricultural situation. Separated by the Congo River from Angola to the south, from the Portuguese enclave of Cabinda to the west, from French Congo to the north, and from the other Belgian colonial provinces to the east, these tropical rainforests had many advantages for those willing to start a cash-crop business. The Mayombe was served by no less than three ports (Boma, Cabinda, and Landana), had many navigable rivers, and was crossed by a newly built railway connecting Boma to the north. T'Serclaes did not mention another important strategic advantage: the district's relatively high population, especially when compared with the rest of the colony. T'Serclaes believed that those fertile and mountainous terrains, "our African Ardennes," were "especially prepared for agricultural conquest."[2] The truth is that "conquest" had begun at least a decade before the baron visited the region. Mayombe already possessed an important cluster of plantations almost entirely devoted to cocoa. The baron went to see almost all of them, but he did not stop at the borders of Congo: He also traveled to São Tomé.

> But why shall I talk about the island of São Tomé? Isn't it a Portuguese possession? The question of nationality is irrelevant here. For a long time, São Tomé has been the example—the model—by which planters across the world have abided. The incredible fertility of its soil and the eminently progressive spirit of its planters have all contributed to make this island a book opened both by nature and by the genius of man, a book that must be read and studied.[3]

T'Serclaes was particularly fortunate, because São Tomé, his source of inspiration, was only 36 hours away by steamer from the Congo. In his lecture, he made use of words, numbers, and dozens of pictures to portray the cocoa plantations of this small island in the Gulf of Guinea, presenting in detail the specificities of the cocoa plant and the island's ecology and sociopolitical environment.

By 1911, plantations had transformed São Tomé into a major player in the global cocoa market. Besides generating massive revenues for planters and for the Portuguese empire, these plantations also embodied the "virtues" of modern colonialism, be they the efforts of Europeans to "improve" African lands, to "rescue" African peoples from local enslavement, or to teach them the "moral value of work."[4] Many foreigners who visited the island in the 1910s chose to ignore that São Tomé's labor system, analogous to slavery, had been the object of harsh international criticism.[5] Some, like T'Serclaes, openly endorsed the Portuguese planters' "spirit of humanity."[6] Besides "philanthropic" motivations, importing the São Tomé plantation complex to the Congo raised Belgian subjects' hopes of producing cocoa for internal consumption in their own imperial territory and making a fortune from it.

Cocoa in the Congo however was not simply an economic and industrial affair: It was very much a political endeavor. In the aftermath of the "red rubber" scandal and the subsequent inquiries that brought the Congo into the spotlight, it was clear that the colony needed to be reinvented through the pursuit of more respectable colonial attributes.[7]

Congo's future depended on a different labor regime. Rubber collectors should be transformed into coffee and cocoa plantation laborers running under the guidance of the White man.[8]

This chapter explores the deep entanglements established between São Tomé and the Congo through projects of cocoa plantations over the course of two decades, from the early 1890s to the early 1910s. By following the circulation of human actors, plantation practices, and material objects across these territories, the chapter shows how São Tomé plantations worked as a model, how this model traveled, and how it took root in new lands. It is important to acknowledge that in the 1910s cocoa production was undergoing a major revolution, driven by peasant farmers growing cocoa on small plots in the Gold Coast (today Ghana).[9] However, plantations remained the primary reference for European colonialists.[10]

Growing cocoa in the Congo relied on the successful transplantation and adaptation of plants, but it would be impossible without agronomic technologies, imperial policies, and racialized labor regimes. Although some of those technologies and policies were new, others had been inherited from previous imperial experiences. This paper will try to unveil the material, social, political, and economic dynamics, old and new, local and global, that allowed for those cocoa "cropscapes" to flourish in the Congo.[11] Looking at the relations established between what the historical scholarship tends to perceive as disconnected territories, this paper will contribute to dislocating the common metropolitan-colonial geographies adopted in the study of modern colonialism in Africa and reveal the limitations of narratives centered on nation-based empires.[12] Casting light on Congo-São Tomé networks reveals how late nineteenth-century African colonial projects were made of interimperial logics of cooperation and competition.[13] This paper also engages with an important body of knowledge interested in decentering free wage labor as the paradigmatic twentieth-century working experience.[14] Labor regulations, together with infrastructures and taxation projects, can thus illuminate the state's role in the development of these capitalist projects.

Circulation is a fundamental component of this story, but this chapter does not seek to naturalize the motion of things, people, and ideas across time and space. As such, it pays close attention to how often movement was halted, and sometimes blocked, by multiple frictions.[15] If motion should be taken not as a given but rather a problem to be solved, it is important to highlight the work required for these cocoa plantations to travel and function as a model. More specifically, this chapter will look at the different organizations and institutions, actors (planters, bureaucrats, financial elites, publicists) and, above all, laborers necessary to bring these plantations into existence.[16] That is, Congo plantations resulted from both a real and metaphorical process of translation.[17]

Making Colonial Congo

While sharing many similarities with other European colonial projects, such as the combination of a reformist discourse against slavery with a reality of plunder and racial violence, the Belgian trajectory in Africa has some unique features.[18] It began to bear its first fruits in 1876, a mere four and a half decades after Belgium became a nation itself, when the philanthropic International African Association, uniting national and foreign scientists, politicians, and financiers was formed under the auspices of the Brussels Geographic Conference and King Leopold II.[19] In 1879, this body morphed into the more economically and politically driven International Congo Association. That same year, Henry Morton Stanley launched his third African expedition, traveling across what would become the Congo by going upstream the Congo River, to establish outpost stations and sign treaties with chiefs on behalf of the association and its patron king. On Stanley's return to Europe, Leopold II began an unparallel diplomatic offensive that resulted in the recognition of the International Congo Association's sovereign powers over the territories it controlled in Central Africa at the Berlin Conference of 1884–1885. An area covering nearly two million square kilometers, almost seventy-six times the size of Belgium, would become the Congo Free State.

The sovereign dimensions of the Congo Free State defy easy classifications even amidst the complicated systems of governance of this colonial period in Africa. The Congo was a colony without a metropolis, thereby lacking any oversight by a European parliament; it was a truly odd element in the geopolitics of its time. As an absolute monarchy, Congo was the private domain of Leopold II, and as such, he owned the products of its lands. Before Congo's annexation by the Belgium state in 1908, the territory was managed like a private enterprise by Leopold II and a group of financial, industrial, and commercial elites who owned, together with the Congo Free State, major commercial societies. Regardless of the free trade agreements that were at the core of the Berlin Treaty, Leopold II and his establishment profited from an extraction economy operating under a monopolistic regime. Despite the goal of maximizing profits while keeping investment as low as possible, under Leopold II, the Congo developed some attributes of a modern state: laws, a hierarchical bureaucracy, a judicial system, and an infrastructure for the collection and transmission information. At the capital, Boma, statistics were compiled, taxes were collected, letters were mailed, cases were judged, and, just as importantly, soldiers were trained. The infamous militia-cum-colonial regular army, the Force Publique, played a critical role in Congo's colonization.[20]

After "pacification" campaigns, Belgians tapped into and greatly expanded the existing African trade in elephant ivory.[21] But it was rubber—an essential material for war, communication, and transport industries, craved by European and US markets and highly profitable—that presented the king with a major business opportunity. The infamous rubber trade, the violence it unleashed, and the international campaigns for its suppression that followed have attracted an impressive body of literature.[22] The horrors of rubber collection quotas, floggings, cutoff hands, rapes, and the burning of villages are rightly portrayed as constituting one of the most atrocious episodes in the history of European colonialism: Leopold's "reign of terror." While rubber constituted by far the most visible dimension of the Congo Free State, its brutalities were rather exceptional.[23] The spectacular violence of ivory and rubber for humans and nonhumans has occluded recognition of the slow, but no less insidious, violence of cocoa in Mayombe plantations.[24] In fact, post-emancipation contract labor and obligatory labor were common techniques taking shape in those same years to organize and command labor. Mayombe plantations are thus a privileged site to analyze the new colonial labor regimes that emerged after the Berlin Conference.

There was no ivory and very few rubber plants in the Mayombe. The region was a tropical forest inhabited by a specific ethnic group that bears the name of the region.[25] Men hunted and harvested palm to make palm wine and palm oil, while women cultivated the land, wove fabrics, made pottery, and cared for their families. Both fished. The dense woodlands were however not enough to isolate Mayombe people from Europeans. Since the 1500s, the country provided an important reserve of enslaved persons transported to plantations in the Americas. The flintlocks, pistols, and muskets that were part of the material culture of those groups by the late nineteenth century dated back from those early times.

According to colonial sources the "excesses" of the slave trade made this people "singularly suspicious," "defiant," and, at the same time, incredibly brave.[26] As such, the Belgian occupation of the region was met with fierce resistance. From 1888 until 1894 the Congo Free State suffered several military setbacks. Even officials, unsympathetic toward native populations, narrated battles where "dozen of Mayombe men armed with flintlocks did not hesitate to open fire against fifty soldiers equipped with advanced rifles."[27] It is important to note that flintlocks, and other devices mobilized by colonized people against European technologies of mass murder, were as much real weapons as tools granting them less tangible powers.[28] To counter resistance, the government promised Mayombe peoples an exemption from serving on the Force Publique. Through that guarantee, an undisclosed excess of violence, and an unknown toll in lives, the colonial state eventually came to control the territory during the late nineteenth century. Gradually, "the state forces were able, without too much difficulty, to cross Mayombe from north to south."[29] However, the continuous military activities in the years that followed indicate that "pacification" was never totally achieved.

If "securing its borders was the first duty of a developing state," the next step was to name, describe, map, and collect the land's resources.[30] As soon as Mayombe territories and people were dominated by the military, experts were called in to provide the state with knowledge about economic possibilities.[31] During the second semester of 1893, Emile Laurent, a professor at the Agricultural Institute of Gembloux, and Félix Fuchs, the Congo State inspector, led a thorough scientific expedition traversing the entire region. Like other experts operating in colonial contexts, Laurent was gathering plant specimens to enrich European scientific collections and identifying all the products (existing or to be introduced) that could be of commercial interest, merging botanical and agronomic knowledge.[32] In Mayombe, he found oil palms and precious woods along a myriad of fruits, vegetables, and tubers. But while "from an economic point of view, there are no serious hopes if one bases oneself on banana, cassava, potato, bean and pigeon pea," Laurent firmly believed that "the coffee and the cocoa tree will be particularly successful in Mayombe, especially in the mountainous regions which are cooled by the fogs and the morning rains." The mission's agricultural goals demanded that Laurent pay close attention to the issue of labor. His conclusions followed a clear racialized reasoning: because "the inhabitants of the temperate regions support with great difficulty the agricultural work under the sky of the tropics," the local population should be used as a work force, but since West African men found agricultural work degrading, it was necessary "to accustom the young blacks to toiling the soil." According to Laurent, in state-run colonial stations and in the "well-organized missions," colonists had already "achieved remarkable results" in transforming "idle" Indigenous men into exemplary agricultural workers. But just like T'Serclaes, Laurent also went to São Tomé to see how the cocoa plantation system operated in practice. In December 1893, before returning to Belgium, he would take some time to visit the island, where he was able to appreciate the "splendor of these cultures."[33] Laurent inaugurated what would be a series of travels of Belgian subjects to the Portuguese colony.

São Tomé as a Plantation Model

Plantation-grown cocoa made São Tomé a compelling destination for Belgians working in the Congo from the early 1890s onward. It is important to pay attention to the specific temporalities and contexts that made this geographical encounter possible and fruitful. Officials of the Congo Free State were looking for models that could serve to guide a long-term strategy of cash-crop production and labor mobilization beyond the raw extraction of ivory, rubber, and human lives. São Tomé, one of the oldest European colonial settlements in Africa, had played a pivotal role in establishing this type of enterprise. Since the early sixteenth century and up to 1850, the island operated as a hinge between Brazil and Africa, allowing for a continuous interchange of plants, peoples, and plantation practices.

São Tomé's cocoa production was just the last piece of a long history of land and labor exploitation drawn along the geographies of capitalism, imperialism, and slavery. Before cocoa, two of most important products central to the making of the modern world economy, sugar and coffee, were also grown in São Tomé as plantation crops. When sugar moved to the Caribbean and South America in the late 1500s, São Tomé became a major entrepot in the transatlantic slave trade. The same ships that carried enslaved people from Angola to the Americas and stopped at the island for provisions brought the first plants of coffee and cocoa from Bahia to São Tomé in the late eighteenth century. However, coffee and cocoa were not immediately turned into cash-crops, as the trade of enslaved persons proved to be much more profitable. It was only in the early 1850s, once the slave trade to Brazil was finally abolished, that former merchants operating on both sides of the Atlantic invested their fortunes in plantations in São Tomé, adapting several technologies of land and labor management from the burgeoning coffee plantations of Brazil.[34]

Coffee plantations thrived in São Tomé until 1875, the year in which the apprenticeship period following the abolition of slavery formally ended.[35] Over the course of the 1875–1876 harvest, formerly enslaved men and women abandoned the plantations and refused to work for their old masters, leaving the coffee cherries unpicked and putting many planters in a difficult financial situation. To worsen the planter's position, those years coincided with the decrease of coffee prices in the global market. Highly indebted coffee growers were forced to sell their properties. New planters soon transitioned to cocoa. Transition was possible because the two plants had rather similar environmental and agricultural requirements. With cocoa, land concentrated in fewer hands, plantations grew in size, and planters applied intensive agricultural practices and adopted technology in every aspect of production.[36]

The *Theobroma cacao* tree, an understory species native to the Amazon, had found in São Tomé a perfect habitat an ocean away from its origin. Of the three main varieties of cultivated cocoa—*criollo*, *forastero*, and *trinitario*—São Tomé plantations grew the *forastero* type, especially the *amelonado* subvariety. *Forastero* trees were more resistant to disease, more productive and earlier bearers than *criollo* or *trinitario*, but their beans, rather flat and lacking aroma, were of a merely ordinary kind and paid accordingly. Besides the specific features of different varieties, there are unique characteristics of the plant itself that can help us understand the relations between labor and cocoa. The reproductive system of the cacao tree, for example, challenges common features of other fruit trees. The tree's tiny flowers do not sprout from branches but emerge directly from the trunk, and contrary to other flowers, they have a lifespan of just twenty-four hours. Additionally, they are unscented and thus attractive only to a unique family of microscopic rainforest insects. Of an average of sixty thousand flowers that grow every year on a single tree, only about five percent are pollinated, and less than one percent of those will become fruit. As it is rather common to see cocoa trees bearing flowers and fruits simultaneously at different stages of maturity, harvest is a complicated, sensitive endeavor. Further, profitable cocoa production required knowledge of not only biology but also chemistry and mechanics, as its beans had to be fermented and dried on site before being shipped. The chemical process that occurred during fermentation and drying was of the outmost importance. Besides the influence in color, fermentation determined cocoa's flavor, texture, aroma, and consequently its price. And just like pollination, fermentation was a very uncontrolled process. Bacteria were rather wild, and unlike other industries that involve fermentation, no starter cultures were ever used.

Cocoa was also a problem of finance. Cocoa trees took between three and five years of hard work before bearing fruit and eight years to give a full harvest, demanding important investments with no immediate return of capital. Capital gains, in turn, depended on the value of the crop that was determined by a highly volatile international market. The environmental conditions of São Tomé posed additional difficulties as its harvest season coincided with the rainy season. The history of cocoa on the island was thus the history of efforts to raise the quality of the *amelonado* subvariety, to grow large amounts of it, to cut production costs, and to sell it at a high profit. Considering that custom duties and freight rates to Lisbon were fixed and expensive—not to mention the high interest rates on loans taken to finance operations—planters could mainly intervene in the variable of labor.

For the system to be implemented, it was necessary to secure a steady flow of workers. At the center of the entire enterprise was the new labor regime that emerged after 1876: contract labor. Together with protective tariffs, this was the most important measure that the imperial state put forward to help São Tomé planters. Under the pretense of "rescuing" men and women from Indigenous enslavement, agents located in the interior of Angola "recruited" people in the Angola Hinterland. Angolan people signed five-year contracts declaring their willingness to work in São Tome plantations in exchange for shelter, food, clothing, and an insignificant wage. What made these contracts even more lucrative was the fact that they were permanently renewed: In practice, no laborer would ever return to Angola at the end of his or her contract. The paternalistic picture painted by a foreign missionary in 1896 was distressful but real: "These poor creatures are redeemed from the status of native slavery into the status of European plantation slavery," arriving at the island with "no other prospect than that of being slowly worked to death."[37] Many contemporaries acknowledged that "the contract system which in the Portuguese colonies has superseded slavery is openly acknowledged by planters, newspapers, and statesmen in Parliament to be nothing but the old slavery legalized under a new name." With the support of the imperial state, planters found a way to obtain labor at a much lower cost than if they would have to enter in the real "free labor" market.

From 1875 until 1890, almost 27,000 Angolan men and women landed in São Tomé. Due to high mortality rates, more than 29,000 followed by 1900.[38] With an unusually caustic tone, a Portuguese colonial engineer critical of the plantation's recruitment system suggested that the regular influx of Angolan laborers seemed to suggest that "the island was constantly increasing its surface area."[39] It was only in the 1900s that a British campaign, led by antislavery societies and chocolate manufacturers, unleashed a major investigation on São Tomé labor regime.[40] It is important to note however that not even these reports questioned labor conditions in the plantations: The main concern had always been the nonrepatriation of laborers at the end of their contracts.[41]

What Belgian travelers saw in São Tomé—and tried to mimic in the Congo—were model plantations: fine-tuned and lucrative production machines with modern agronomic technologies employing an army of contract workers and exploring their labor in a scientific and militarized fashion. The use of the term *militarized* is not a mere metaphor. There were several retired officials ruling over São Tomé plantations, and the paradigm of military organization influenced the management of daily life in the fields, the hierarchical organization of plantations spaces and peoples, and their bureaucratic apparatuses.

Terreios (terraces), for example, had a structural role on São Tomé plantations. While conceived in the first instance as place for the desiccation of cocoa, these were also where laborers assembled for morning and evening roll calls. These roll calls were organized very much like military parades: It was not by chance that contemporaries used martial language, such as *forma* (rank) and *destroçar*! (fall out!), to describe these daily routines. Required to stand in silence, laborers were counted, inspected, and grouped at dawn before going to work. At dusk, upon returning from the fields, they were once again tallied, examined, and sometimes punished whenever they had not attained the predefined labor quotas. In 1904, a French botanist noted that "the discipline to which all workers are subjected is much more rigorous than the rules imposed in the French colonies, not only for workers in our railway construction sites but even the militias in Senegal."[42]

Belgian agronomists analyzed and measured the success of São Tomé agricultural operations in terms of cocoa productivity, while colonial propaganda journals stressed their massive and almost instant fortunes, amplifying Belgian expectations.[43] In fact, numbers were solid. In 1894 the island's plantations exported 6,000 tons of cocoa, but by 1903 they were producing more than 22,000 tons.[44] In just a decade, the island had become a major player in the global cocoa market. A specific network combining science, technology, capital, and coerced labor had created a stable commodity and a stable colonial power, making São Tomé a successful plantation story in Africa and a main reference for foreign colonialists.

Cocoa as l'avenir du Congo

In 1898, Belgian authorities expected that "in the not-too-distant future the Independent State will be able to supply Belgium with the 2 million kilograms of cocoa (not including cocoa butter; and prepared cocoa) that it imports annually."[45] To achieve that goal, the Congo Free State's Board for Industry and Agriculture (Direction de l'Industrie et de l'Agriculture) instructed its experts to imitate the best examples of foreign colonies. It became a standard practice to send "several officers . . . to the island of São Tome to gain familiarity with the agronomic methods in place."[46] These experts were those who carried the first cocoa seeds to the Congo in the early 1890s. They were also the ones in charge of acclimatizing those plants at state-run agronomic stations. However, many of the first coffee and cocoa experiments in the Congo had failed. Following the absorption of the Congo Free State as a directly ruled Belgian colony in 1908, the head of the recently founded General Board for Agriculture at the Ministry of the Colonies in 1910 summarized the Congo's agriculture situation in the following terms: "We had in the beginning great illusions regarding Congo's agriculture. People less educated in agricultural matters can successfully sow and transplant colonial plants, but between this amateur work and true colonial agriculture lies an abyss. The difficulties lie not in the seeds or in the growing methods, but in the economic maintenance of such cultures to obtain sufficient and lasting results."[47] In fact, growing cocoa was a matter greater than just expertise with plants and agronomy; it also required a specific production system, the plantation. To get a sense of how cocoa plantations traveled from São Tomé to the Congo, adapted to the Mayombe's ecological environment, and created new social and political relations in the Belgian colony, this section follows the trajectory of several Belgian colonial officers and entrepreneurs, including Victorien Lacourt, one of the earliest planters in the Congo.[48]

Lacourt was an agronomist trained at the École d'Horticulture et d'Agriculture de l'État at Vilvorde. As with so many other highly qualified professionals of his generation, he emigrated and accepted a mission in the Congo.[49] Lacourt reached Léopoldville (now Kinshasa) in mid-1891, where he would become the chief agronomist of the district of Stanley Pool. His main work consisted of experimenting with new crop varieties, including coffee and cocoa. In addition to the normal tasks expected of an agronomist, including writing essays and conducting land surveys, he took part in judiciary inquires and military operations.[50] His deep commitment to the Congo cause earned him an Étoile de Service on his return to Belgium in 1893, the highest honor for services and achievements in the colony.

After three years of colonial proselytizing in his homeland, Lacourt embarked back to the Congo in February 1897, this time to establish his own agricultural enterprise.[51] That was the same year the Congo Free State forced native chiefs to grow cocoa and coffee on state-owned lands.[52] It is known that in the Congo this initiative produced few outcomes, but it was part of a broader campaign linking *l'avenir du Congo* (the future of the Congo) to those specific plants. In 1897, the colonial section at the Brussels International Exposition in Tervuren had a "salon des grands cultures" where cocoa, along with coffee and tobacco, was given great prominence.[53]

Lacourt had been able to acquire one thousand hectares in the Kasai region, ideally suited for rubber, coffee, and cocoa trees. If accessing land was the first task in developing a plantation, it was then necessary to amass the workers to cultivate it. And contrary to São Tomé, where labor was imported, in the Congo, as Belgian socialist leader Emile Vandervelde put it, "the labor on which it was possible to depend in a permanent way was the native labor recruited on the spot."[54] Since 1888, the Congo Free State had decreed the rules by which "voluntary engagement" in labor contracts should abide. Even the unsuspicious Roger Casement recognized that the decree "entered into the most minute details concerning the length of the engagement, the form of the contract, and the payment of wages."[55] If meticulously defined working contracts were also the legal documents governing the relations between São Tomé plantation owners and Angolan laborers, in the Congo contracts came accompanied by taxes enforced on African subjects in the form of money, labor, and/or in kind.[56] Taxes and the infamous Force Publique, which terrorized tax payers created a situation in which workers were coerced into "free" wage labor relations.[57]

This was the backdrop in which Lacourt operated. In 1897, the magazine *La Belgique Coloniale* advertised the success of this "first planter settler in the Congo."[58] As an agronomist, he had examined the terrain, tested methods of cultivation, and chosen the most useful species to propagate. He was also fully "aware of the needs, habits, and customs of the natives." Before embarking to the Congo "he provided himself with a whole set of objects for exchange, mainly fabrics, which constitute the common currency, which will pay for the work he will ask of the natives."[59] However, all this knowledge about "needs, habits, and customs" would be useless without the state's exertion of authority and coercive power "through active and complete cogs: military, justice, administration, missions."[60] Given the thin presence of Europeans across the territory, whether Belgians or others, the state relied heavily on the Force Publique. Lacourt completely depended on them to recruit labor at his plantation on the Sankuru River. Contemporary accounts narrate how he was received as "a great lord" at local villages and how he was able to choose between the "natives that came to enlist *voluntarily* in groups of ten to twenty-five at a time" [italics original]. But it was the complex taxation system—complete with the threat and delivery of violence—that led three hundred of these "voluntary" workers to resettle near his plantation in self-constructed huts "erected according to the indications of an overall plan." The labor regime was very similar to those practiced at São Tomé plantations in terms of organization and schedule. Laborers were grouped in teams of twenty-five men commanded by an overseer, the working day consisted of eight to twelve hours, and men were paid ten centimes a day. Lacourt's plantation arrangements depended on a mixture of punishment and incentive that allowed the system to operate. The stick and carrot metaphor was overtly used to describe the methods deployed to ensure the cooperation of overseers and village chiefs. Lacourt granted gifts as "tokens of friendship" after securing his goals, noting that "salt in particular is of great value" and "recruitment agreements were always accompanied by free libations of malafu [palm wine]."[61]

After obtaining land and labor, Lacourt needed plants. In January 1898, Lacourt already had fifty thousand coffee plants and two hundred cocoa trees under cultivation. The low number of cocoa trees was due to the difficulty in getting seeds, which was to be soon overcome by a trip "to San Tome [sic], to obtain the one hundred thousand cocoa seeds he has ordered."[62]

Cocoa was not difficult to grow in a humid rainforest environment, but the extremely short viability of its seeds—with their germination capacity lasting less than a week—restricted the ability to transport and store it. This led to seeds becoming the subject of a delicate diplomatic affair in 1898 involving the highest members of government in Portugal and Belgium. Following a complaint issued by a minister of His Belgian Majesty in Brussels, the head of the Portuguese Ministério da Marinha e do Ultramar (Overseas and Naval Ministry) sent a confidential letter informing the governor of São Tomé of how to proceed in an episode where Lacourt and his requested seeds were the main protagonists. Following a briefing sent by the governor of the Congo Free State, the Belgian representative decried that while plants had previously traveled smoothly between São Tomé and the Congo, this time Portuguese planters had denied Lacourt his promised cocoa seeds. The Portuguese minister recognized "the inconvenience of directly or indirectly favoring the development of cocoa cultivation in colonies other than ours," but he also admitted the need to maintain highly cordial relations with the Congo Free State. Moreover, he acknowledged that free trade agreements limited the government's ability to prohibit the export of seeds. Even if authorities could prohibit or tax these transactions, it would prove totally inefficient: Given that "one kilogram of seeds could produce 800 plants," foreigners could always smuggle small portions away. After some consideration, the minister instructed the governor of São Tomé to claim that "prohibition was motivated by the necessity of expanding the plantations on the island, where large tracks of uncultivated land demanded all possible seeds."[63]

It is impossible to know where and how Lacourt got his cocoa seeds, but his business was certainly prospering. In Brussels in February 1899, he founded the limited company Plantations Lacourt with a capital of eight hundred thousand francs, together with his brothers.[64] Lacourt confidently calculated the success of the entire enterprise by drafting his budget forecasts with São Tomé in mind. He had established contact with a great São Tomé planter, "Mr. Az . . . ," who shared his balance sheets with him. It can only be surmised that the mysterious "Mr. Az . . ." was Jacob Levy Azancot, owner of the Java Plantation in São Tomé and a prominent figure on the island. In those years, it would have been easy to meet São Tomé planters in Parisian hotels or lavish Swiss resorts. Lacourt recognized, not without some exaggeration, that São Tomé plantations provided their owners "with as much as a 45% margin," but he believed "the operating conditions there are actually inferior to those observed in the Congo."[65] Land cost fifty times more in São Tomé than in the Congo, and labor was six times more expensive.

The success of Lacourt's operations can be measured, like that of São Tomé planters, by his investments in the metropole. By 1908, he had accumulated enough money to buy twenty-four hectares in his hometown Grez-Doiceau, a village thirty kilometers southwest from Brussels, where he built the Château Lacourt. Many postcards of the time labeled the house Vila Sankuru, recognizing the Congolese origins of his fortune. Lacourt's pioneering plantation on the banks of the Sankuru in Kasai province set the terms for the plantations of Mayombe, wherein he would also be an important protagonist.

As in the case of Lacourt's plantations, the power of capital and state united to shape new agricultural projects in the Mayombe. The very first plantation society in the region, the Société Anonyme d'Agriculture et de Plantations du Congo, was founded in 1896 with a capitalization of six hundred thousand francs, thirty percent of which belonged to the Congo Free State. The society received ten thousand hectares of the most fertile land in the region, including terrains in Lenghi and Temvo, sites to the first experimental stations in the Mayombe.

However, the Mayombe railway was the most important state-sponsored initiative to promote plantations. In July 1898, the Société des Chemins de Fer Vicinaux du Mayombe was created to build a narrow-gauge railway linking Boma to the navigable Chiluango River basin. The Congo Free State, the largest stockholder, amassed three million francs of capital together with two important credit institutions and a group of Anvers capitalists. Through a convention signed between the Society and the Congo Free State in September of that year, the company received a concession of one thousand hectares of land for each kilometer of railway built, to be sourced from the public lands of the Lower Congo.[66] In other words, the concession allowed for the privatization of communal lands on both sides of the railway and its gratuitous commercialization. To cope with financial difficulties, the society had already disposed of one hundred thousand hectares of land by 1899, prior to the inauguration of the railway's first kilometers. To put the scale of those concessions into perspective, the island of São Tomé measures only 85,900 hectares, including large tracks of uncultivatable mountains. As contemporaries put it, "the island of São Tomé would disappear like a speck in the immense Congo basin."[67]

The Mayombe railway preceded the development of the territories it would cross, giving rise to a process of land grabbing and capitalist speculation (Fig. 7.1). Until 1900, seven companies were created to explore the region's bounty.[68] These were large-scale limited liability companies whose capitalization amounted to more than eleven million francs. The shares of these agricultural societies were held by colonial officers, industrialists, bankers, and professionals of all sorts, weaving a dense network

Figure 7.1. Map of agricultural concessions in the Mayombe, Ministère des Colonies—administration de l'Agriculture. *Source:* Notes pratiques pour les Colons agricoles: L'amélioration et l'extension de la culture du cacaoyer au Congo belge (Imprimerie Industrielle et Financière, 1914). Public domain.

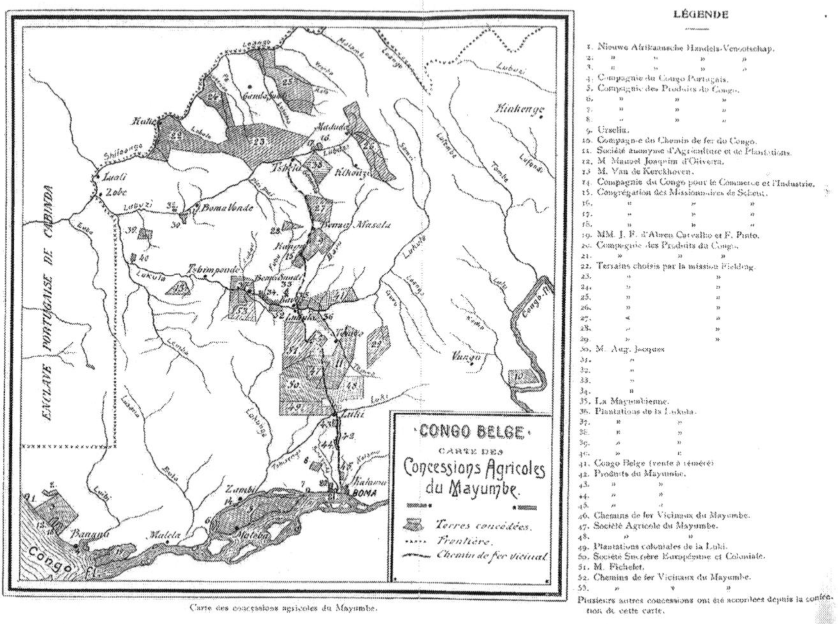

that linked the Congo with industrial and financial interests in Belgium. It is important to note the presence of aristocratic families among the stockholders, demonstrating that plantations were seen as respectable businesses.

The Urselia plantation, owned by the members of the aristocratic d'Ursel family, reveals the extent to which São Tomé's plantations served as the blueprint for the exploration of the Mayombe.[69] Urselia occupied four thousand hectares along the Mayombe railway, and its main business was cocoa production. Hippolyte d'Ursel's powerful ties with the higher echelons of Belgian politics and industry were essential in the process of land acquisition. He obtained the property in 1898 from the French firm Daumas et Compagnie, which had operated in the Mayombe before the existence of the Congo Free State. The estate itself was put under the direction of Norbert Diderrich.[70] Diderrich, a civil and mining engineer from the Université de Louvain, went to the Congo in 1890 as a geologist in the service of the Compagnie du Congo pour le Commerce et l'Industrie, one of the earliest and most powerful companies to operate in the colony. Upon his return to Belgium, he was praised for his surveys of the Katanga region and nominated as director for the Congo Free State's recently created Board for Industry and Agriculture. In 1894, Diderrich would be the person in charge of founding the agricultural stations of Lenghi and Temvo. Diderrich would also conduct the survey for the Mayombe railway line, serve as its first director, and involve himself, like Lacourt, with other plantations in the region.[71] He traveled to São Tomé in July 1898 to learn from the agricultural techniques practiced there.

T'Serclaes's travel companion, Jacques, was the one who actually ruled over Urselia in its first years.[72] Unlike Lacourt and Diderrich, Jacques had no education beyond elementary school when he embarked for the Congo in 1889 to serve in the First Lancers Regiment. His fate changed when he joined the Force Publique operating in the Mayombe. He became famous after taking part in some of the most violent military operations in the region, his contemporaries dubbing him the "King of the Mayombe." In late 1898, after a sojourn in Belgium, the Congo Free State "lent" him to the d'Ursel family to work on their estate. During the rainy season of 1899 and 1900, he oversaw the planting of more than five hundred thousand cocoa trees.[73] The seeds were sourced from the nearby Temvo experimental station. The spacing of the cocoa trees four meters from each other resembled practice at São Tomé plantations, as did the processing of their fruit, including the drying trays and fermentation boxes (Figs. 7.2 and 7.3).[74] The diet of Urselia laborers, composed of dry fish from Moçamedes, slated meat from Argentina, and rice also mimicked that of São Tomé plantations.

Jacques visited São Tomé in 1901, and eight laborers were later recruited from São Tomé to teach Congo natives the routines of the cocoa tree.[75] In 1908, Urselia had one thousand hectares of virgin forest under cultivation, produced two hundred tons of cocoa that were grown, and harvested and processed by four hundred Mayombe men. In São Tomé, Belgian planters had learned that military-like discipline was an essential component of putting Native peoples to work. Octave Louwers, a magistrate and an influential figure of the Belgian colonial milieu, described "a magnificent and impressive scene" on his visit to Urselia to regularize

Figure 7.2. Cocoa drying trays at the Urselia plantation, Mayombe. *Source:* Author's collection.

Figure 7.3. Cocoa Drying Trays at the Vista Alegre plantation, São Tomé. *Source:* Author's collection.

working contracts. In the morning, "workers lined up like soldiers, well-disciplined . . . under the State's flag which one could hear flapping in the wind in the profound silence that prevailed."[76]

The life of Jacques is also a good reminder of the widespread use of violence in the plantation economy, especially in frontier regions. During the years in which he administered, he also participated in several military expeditions against "revolting natives." These raids were meant to force chiefs to supply workers or to recuperate those who had fled the plantations. His accumulated experience in agriculture, the army, and seed capital amassed during his employ as an administrator for the Ursel family allowed him to eventually venture out for himself. In 1904 he obtained a concession of three hundred hectares to grow his own cocoa (Fig. 7.4).[77]

Creating, maintaining, and developing plantations in the Mayombe depended on constant travel and transits between the Congo and São Tomé. Besides T'Serclaes, Lacourt, Diderrich, and Jacques, many other Belgians crossed the imperial boundary. A quick and incomplete survey shows how officials, entrepreneurs, capitalists, and experts like Óscar Michaux (1894); Alex Delcommune, Albert Thys and Valere Mabbile (1899); Theodore Masui (1900); Pierre Danco (1902); Louis Joseph Royaux (1908); and Paul Drousie (1911) moved in and out of the Congo to São Tomé to understand how Portuguese colonialists explored land, managed labor, and grew cocoa.[78] It is probable that many others engaged in these same fact-finding journeys for plantation exploitation.

Figure 7.4. The plantation of Auguste Jacques in Makaïa-Vuabi, Charles de T'Serclaes de Wommersom. *Source: À travers les plantations du Mayombe et de San Thomé* (Maison d'Editions "L'editorial," 1911): 24–25. Public domain.

Conclusion

Plantations in the Mayombe reached their apogee in 1910, when the region exported nine hundred tons of cocoa. However, the Congo would never supply more than ten percent of all the cocoa consumed in Belgium. This can be seen as a meager result compared to the thirty-five thousand tons that São Tomé plantations put on the market that same year. But such indicators of success or failure do not properly explain the relevance of these production systems in feeding the imagination of colonialists about how to make African workers capable of supplying the industries in the global north with their much needed raw materials.[79] Mayombe plantations set the stage for other experiments in cotton, palm oil, and coffee, and the labor struggles relating to cocoa would inform the development of alternate forms of forced labor that would structure the agricultural sector in the Congo in the following decades. Coerced crop production through obligatory cash crop schemes—mainly practiced for cotton in the 1920s in the Belgian Congo—would serve as a reference for other imperial powers in Africa. Inverting the circulation, the Congo's regime of cotton production would inspire the policies of Portuguese imperial authorities in Mozambique with the most atrocious consequences.[80]

In 1912, expectations of the virtuous potential of Mayombe plantations were still high, coming even from men like the Protestant Reverend John Harris, who drew on an impressive abolitionist resumé as secretary of the Anti-Slavery and Aborigines' Protection Society. In a "report for private use" addressed to an important British chocolate manufacturer, he claimed that after crossing the Mayombe, he could hardly "imagine a track of country more ideally suited to the cultivation of cocoa."[81] Jacques's plantation, for instance, was "the most admirably organized we have seen." Although Jacques was "by no means an ideal character," and "a certain amount of harshness is occasionally practiced upon the employees," Harris distanced these labor practices form the slave-like ones he denounced in São Tomé.[82] He even suggested that British manufactures should "enter into a contract directly with the free planters of Mayombe" to buy their crop. This "would render a signal service to the cause of progress in the Congo and to the native races of this land." He was more suspicious of Catholic priests and the "fake orphanage system" that sustained the cocoa farms of Mayombe Catholic Missions. Harris's position shows the blurred lines that defined what was acceptable and unacceptable in terms of labor and rule and how this reflected specific prejudices.

Politics of comparison, be it the ways colonial governments continuously measured their differences and policed each other's initiatives, were the norm of colonial relations.[83] Experiments of cocoa interlinking Belgian Congo and São Tomé exhibit such politics in action. These neighboring colonies, lacking any imperial connection, were stages for multiple exchanges forged by people (planters, colonial officials, experts, and laborers) but also enacted by plants, technological regimes, and coerced labor systems. This chapter discussed how comparison and the politics of colonial cooperation and competition helped actors imagine a new future for the Congo after the "red rubber" scandal, one centered around cocoa, plantations, and contract labor.[84] Additionally, this chapter demonstrated how the process of building actual plantations was a much patchier and conflictive process than actors wanted to acknowledge. Converting the Mayombe into a civilized territory similar to São Tomé was never entirely possible, but the experimental nature of the initiative is nonetheless a good reminder of the transformative aspect of these transimperial relations. Cocoa sowed the seeds of modern race and labor relations that would be reaped some decades later in the form of cotton bales and palm oil barrels.

Notes

1. Charles de T'Serclaes de Wommersom, *À travers les plantations du Mayombe et de San Thomé* (Maison d'Editions "L'editorial," 1911), 11. All translations are my own.

2. T'Serclaes de Wommersom, *À travers les plantations*, 8, 17.

3. T'Serclaes de Wommersom, *À travers les plantations*, 19.

4. Miguel Bandeira Jeronimo, *The "Civilizing Mission" of Portuguese Colonialism, 1870–1930* (Palgrave Macmillan, 2015). On São Tomé plantations, see Marta Macedo, "Standard Cocoa: Transnational Networks and Technoscientific Regimes in West African Plantations," *Technology and Culture* 57, no. 3 (2016): 557–585. See also Ted McCormick's, Moritz von Brescius', and Theresa Ventura's chapters in this volume.

5. On the São Tomé labor system and the international campaigns against it, see Kevin Grant, *A Civilised Savagery: Britain and the New Slaveries in Africa, 1884–1926* (Routledge, 2005); Catherine Higgs, *Chocolate Islands: Cocoa, Slavery, and Colonial Africa* (Ohio University Press, 2012).

6. T'Serclaes de Wommersom, *À travers les plantations*, 63.

7. *Red Rubber* was the title of the British journalist and activist E. D. Morel's monograph denouncing the rubber labor practices in the Congo. E. D. Morel, *Red Rubber: The Story of the Rubber Slave Trade Flourishing on the Congo in the*

Year of Grace 1906 (Nassau Print, 1906). On that subject, see Adam Hochschild, *King Leopold's Ghost: A Story of Greed, Terror and Heroism in Colonial Africa* (Macmillan, 1999); Grant, *A Civilised Savagery*. For a reappraisal of this and other themes of Congo's colonial history, see Idesbald Goddeeris et al., eds., *Le Congo colonial: une histoire en questions* (Renaissance du livre, 2020).

8. Literature has already made clear that violence would also be central in the making and sustaining of the plantation system in the Mayombe. See for example Kajsa Elkholm Friedman, *Catastrophe and Creation: The Transformation of an African Culture* (Harwood Academic Publishers, 1991).

9. Francesca Bray et al., *Moving Crops and the Scales of History* (Yale University Press, 2023), 48–52.

10. The European cultural bias toward the plantation mode of production of cocoa in Western Africa has been addressed by Corey Ross, "The Plantation Paradigm: Colonial Agronomy, African Farmers, and the Global Cocoa Boom, 1870s–1940s," *Journal of Global History* 9, no. 1 (2014): 49–71.

11. The concept of "cropscape," exploring the ever-mutating assemblages of human and nonhuman, symbolic, and social elements within which a particular crop flourishes or fails in a specific place and time, has served as an inspiration to narrate this cocoa story. See Bray et al., *Moving Crops*.

12. The importance of following transnational movements and networks when discussing colonial histories has been put forward eloquently by Frederick Cooper, *Colonialism in Question: Theory, Knowledge, History* (University of California Press, 2005).

13. Daniel Hedinger and Nadin Heé, "Transimperial History: Connectivity, Cooperation and Competition," *Journal of Modern European History* 16, no. 4 (2018): 429–452; Ulrike Lindner, "New Forms of Knowledge Exchange Between Imperial Powers: The Development of the Institut Colonial International (ICI) since the End of the 19th Century," in *Encounters of Empires: Interimperial Transfers and Imperial Manifestations, 1870–1950*, eds. Volker Barth and Roland Czetowski (Bloomsbury, 2015).

14. Marcel van der Linden, *Workers of the World: Essays toward a Global Labor History* (Brill, 2008); Marcel van der Linden, ed., *Humanitarian Intervention and Changing Labor Relations: The Long-term Consequences of the Abolition of the Slave Trade* (Brill, 2011); Clare Anderson, *Convicts: A Global History* (Cambridge University Press, 2022).

15. On the operative uses of the "friction" metaphor to explore the multiple conflicting interactions that are part of global movements of things and people, see Anna Lowenhaupt Tsing, *Friction: An Ethnography of Global Connection* (Princeton University Press, 2005).

16. Jane Burbank and Frederick Cooper, *Empires in World History: Power and the Politics of Difference* (Princeton University Press, 2010). The International Colonial Institute, studied by Ulrike Lindner and Benoit Daviron, as an example of the circulation of knowledge between European empires, is particularly relevant.

However, in this article I propose that less formal institutions and actors need to be incorporated to understand the making of collective imperial knowledge. See Lindner, "New Forms of Knowledge Exchange"; Benoit Daviron, "Mobilizing Labour in African Agriculture: The Role of the International Colonial Institute in the Elaboration of a Standard of Colonial Administration, 1895–1930," *Journal of Global History* 5, no. 3 (2010): 479–501.

17. The idea of "translation" is developed in Fa-ti Fan, "The Global Turn in the History of Science," *East Asian Science, Technology and Society: An International Journal* 6, no. 2 (2012): 249–258.

18. For the history of colonial Congo, see David Van Reybrouck, *Congo: The Epic History of a People* (Harper Collins, 2014); Jean-Luc Vellut, ed., *La Mémoire du Congo: le temps colonial* (Snoeck, 2005); Idesbald Goddeeris et al., *Le Congo colonial*; Patricia Van Schuylenbergh et al., eds., *L'Afrique belge aux XIXe et XXe siècles* (Peter Lang Verlag, 2014).

19. Guy Vanthemsche, *Belgium and the Congo, 1885–1980* (Cambridge University Press, 2012); Vincent Viaene, "King Leopold's Imperialism and the Origins of the Belgian Colonial Party, 1860–1905," *Journal of Modern History* 80, no. 4 (2008): 741–790.

20. Jean-Luc Vellut, "La violence armée dans l'État Indépendant du Congo. Ténèbres et clartés dans l'histoire d'un État conquérant," *Cultures et Développement* 16, no. 3–4 (1984): 671–707.

21. Listed as one of the main achievements of 1893, the propagandist journal *Le Mouvement Géographique* celebrated "the largest public sale of ivory that has taken place so far on the European continent" in October that year. Alphonse-Jules Wauters, "État Indépendant du Congo," *Le Mouvement Géographique* 11, no. 1 (1894): 2. To gather the seventy-one tons of ivory traded in Anvers, almost three hundred elephants had to be killed.

22. Hochschild, *King Leopold's Ghost*; Grant, *A Civilised Savagery*; Dean Pavlakis, *British Humanitarianism and the Congo Reform Movement, 1896–1913* (Routledge, 2018).

23. Jean Stengers, *Congo, mythes et réalités* (Racine, 2005).

24. Friedman, *Catastrophe and Creation*.

25. Information about the Mayombe people had been collected by Cyrille Van Overbergh, *Les Mayombe: Collections de monographies ethnographiques* (Institut International de Bibliographie, 1907). These colonial ethnographies are incredibly rich and problematic sources that deserve close scrutiny. See Jan Vansina, "The Ethnographic Account as a Genre in Central Africa," *Paideuma* 33 (1987): 433–444.

26. Lieutenent Maurice Gilmont, quoted in Overbergh, *Les Mayombe*, 73.

27. Overbergh, *Les Mayombe*, 78.

28. On the multiple meanings of these technological artifacts in Central Africa, see Giacomo Macola, *The Gun in Central Africa* (Ohio University Press, 2015).

29. Norbert Diderrich, quoted in Overbergh, *Les Mayombe*, 434.

30. Norbert Diderrich, quoted in Overbergh, *Les Mayombe*, 434.

31. Émile Laurent, "Le Bas-Congo: sa flore et son agriculture," *Bulletin de la Société Royale de Botanique de Belgique* 33 (1894): 37–56.

32. Émile Wildeman, *Plantae Laurentianae: ou énumération des plantes récoltées au Congo en 1893 et 1895–1896 par Émile Laurent* (Ve Monnom, 1903).

33. *Musée Royal de l'Afrique centrale*, Tervuren, Fonds Théophile Wahis, correspondence form Émile Laurent, HA.01.0202.236.

34. Marta Macedo, "Coffee on the Move: Technology, Labour and Race in the Making of a Transatlantic Plantation System," *Mobilities* 16, no. 2 (2021): 262–272. Other discussions of specific forms of management knowledge on plantations can be found in the chapters by Theresa Ventura, Gillian McGillivray, Claudia Roesch, and Rebekah McCallum in this volume.

35. The abolition of slavery in the Portuguese colonies in Africa was a gradual, convoluted process that began in 1856 with the mandatory registration of slaves and "freed Africans" (*libertos*) followed by an abolition decree in 1869. A postabolition "apprenticeship" period ended in 1875 in São Tomé. After 1876, other forms of coerced labor recruitment were established. These lasted well beyond the second half of the twentieth century. On the history of São Tomé, see Isabel Castro Henriques, *São Tomé e Príncipe: A Invenção de Uma Sociedade* (Vega Editora, 2000); Augusto Nascimento, "S. Tomé na segunda metade de oitocentos: nascimento de uma sociedade colonial" (Master's thesis, Faculdade de Ciências Sociais e Humanas, Universidade Nova de Lisboa, 1992); Augusto Nascimento, *Poderes e quotidiano nas roças de S. Tomé e Príncipe: de finais de oitocentos a meados de novecentos* (Tipografia Lousanense, 2002).

36. Macedo, "Standard Cocoa."

37. Heli Chatelain, "African Slavery: Its Status and the Anti-Slavery Movement in Europe," in *Africa and the American Negro*, ed. John Bowen (Gammon Theological Seminary, 1896), 103–112, 108.

38. Mortality rates sometimes reached fifteen percent; see *Diário de Notícias*, November 4, 1904.

39. Ezequiel de Campos, quoted in Teresa Nunes, "O ideário republicano de Ezequiel de Campos: 1900–1919" (PhD diss., University of Lisbon, 2011), 207.

40. See note 3.

41. See for instance, William Cadbury, *Os Serviçais de S. Tomé. Relatório de uma visita às ilhas de S.Tomé e Príncipe e Angola, feita em 1908, para observar as condições da mão—de-obra empregada nas roças de cacau da África Portuguesa* (Livraria Bertrand, 1910).

42. Auguste Chevalier, *Le Cacaoyer dans L'ouest Africain*, vol. IV: *Les végétaux utiles de L'Afrique tropicale française* (A. Challamel, 1908), 64.

43. Théodore Masui, "Voyage a l'ile de san-Thomé," *Bulletin de la Société d'Études Coloniales* 8, no. 4–5 (1901): 223–249, 293–320; Marcel de Blochouse, "La Colonie portugaise de l'Ile de San Thomé sous l'Equateur." *Annales de Gembloux*

15, no. 5 and 7 (1905): 250–259, 381–393; Paul Drousie, "Notes sur l'agriculture à Sao Thomé," *Bulletin Agricole du Congo Belge* 3 (1912): 867–910. L'Île de San Thome et ses plantations de caféiers et cacaoyers," *Le Mouvement Géographique* 14, no. 8 (1897): 89–91; "L'Île de San Thome," *Le Mouvement Geographique* 16, no. 59 (1899): 601–603.

44. Auguste Chevalier, "Le cacao: sa production et as consommation dans le monde," *Annales de Geographie* 15, no. 82 (1906): 289–298.

45. René Vauthier, "La taille du cacaotier," *La Belgique Coloniale* 4, no. 39 (1898): 459.

46. Edmond Leplae, *L'Agriculture du Congo Belge. Rapport sur les années 1911 and 1912* (Imprimerie Industrielle et Financière, 1913), 21.

47. Leplae, *L'Agriculture du Congo Belge*, 21.

48. P. Van den Abeele, "Lacourt (Victorien Joseph Prosper)," *Biographie Coloniale Belge*, vol. 4 (1955): col. 467–472.

49. From the 1880s onward, the Congo and several countries in South America were the logical destination for many young men with university degrees that could not find work in Belgium. To have a sense of the numbers, around 1887, Belgian universities produced 1,500 graduates every year. See Eddy Stols, "Penetração econômica, assistência técnica e 'brain drain': aspectos da emigração belga para a América Latina por volta de 1900," Jahrbuch für Geschichte von Staat, Wirtschaft und Gesellschaft Lateinamerikas (1976), 361–385.

50. On the use of land surveys, see Ted McCormick's chapter in this volume.

51. René Vauthier, "Initiative Individuelle," *La Belgique Coloniale* 3, no. 7 (1897): 80–81.

52. "Établissement de plantations de café et de cacao sur les terres vacantes appartenant à l'État," Décret du 30 Avril 1897, *Bulletin Officiel de L'État Indépendant du Congo* 13, no. 7–8 (1897): 236–237.

53. René Vauthier, "A Tervueren," *La Belgique Coloniale* 3, no. 44 (1897): 519.

54. Emile Vandervelde, *La Belgique et le Congo: le passé, le présent, l'avenir* (F. Alcan, 1911), 54.

55. Roger Casement, *Correspondence and Report from His Majesty's Consul at Boma Respecting the Administration of the Independent State of the Congo* (Harrison and Sons, 1904), 165.

56. Bas De Roo, "Taxation in the Congo Free State, an Exceptional Case? (1885–1908)," *Economic History of Developing Regions* 32, no. 2 (2017): 97–126. In fact, taxation as a way to force people into the labor market was a common practice in many colonial contexts across Africa, see for example, Philip J. Havik et al., *Administration and Taxation in Former Portuguese Africa, 1900–1945* (Cambridge Scholars, 2015); Leigh Gardner, *Taxing Colonial Africa: The Political Economy of British Imperialism* (Oxford University Press, 2012).

57. Julia Seibert, "More Continuity than Change? New Forms of Forced Labor in Colonial Africa: The Case of the Belgium Congo 1908–1960," in van der

Linden, *Humanitarian Intervention*; William J. Samarin, *The Black Man's Burden: African Colonial Labor on the Congo and Ubangi Rivers, 1880–1900* (Westview Press, 1989).

58. Vauthier, "Initiative Individuelle," 80.

59. Vauthier, "Initiative Individuelle," 80.

60. René Vauthier, "Une Ferme au Congo," *La Belgique Coloniale* 4, no. 5 (1898): 56.

61. Vauthier, "Une Ferme au Congo," 56–57.

62. René Vauthier, "Nouvelles Congolaises," *La Belgique Coloniale* 4, no. 23 (1898): 272.

63. Arquivo Histórico de São Tomé e Príncipe, Confidenciais 1897–1900, Letter from the Governor of the Province of São Tomé to Francisco da Costa Silva, General Director of the Ultramar, June 29, 1898.

64. "Plantations Lacourt," *Bulletin Officiel de L'État Indépendant du Congo* 15, annex to no. 5 (1899): 46–55.

65. René Vauthier, "Agronomie Coloniale: Parallèle entre San-Thomé et le Congo," *La Belgique Coloniale* 4, no. 7 (1898): 79–80.

66. "Société des Chemins de Fer Vicinaux du Mayombe, Convention avec l'État, 21 Septembre de 1898," *Bulletin Officiel de L'État Indépendant du Congo* 14, no. 8–9 (1898): 197–212.

67. Vauthier, "Agronomie Coloniale," 79–80.

68. These companies were (1) Société Agricole du Mayumbe (May 9, 1899); (2) Société Anonyme des Produits du Mayumbe (May 27, 1899); (3) Plantations de la Lukula (June 27, 1899); (4) Société Anonyme Urselia (January 12, 1900); (5) La Mayumbiene: Commerce, Elevage, Plantations et Agriculture (April 12, 1900); (6) Société Anonyme des Plantations Coloniales La Luki (October 5, 1900); and (7) Compagnie Sucrière Européenne et Coloniale (October 5, 1900). See, for (1) *Bulletin Officiel de L'État Indépendant du Congo* 15, annex to no. 5–6 (1899): 71–83; for (2) *Bulletin Officiel de L'État Indépendant du Congo* 15, annex to no. 9–10 (1899): 85–83; for (3) *Bulletin Officiel de L'État Indépendant du Congo* 16, annex to no. 10–12 (1900): 117–130; for (4) *Bulletin Officiel de L'État Indépendant du Congo* 16, annex no. 1–2 (1900): 14–21; for (5) *Bulletin Officiel de L'État Indépendant du Congo* 16, annex to no. 8–9 (1900): 69–86; for (6) *Bulletin Officiel de L'État Indépendant du Congo* 16, annex to no. 10–12 (1900): 152–166; and for 7() *Bulletin Officiel de L'État Indépendant du Congo* 16, annex to no. 10–12 (1900): 166–179. See also Leen Vantieghem, "La culture du Cacao au Mayombe (Congo Belge), 1885–1914: Les bases d'une économie de plantation capitaliste," in *Chocolat: De la Boisson Elitaire au Bâton Populaire, XVIe–XXe siècle*, ed. Emmanuel Collet and Sylvie Estève (CGER, 1996), 145–160; Jean-Luc Vellut, "Le cacao dans l'économie politique de l'ancien Congo Belge," in Collet and Estéve, *Chocolat*, 123–142.

69. Just like Boa Entrada in São Tomé, Urselia was seen as the model plantation in the Congo. Emile Vandervelde, *Les derniers jours de l'État du Congo, journal de voyage: Juillet Octobre, 1908* (La Société Nouvelle, 1909), 70–71.

70. M. Van den Abeele, "Diderrich (Norbert)," *Biographie Coloniale Belge* 3 (1952): col. 239–244.

71. Diderrich owned stocks of the Société Agricole du Mayombe (he would also act as administrator in this society) and of the Compagnie Sucriere Europeene et Coloniale. Lacourt owned stocks of the Société Anonyme des Produits du Mayombe and of the Plantations de la Lukula.

72. Marie-Louise Comeliau, "Jacques (Auguste-Joseph)," *Biographie Coloniale Belge* 5 (1958): col. 469–470.

73. T'Serclaes de Wommersom, *À travers les plantations*.

74. Charles d'Ursel, "Une visite a l'état indépendant du Congo," *Revue des Deux Mondes* 162, no. 1 (1900): 127–162.

75. Vellut, "Le cacao dans l'économie politique."

76. Octave Louwers quoted in Overbergh, *Les Mayombe*, 439.

77. In 1913, he would also establish two plantations with T'Serclaes.

78. See the nine volumes of the *Biographie Coloniale Belge*, accessed on May 12, 2023, https://www.kaowarsom.be/fr/ebooks.

79. Even if Belgian chocolate was not yet famous worldwide, there were already more than seventy chocolate companies operating in the country in 1910, employing more than two thousand workers. Peter Scholliers, "De la boisson élitaire à la barre populaire: la production et la consommation du chocolat en belgique aux XIXe et XXe siècles," *Chocolat*, in Collet and Estéve.

80. Allen Isaacman and Richard Roberts, eds., *Cotton, Colonialism, and Social History in Sub-Saharan Africa* (James Currey, 1995).

81. Mondelez International Archives, 660-11761, Report on Cocoa Plantations in the Congo, Reverend John H. Harris, 1912.

82. John Harris, *Dawn in Darkest Africa* (Smith, Elder, 1912).

83. Ann Laura Stoler and Carole McGranahan, "Introduction: Refiguring Imperial Terrains," in *Imperial Formations*, eds. Ann Laura Stoler et al. (School for Advanced Research Press, 2007).

84. Hedinger and Heé, "Transimperial History"; See also Ulrike Lindner, "Imperialism and Globalization: Entanglements and Interactions Between the British and German Colonial Empires in Africa Before the First World War," *German Historical Institute London Bulletin* 32, no. 1 (2020): 4–28.

Chapter 8

Copra and Conquest

Penal Colonies and Botanical Knowledge in the American Colonial Philippines

Theresa Ventura

"After fifteen years of observation on the ground in the Philippines," wrote Dean Conant Worcester, "I have reached the conclusion that no branch of agriculture there offers such certainty of steady and assured culture from comparatively small investments as does the growing of coconuts."[1] Worcester was not wrong. When the United States began its occupation and colonization of the Philippines in 1898, the fruit and oil of the coastal palm tree were locally traded goods that provided small growers a degree of protection from the precarity of capitalist agriculture. Neither coconuts nor copra, the dried cakes from which coconut oil is pressed, had been a major export crop. Less than a decade after the American annexation, copra was the Philippines's third largest export commodity, trailing behind only the far more established sugar and hemp industries. Worcester, a University of Michigan–trained zoologist turned colonial administrator and agricultural entrepreneur, attributed this phenomenal growth to the "soil and climatic conditions in many parts of the Philippines [that] are ideal for coconut production." By claiming the tree "may be raised to advantage as far north as Pangasinan . . . and [could] flourish in the Southern Philippines to a degree nowhere excelled and seldom equaled in other countries," Worcester naturalized the place of the coconut in the Philippine landscape, turning the archipelago into an exemplar of what the American botanist Edwin Copeland called "ideal coconut country."[2] In the process, Worcester elided the main source of his observation—a knowledge infrastructure composed of penal farms in the southern Philippines. The unremunerated labor of prisoners and the American appropriation, codification, and circulation of their experiential knowledge turned these sites of punitive relocation into the furthest edge of an expanding copra commodity frontier.[3]

This chapter approaches the two largest penal farms—the Iwahig Penal Colony in Puerto Princessa, Palawan, and the San Ramon Penal Farm in Zamboanga, Mindanao—as a lens into the construction of knowledge infrastructures in frontier settings and the attendant frictions of scientific appropriation and codification taking place therein (Fig. 8.1). Its focus is on the American "civil scientists" whose fieldwork in

Figure 8.1. Map of Iwahig Prison and Penal Farm, Puerto Princessa, Palawan; San Ramon Prison and Penal Farm, Zamboanga, Mindanao. Both are still in operation today, with Iwahig still hailed as a model of rehabilitative penology. *Source:* Created by the author.

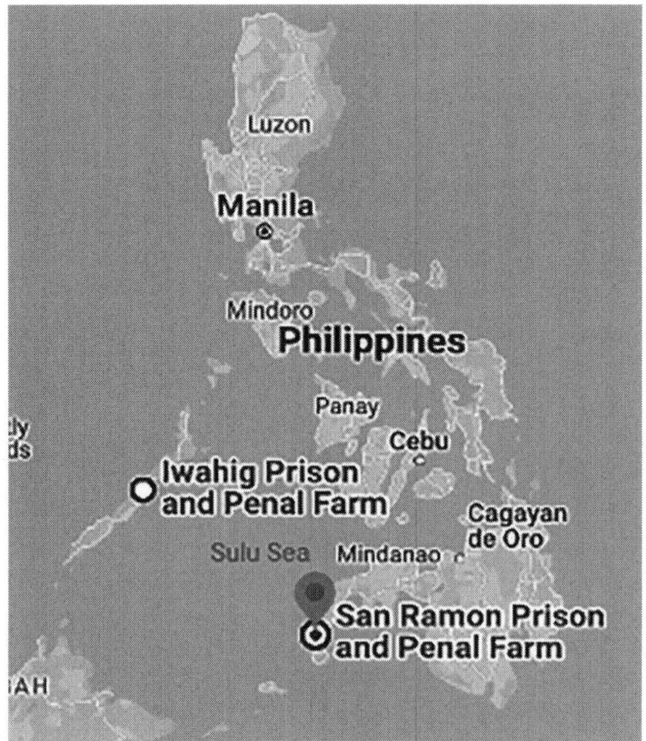

the Philippines was enabled by the colonial state and the Philippine prisoners whose fieldwork was directed, redirected, and observed by these scientists.[4] "Fieldwork" here thus refers to agricultural labor and to the collection of specimens for scientific research. This duality, notes Daniel Rood, is especially apt in commodity frontier settings in which coerced labor produced scientific knowledge but also became separated from it.[5] Foregrounding agricultural fieldwork in the history of science therefore entails asking how the "methods and languages" of botanical science emerged as "techniques for managing racialized labor."[6] In other words, to understand the coproduction of agricultural and scientific fieldwork on the copra commodity frontier, scientific knowledge must be seen as a form of racial and labor management and scientific expertise as another frontier-produced commodity.

In the southern Philippines, the entangled fieldwork of prisoners and civil scientists produced the modern coconut palm. This stout and squat tree could produce more than two hundred nuts throughout the year, ensuring a constant flow of copra for distant markets in industrial processing centers. But by laying claim to the tacit and propositional knowledge needed to cultivate these stout trees—that is, knowing *how* and *why* a coconut palm could be made prolific—civil scientists asserted their expertise. They packaged this know-how in lavishly illustrated and highly detailed planter manuals and investment guides that recast locally produced and historically contingent information into universal knowledge.[7] After all, as Copeland wrote, the prolific palm of the southern Philippines was reproducible "the same the world over."[8] These manuals and guides drew more Euro-American capital to the copra frontier even as American colonial administrators ceded their positions to Filipinos and provided civil scientists with the means to move within and between Euro-American plantation empires and an epistemic community of tropical agriculturalists. Penal farms, in this sense, were the American nodes in a transnational network of Dutch and British botanical gardens and research stations that entrenched plantation agriculture in the global South in the name of scientific agriculture and modernization. Penal farms, however, did not just become such nodes because of a natural relationship between punitive relocation and experimental science. Rather, it resulted from the frictions and contradictions of US colonialism in the Philippines. The chapter thus first turns to these productive frictions—namely that of an imperial war of occupation framed as one of liberation and its critics, between American civil scientists and the Philippine-born *mestizo* landowners on whom they depended yet vied for power and between the ambitions of civil scientists and the constraints of colonial state building—before moving to the Southern Philippine prison farms on which these tensions were worked through.

Punitive Relocation and Knowledge Infrastructure

Penal colonies have long served as spaces of experimental labor control, resource extraction, and knowledge production as states have relied on punitive relocation to advance empire- and nation-building goals since the sixteenth century. Captives, in turn, have contributed to the natural and human sciences as labor pioneers in "relatively pristine spaces," as assistants to recognized authorities and as objects of biomedical and sociological study.[9] It should come as no surprise then that the early twentieth-century American iterations of the Iwahig Penal Colony and the San Ramon Penal Farm built on a foundation first erected by the Spanish. Spanish Crown authorities in the Americas began relocating convicts and other "social undesirables" to remote Pacific territories and dependencies in the sixteenth century, a practice that persisted for Puerto Rican and Cuban exiles despite an 1842 ban. By the mid-nineteenth century, Philippine colonial authorities turned to intra-archipelago relocation to ease unrest in the north and exert crown sovereignty in the largely Muslim south.[10] But the relocations did not necessarily result in commodity frontiers. Banishment to the Iwahig River Valley in Puerto Princessa, Palawan, nearly five hundred miles south of Manila, was often a death sentence by malaria, and Spanish authorities abandoned efforts to open a prison, leaving a small community of settlers behind. Prisoners at the San Ramon colony in Mindanao fared somewhat better. Established in 1869, the penitentiary and farm were roughly fifteen miles northwest of the principal Spanish settlement in Zamboanga. Ostensibly reserved for the "most desperate class—assassins, thieves, conspirators," San Ramon fell to US forces in 1898. The US Army released approximately one thousand prisoners and razed all buildings except for the sugar and sawmills.[11] A brewing crisis of incarceration in Manila would soon lead US officials to reopen San Ramon and redouble efforts to conquer mosquitoes in Palawan. Recounting this crisis avoids naturalizing penal relocation and US imperial power.

A surging number of prisoners were behind the incarceration crisis. Faced with a fierce anticolonial resistance and declining domestic support for a war that claimed more than one million Philippine lives, US

President Theodore Roosevelt declared victory in 1902. This "peace" was only on paper, which quickened an official transfer of power from the US military to an appointed civilian government led by William Howard Taft. Taft's 1901 Sedition Act outlawed political views, publications, and acts in support of independence or critical of US authority. In the process, he transformed combatants and insurgents into "outlaws" and "bandits" to be policed by the Philippine Constabulary, an archipelago-wide force composed of Filipino recruits led by former US Army officers. Throughout Luzon and the Visayas, the constabulary pursued peasant followers of messianic leaders, many of whom prophesied independence and an end to plantation regimes.[12] Between 1903 and 1905, US authorities tried more people for sedition and banditry than any other crime.[13] But housing the convicted at Manila's centrally located Bilibid Prison generated new problems. Founded in 1865, Bilibid's outdated and overcrowded facilities attested to the continuity of an imperialism rejected by Filipinos, turning the treatment of prisoners into a "flashpoint for anti-colonial and anti-imperial critiques of U.S. rule."[14] Punitive relocation offered to ease overcrowding and, just as importantly, allowed US officials to distinguish their rule from that of Spain through engagement with a global discourse on penal reform and an emphasis on the rehabilitative power of agricultural labor and gradual self-governance in a controlled setting. The framing, notes Michael Salman, turned penal colonies into miniaturized simulacra for a progressive imperialism that colonized the future by pegging independence to a series of American-determined and perpetually shifting benchmarks.[15]

Iwahig received its first sixty-one prisoners in 1904 and San Ramon reopened in 1907, with US officials boasting the facility had "every modern feature known for the comfort, health and reformation of prisoners confined therein."[16] High mortality, prisoner mutinies, and escapes indicate otherwise. Several years after opening, Iwahig's death rate was more than twenty-five percent, with beriberi, malaria, and dysentery pointing to chronic food shortages and a sanitary infrastructure ill-suited for its watershed location.[17] The Constabulary suppressed an organized outbreak of one hundred prisoners in 1905 while others fled to the mountainous interior, seeking refuge with the Indigenous Tagbanua. An illicit trade in sex, food, and favors took shape between prisoners and a small community of settlers around the bay—a palimpsest of Spanish colonization attempts.[18] San Ramon escapees absconded to Basilan, the largest and northernmost island of the Sulu Archipelago where at least two evaded recapture for nearly a decade.[19]

Constabulary officer John R. White assumed control of Iwahig in 1906 and, finding it a "doleful colony," implemented an incentive system that rewarded male prisoners for good behavior with access to land and the labor to work it in the form of wives and children. This system sorted prisoners into three hierarchical categories: prisoners, colonists, and freeholders. The status of prisoner was reserved for the poorly behaved and new arrivals, forced to perform the arduous physical labor of forest felling and road building while clothed in the prison stripes of Bilibid. Prisoners could aspire to become a middling group of colonists, who were rewarded for good behavior with two-hectare plots. At the top of this hierarchy stood freeholders, who had received an outright land grant of two hectares—becoming landowners within the confines of prison boundaries. Colonists and freeholders could request that wives and children join them on their two-hectare plots. If unmarried, they could call for a fiancée, provided the couple wed immediately.[20] In this way, Iwahig, soon to be followed by San Ramon, assumed a model of family labor characteristic of the post-emancipation US southern cotton belt. There, freed-people's desires for an economic and political autonomy rooted in land ownership was countered by former slave-owners' continued monopolization of land even after their loss of human property. In the absence of federally mandated land redistribution, sharecropping emerged as a compromise in which freed people gained some privacy in exchange for continued cotton cultivation. Over time, "the more abstract compulsions" of contracts, debt, and the law bound agrarian households both to place and long-distance markets, guaranteeing the production and export of cheap materials for industrial processing. By the late nineteenth century, as Angela Zimmerman writes, Euro-American social scientists hailed heterosexual family farming as an ideal model for controlling emancipated workers.[21] White's Iwahig program, then, brought the family homesteading model of the post-plantation US South to the prison plantation of the southern Philippines.

Family sharecropping as a form of labor control was, at least on paper, successful. Wives and children planted the cash crops that supplemented diets, while fathers performed the fieldwork needed to make the prison self-sufficient and revenue generating. By 1926 Iwahig was "said to be the largest penal colony in the world," home to over 1,200 prisoners and their families spread out over one hundred thousand acres. San Ramon housed six hundred prisoners, mainly Muslim from Mindanao and Sulu, on 1,415 acres.[22]

Even with family labor in place, understanding Iwahig and San Ramon's leap from penal colony to the knowledge infrastructure of the copra commodity frontier requires looking at the frictions of forging a collaborative colonial state with Philippine sugar planters. These planters, most of whom descended from Chinese merchants and Indigenous women, vied with the Spanish Crown and the Catholic Church for recognition as equals and, in the face of opposition, refashioned themselves as Filipino with the right to govern an independent nation.[23] The imperial transition from Spanish to US rule was simultaneously a denial of independence and an opportunity for large planters. The sugar planter Juan Araneta, for instance, welcomed the Constabulary's policing of rebellious sugar workers led by the spirit medium, Dionisio Sigobela, on his vast estates Negros island estates. Araneta also welcomed the civil scientists staffing the Philippine Bureaus of Agriculture, Forestry, and Science, ceding oversight of Negros' La Granja Modelo to the Agriculture Bureau before the end of the war, in the hope of improving his estates. He and fellow large planters pushed for agrarian policies aimed at expanding agricultural credit, improvements in sugar refining, and a concerted effort to bring Rinderpest, the cattle disease felling water buffalo, under control.[24] But these interests were at odds with the mission of American civil scientists who had arrived alongside the occupying army in 1898 to identify fodder for calvary horses, survey the agricultural resources of the archipelago, and return seeds to the continental United States.

The latter goal of circulating seeds back to America was tied to the US Department of Agriculture's (USDA) new Office of Foreign Seed and Plant Introduction (OFSPI), founded in 1898 with a mandate to help White settler farmers diversify and fortify crops with seeds gathered from the globe. The office was a technocratic response to the political problem of rural anger at plummeting crop prices, monopolistic rail practices, and near-usurious bank loans. Yet, the federal government's attempt to constrain rural unrest in the United States meant that agricultural development in the annexed insular territories could not compete with US beet and cane sugar growers or Louisiana's rice industry. To this end, USDA Secretary James Wilson advised his counterpart in the Philippine colonial government, Bureau of Agriculture director Frank Lamson Scribner, that "fibers, coffee, rubber, spices, and such things as we cannot produce should have most attention."[25] Scribner was well familiar with the management of an agricultural empire. Though born in Maine, he had worked at USDA outposts in Montana, Wyoming, and Idaho as a fodder expert before his Philippine appointment. But his mandate to focus on novel exports invariably conflicted with the interests of sugar planters like Araneta. Editorials in the nationalist Philippine press rechristened the Bureau of Agriculture the "Bureau of Failure," highlighting the rotating cast of American directors "who come to save the country or its wealth; but, in truth, what hopes can the last to arrive, ignorant of the very peculiar conditions of the country."[26] Another editorial referred to the civil scientists in the colonial administration as a "plague of experts imported from the United States . . . more disastrous for the country than the calamities they seek to exterminate."[27]

One signal of failure of civil scientists was their inability to open and staff a tropical research institute and botanical garden modeled on the Lands Plantentuin in Buitenzorg, Java.[28] Buitenzorg was fast becoming synonymous with a "progressive colonialism" of improved seeds and support for small-holder farming like that taking shape at Iwahig and in the post-emancipation US South.[29] Under the direction of botanist Melchoir Treub, Buitenzorg strengthened its international influence by offering foreign researchers transportation, accommodation, working space in one of its eight laboratories, and access to the two hundred thousand specimens in its herbarium and the more than six thousand volumes in its library.[30] David Grandison Fairchild, future head of the OFSPI, wrote that his visit had awakened him to "the possibilities there are in the organizing of such colonies if they are properly managed."[31] Thus, for botanists and agricultural scientists, the US foothold in the Philippines turned the archipelago into a metaphorical "stepping stone" to transimperial scientific networks, while those networks further informed American expectations of and for the Philippines. After a stay at Buitenzorg, botanist Elmer D. Merrill, who had followed Scribner's path from Maine to the continental US West to the Philippines, concluded that, "[i]f the American agricultural and forestry administration in these islands are to succeed both must be established on practically the same lines followed by the English and Dutch in their colonial possessions."[32]

Claiming the land for a research institute equivalent to Buitenzorg was much easier than securing the labor and funds required to build it. In 1904, the Philippine Commission authorized construction on the Lamao Botanical Garden and Reserve in Bataan to be housed in the Interior Bureau overseen by Worcester. The twelve-thousand-acre reserve began in the Lamao River delta at Manila Bay and encompassed the summit of Mount Marvieles at an elevation of 4,500 feet. Like Buitenzorg, the location encompassed multiple temperatures and terrains. Lamao's biosphere was home to the Aeta, a migratory group the Spanish had called Negrito.[33] Lamao officials sought to discipline the Aeta into a landscaping labor force, the need for which cannot be underestimated. Interimperial travel to research stations and botanical gardens informed American ideas about what the grounds of Lamao should look like. Farm machinery expert Thomas Hanley gushed upon his return from Peradeniya that passing through the gates "produces a feeling of wonder and delight in the visitor from a temperate climate . . . the almost unanimous opinion of the visitors is that the garden cannot be surpassed."[34]

Nevertheless determined to try, Thomas Richmond, a bureau employee in charge of nurseries, returned from trips to Ceylon, Singapore, and Hong Kong with maps of the "arrangement of plants, construction of plant houses, kinds of labels used, methods of recording the history of seeds and plants received, the system of arrangement of plants and care of the same."[35] The basic groundwork of clearing thickly forested jungle, planting and maintaining grass lawns, and building propagating houses was not simply an aesthetic matter. Whereas Dutch East Indies planters financed Buitenzorg's research in exchange for seeds and advice, the austerity of the American colony and antagonism with Philippine planters required that Lamao become self-supporting and revenue generating.[36] Hanley began his attempt to discipline the Aeta into a garden labor force with an offer of an unspecified wage and a "metal tag and a certificate to the effect that [the holder] is under the protection of the Philippine government."[37] The project disappeared from the official colonial state archive nearly as soon as it appeared, perhaps a reflection of Aeta indifference.[38]

Ambitions for Lamao fizzled just as Iwahig and San Ramon began receiving prisoners, providing through force the labor force that Lamao lacked. The timing resulted in an effective merger between the environmental management institutions and the Bureau of Prisons. The economic botanist William S. Lyon, who began his career as an agricultural expert by serving on California's first board of forestry officials before authoring a report on the global copra trade for the Philippine Bureau of Agriculture, worked with prison officials to select Iwahig's location.[39] Merrill personally packed Lamao's seedlings of oranges, "Bontoc" lemons, mango, pineapple, and bananas, along with coffee trees imported from Java and Ceylon.[40]

The material exchange affected a larger ideological transformation of the penal colonies into demonstration farms. Beyond rehabilitating prisoners through fieldwork, civil scientists hoped the penal farms would uplift Philippine agriculture by modeling the scientific agriculture that they maintained "native" farmers rejected. In the words of one bureau scientist, "after the natives see the advantages to be gained, they will take to it [American methods], and not before. No amount of talking will convince them that their method is a poor one, but they must themselves see the work done."[41] A 1907 news article concurred: "It is well known to be almost impossible to introduce modern farming implements and methods among a conservative native population, but the colonists from Iwahig returning to their homes may well prove the leaven to improve agricultural methods in all the provinces of the archipelago."[42]

Copra's Conquest and Plantation Knowledge

The merging of the Bureaus of Prisons and Agriculture turned the penal farms into a knowledge infrastructure that paved the way for copra's conquest in Palawan and Mindanao. The reasons for copra's ascendancy were threefold. First, each penal farm was situated in a watershed area, thereby containing the thin sandy soil and circulating groundwater in which coastal palm trees had evolved. The tree's roots systems absorbed wash over, while the tall and spindly trunks bore strong winds and prevented coasts from erosion. Of the plant materials transferred from Lamao to the penal farms, coconut seedlings did best. Considering this, the head of the Bureau of Agriculture, Scribner, urgently recommended that "labor, farming tools, and draft animals be found to ready the ground for an additional 200,000 coconut trees" on San Ramon.[43] Second, and no less important than the suitability of land, was prisoner familiarity with coconut propagation and planting. The plant's multiple uses as food, medicine, and raw material for housing, utensils, and fibers had earned it the Tagalog title *puno ng buahy* (tree of life). Without coconuts and bamboo, the physician Trinidad Pardo de Tavera wrote in a nineteenth-century guide to the plants of the archipelago, "the people of the archipelago would not know how to live."[44] Rendering coconuts into copra, the dried cakes from which oil is pressed, required little additional investment beyond an iron spike for husking the meat and bamboo mats for sun drying. The myriad uses of the whole tree and the simplicity of processing lent smallholders a degree of relief from debt tenancy during the long nineteenth century transition to commercial agriculture, while at the same time giving the tree an additional reputation as a lazy man's crop.[45] Prisoner knowledge of nut propagation (Fig. 8.2), the

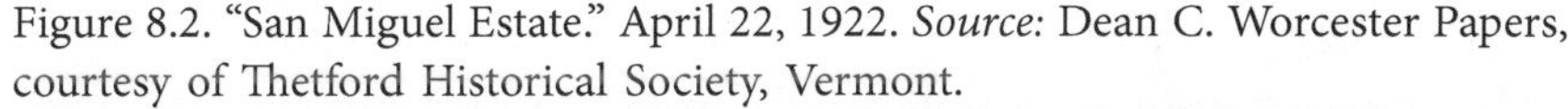

Figure 8.2. "San Miguel Estate." April 22, 1922. *Source:* Dean C. Worcester Papers, courtesy of Thetford Historical Society, Vermont.

low capital costs of processing, and the increasing international demand for oleochemicals (vegetable fats with industrial applications) combined to turn the penal farms into commercial coconut plantations.

Industrial chemists impressed the "tree of life," and more specifically copra, into an emerging military-industrial complex at the turn of the twentieth century. Copra was a source of cheap calories, much like sugar, but it also had industrial applications. Bureau of Agriculture botanists noted these uses in their travels across a copra commodity chain that began in Oceania and extended west to the United States. Lyon, the California forester turned economic botanist who helped select the location for Iwahig, had earlier reported that chemists in Marseilles had "produced from the cocoanut a series of food products whose manufacture has revolutionized the industry and placed the business of the manufacturer and of the producers upon a plane of prosperity never before enjoyed."[46] This revolutionary product was oleomargarine, a shelf-stable butter substitute made from coconut oil among other vegetable fats. British chemists turned the comestible into a combustible. When heated under pressure with an alkali such as lye, coconut oil's high lauric acid content converted into nitroglycerin at a rate 25%–30% higher than other high lauric acid vegetable oils.[47] Indigenous growers across Oceania, notably Samoa and Micronesia, as well as Seletar in Indonesia and Sri Lanka, initially met growing demand for copra through a trade commanded by German, British, French, and Dutch trading companies and colonial governments, with Indigenous labor soon supplemented by South and East Asian indentured laborers.[48] Iwahig and San Ramon's botanical gardens thus capitalized on prisoner familiarity with the crop, the sandy soils of the prisons, and rising demand to reconfigure the penal colonies into copra commodity frontiers.

Civil scientists and prisoners on the copra commodity frontier performed their fieldwork through different lenses. For civil scientists, coconut trees were a source of future copra profits: the more nuts, the more profits. But, as some learned through travel and transimperial exchange, planting more trees did not automatically translate into a higher yield of nuts. Hanley reported that a chance train ride from Colombo to Kandy placed him "in the acquaintance of an educated Singhalese" who owned a plantation "upon which he made coconut growing a specialty." The unnamed informant shared that spacing the trees twenty-five to thirty feet apart generated more nuts than if the trees were planted closely together.[49] Armed with this knowledge, civil scientists sought optimal spacing practices to produce trees capable of meeting the factories' constant demands for raw materials, a project they called "improvement." Prison fieldworkers, however, perceived the tree through its everyday life-sustaining uses—fronds, trunks, coir, and husks—therefore spacing seedlings at distances and depths Americans judged too close for maximum fruiting. "Such extreme economy of labor," Copeland argued, "certainly does not pay."[50] Copeland, in his role as San Ramon's chief botanist, therefore carved out zones for spacing experiments, directing prisoners to plant trees at varying distances and depths, the growth of which he monitored and compared to old groves. By the end of the experiment, Copeland determined that seedlings be placed in holes at least 12–13 inches (30–33 cm) wide and deep at distances no closer than 32 feet (9.75 m), with the land in between given to soil-enhancing cover-crops while additional pruning encouraged further year-round fruiting.[51] The careful spacing and pruning demanded by this project of improvement yielded squat trees with fat trunks, the cultivation of which was too important to leave to Iwahig and San Ramon's settlers and freeholders (Fig. 8.3). Accordingly, the experimental zones were turned into distinct agroforests

Figure 8.3. "San Miguel Estate, typical coconut tree." April 22, 1922. Base of tree showing a swollen portion of the trunk, which indicate healthfulness and vigor. *Source:* Dean C. Worcester Papers, courtesy of Thetford Historical Society, Vermont.

called "permanent plantations." Copeland and prison botanists deemed the maintenance of the permanent plantations as too important to be performed on the family plots of settlers and colonists. By 1911, Iwahig had three acres set aside for five hundred coconut trees along the lower Iwahig River. San Ramon's agroforest, by 1915, contained twenty-five thousand mature trees, nine thousand seedlings awaiting plantation, and five thousand sprouts in seed beds.[52]

Copeland translated the results of his San Ramon work into a 1914 manual entitled *The Coco-nut*. At the time of its publication, he was professor of Plant Physiology and dean at the University of the Philippines College of Agriculture in Luzon's Batangas Province. The college opened to students in 1912, the entrance gates lined with coconut trees. In his manual, he exclusively referred to San Ramon as a "government plantation," not a penal colony, thus erasing the prison fieldworkers and their labor on which his knowledge had been derived. The manual was typical of plantation guidebooks that transformed knowledge obtained from prisoners and local actors into universal science. Copeland acknowledged that the book was "written in the Philippines and may seem to deal to an unreasonable extent with the coconut industry of these islands" but assured prospective readers that "it contains everything that a planter anywhere in the tropics has most need of knowing. The behavior of the coconut is intelligible in the light of knowledge of its physiology, and surely in no other way; and the physiology of the tree is the same the world over."[53] His overall aim was to popularize a set of practices that marked the differences between "good planters" and those who treated the tree as a lazy man's crop. "In most places," he wrote, "a large part of the trees will survive if left to themselves, but no good planter will be contented with merely seeing his trees survive. What the planter wants is not coconut trees for themselves, but the profits which they can be made to yield, and merely surviving does not yield returns."[54] Good planters, however, did not simply aspire to profit. They understood the physiology of the tree, the propositional knowledge on which the rules of good practice "must rest."[55] Copeland borrowed an industrial metaphor to further describe the relationship between the good planter and physiological knowledge. A chauffeur, he suggested, was equipped to drive a car and could do it well: "If everything runs smoothly, the training by rule and example will be sufficient. But when things go wrong, it will leave him helpless."[56] The scientific planter ran his plantation as an organic machine. As examples of this efficiency, each penal farm produced enough copra for direct sales to oil refiners by the second decade of US occupation at which point copra constituted thirty percent of Philippine exports.[57] In Worcester's estimation, the 1909 output of "approximately 231,787,050 pounds of copra" excelled "that of Java, of the Straits Settlements, of Ceylon, or of the South Sea Islands, and places the Philippines at the head of the list of coconut growing countries. In fact, during the year mentioned the Philippines produced about one third of the world's output."[58]

Although Copeland did not explicitly assign a racial identity to his "good planter," its racialized counterpart was the "native." Native planters valued their plantations "by the tree instead of by its area or even by its production," thus having no incentive to cultivate stout trees for the copra trade.[59] Worcester too contrasted good planters with native practices, albeit far more bluntly: "The agricultural methods of the natives have violated every known rule. Seldom has the ground been really prepared for planting. The trees invariably stand too thickly. The Filipino cannot rid himself of the idea that the more seed he sows the greater will be his harvest." This perceived carelessness produced the dreaded "tall spindling trees" that bore "nuts sparingly"—and were thus at odds with their scientific plantation.[60] Likewise, Worcester judged native planters to be unreliable interlocutors and knowledge translators. He deemed "the Filipino" unable to convey "reliable information as to cost of production and average annual value of crop . . . one man will tell you that his trees average ten nuts per year, while another will solemnly assure you that fairly good trees produce three or four hundred."[61]

Photography was an important medium through which scientific agriculturalists distinguished between good planters and native practices. Worcester, who transitioned from government employment to private investment, deployed before and after photographs of cleared coconut groves to illustrate the productive differences of improvement. His company's purchase of the San Miguel Estate on the island of Mindoro, for instance, transformed an overgrown forest into a well-ordered and spaced field (Fig. 8.4 and Fig. 8.5). Copeland extolled the clearly defined rows as a tool for labor management: While well-arranged rows made cultivation easier,

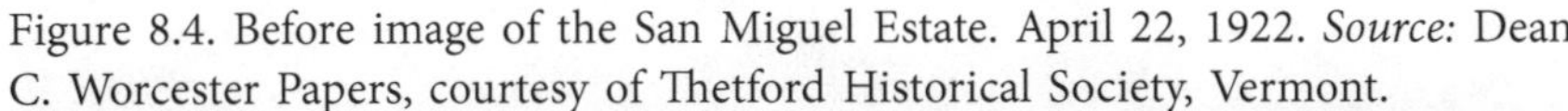
Figure 8.4. Before image of the San Miguel Estate. April 22, 1922. *Source:* Dean C. Worcester Papers, courtesy of Thetford Historical Society, Vermont.

Figure 8.5. After image of the San Miguel Estate, with the caption, "A grove of old trees a year after the brush has been cleared away. Note their fine condition." April 22, 1922. *Source:* Dean C. Worcester Papers, courtesy of Thetford Historical Society, Vermont.

"[m]ore important than this, however, is ease in supervision. Whether or not the management and care of the farm be handled by contract, it is very desirable that it be easy to check at all times the work which is done on the field. This will of course be much easier if the trees are regularly arranged so that the grove can easily be divided up into units."[62] Other photographs from the San Ramon Penal Colony hint at the tensions behind this need for supervision. Copeland, writing with an eye toward the production of the "greatest quantity and best quality of oil," advised that the harvesting of nuts should wait until they were ripe enough to have fallen from the tree at which point the interior meat had shrunk and the oil content had increased. This did not stop prisoners from scaling trees with twists made of hemp or carving notches in the trunk to climb (Fig. 8.6 and Fig. 8.7). "The force of custom," Copeland complained, was strong, though the prisoners' devotion to the forced production of copra was of course likely weak; it is unclear, too, if monetary rewards or payments incentivized prisoners to collect as many nuts as possible.[63] When climbers did make notches in the tree, Worcester complained that they were too deep, extending into the wood. Drawing on another industrial metaphor, he proposed providing

Figure 8.6. “Thong of twisted hemp used by climbers in ascending coconut trees.” San Ramon Penal Farm, Zamboanga, Mindanao. April 22, 1922. *Source:* Dean C. Worcester Papers, courtesy of Thetford Historical Society, Vermont.

Figure 8.7. “Climbing a coconut tree by means of notches in the bark preparatory to cutting down the nuts.” San Roman Penal Farm, Zamboanga, Mindanao. April 22, 1922. *Source:* Dean C. Worcester Papers, courtesy of Thetford Historical Society, Vermont.

pickers with the "climbers used by linemen in ascending telegraph poles" so "they could go up and down the trees easily and safely without doing them the slightest injury."[64] Worcester's likening of the living trunks to dead lumber overlooked the possibility that prison fieldworkers had been tapping the trees for *tuba*, a sweet alcohol made from fermented sap. As the sap came from a cut under the blossom stalk from which the nuts grew, civil scientists judged *tuba* production as incompatible with the copra trade. Thus, the surveillance enabled by avenue-like rows of the agroforest sought to guarantee copra exports.

As an act of colonial-state primitive accumulation, the copra knowledge gleaned from Iwahig and San Ramon became an invitation to private investment. The Bureau of Agriculture published a series of investment guides, including Worcester's 1911 treatises, drawn from penal farm sources. Iwahig's superintendent, C. H. Lamb, translated the poorly remunerated labor of prisoners into dollar amounts for potential investors, holding that it would cost $15.80 to clear one acre of land at a daily wage of $0.25. He judged that "coconut planting for a permanent crop cannot be equaled by any other known permanent crop, not even rubber."[65] Worcester boasted to the army general Frank McIntyre that his 1911 guide "has already brought a good bit of money out here for investment in coconut growing. There are two men in the islands now hunting land. One of them has $250,000 available, and the other has $50,000 with the assurance of more as fast as it is needed."[66] The largest firm to invest in the southern Philippine copra industry was the International Banking Corporation (IBC), the first American bank with a charter granting it the power to open branches outside the continental United States. Its executive board and shareholders included rail and shipping magnates, many with close connections to the Theodore Roosevelt administration. Roosevelt, in turn, authorized the IBC to act as the fiscal agent of the state in the Caribbean, notably Panama during the canal's construction; in China, to collect indemnities from the Boxer Rebellion; and in the Philippines.[67] IBC credit smoothed the transition from colonial administrators to private business. Worcester and the former director of prisons, M. L. Stewart, used an IBC loan to form the American-Philippine Development Company in 1913. The company operated a private plantation near San Ramon managed by J. B. Cooley, a former San Ramon superintendent. These connections effectively created a pipeline directing former prisoners to contract work on the American-Philippine Development Company plantation. Ever the agricultural entrepreneur booster, Worcester portrayed the conversion of the prisoners from Muslim dissidents to disciplined laborers as complete. "Our laborers," he wrote to a family member in the United States in 1923, "are all either Samal Moros or ex-convicts from the San Ramon penal station, and they are real workers, who work by the hour, and complain of a SHORT day, never of a long one."[68]

The prison-to-plantation laborer pipeline suggests the ways in which the penal farms served as a commodity frontier knowledge infrastructure and a material infrastructure. San Ramon's success encouraged American settlers in the surrounding district of Zamboanga to become coconut planters. The mutually constitutive relationship between the penal farm and the developing American planter class is captured in a front-page headline in *The Mindanao Herald* declaring, "SAN RAMON IS OURS." The penal farm was to "be used as a nursery for hemp plants, cocoanuts, etc., for the benefit of the planters of the Province."[69] World War I demand for oleochemicals and nitroglycerin sparked a rush to clear more land for coconut plantations and to open facilities for oil refining in the Philippines—an expansion that would not have been possible without the infrastructure and botanical knowledge of the penal colonies-cum-plantations. Worcester himself moved from civil service to private plantation. In 1915, he took over the management of the American-owned Visayan Refining Company's two-million-peso facility in Cebu, strategically located near that island's deep port and a short distance from the penal colony and plantations of northern Mindanao. He would amalgamate this facility with two other firms, selling a large share of the capital stock to Lever Brothers of London.[70] In this way, punitive relocation and colonial scientific agriculture created the knowledge infrastructure for the expansion of a copra commodity frontier.

The copra commodity frontier soon became a site of contestation and competition between Americans and the elite landowning families who benefited from and sought to control US rule. This competition did not hinder copra's conquest but rather advanced the commodity's development as Americans and Filipinos fought for control over its trade. The Philippine National Bank extended credit to Philippine landowners and businessmen eager to enter the market and to limit American control of the economy. For example, Cebuano tycoon Vicente Madrigal, son of a Spanish father and Philippine-born mother who, like other landed elite, embraced a national Filipino identity, opened a competing oil refining facility near Worcester's. A promise from the Philippine National Bank to compel a Manila-based shipper to buy from Madrigal at an inflated price allowed him to offer local growers and pickers higher prices than those paid by Worcester. Such competing infusions of capital, high demand, and inflated copra prices brought small farmers into the coconut market. By the end of World War I, the total area planted to coconuts had trebled.[71] Between 1910 and 1918, imports of Philippine copra into the continental United States grew from 9,914,000 pounds to a staggering 326,774,000 pounds.[72] Copra's conquest of the southern frontier was complete.

Conclusion

The Iwahig Penal Colony in Palawan and San Ramon Penal Farm in Mindanao lend insight into the construction of knowledge infrastructures in frontier settings and to the frictions of scientific appropriation and codification taking place therein. Punitive relocation provided American colonial administrators in the Philippines with a solution to the crisis of imprisonment—a crisis arising from the fiction that the Philippine-American War had ended even as resistance to the US occupation and plantation regimes continued in the countryside. Penal farms in the southern Philippines became a way to manage Manila's burgeoning prison population while at the same time placing US initiatives in the Philippines in dialogue with transnational penal reform currents. Even though Iwahig and San Ramon were built upon a preexisting Spanish infrastructure, Americans cast each as a novel space in which to reform individuals and, through the subsequent relocation of family members, to discipline agricultural labor to market requirements. In this regard, the penal farms, at least rhetorically, resembled sharecropping relations in the post-emancipation US South and anticipated the kind of progressive colonialism that scientific agriculturalists at Buitenzorg in Java were beginning to articulate. The link between the reform of individual prisoners and the improvement of tropical agriculture was solidified as US civil scientists turned to penal farms as a source of agricultural labor and a refuge from the criticisms of Philippine sugar planters. Penal colonies, in this sense, were experimental farms, demonstration stations, and nodes in a network of colonial botanical gardens facilitating the export of plantation commodities from the global South to the industrialized North.

The process by which Iwahig and San Ramon became coconut plantations, however, depended on the entangled fieldwork of prisoners and civil scientists. As the policing of rural insurgents moved agricultural labor from sugar plantations to an initially undetermined commodity frontier, prisoners brought their knowledge of the "tree of life" to the sandy soils of Iwahig and San Ramon. There, prisoner familiarity with sprouting, transplanting, and tending to the trees informed American civil scientists' understandings of what the penal farms could usefully produce, just as transimperial knowledge exchanges further shaped their knowledge of copra's economic potential. Eager for the coconut trees to bear the fruit of copra-derived profits, penal farm botanists carved out distinct agroforests wherein "improvement" limited prisoner use of the coconut as a source of food, alcohol, or fibers.

Frontiers, by definition, are not static but neither is the movement of a frontier natural or predetermined. Penal farms created the southern Philippine copra commodity frontier, serving as an infrastructure for the generation and global circulation of botanical knowledge and as an invitation to nonstate investment. The movement of capital to the copra frontier generated further movements: Laborers in Iwahig and San Ramon moved from the penal farms to work on the privately owned plantations nearby; Worcester moved from state-work to ownership of plantations; and Copeland moved from state botanist to the deanship of the University of the Philippines's College of Agriculture. Copeland's 1914 coconut plantation manual would see several reprints. The manual translated prisoner experiential knowledge into propositional knowledge, distinguishing between presumed Euro-American good planters who ran their plantations as engineers and Natives who cultivated according to tradition with little understanding of physiology. While Copeland's manual referred to San Ramon as a government farm and never a prison, the ties between penal farms and the university persisted. In 1930, the Philippine legislature considered a bill to cede control of Iwahig from the Bureau of Prisons to the University of the Philippines while transferring the remaining prisoners to San Ramon. The measure, the bill's sponsors hoped, would provide the financially ailing university with a dependable income stream. Though unsuccessful, the proposal was nonetheless a reminder of the forced labor and agricultural fieldwork behind the production of scientific knowledge.[73]

Notes

1. Dean C. Worcester, *Coconut Growing in the Philippine Islands* (US Bureau of Insular Affairs, 1911), 1, in Articles, 1898–1915, and undated, concerning the

Philippines, Box 2, Dean C. Worcester Papers, Bentley Historical Library, University of Michigan (henceforth, DCW).

2. Edwin Bingham Copeland, *The Coco-nut* (Macmillan, 1914), x. Reports of the Philippine Commission from 1900 to 1915, published annually in Washington, DC, at the Government Printing Office, give insight into the growth of the copra industry during the early years of the US occupation. Secondary literature on the growth of coconut plantations and copra exports remains scant. One of the best brief histories is Resil B. Mojares, "Worcester in Cebu: Filipino Response to American Business, 1915–1924," *Philippine Quarterly of Culture & Society* 13, no. 1 (1985): 1–13. See also Rigoberto Tiglao, "The Political Economy of the Philippine Coconut Industry," in *Political Economy of Philippine Commodities*, ed. Randolf S. David (University of the Philippines Press, 1983). For a sense of the size and scale of coconut plantation and copra exports in the contemporary Philippines, see Monica B. Castillo and Princess Alma B. Ani, "The Philippine Coconut Industry: Status, Policies, and Strategic Directions for Development," Food and Fertilizer Technology Center for the Asian and Pacific Region Agricultural Policy Platform (FFTC-AP) (June 2019), https://ap.fftc.org.tw/article/1382.

3. My understanding of commodity frontiers as regions integrated into transnational networks of environmental exploitation and capitalism most often through force is informed by the work of Jason Moore. See, in brief, Jason Moore, "The Rise of Cheap Nature," in *Anthropocene or Capitalocene? Nature, History, and the Crisis of Capitalism*, ed. Jason W. Moore (PM Press, 2016). For other cases of economy botany, see also the chapters by Jennifer R. Saracino, Moritz von Brescius, Christina Skott, Marta Macedo, and Gillian McGillivray in this volume.

4. By "civil scientists," I mean scientists who were employed in the American colonial civil service. I use the term to reinforce and build on Jessica Wang's argument that the nineteenth-century internationalism of science was as much a product of government as it was of science. In the American colonial Philippines, civil scientists were employed by the colonial state as experts. In a circular fashion, these experts' expertise guided all manner of state policies concerning resource extraction and management. See, Jessica Wang, "Knowledge, State Power, and the Invention of International Science," in *Knowledge Flows in a Global Age: A Transnational Approach*, ed. John Krige (University of Chicago Press, 2022).

5. Daniel Rood, "Toward a Global Labor History of Science," in *Global Scientific Practice in the Age of Revolutions, 1750–1850*, eds. Patrick Manning and Daniel Rood (University of Pittsburgh Press, 2016).

6. Rood, "Global Labor History of Science," 256.

7. Rood, "Global Labor History of Science," 257.

8. Copeland, *The Coco-nut*, 28.

9. Clare Anderson, *Convicts: A Global History* (Cambridge University Press, 2022), 10, 251.

10. Greg Bankoff, "Deportation and the Prison Colony of San Ramon, 1870–1898," *Philippine Studies* 39, no. 4 (1991): 445; Michael Vincent P. Caceres,

"Colonial Penal de San Ramon: Images of the Oldest Existing National Penitentiary in the Philippines (circa 1870)," *Liceo Journal of Higher Education Research* 5, no. 1 (2007): 133–153; Christian G. De Vito, "Punitive Entanglements: Connected Histories of Penal Transportation, Deportation, and Incarceration in the Spanish Empire (1830s–1898)," *International Review of Social History* 63, no. S26 (2018): 1–21.

11. John Foreman, *The Philippine Islands* (New York, 1899), quoted in Bankoff, "Deportation and the Prison Colony of San Ramon," 452.

12. Rural messianic movements included those of Ruperto Rios in Tayabas (now Quezon) Province; Simeon Ola in Albay Province; and Dionisio Sigobela, also known as Papa Isio, in Negros Occidental. On the Constabulary suppression, see, in brief, Moon-Ho Jung, *Menace to Empire: Anticolonial Solidarities and the Transpacific Origins of the US Security State* (University of California Press, 2022), 41; Alfred McCoy, *Policing America's Empire: The United States, the Philippines, and the Rise of the Surveillance State* (University of Wisconsin Press, 2009), esp. 147–148 and chapter 3, "Surveillance and Scandal."

13. Michael Salman, "The Prison that Makes Men Free," in *Colonial Crucible: Empire in the Making of the Modern American State*, eds. Alfred W. McCoy and Francisco A. Scarano (University of Wisconsin Press, 2009).

14. Benjamin D. Weber, "Fugitive Justice: The Possible Futures of Prison Records from US Colonial Rule in the Philippines," *Archive Journal*, August 2017, http://www.archivejournal.net/essays/fugitive-justice/.

15. Salman, "The Prison that Makes Men Free," 116–128. The Pacific, just like the Atlantic, writes Alfred W. McCoy, was "an avenue for a criss-crossing of carceral innovations in the era of high imperialism;" Alfred W. McCoy, "Introduction: Police, Prisons, and Law Enforcement," in McCoy and Scarano, *Colonial Crucible*, 84.

16. Manuel A. Alzate, *Convict Labor in the Philippine Islands; Presented at the Ninth International Prison Congress Held in London, August 1925* (Manila Bureau of Printing, 1926), 22.

17. John R. White, *Bullets and Bolos: Fifteen Years in the Philippine Islands* (Constabulary Books, 1928; repr., 2019), 238. "Heavy Rainfall Causes Trouble in Palawan," *Cablenews-American* (Manila), December 21, 1910.

18. White, *Bullets and Bolos*, 245.

19. "Escaped Prisoners Are Captured," *The Mindanao Herald*, July 21, 1906, 1–2.

20. This division of labor is described in Alzate, *Convict Labor in the Philippine Islands*, 37.

21. Karen R. Miller, "Agents of the Settler State: Incarcerated Filipino Workers, Conjugal Migration, and Indigenous Dispossession at the Iwahig Penal Colony," *American Quarterly* 76, no. 1 (2024): 25–53. On the emergence of sharecropping in the US South, see, in brief, the essays in *Freedom: A Documentary History of Emancipation, 1861–1867, Series 3, Vol. 1, Land and Labor, 1865*, eds. Steven Hahn

et al. (University of North Carolina Press, 2008); Alex Lichtenstein, "Introduction: Rethinking Agrarian Labor in the US South," *Journal of Peasant Studies* 35, no. 4 (2009): 621–635. On the reconstitution of emancipated labor as family labor and social control, see Angela Zimmerman, *Alabama in Africa: Booker T. Washington, the German Empire, and the Globalization of the New South* (Princeton University Press, 2010), 15. On links between the US South and insular colonies, see Natalie J. Ring, *The Problem South: Region, Empire, and the New Liberal State, 1880–1930* (University of Georgia Press, 2012).

22. Alzate, *Convict Labor in the Philippine Islands*, 20, 22.

23. See in brief, Richard Chu, *The Chinese and Chinese Mestizos of Manila: Family, Identity, and Culture, 1860s–1930s* (Brill, 2010); Filomeno V. Aguilar, "Between the Letter and the Spirit of the Law: Ethnic Chinese and Philippine Citizenship by Jus Soli, 1899–1947," *Southeast Asian Studies* 49, no. 3 (2011): 444. See also Resil B. Mojares, *Brains of the Nation: Pedro Paterno, T.H. Pardo de Tavera, Isabelo de los Reyes and the Production of Modern Knowledge* (Ateneo de Manila University Press, 2006).

24. Alfred McCoy, "Sugar Barons: Formation of a Native Planter Class in the Colonial Philippines," in *Proletarians and Peasants in Colonial Asia*, eds. E. Valentine Daniel et al. (Frank Cass, 1992); Filomeno V. Aguilar, *Clash of Spirits: The History of Power and Sugar Planter Hegemony on a Visayan Island* (University of Hawai'i Press, 1998). On Araneta and civil scientists, see Alonzo Stewart, "Agricultural Conditions in the Philippine Islands," in *Senate and House Documents and Reports: Hearings*, 60th Congress, 1st Session, Document No. 535 (US Bureau of Insular Affairs, 1908), 23.

25. Wilson to Lamson-Scribner, October 17, 1903, Box 1, Letterbooks, 1888–1903, Vol. 3, F. Lamson-Scribner Papers, Manuscript Division, Library of Congress. On the politics of insular sugar imports after 1898, see April Merleaux, *Sugar and Civilization: Empire and the Cultural Politics of Sweetness* (University of North Carolina Press, 2015). US President William McKinley's December 1900 State of the Union address highlighted the beneficial impact of empire on farming: "The Department of Agriculture has been extending its work during the past year, reaching farther for new varieties of seeds and plants." The Philippines, along with Hawai'i and Puerto Rico, McKinley continued, were not foreign threats but were "being considered so that their peoples may be helped to produce the tropical products now so extensively brought into the United States." The Agriculture Pavilion at the 1901 Pan-American Exposition displayed this new bounty and its promise for American farmers. Grapevines and coconut palms—just two of the more than five thousand crop samples on display—hung above the entrance arch and draped the plaster moldings. See, William McKinley, State of the Union, December 3, 1900, http://www.let.rug.nl/usa/presidents/william-mckinley/state-of-the-union-1900.php. Heroic treatments of the OFSPI's plant exploration include Amanda Harris, *Fruits of Eden: David Fairchild and America's Plant Hunters* (University of Florida

Press, 2015), and Daniel Stone, *The Food Explorer: The True Adventurers of the Globe-Trotting Botanist Who Transformed What America Eats* (Dutton, 2018). On the OFSPI as a form of colonial extraction and plant transfer as a template for neoliberal seed banking, see Xan Sarah Chacko, "When Life Gives You Lemons: Frank Meyer, Authority, and Credit in Early Twentieth-Century Plant Hunting," *History of Science* 56, no. 4 (2018): 432–469.

26. "The Bureau of Failure," *La Vanguardia* (Manila), July 31, 1911, Box 3, Translations from Spanish and Filipino of Newspaper Articles, Charles B. Elliott Papers, Manuscript Division, Library of Congress, Washington, DC (henceforth, CBE).

27. "Serum and the Experts," *La Democracia* (Manila), April 15, 1911, CBE. This article referred specifically to the Rinderpest epidemic.

28. For other examples of "failure," see the chapters by Christina Skott, Marta Macedo, and Moritz von Brescius in this volume, as well as Rebekah McCallum on ignorance.

29. Florian Wagner, "From the Western to the Eastern Model of Cash Crop Production: Colonial Agronomy and the Global Influence of Dutch Java's Buitenzorg Laboratories, 1880s–1930s," in *Agrarian Reform and Resistance in an Age of Globalisation: The Euro-American World and Beyond, 1780–1914*, eds. Joe Smith and Cathal Regan (Routledge, 2019). For an alternative form of labor organization in the US South, see Claudia Roesch's chapter in this volume.

30. Wagner, "Colonial Agronomy," 137–138.

31. Fairchild to Steere, May 11, 1898, Joseph Beal Steere Papers, Bentley Historical Library, University of Michigan. On Fairchild's entanglements with empire, see Stuart A. McCook, "The World Was My Garden: Tropical Botany and Cosmopolitanism in American Science," in McCoy and Scarano, *Colonial Crucible*.

32. Elmer D. Merrill, *Report on Investigations Made in Java in the Year 1902* (Manila Bureau of Public Printing, 1903), 10. Merrill arrived in Buitenzorg without an official appointment, but he did bring a gift of six hundred Philippine plant specimens with native names, which he then sought to match to material in Buitenzorg's herbarium, indicating how these networks made the local legible to experts and, as Merrill wrote, "anyone outside of the Philippine Islands," 11. On another trip, see Elmer D. Merrill, "Report of the Chief of the Bureau of Agriculture for the Year Ending August 31, 1902," in *Third Annual Report of the Philippine Commission, 1902* (Washington Government Printing Office, 1903), 600–601. It is worth noting that Merrill had been Scribner's assistant in Wyoming, Montana, and Idaho.

33. Luke E. Wright, "Executive Order No. 33," July 26, 1904, in *Executive Orders and Proclamations Issues by Governor-General* 2, no. 1, 61–67.

34. Thomas Hanley, "Notes on Agriculture in Ceylon and on the Botanical Gardens at Peradeniya by Thomas Hanley," in *Philippine Commission, 1902*. See also, "Report of the Chief of the Bureau of Agriculture for the Year Ending August 31, 1902," in *Third Annual Report of the Philippine Commission, 1902*, 587–596.

35. *Report of the Chief of the Bureau of Forestry, 1905. From the Report of the Philippine Commission, Part 2, Pages 265–290* (Washington Government Printing Office, 1906), 282.

36. On Buitenzorg, see Wagner, "Colonial Agronomy." On revenue generation at Lamao, see Wright, "Executive Order No. 33."

37. *Report of the Chief of the Bureau of Forestry, 1905*, 282.

38. The 1918 report of the Bureau of Agriculture noted that the Lamao Horticultural Station was having difficulty retaining workers due to higher wages offered by the Limay sawmill: "To overcome the shortage of farm hands," the report states, "women and young boys were employed during the latter part of the year at an average daily wage of 55 centavos each" for weeding by hand, watering vegetables and plants, and shelling beans. The women and young boys could do as good work as the regular laborers, if not better. The report did not indicate if the workers were connected to the Aeta group from 1904. "Lamao Horticultural Station," *Eighteenth Annual Report of the Bureau of Agriculture for the Fiscal Year Ended December 31, 1918* (Manila Bureau of Printing, 1919), 61.

39. "A Valley of Life," *The Review: A Monthly Periodical, Published by the National Prisoners' Aid Association* 1, no. 3 (1911): 2–4.

40. *Report of the Chief of the Bureau of Forestry of the Philippine Islands for the Period from September 1, 1903, to August 31, 1904* (Manila Bureau of Public Printing, 1905), 41–42.

41. James H. Shipley, "Report of the Farm Machine Expert. Report of the Chief of the Bureau of Agriculture for the Year Ending August 31, 1902. Exhibit C," in *Third Annual Report of the Philippine Commission, 1902*, 604–605.

42. "Hope for Iwahig Plan—the Colony Now on Better Footing—Prisoners Learning Agriculture and are Interested in It," *Cablenews-American* (Manila), September 17, 1907.

43. *Third Annual Report of the Philippine Commission, 1902*, 656.

44. T. H. Pardo de Tavera, *The Medicinal Plants of the Philippines*, trans. Jerome B. Thomas Jr. (Blakinston's Son, 1901), 236.

45. On the coconuts as protection from debt, see Rigoberto Tiaglo, "The Political Economy of the Philippine Coconut Industry," in David, *Political Economy of Philippine Commodities*. Norman G. Owen, *Progress Without Prosperity: Manila Hemp and Material Life in the Colonial Philippines* (University of California Press, 1984), 177, cites the Abaca landlords' practice of allowing fallen nuts to compost as evidence of the noncommercial nature of coconut growing in the Kabikol region. Christiaan G. Heersink has written about the tree's reputation as the kind of crop on which an idle man can grow rich in an Indonesia context. See, Christiaan G. Heersink, "Selayar and the Green Gold: The Development of the Coconut Trade on an Indonesia Island 1820–1950," *Journal of Southeast Asian Studies* 25, no. 1 (1994): 47.

46. William S. Lyon, *The Cocoanut, with Reference to Its Products and Cultivation in the Philippines*, Bureau of Agriculture, Bulletin No. 8 (Manila Bureau of Public Printing, 1903), 6.

47. By World War II, other industrial uses of coconut oil included ammunition, cordite explosive, protective coating for ordnance, and alkyd resin in the manufacture of shatterproof glass, and as nitroglycerin for the treatment of heart problems. US Senate, Seventy-Seventh Congress, Second Session, Subcommittee of the Committee on Finance, *S. 2079: A Bill to Authorize the Condemnation of Materials Which Are Intended for Use in Process or Renovated Butter and Which Are Unfit for Human Consumption, and for Other Purposes* (US Government Printing Office, 1942).

48. See, for instance, Josh Levy, "Ideal Coconut Country: Commodified Coconuts and the Scientific Plantation in Pohnpei, Micronesia," *Journal of Pacific History* 53, no. 4 (2018): 435–436; Holger Droessler, *Coconut Colonialism: Workers and the Globalization of Samoa* (Harvard University Press, 2022); Heersink, "Selayar and the Green Gold."

49. Hanley, "Notes on Agriculture in Ceylon," 630.

50. Copeland, *The Coco-nut*, 138.

51. Copeland, *The Coco-nut*, 135–136.

52. On Iwahig, see "Farming on Big Scale," *Cablenews-American* (Manila), December 4, 1908; On San Ramon, see *Report of the Philippine Commission* (1915), 178.

53. Copeland, *The Coco-nut*, xii.

54. Copeland, *The Coco-nut*, 146.

55. Copeland, *The Coco-nut*, x.

56. Copeland, *The Coco-nut*, xi–xii.

57. George L. Hicks, *The Philippine Coconut Industry: Growth and Change, 1900–1965* (Center for Development Planning, 1967), 6.

58. Worcester, *Coconut Growing*.

59. Copeland, *The Coco-nut*, 134.

60. Worcester, *Coconut Growing*.

61. Worcester, *Coconut Growing*, 1.

62. Copeland, *The Coco-nut*, 133.

63. Copeland, *The Coco-nut*, 175.

64. Worcester, *Coconut Growing*, 2.

65. C. H. Lamb, cited in Worcester, *Coconut Growing*, 8, 19.

66. Worcester to McIntyre, October 30, 1912, Articles, 1898–1915, and undated, concerning the Philippines, Box 2, DCW.

67. Peter James Hudson, *Bankers and Empire: How Wall Street Colonized the Caribbean* (Chicago University Press, 2017).

68. Dean C. Worcester to George Worcester, 1923, Dean C. Worcester Papers, Folder 57, Thetford Historical Society. Capitalization in the original.

69. *The Mindanao Herald* 2, no. 19 (April 1, 1905), 1.

70. My numbers are drawn from Mojares, "Worcester in Cebu," 1, 3.

71. Mojares, "Worcester in Cebu," 8.

72. Grayson L. Kirk, *Philippine Independence: Motives, Problems, and Prospects* (Farrar & Rinehart, 1936), 74.

73. "House Bill Would Cede Iwahig Penal Colony to State University," *Progress*, July 27, 1930.

Part V

Reform

Chapter 9

Cane Farmers versus Sugar Factories in Post-Emancipation Era Cuba and Brazil

GILLIAN MCGILLIVRAY

Cane farmer Juan Bautista Jiménez opened the prologue of his book *White Slaves of Las Villas* with this lament: "Some people say that there's no business like cane farming, but we, the *colonos* of Las Villas, are just the White slaves of the sugar factories."[1] At the time of writing, *colonos*—the universal term used for cane farmers in Cuba—were paid the equivalent of only four arrobas of sugar at the Havana market price in exchange for each one hundred arrobas of cane delivered to factories.[2] By the time *White Slaves* came out in 1893, the newly formed Colono Association had succeeded in pressuring Las Villas factory owners to raise the amount they paid colonos to five arrobas. Higher sugar prices related to the 1891 Spanish-US Reciprocity Treaty drove this nascent colono movement for improved pay. When the Spanish Crown ended the treaty in 1894, the movement was cut short, and Cubans took up arms in their Independence War of 1895 to 1898.[3] Bautista Jiménez belonged to a social class relatively new to Cuba, dating back to Cuba's first war for independence (1868–1878).[4] Brazil had a much deeper history with cane farmers (called *lavradores*), but other cane subcontracting systems that included colonos and suppliers (*fornecedores*) in the Southeast and *moradores* (tenants) in the Northeast expanded exponentially in the late nineteenth and early twentieth centuries.

This chapter speaks to the volume's argument that plantations relied on diverse forms of hierarchies and coercive labor. By contrasting the Cuban and Brazilian cases, it demonstrates how local contexts and global contingencies profoundly affected the hierarchies between industrialists, landowning farmers, and the workers below them. Cane farmers constituted an important category between the factory owners and field workers, brokering their knowledge and expertise with paternalistic labor management tactics to defend themselves against rising agro-industrialists. Because cane farmers mobilized in regionally specific ways, the chapter opens with an overview of the geography of sugar production and the origins of the colono system in Cuba and Brazil. Next, it highlights conflicts between cane farmers and factory owners, showing how, in both countries, cane farmers tapped into populist nationalist rhetoric in the mid-twentieth century to gain protection from the state. The question the chapter seeks to answer is, why did Cuban farmers manage to protect their interests against the powerful industrial sugar-factory owners above them when their Brazilian counterparts largely failed?

Sugar Regions, Industrial Knowledge, and the Origins of the *Colonato*

Cuba's central province of Las Villas served as a ranching zone for much of the colonial era, leaving the bulk of sugar production to the Western provinces of Havana and Matanzas. This changed during the second half of the nineteenth century, when foreign and domestic investors set up large, industrially sophisticated sugar factories on Las Villas' southern coast and in the center of the province. By the beginning of the twentieth century, Las Villas produced over one-third of the island's sugar. The second-largest producer was Matanzas to the west, with just under one-third in 1904. Oriente to the east ranked next, at seventeen percent.[5] Oriente had only recently reached this position thanks to a few very large, new sugar factories set up during or after the US occupation of Cuba from 1898 to 1902 that included the Francisco Sugar Company, the Chaparra Sugar Company, and two United Fruit Company factories. Investors in Oriente and neighboring Camagüey continued to add state-of-the-art factories, cutting down forest to make space for cane in fertile virgin lands as the twentieth century progressed.[6] By 1942, the eastern provinces including Oriente and Camagüey produced fully 55 percent of the island's sugar.[7]

Cuba's East was like Brazil's São Paulo: In both places, modern factory owners expanded sugar (and coffee) production into virgin frontiers in the early to mid-twentieth century. The difference between the two cases was that, in Cuba, the state intervened to assure that cane farmers across the island—who grew a vast majority of the cane in Cuba—could access a fair share of the sugar factories' profits. Most of these profits were made through export to the United States. In Brazil, the state intervened for regional rather than class interests, aiming to protect factory owners from Brazil's northeastern region from too much competition. Quotas were set to slow São Paulo's rise and to guarantee the traditional zone a share of Brazil's domestic market.

Cane sugar producers across Cuba, Brazil, and the world, faced rising European competition in the late nineteenth century. Protected by their national governments, beet sugar producers on the continent had developed the knowledge and technology that allowed them to expand from taking five percent of the world market in 1840 to fifty percent by the 1880s.[8] Cane producers in European colonies and newly independent nations adapted many of these new technologies from European beet to sugar cane, radically changing the sugar-making process in the later nineteenth century as rustic "mills" became "factories." Vacuum pans and steam power allowed factory owners to vastly increase the amount of cane they could grind in contrast to the humans, animals, or rivers that turned the rustic mills at slower speeds.[9] New railroad lines and river canal systems allowed factory owners to quickly access and grind cane from farther afield within twenty-four hours of workers cutting it thus guaranteeing high sucrose content.

Cuban and Brazilian mill owners needed to introduce new technologies to remain competitive on the world market just as enslaved workers achieved freedom, respectively, in 1886 and 1888. To cope with the higher costs of sugar factory equipment, the challenge of recruiting and controlling paid labor, and giant factories' need for ever-larger amounts of cane, reformers in both countries sought to separate the process of growing cane from that of making sugar.

Cuba fared better than Brazil. Sugar refineries on the densely populated East Coast of the United States purchased semirefined sugar from Cuba in ever-expanding amounts. The English, French, and Dutch refineries used European beet for their factories or purchased from cane-sugar producers in their colonies or former colonies in the Caribbean or Asia. Independent Brazil was largely excluded from the world market; producers therefore shifted their focus to the expanding numbers of consumers in southeastern Brazil drawn by Brazil's coffee boom.[10]

Brazil modernized, but sugar production in Cuba forged way ahead with access to Spanish, British, Canadian, and US financing for factories and infrastructure development. Cuba's independence wars destroyed older mills and made room for factories with enormous metal tandems to extract more juice per ton of cane. These factories could source cane from the vast plains and virgin forests of Eastern Cuba. In contrast, locals and foreigners wishing to establish factories in Brazil had to try to access capital and simultaneously work with the powerful rustic mill owners on the more hilly and older fields of the Northeast and Rio de Janeiro. The gap between Cuba and Brazil expanded so that by 1908, total productivity of Cuba's sugar factories was seventy percent greater than those of Brazil.[11] Despite these different scales of development, both countries witnessed clashes between the farmers who controlled the planting of cane and the factory owners whose workers and machinery turned the cane into sugar.

Colono-Factory Negotiations in Cuba

A 1925 *Cuba Review* article looking back at the origins of Cuba's colonato system identifies Francisco Feliciano Ibáñez, owner of the San Joaquin factory in Matanzas, as its pioneer. Ibañez encouraged smaller outlying landowners to stop processing cane in their rustic mills and to send bundles by oxcart and railroad to larger, more central sugar factories like his.[12] The larger factories were appropriately renamed *centrales*.

Ibáñez faced an uphill battle to convince neighbors they should stop grinding cane in their own rustic mills because they feared a loss of status. Their holdings would be classified as *colonias* (sugar cane farms) rather than *ingenios* (plantation mills), so they would become mere "farmers." Ibáñez published a series of pamphlets explaining how much labor and money could be saved if each district had one large factory instead of ten smaller ones. When he offered the equivalent of four US dollars for each one hundred arrobas of cane delivered to his loading stations, former mill owners finally agreed to sell him their cane. The nearly one thousand rustic sugar mills across the island in the nineteenth century consolidated or closed so that, by the 1920s, Cuba had virtually no mills but more than two hundred centrales that processed massive amounts of cane.[13]

When the price of sugar declined to the point that Ibañez could no longer pay four dollars, he and other factory owners began to pay in kind, giving colonos a certain proportion of sugar for every ton of cane delivered. Spanish water mill owners used this technique—farmers getting a proportion of flour from the corn or wheat that they delivered to each water mill. Despite the insecurity of market variations in the price of sugar, getting sugar for their cane gave cane farmers some power. As sugar stakeholders, they could bargain and receive credit from more than just one factory owner; they could negotiate with warehouse men, sugar brokers, provision merchants, or bankers.[14]

The colonos Ibañez was dealing with were prestigious rustic mill owners. On the other end of the colono spectrum, Ibañez could offer sharecropping contracts to very humble, recently arrived immigrants or formerly enslaved workers, granting them access to small plots of land in exchange for part of their harvest. Factory owners offered these colonos contracts to plant cane alongside subsistence crops, thus keeping them tied to land and factory. As a whole, most formerly enslaved individuals either preferred to work for pay or were not offered contracts: Afro-Cubans of all ranks were squeezed out of access to land in most of Cuba's sugar zones. The 1899 Census carried out during US occupation following the Spanish-American War reported that Afro-Cubans owned only four and one-half percent of the roughly fifteen thousand "sugar plantations" that included sugar factory and cane farmer–owned lands. White Cubans and immigrants controlled the remaining ninety-five percent.[15] Despite the Independence War struggles for racial equality, the Cuban government ended up imposing a US-inspired 1902 ban against non-White immigration. It allowed Spaniards to remain and keep their resources after the war and let some nine hundred thousand more Spaniards settle on the island between 1900 and 1929. In effect, elites embraced a "Whitening" project similar to that adopted a decade earlier by their Brazilian and Argentinian counterparts.[16] Humble Cubans and Spaniards rented land, while those with more resources purchased it. Both groups began to allocate a portion of land to cane as expanding rail lines made factories accessible. New entrepreneurs as well as former estate owners also bought up large plots of land and employed managers and substantial numbers of laborers. This vastly differentiated group of people on the island fell under the category of colonos.[17]

Whether they were sharecropping freedmen or large landowning colonos, all found themselves in a dependent position in relation to the factories because their cane was only valuable if processed within twenty-four hours of cutting. Most central owners tried to lock suppliers into multiyear contracts prohibiting sale to other factories.[18] Bautista Jiménez's

White Slaves accused owners of signing contracts for more cane than they needed to ensure a continuous supply for their factories.[19] This left colonos with useless ripe cane standing in their fields, unable to pay off their debts to their creditors or salaries to their workers—many of whom were Afro-Cuban freedmen or low-paid Afro-Caribbean laborers.

Colonos could fight back by threatening to withhold cane or sell to other factories. In 1905, farmers along the Cuba Company rail lines refused to grow and sell cane to the Tuinucú sugar factory in central Cuba unless the manager agreed to pay for cane pickup at the company loading stations at a rate of five arrobas of sugar per one hundred arrobas of cane. Because the Cuba Company railway owner, William Van Horne, had set up a new factory just east of Tuinucú, colonos had real bargaining power.[20]

Many other colonos in Western and Central Cuba could use this tactic of playing one factory off another because of the dense concentration of factories in these regions. Figure 9.1 shows the Cuba Company rail line and the larger number of factories in Western and Central Cuba compared to those of the East in 1917. Factory owners fought back as best they could. Tuinucú owner Manuel Rionda successfully lobbied Van Horne not to allow yet another factory on Cuba Company's rail line, squeezing out a third possible competitor from the region. Farther West, in Matanzas, a manager boasted that he "tied" and "locked" colonos to his factory by offering cash-strapped farmers credit to pay their workers and purchase seeds; in general, companies had access to far more capital.[21]

Colonos in Cuba's East were tied to single buyers since most eastern factories carved out exclusive landholdings. Many companies also controlled private ports and railroads. Eastern colonos complained that lack of competition allowed companies to pay whatever they wanted for cane, and they were, in fact, paid less than their western counterparts. In the very early twentieth century, factory owners could justify this because western colonos extracted significantly more cane in the fertile virgin soils.[22] By the 1920s, though, cane yield was leveling off between the regions, and western and central colonos who owned their own lands found themselves in a much stronger position than the majority of colonos in the East who planted cane on land rented from isolated factories.

In the East, Center, and West, some very powerful Cubans became colonos. Especially just after World War I when sugar prices peaked, many former Independence heroes bought land and became what historian Jorge Ibarra Cuesta called "Liberator-Landowners." Ibarra identified at least one hundred Independence veteran colonos selling cane to factories across the

Figure 9.1. Cuba's 198 sugar mills in 1917. *Source:* Drawn for the author by Carolyn King, Geography Department, York University.

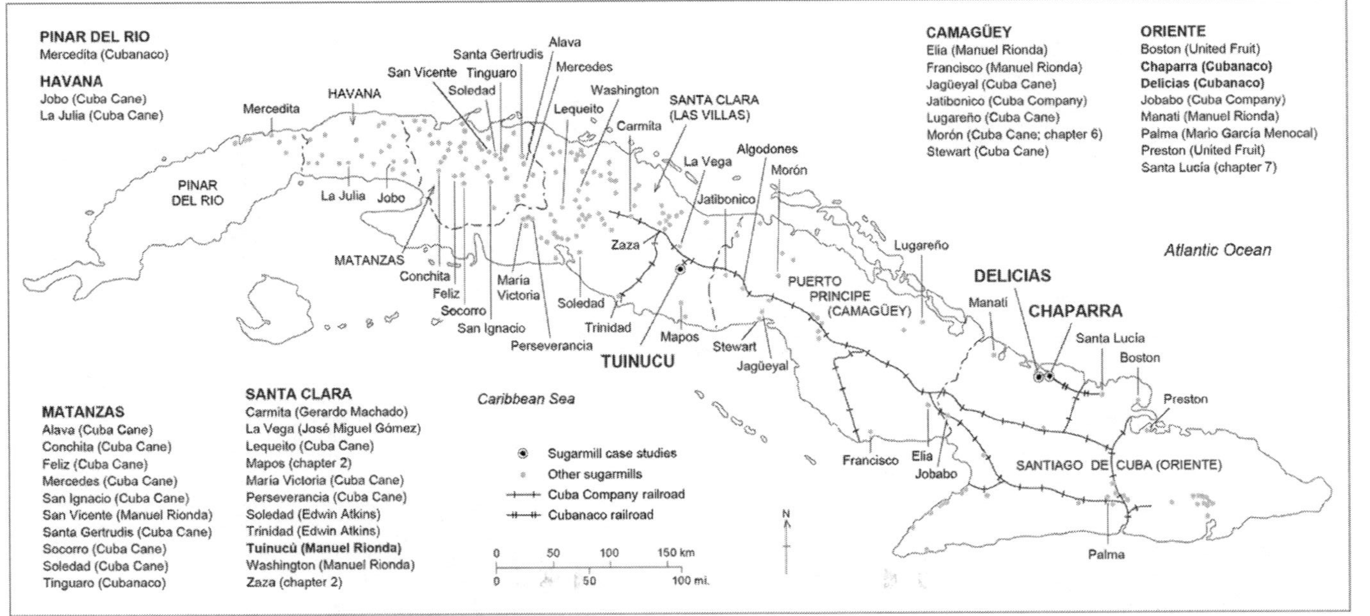

island.[23] These powerful new colonos and their predecessors developed effective strategies to push back against factory control. For example, a 1918 *Louisiana Planter and Sugar Manufacturer* article noted that it was "not at all uncommon" for colonos to light their fields on fire to force the factory to send factory employees and carts to harvest and grind the cane before it lost its sucrose.[24] Labor was expensive during World War I, so this was an important strategy that forced factories to cover the cost of field labor. Moreover, factories planned when to harvest each field according to readiness, so by forcing the factory to harvest—rather than completely lose—the burned cane, the colono could jump the queue.

Colonos could also challenge factories by compromising cane quality. For example, when the Great Depression hit in 1929, colonos at Tuinucú refused to pay for seed and threatened to plant ratoons from the previous season's harvest regardless of risk of disease. This pushed the company to give colonos more than $13,000 worth of seeds, write off debts, and offer enough credit to ensure that colonos would pay workers to plant and weed new cane. The company opted to do this to ensure a healthy cane supply for future harvests.[25]

Rionda, who owned the above-mentioned Tuinucú, summed up the colonato's many advantages in a 1913 study. Colonos shouldered most of the risks and expenses related to crop diseases, droughts, floods, fires, and the raising of the oxen required to move the cane.[26] Moreover, colonos spared factory administrators from the many details of cultivation and the "annoying" tasks of dealing with labor. It was easier to make colonos negotiate with field workers, especially as they demanded ever-higher rates. The colonato allowed sugar company managers to dedicate their full attention to the factory, railroad, shipments, and many other branches of the business. Rionda granted a $2.25 minimum price for one hundred arrobas of cane to Francisco's colonos and removed the ten-cent railroad freight charge, reasoning that "Men must be well remunerated. If not, disorder sets in."[27] The company had recently tripled the factory's capacity to three hundred thousand bags, and despite the fact colonos did not pay for these improvements, Rionda felt it reasonable that they be given a share of the increased earnings. Rionda's final sentence communicates well the reciprocal nature of the relationship: "The Company, by now being larger, has become more dependent on the colonos . . . I believe in anticipating advances to all employees, rather than [being] forced to give them. The colonos is nothing but an employee after all."[28]

Colonos did not see themselves as mere employees. An Almanac that the Association of Colonos of Chaparra and Delicias published in 1926 constitutes a powerful sample of how Eastern colonos saw themselves in relation to the company, the community, and the nation.[29] Approximately ninety percent of the two factories' 1,300 colonos belonged to the Association.[30] When addressing company administrators or President Gerardo Machado (1924–1933), they described themselves as partners of capital and natural mediators between company and field workers. That they employed thousands of workers could be used to threaten the company: They could easily paralyze cane supply if their demands were not met. It could also be used to show President Machado that they were worthy of state protection as middle-class (mostly White) Cubans employing thousands of (often Black) workers. A vast majority of Chaparra and Delicias colonos were Cuban nationals. In contrast, the Cuban American Sugar Company owners were foreign, and half of the roughly ten thousand field workers below the colonos were also foreign, many from neighboring Caribbean islands.[31] To attract sympathy and solidarity from other Cubans, the rich, educated colonos had the resources to travel to Havana or publish manifestos in the press. There, they could emphasize the plight of their poor, humble Cuban sharecropping counterparts within the same category of colonos.[32]

Three images (Fig. 9.2 a, b, and c) reproduced from the 1910 *Album de vistas del gran central Chaparra* help sketch out the profile of Chaparra and Delicias's top-tier colonos. The first shows an intimidating line-up of colonos riding toward the office on horseback, clad in fine-looking white clothing and wide-brimmed hats. The next image features a close-up of these same well-dressed men sitting on a staircase waiting for their pay. The third shows colono José M. Lasa's wife and child standing by an American-style two-story house in wide-brimmed skirt and stylish white rompers, adding to the impression of middle-class respectability. The pictures clearly demonstrate that Spanish immigrants and Cubans of Spanish-descent successfully instrumentalized the Cuban government's Whitening project to climb the social ladder.

Organizations forged by cane farmers in the East, like those of Chaparra and Delicias, gained support and solidarity from colonos in the West. Machado, who had campaigned as a populist man of the people, despite his elite status, received hundreds of letters from individuals, local chambers of congress, colono associations, and agricultural blocks across

Figure 9.2a–c. Selected images, "Album de vistas del gran central Chaparra, 1910."
Source: Biblioteca Nacional de Cuba, Havana. Public domain.

the island supporting the colonos of the East.[33] The Cuban and foreign sugar factory owner these colonos were protesting against were Machado's most lucrative supporters, but Machado faced a challenging juggling act because many colonos belonged to the well-educated, vocal bourgeoisie (including the Liberator-Landlords) that also constituted an important power base for him.

The Chaparra and Delicias colonos resolved to put their problems in Machado's hands in November 1925.[34] The president organized a meeting in Havana for company administrators and the association directors, and the company agreed to pay farmers five arrobas of sugar per one hundred arrobas of cane, as long as it could abolish the minimum price of $2.25 per one hundred arrobas. The colonos agreed, and their almanac expressed their gratitude for "the Honorable President of the Republic."[35]

The Cuban president was careful to include colono needs when he proceeded to introduce significant controls over the sugar industry. Machado's 1926 Verdeja Act imposed a ten percent decrease on the nation's crop but included a clause prohibiting factories from displacing cane-farmer cane with "administration cane" (the name given to cane cultivated directly by factories). As Ramiro Guerra y Sánchez noted in his 1927 book *Azúcar y población en las Antillas*, by protecting weak producers, Machado protected cane farmers from losing ground to larger sugar factories that might otherwise have expanded production to concentrate profits.[36]

Ramiro Guerra was an influential journalist, and his book was widely read. *Azúcar y población* would eventually land in the hands the president of Brazil's Institute for Sugar and Alcohol (IAA), Barbosa Lima Sobrinho, who cited it in his 1941 text defending greater protection for cane farmers entitled *The Economic and Social Problems of Sugar-cane Cultivation*. The text noted that, because Brazil's 1933 IAA legislation did not sufficiently detail sourcing for quotas, factory owners (*usineiros*) were squeezing out cane farmers, taking over their lands, and hiring managers and workers to plant and grind the factory's cane.

Cuban colonos fared better than their Brazilian counterparts, in part, because of the early twentieth-century solidarity building and state lobbying sampled above. The fact that Colono Association leaders were predominantly White, middle-class Cubans facing down often foreign-owned sugar companies made their fight much easier than the Brazilian-on-Brazilian struggles that would take place between agrarian cane farmers and industrial factory owners in the 1930s and 1940s. Cuba's legislation was constructed from the start with attention to cane farmer and sugar factory owner concerns. In contrast, Brazil's evolved more as part of President Getúlio Vargas's goal to balance out regions and organize the economy from above.[37]

Cuban President Machado's populist moves to help cane farmers, among other important initiatives like trying to diversify the economy and build a stronger state, gave way to repression and corruption as the Depression deepened. Cubans had to fight a revolution in 1933 to remove his regime. The Depression prompted factory owners like Rionda to remove many concessions that colonos (and workers) had come to expect. Rionda reported from Tuinucú's headquarters in New York to his on-site factory manager that sales from 1928 had yielded a profit of only $194,000. They would have to stop paying dividends, which meant "out with the idea of paying the colonos but just what they are entitled to."[38] The manager responded that, because Tuinucú was paying, on average, only $2.32 per one hundred arrobas of cane, from which they deducted rent, colonos could not pay back most of their debts and lacked the funds to pay workers to weed, cut, and haul their cane even though salaries were lower than ever. Colonos fell deeper into debt, and workers lost their jobs.[39]

Farther to the East, the on-site manager of the Chaparra and Delicias factories sought to convince New York directors that colonos should be protected from harsh cuts. It was neither a legal nor a moral matter, but rather practical. The actual cost for the company to grow its own cane averaged more than $3.00, far more than the colono minimum of $2.56.[40] Directors ignored this sound advice and insisted that, to receive payment for the 1931 harvest, cane farmers should sign a waiver agreeing that the minimum be removed for the 1932 harvest. They refused to sign. They did not get paid, nor did their thousands of agricultural workers. The entire region that depended on these workers' and farmers' purchases suffered. Colonos played the nationalist card in a 1931 *El Colono* magazine cartoon: A fat, cigar-smoking American in a fancy suit sits at his desk waving a contract at a barefoot colono who stands, shoulders slumped, with machete in hand. The colono states: "I need my money. It's been five months since you milled my cane. I cannot tend to my fields or provide for my most pressing household needs." The administrator responds, in terrible Spanish, that he is not the colono's friend and cannot pay, unless the colono signs the contract. The colono refuses, stating: "I do not want to be a slave in my nation [*en mi patria*]."[41]

Before turning to the Brazilian case, a brief reflection on Cuban colonos' rhetorical strategy is required. In their successful campaign for government protection, they drew on racialized and gendered nationalist arguments, claiming that they could protect the nation from chaos as the rural "yeomen" farmers softening conflicts between big companies and masses of workers.[42] Cuban cartoonists depicted the "typical Cuban" as a White, bearded country-bumpkin named Liborio.[43] Cane farmers—many of them former sugar mill owners unable to consolidate and modernize their mills after the independence wars, others, newer Spanish immigrants—cast themselves as White fathers unable to feed and clothe their wives and children because of greedy foreign-owned sugar factories underpaying for cane, or rapacious North American banks repossessing their lands. Important public intellectuals including Ramiro Guerra helped to propagate the defense of the idealized White male head-of-household in need of protection.[44]

First Machado (1925–1933), and then presidents Ramón Grau San Martín, Carlos Mendieta, Fulgencio Batista, and others (1934–1944) responded consistently to colono demands. Mendieta declared a moratorium in August 1934 to help colonos pay their debts. The National Colono Association was inaugurated in 1934, and the Cuban Institute for the Stabilization of Sugar created a program of land reform that essentially guaranteed tenant colonos the right to stay on the land that they cultivated permanently.[45] This was significant because, as noted earlier, most colonos were Cuban, and many of the land-owning factory owners were American. The colonos did not gain full ownership of the land, but they gained protection from eviction.

The Cane Farmers of Brazil

I have yet to come across an example of Brazilian cane farmers likening their situation to that of slaves. Evidence from the traditional sugar zones of the Northeast and Rio suggests that sugar factory owners in both regions tried to retain their former enslaved workers (*libertos*) and to attract other humble Brazilians through colono contracts. Sugar factory owners could not afford to subsidize passages for White European immigrants as their wealthy coffee planter counterparts did in the state of São Paulo. But libertos wanted to avoid dependency. An 1893 northeastern newspaper article noted that libertos embraced freedom of mobility "to the point that they would even wander around starving."[46] Even some thirty years after abolition, a 1922 agricultural ministry circular on rural Brazil reported that many workers in Pernambuco continued to opt for miserable hovels over working as wage laborers under the direction of overseers, administrators, or owners. The circular, to the inspectors' credit, also criticized employers for failing to provide benefits and treat rural workers with the civility that might have made the situation otherwise.[47]

Many libertos did remain in Brazil's sugar zones (pictured in Fig. 9.3). They tried to secure work as day laborers, but many had to accept the status of sharecroppers or resident laborers, especially in the Northeast. They risked losing access to land and jobs altogether if they ceded their limited opportunities on cane plantations to the abundant potential workforce from the nearby drought-prone regions. Libertos in Rio and their counterparts in São Paulo had more options. They could try their luck in booming cities, grow subsistence foods, and raise livestock in

Figure 9.3. Map of Brazil showing the three major sugar zones. *Source:* Map CC BY-SA 2.5 by Stefan Ertmann and João Felipe, Textugo, Joelf; sugar zones added by the author.

frontier zones, or squat in abandoned coffee zones to feed themselves and sell surplus in the local markets.

The sugar region of Campos dos Goytacazes had the highest number of enslaved people in the province of Rio de Janeiro at the time of abolition, so it offers a useful post-emancipation case study.[48] When abolition came, libertos there, like their counterparts in the Northeast and São Paulo, aimed to take control over their lives and labor, and this included family gender roles.[49] Historian Sheila Faria found evidence that formerly enslaved men preferred to avoid the colonato, and wives performed jobs outside of cane fields.[50] Journalist Arrigo de Zetirry's 1894 newspaper series on rural labor in Rio de Janeiro reported that women "claimed to have too much to do in the home," so only their husbands worked in the fields and paid "good daily wages to strangers" rather than accumulate savings.[51]

The libertos were not wrong to try to avoid contracts. Their humble counterparts who did opt to sign contracts depended on factories for credit, finding themselves tied by debt. A Rio de Janeiro colono quoted in Zetirry's same 1894 series stated that "our cane merely covers the cost of paying off the debt for the necessities we buy from the company store during the year. Our real profits come from selling our corn, manioc, and beans, since we do not need to share with anyone."[52]

As in the Cuban case, Brazilian colonos could neglect their fields, threaten to withhold their cane, sabotage it, or sell it to another factory. Sugar factory owners, on the other hand, could evict families from their houses and cut off access to cane and subsistence plots without fear of reprisals since state authorities left control largely in the hands of landlords. Colonos had much to gain in the form of housing, access to land, credit, and sometimes other benefits such as medical support or education. They had lots to lose if they disagreed with the company's price for their cane or labor.

The factory owners who gave colonos access to land depended on their agricultural knowledge—when and how to plant, weed, and harvest—but landowners also held significant power. The level of power depended on whether colonos owned or rented land, on how much land they were working, and on what sort of contract they signed (or agreed to orally) with factory owners. We saw that all who farmed cane in Cuba were called colonos. This term was also used for sharecroppers of cane in Rio de Janeiro and São Paulo. In Brazil's Northeast, the equivalent of these colonos would include groups (self-defined or labeled by others) as *fornecedores de cana, senhores de engenho, lavradores, cultivadores, arrendatários, sitieiros, moradores*, or other names according to their status. Rustic mills continued to coexist with modern factories up to and sometimes beyond the 1930s since local populations often opted for the less expensive, less refined sugars produced in these mills. Northeasterners might have sharecropping contracts (*à meação* or *à parceria*) or access to land in exchange for provision of unpaid labor (*à cambão* or *à condição*). Campos dos Goytacazes cane farmers in Rio might call themselves *agricultores, lavradores, pequenos produtores de cana, plantadores, alugados, diaristas*, or *empreiteiros*.

There is much in a name: Class-formation and political lobbying were accomplished far more quickly in major sugar-producing countries including Cuba and Puerto Rico in part because rich cane farmers were willing to throw in their lot with poor sharecroppers, and vice versa, as a single-class category of colonos. Well-educated and politically connected colonos in Cuba projected the image of the downtrodden farmer to court public opinion, tap into nationalist populist respect for the "farmer" and the "worker," and lobby the government for protection and subsidies for farmers. This was not the case in Brazil.

Brazilian farmers were in fact far more likely to emphasize their status as a traditional rural middle class of patriarchs guaranteeing stability in the countryside. Until the late 1920s, Brazil's cane farmers frequently joined factory owners, struggling to organize against merchant speculation or demanding help from the government for Brazil's sugar industry as a whole or for their region.[53] This tendency for collaboration versus conflict between cane farmers and factory owners in the early twentieth century helps explain why the Brazilian legislators intervening in the sugar industry paid less attention to cane farmers than those of Cuba.

Pernambuco cane farmers reached out directly for government assistance in a 1931 letter. These "producers of raw material," in their request to Getúlio Vargas's labor minister Lindolfo Collor, complained that their former appeals to the Labor Ministry had been bounced to the minister of agriculture. There, they remained unattended, thus this second appeal to the Ministry of Labor. The cane farmers wanted a new pay scale to increase the amount of sugar they should be credited for each kilogram of their cane. They argued that the modern *usina* factories yielded more sugar from their cane than the animal and water-run *engenho* mills that had determined the then-reigning price of thirty-eight kilograms of sugar per one thousand kilograms of cane, and they also complained that sugar factories were taking over land to plant their own cane. The cane farmers marshaled comparative evidence and arguments from around the world to support an increase, pointing out that in Cuba, sugar factories paid between forty-five and seventy-five kilograms of sugar per one thousand kilograms of cane. The farmers cited the fascist Italian Benito Mussolini's statement that "the real wealth of a people comes from the land, that is, from agriculture," and added that "the new *latifúndio* are contrary to the modern spirit moving towards the division of property as a solution to the labor problem and to promote the general progress of the state."[54] The word *latifúndio* means a large estate, and, ironically, some of the large cane farmers could be considered large estate holders themselves; their critique targeted sugar factory owners, who were expanding landholdings and hiring workers to plant and harvest cane adjacent to their factories.

Sources indicate that the labor minister supported their demand, in principle, but the state lacked the capacity to impose a new scale. Regulating pay for cane did not become possible until the IAA, established in 1933, got involved in the slow and contentious process of getting each sugar factory to submit lists of their cane farmers to determine the amount of cane each had the right to sell according to its quota. The IAA archive is full of threatening letters to sugar factories across the country demanding that they comply with the legislation to submit cane farmer maps to the IAA, from the 1940s and thereafter.[55]

At least rhetorically, Vargas reached out to farmers in the same year cane farmers wrote to his labor minister in 1931: "Regarding sugar production, support for improvements must be extended to all, including small cultivators whose needs, in general, have been sacrificed for the large industrialist sugar factory owners."[56] Vargas's *interventor* (replacement governor) to the state of Pernambuco, Lima Cavalcanti also declared, when presenting his 1932 budget proposal, that "the state government must take responsibility to stimulate production, facilitating growth by all possible means while at the same time protecting the productive classes including industrial sugar factory and sugar mill owners, and through them, the cane farmers."[57]

Vargas and Cavalcanti's quotations reveal a strategic flattening of the complex and competing groups within the "productive classes." Cavalcanti was a small industrialist whose opposition to Pernambuco's former governor Estacio Coimbra made him a clear choice as Vargas's interventor. He had ingratiated himself with the cane farmers through his family's prominent participation in the Pernambuco Cane Supplier's Association

(Centro de Fornecedores de Cana de Pernambuco), formed in 1928, but once in power he clearly favored the interests of industrialists over farmers.[58] He was not alone: The Vargas regime, as a whole, supported sugar industrialists for over a decade before they turned more explicitly to agrarian middle-class demands.

The Pernambuco Cane Supplier's Association's request to the state for mediation between themselves and the industrialists was something novel, prompted by the agricultural crises of the 1920s. Campos cane farmers (much closer to the nation's capital) had marched to Rio to engage President Artur Bernardes as early as the mid-1920s, but he was near the end of his mandate (1922–1926) and did little. Cane farmers from Campos, Pernambuco, and other sugar-producing regions had to marshal significant lobbying efforts in Rio and with the governors in their states before they finally got more significant protection through the Sugar-cane Growing Statute of 1941.[59]

In 1941, IAA President Barbosa Lima Sobrino noted with distress that sugar factory owners were taking advantage of the more stable sugar prices prompted by the IAA's quota system. Claiming that they could not meet their quotas if they had to depend on cane farmers, sugar factory owners used their superior access to credit to absorb large expanses of former cane farmer–controlled lands and to exclude independently produced cane from their factories. "Before," Lima Sobrinho wrote, "the factory would conquer land: it was the sugar *latifúndio*. Today, it is absorbing quotas." The solution that Lima Sobrinha proposed was to divide the quotas in half, between the factory and the cane farmer. He advocated this division "to guarantee the survival of the [cane farmer] class of producers that was heading towards extinction and flooding the ranks of the proletariat."[60]

The factory owners justified their expansion through economy-of-scale arguments and by emphasizing their status as modern, progressive agro-industries. A glance through the literature that they were likely reading, magazines such as the Pernambuco Agricultural Society's *A Auxiliadôra da Agricultura* and the IAA's magazine *Brasil Açucareiro* suggests that they could, indeed, learn a lot about—and consult other countries' examples of—how to improve irrigation, planting, and cane farmer varieties, but agronomists complained that factory owners (usineiros) ignored their advice as much as cane farmers.[61] The factory owner land grab may also have been a response to the cane farmers' mobilization; it made sense for factories to exclude farmers before a united movement emerged.

They were right to be concerned; many farmers and their new associations sent letters and telegrams to Vargas and his ministers asking for help. One such missive begged the president to ask the IAA to buy up their cane as a means to avoid the "complete ruin of the traditional farming class of Pernambuco."[62] Gilberto Freyre, José Lins do Rego, and many other public intellectuals got involved in the defense of the smaller producers versus the modern, capitalist factories. The cane farmers and rustic producers cast the expansion of the modern agro-industrial factory complexes as a new version of the latifúndio that put at risk the "peaceful social fabric" and *peculiar* relations in the countryside. The term "peculiar" comes from a 1943 article and could be translated as "unique" or "special"—meaning: paternalistic, versus the big sugar factories with their armies of agrarian and industrial workers.[63]

Cane farmer advocates in Brazil, as in Cuba, presented farmers as an agrarian middle-class barrier against proletarian revolution, arguing that if farmers were paid more, they could pay their workers more and keep them separate from other workers, "content" on cane farmers' imagined agrarian paternalist utopia. Brazil's Lima Sobrinho used a direct quote from Cuba's Ramiro Guerra to make this argument: "The sugar latifúndio is eradicating farmers from the soil by purchasing their lands on a grand scale, swelling the ranks of the proletariat in urban centers while exploiting others as dependent workers and sharecroppers. The latifúndio is causing the entire independent farming class to suffocate, bit by bit, impoverishing and lowering their standard of living, creating unbearable living conditions for them. The latifúndio is thus a formidable agent contributing to poverty and urbanization . . . disturbing the entire rural economy."[64] The IAA gradually realized that state intervention had undermined the cane farmers, and the 1941 Sugar-cane Growing Statute was conceived as a response to this. Factory owners mounted a huge lobbying campaign against reform, sending representatives and delegations to badger the IAA in Rio de Janeiro and mounting press campaigns. They succeeded in getting quotas for cane farmers watered down from seventy-five to fifty percent. Cane farmers, in turn, mounted their own campaigns that succeeded in keeping the quota at fifty percent and closed loopholes that might have allowed sugar factory family members or close associates to be rebaptized "cane suppliers" as a factory work-around to the new laws.

Taking a turn back to Cuba, the island's 1937 Sugar Coordination Law guaranteed cane farmers quotas at each factory, the right to permanent tenure, and higher standardized prices for their cane, among other benefits. The legislation also established a fixed cap that could be charged for land and tables indexing worker salaries to the price of cane. It is significant that Brazil's otherwise similar Sugar-cane Growing Statute did not include these last two measures because powerful factory owner and cane farmer lobby groups had convinced legislators that the "special (*peculiar*)" conditions reigning in each different sugar zone of the Brazil needed to be understood before establishing such caps and payment tables.[65]

Conclusion: The Circulation of Political Knowledge and State Capacity

Ideas and legislation relating to sugar and labor policy circulated widely. Brazil's Lima Sobrinho was evidently inspired by Ramiro Guerra's writings, and Brazil's Sugar-cane Growing Statute passed in 1941 was in many ways similar to Cuba's 1937 Sugar Coordination Law. Critics accused the Brazilian IAA of being Marxist, as had critics of Cuba's Sugar Stabilization Institute and other nation's dirigiste efforts to limit, impose quotas, and distribute the benefits from their national sugar industries more evenly among producing sectors. It took a lot of institution building for these societies to be able to map, document, and regulate production across their nations. The process that began in 1930s Cuba and Brazil took place under corporatist authoritarian regimes inspired by models such as Mussolini on the Right, and the Mexican Revolution on the Left.

These ambitious state regulatory projects were particularly complex when it came to decisions on how to regulate an agro-industry like cane sugar production, as demonstrated by the 1931 cane farmer association letter that got bounced back and forth between the Ministries of Labor and Agriculture. Those cane farmers quoted Mussolini, as did Lima Sobrinho, who also quoted eclectically from John Stuart Mill, Franklin Delano Roosevelt, and others. The IAA's magazine, *Brasil Açucareiro*, includes extensive coverage over the course of the 1930s of the US New Dealer's approach to sugar quotas as well as a direct transcription of Cuba's complex laws. The specter—or inspiration, depending on one's perspective—of Mexican Revolutionary land reform also entered the discussions surrounding protection for cane farmers in the debates over Brazil's 1941 Sugar-cane Growing Statute.[66] Well-read Brazilians may, indeed, have feared or been inspired by the populist example of Lázaro Cárdenas, who redistributed lands among workers in the 1930s to create the Emiliano Zapata cooperative sugar factory in Morelos and the Los Mochis cane farmer cooperative in Sinaloa. Such transnational circulation was not just theoretical in the case of Cuba and Mexico: Cuba's Fulgencio Batista visited the Emiliano Zapata mill in Mexico, and Cuban sugar workers formed the first national association of sugar workers during a visit to Mexico City.

Before state intervention into sugar, cane farmers and factory owners had to negotiate many challenging issues one-on-one. Who weighed the cane? What price or portion of sugar cane did farmers get from the final product? Were they paid according to weight or quality? Colonos could have their workers mix sticks in among the cane to make it weigh more. They could send cane to other factories despite factory-sunk costs in railroads, cane loading stations, and other infrastructure. Factory owners could make strategic use of ignorance, taking advantage of low literacy and math skills to skew weighing scales or toy with how quality was measured. In most places, cane farmers and factory owners managed to negotiate these tensions to achieve an uneasy coexistence/alliance through World War I, the two groups seeing themselves as part of the same elite "owner/producer" class needing to control the workers below them.

When sugar's price bounced dramatically up and down during World War I and the postwar years, cane farmers began to organize separately from factory owners—in Cuba, *Associaciones de Colonos* branched off from *Associaciones de Hacendados*; in Brazil, *Associações de Fornecedores de Cana* or *Plantadores* emerged as separate from *Usineiro* associations. Both groups turned to national states to demand intervention and mediation. Cane farmers in Brazil did not emerge as triumphantly as their Cuban counterparts. The colono umbrella name helped Cubans, as did their lobbying strategies. The argument Charles Bergquist presented in his comparative study of labor in Latin America may also apply. He noted that "where export production involved a class and national dichotomy, one of national labor versus foreign capital, export workers were better able to mobilize the powerful sentiment of patriotism—a sentiment fostered by the dominant culture—in support of their class interests."[67] Cuban cane farmers needed only make the case that they were Cuban and that they were a middle class worthy of protection against large foreign companies. Brazilian farmers had to convince the state that farmers were as important as industrialists. This, in the context of World War II developmentalist Brazil, was a tough case to make.

Notes

1. Thanks to Nicholas B. Miller, Ulrike Lindner, and the Plantation Knowledge participants for their feedback on this chapter; to the Social Sciences and Humanities Council of Canada for research support; and to Duke University Press for permission to include references from my previous book on Cuba and forthcoming book on Brazil. Translations from the Spanish and Portuguese are mine, unless otherwise noted. Thanks also to James Cypher and Mark Jurdjevic. Juan Bautista Jimenez, *Los Esclavos Blancos: por un colono de Las Villas* (Havana, 1893), 3. Rebecca J. Scott was kind enough to help me locate this source, referenced in her pioneering comparative research on post-emancipation Cuba, Brazil, and Louisiana.

2. Four arrobas were roughly forty kilograms. From this, factory owners deducted additional fees to cover transportation costs. "El concepto de colono en Cuba es . . . en general, la persona que se dedica al cultivo de la caña de azúcar; siendo la clase de cultivo la característica distintiva del colono cubano." Angel Usategui y Lezama, *El Colono Cubano: Ensayo de Derecho Agrario* (Jesus Monteiro, Obra laureada y premiada por el Colegio de Abogados de la Habana, en el Concurso de Obras Jurídicas de 1938), 19.

3. Gillian McGillivray, *Blazing Cane: Sugar Communities, Class, and State Formation in Cuba, 1868–1959* (Duke University Press, 2009), 158; Rebecca J. Scott, *Slave Emancipation in Cuba: The Transition to Free Labor, 1860–1899* (Princeton University Press, 2005), 279–293.

4. The war failed, in part, because planters in the West preferred to remain part of the empire to protect sugar and slavery, but that war and the Little War of 1879 did succeed in paving the way for slave emancipation in 1886.

5. Las Villas produced thirty-five percent, Matanzas produced thirty-one percent, the western province of Havana produced thirteen percent, and Pinar del Rio (in the West) and Camagüey (in the East) produced roughly two percent each. See L. V. de Abad, *Azúcar y caña de azúcar: Ensayo de orientación cubana* (Mercantil Cubana, 1945), 396.

6. Reinaldo Funes documents the environmental impacts in *From Rainforest to Canefield: An Environmental History since 1492* (University of North Carolina Press, 2008).

7. de Abad, *Azúcar y caña de azúcar*, 396.

8. Luis González, "Law, Hegemony, and the Politics of Sugar Cane Growers Under Getúlio Vargas: Campos, Rio de Janeiro, Brazil, 1930–1950" (PhD diss., University of Minnesota, 1998), 51.

9. See also Christina Skott's chapter in this volume.

10. Consul-General George T. Colman, "Increase in Brazilian Sugar Exportation," May 14, 1923, in US National Archives, RG 166 Foreign Agricultural

Service, Box 66, File: "Brazil: Sugar & Molasses, 1908–1933." Rio had always had more of a focus on the domestic market and on consumers in nearby Argentina and Uruguay, but its producers had to battle it out with the Northeast and São Paulo for Brazil's domestic consumer market in the twentieth century.

11. McGillivray, "The Colonial Compact, 1500–1895," *Blazing Cane*; Funes, *From Rainforest to Canefield*; David Albert Jr. Denslow, "Sugar Production in Northeastern Brazil and Cuba, 1858–1908" (PhD diss., Yale University, 1974).

12. Manuel Rionda (presumed author), "The Cuban Colono System," *Cuba Review* 24, no. 1 (December 1925): 19–28. As early as 1862, the Conde Pozos Dulces Francisco de Frías wrote that Cuba's salvation lay in separating agriculture from industry: "la caña cultivada intensivamente y con todos los recursos de la ciencia, tan hábilmente expuestos por el autor, presupone desde luego la separación del cultivo de la fabricación. . . . En esa división y en esos progresos está cifrada la salvación de Cuba como pueblo agricultor." Prologue to Alvaro Reynos, *Ensayo sobre el cultivo de la caña de azúcar*, 4th ed. (Talleres Tipográficos de "El magazine de la raza," 1925), xxviiii.

13. Rionda (presumed author), "The Cuban Colono System," 19–28.

14. Rionda (presumed author), "The Cuban Colono System," 19–28.

15. US War Department, *Report on the Census of Cuba* (1900), 556–557, cited in Rebecca J. Scott, "Defining the Boundaries of Freedom in the World of Cane: Cuba, Brazil, and Louisiana after Emancipation," *American Historical Review* 99, no. 1 (February 1994): 82.

16. Aline Helg, "Race in Argentina and Cuba, 1880–1930: Theory, Policies, and Popular Reaction," in *The Idea of Race in Latin America*, ed. Richard Graham (University of Texas Press, 1990), 56; Aline Helg, *Our Rightful Share: The Afro-Cuban Struggle for Equality, 1886–1912* (University of North Carolina Press, 1995); Ada Ferrer, *Insurgent Cuba: Race, Nation, and Revolution, 1868–1898* (University of North Carolina Press, 1999); Alejandro de la Fuente, *A Nation for All: Race, Inequality, and Politics in Twentieth-Century Cuba* (University of North Carolina Press, 2001).

17. Scott, "Defining the Boundaries of Freedom," 82.

18. For another example of insubordination and resistance, see Moritz von Brescius's chapter in this volume.

19. Bautista Jiménez, *Los Esclavos Blancos por un colono de Las Villas*, 7.

20. Pedro Alonso, Tuinucú, to Manuel Rionda, April 6, 1905, Braga Brothers Collection (University of Florida), Record Group 2, Series 1, file: Alonso, Pedro (1902–8), Tuinucú.

21. Bolivar Moyano-Fraga, "*Central-Colono* Relations Within the Cuban Sugar Industry, 1914–1993: Exploring the Local Consequences of Global Changes, the Case of San Vicente from World War I to the Great Depression" (MA thesis, University of Florida, 1997), 60.

22. McGillivray, *Blazing Cane*, 143.

23. "Libertador-Terratenientes," Ibarra Cuesta, *Cuba 1898–1921*, Apendice F, Relación de oficiales del Ejército Libertador que se convirtieron en grandes colonos, 418–425. "Large" is defined as capable of producing more than five hundred thousand arrobas.

24. "News Letter from Our Havana Office," *Louisiana Planter* 60 (February 16, 1918), 103.

25. Oliver Doty, Tuinucú, to Manuel Rionda, February 6, 1929, Braga Brothers Collection (University of Florida), Record Group 2, Series 10a–c, file: Tuinucú: Doty, Oliver K., Letters (1929), Tuinucú.

26. For other instances of ecological precarity, see also the chapters by Rebekah McCallum, Christina Scott, Claudia Roesch, and Moritz von Brescius in this volume.

27. Manuel Rionda, "Study Made January 22, 1913, Relative to Colonos at FRANCISCO," Braga Brothers Collection (University of Florida), Record Group 2, Series 10, file: Miscellaneous.

28. Manuel Rionda, "Study Made January 22, 1913."

29. *Memoria de la Asociación de Colonos de los Centrales "Chaparra" y "Delicias" Correspondiente a los años 1924 a 1925 y 1925 a 1926* (National Library of Cuba).

30. Manager memo from R. B. Wood, October 6, 1930, Archivo Histórico Provincial de Las Tunas, Fondo Cuban-American Sugar Company, legajo 41, expediente 473.

31. A few years before the Almanac was published, the *Agricultura y Zootecnia* feature on the mills noted there were 1,390 Cuban colonos and only ten foreigners (July 1924): 39–40.

32. McGillivray, *Blazing Cane*, 165.

33. These rich letters and manifestos can be found in the Archivo Nacional de Cuba's Fondo Secretaría de la Presidencia, legajo 97, expediente 1.

34. The colonos also lobbied senators and representatives from the East to support or vote down legislation that affected them, the almanac publishing several cases whereby politicians voted as the colonos requested. This demonstrates the strength of nationalist politics whereby colonos had more power during the extremely mercurial sugar price decade of the 1920s.

35. McGillivray, *Blazing Cane*, 183.

36. Ramiro Guerra y Sánchez, *Azúcar y población en las Antillas* (Cultural S. A., 1927).

37. Sobrinho published a study to defend the new *Estatuto de Lavoura Canavieira* (Sugar-cane Growing Statute). Barbosa Lima Sobrinho, *Problemas econômicos e sociais da lavoura canavieira* (Ed. Z. Valverde, 1941). For context, see Joan L. Bak, "Cartels, Cooperatives, and Corporatism: Getúlio Vargas in Rio

Grande do Sul on the Eve of Brazil's 1930 Revolution," *Hispanic American Historical Review* 63, no. 2 (May 1983): 255–275.

38. Manuel Rionda to Oliver Doty, January 31, 1929, BBC, RG 2, S. 10, file: Tuinucú, Colonos—A&L.

39. McGillivray, *Blazing Cane*, 193.

40. R. B. Wood to Directors, New York, October 6, 1930, APLT, CASC, leg. 41, exp. 473.

41. In most cases, colonos had shoes and would hire workers to use machetes, but the fact that there were some humble colonos made the cartoon effective. *El Colono (junio/julio* 1931): 19, APLT, CASC, Fuera de Caja #224, leg. 41, exp. 474.

42. Thomas Jefferson praised small independent "yeomen" farmers as the backbone for democracy in nineteenth-century America; various American and Latin American thinkers have echoed this argument since.

43. Gregory T. Cushman, "De qué color es el oro? Race, Environment, and the History of Cuban National Music, 1898–1958," *Revista De Música Latino Americana - Latin American Music Review* 26, no. 2 (Autumn/Winter 2005): 169.

44. Antonio S. Pereira did much the same thing in Puerto Rico.

45. Louis A. Pérez Jr., *Cuba: Between Reform and Revolution*, 2nd ed. (Oxford University Press, 1995), 268.

46. Cited in Michael Hall and Paulo Sergio Pinheiro, *A classe operária no Brasil 1880–1930* (São Paulo: Editora Brasiliense, 1981) 2:19–23; see Scott, "Defining the Boundaries of Freedom," 97.

47. Brazil, Ministerio da Agricultura, Industria e Commercio, Directoria do Serviço de Inspecção e Fomento Agrícolas, *Aspectos da economia rural brasileira* (Rio de Janeiro, 1922), 347–348, cited in Scott, "Defining the Boundaries of Freedom," 98.

48. Waldick Pereira, *Cana, Café & Laranja: História Econômica de Nova Iguaçu* (Fundação Getúlio Vargas, 1977), 104. Hildete Pereira de Melo noted that when abolition came in 1888, the coffee harvest was just beginning, but there were no losses because the price of coffee was high. In contrast, sugar factories around Campos stopped operating as the price of sugar was so low as to make it impossible to pay workers. Hildete Pereira de Melo, "Coffee and Development of the Rio de Janeiro Economy, 1888–1920," in *The Global Coffee Economy in Africa, Asia, and Latin America, 1500–1989*, eds. William Gervase Clarence-Smith and Steven Topik (Cambridge University Press, 2003), 378.

49. Research from São Paulo and Pernambuco shows libertos preferring to keep mothers and daughters close to home to care for younger children, take care of animals and kitchen gardens, cook, and do household chores. Parents tried to keep their daughters away from predatory male overseers. Christine Rufino Dabat wrote: "Para as moças e meninas o trabalho na roça era preferido, pois era considerado mais seguro, talvez mais decente." Christine Rufino Dabat,

Moradores de Engenho: Relações de trabalho e condições de vida dos trabalhadores rurais na zona canavieira de Pernambuco segundo a literatura, a academia e os próprios atores sociais (Editora Universitária da UFPE, 2007), 457. See, in particular, sections "Questão de gênero" up to "Trabalho na roça," 456–461, and "Produção alimentícia familiar no contexto de plantação," 628–635. This was also the case for freed slaves in São Paulo; see George Reid Andrews, *Blacks and Whites in São Paulo, Brazil 1888–1988* (University of Wisconsin Press, 1991), 84: "Following emancipation, the most intractable of the Libertos' labor demands, and the most significant, as viewed both by the planters and the ex-slaves themselves, was that women and children no longer be employed in field labor."

50. Sheila Siqueira de Castro Faria, "Terra e Trabalho em Campos, 1850–1920" (MA thesis, Universidade Federal Fluminense, 1986).

51. Arrigo de Zetirry, "Artigo no. VIII. A Lavoura no Estado do Rio," *Jornal do Comércio*, 14/07/1894 a 21/10/1894, quoted in Faria, "Terra e Trabalho," 295.

52. Zetirry, "Artigo no. X. A Lavoura no Estado do Rio," quoted in Faria, "Terra e Trabalho," 291.

53. Guillermo Palacios, "Os plantadores de cana de Pernambuco na primeira metade do século XX: nascimento, crise e consolidação de uma 'classe' agrária," *FGV/EIAP Cadernos da EIAP—Série Desenvolvimento Agricola* 1 (1979), 133.

54. Translation by the author. Letter, Augusto Cavalcanti e comissão representando a grande classe dos fornecedores de cana de Pernambuco, Recife, to Lindolfo Collor, Ministerio do Trabalho dos Estados Unidos do Brasil, July 3, 1931, LC c1931.07.03, FGV. The Brazilian architects of the *Estado Novo* were also inspired by Mussolini; see Angela de Castro Gomes, *A Invenção do Trabalhismo*, 3rd ed. (Fundação Getúlio Vargas, 2005), and John French, *Drowning in Laws: Labor Law and Brazilian Political Culture* (University of North Carolina, 2004).

55. Arquivo Nacional, Gabinete Civil de la Presidencia de la República, Lata 459, Código do Fundo 36, Seção de Guarda SDE, IAA, 1942.

56. Translation by the author. The exact date of the speech is not mentioned. Mario Bulhão, "O Estatuto da Lavoura Canavieira," *Brasil Açucareiro* 20, no. 3 (September 1942): 91.

57. "O governo do Estado tem o dever de estimular a producção, facilitando-a por todas as formas, amparando as classes productoras, uzineiros e banguêzeiros, e, por intermedio d'aquelles, os plantadores de canna." This article uses the term "sugar factory" for *usina* and "sugar mill" for the less sophisticated *bangüe/engenho* category.

58. Called the *Estatuto de Lavoura Canavieira*. Palacios, "Os plantadores de cana," 148.

59. González, "Law, Hegemony, and the Politics of Sugar Cane Growers," 336.

60. It reads "*aumentando as fileiras do proletariado*" in the original letter, Alexandre Barbosa Lima Sobrinho, Rio de Janeiro, to Agamenon Magalhães, Recife, May 3, 1941, AGMc1941.05.03, microfilm foto 354, FGV. Lima Sobrinho explained

that "muitos fornecedores passaram de donos de quotas a simples administradores de engenhos dessas usinas reajustadas." This managerial role was certainly a step down from land ownership, but Lima Sobrinho exaggerated in calling them part of the "proletariat." Lima Sobrinho, Rio de Janeiro, to Magalhães, Recife, July 5, 1941, AGMc1941.07.05/2, FGV.

61. Thomas Rogers, "Chapter 4: Modernizing the Sugar Industry: Cane Expansion and the Path toward Rationalization," in *The Deepest Wounds: A Labor and Environmental History of Sugar in Northeast Brazil* (University of North Carolina Press, 2010).

62. Original reads: "ruina completa tradicional classe lavoura Pernambuco" Telegram, Novais Filho, Presidente Assembléia, Neto Campelo Junior, Presidente Sindicato Plantadores, Antonio Alves Araujo, Presidente Sociedade Auxiliadora, Recife, to Getúlio Vargas, Maior Bemfeitor Regimen Republicano, Rio de Janeiro, November 18, 1938, Fondo Gabinete Civil Presidencia de la República, Lata 458, Arquivo Nacional, Rio de Janeiro.

63. M. Lacerda de Melo, "Lavradores de engenho e fornecedores de usinas," *Brasil Açucareiro* 22, no. 6 (December 1943): 502–507.

64. Translation by the author. Lima Sobrinho, *Problemas econômicos e sociais da lavoura canavieira*, 47.

65. de Melo, "Lavradores de Engenhos e Fornecedores de Usinas," 502–507.

66. Palacios, "Os plantadores de cana," 166.

67. Charles Bergquist, *Labor in Latin America: Comparative Essays on Chile, Argentina, Venezuela and Colombia* (Stanford University Press, 1986), 11.

Chapter 10

Managing Regulation

Changes of Policy and Continuities of Practice on Indian Tea Plantations, 1901–1931

Rebekah McCallum

In 1929, John Henry Whitley (1866–1935), a British Member of Parliament from 1900 to 1928 and speaker of the House of Commons from 1921 to 1928, was made chairman of the Royal Commission on Labour in British India, which had been established to gain knowledge about conditions of labor on local plantations.[1] The commission's report, compiled and published in 1931, stated that "the plantation represent[ed] the development of the agricultural resources of tropical countries in accordance with the methods of Western industrialism" and also noted that in 1931, "about 90% of the [tea, coffee, and rubber] plantations in North India and nearly all those in Madras and Burma [were] controlled and managed by Europeans."[2] In 1939, approximately thirteen managing agencies in Calcutta, associated with international companies, controlled more than seventy-five percent of India's total tea production.[3] In 1946, just before Indian independence, "interests in the United Kingdom—mainly limited liability companies" still owned sixty percent of India's tea acreage, with eighty percent of that percentage "represented by ten leading agency houses in Calcutta."[4]

The managing agency system that underpinned the tea industry in India included British agents who acted on behalf of the boards of joint stock companies in Glasgow and London to make decisions concerning legality, recruitment, contracts, shipping, trade, policy, legislation, labor, and more.[5] The agents were usually British or European men with prior experience in India who were thought to have the in-country expertise and knowledge of local and global networks from South Asia that were considered invaluable to British boards. These agents operated from the big cities of South Asia (for example, Calcutta and Colombo) and as partnerships or small companies; by 1868, almost two-thirds of the established tea companies in South Asia had managing agents.[6] Because of their power and exclusionary practices, the autonomy of these agencies was significantly reduced by the Companies Act of 1956 before eventually being outlawed by the independent Indian government in 1970.[7]

During the first half of the twentieth century, managing agencies held significant control over tea production, including the policies adapted by the wider tea industry. Agents accumulated various companies under their control and formed them into a network of smaller companies (and sometimes subsidiaries) that controlled the entire supply chain: from shipping and warehousing to plantation recruitment and management. Their decision-making power in the principal-agent relationship was protected from shareholders through long-term legal contracts with the companies' directors and was not dependent on whether the company turned a profit. Proxy votes, control stock, and tax-exempt joint reserves for their companies also gave them sway on company boards that enabled them to wield power in a way that was beneficial and low risk to themselves.[8]

These agents, their companies, and other (mostly) British tea planters formed a network of operation resulting in the formation of regional associations—like the Indian Tea Association (ITA). While the government formed labor boards and enquiries to understand the industry, these associations lobbied the government for industry policies that favored their influence.[9] Although they were externally focused, these regional associations also shaped the industry by calling for mutual agreement from their constituent companies to comparable business strategies and policy measures for running their plantations. The companies that advocated for these measures enjoyed greater representation and freedoms in labor boards, legislation, recruitment, and self-management. The agreements formed in these associations strengthened their collective position and solidified their place as experts and authorities in the industry.

The Royal Commission on Labour of 1931 was one of the first government commissions that included interviews with laborers.[10] Until that point, most government commissions had simply asked the directors, agents, and managers of companies and plantations to give their insight into the conditions of laborers on the estates, including their needs, wants, and living conditions. They declined to interview laborers even for official labor inquiries, citing several reasons: Lack of precedent, the putative unreliability of information given by uneducated laborers, and the worry that asking laborers to voice their concerns and experiences might lead to greater labor unrest.[11] One such committee justified their approach on the basis of the well-being of the laborers and provided the managers of the plantations with questionnaires to offer their viewpoints in the laborers' best interests. Included were some leading questions, such as: "How far do you think it true that an appreciable rise in the rate of wages would result in the coolie not earning more from the garden, but in his doing less work for the same pay?"[12]

This chapter examines how managing agents and companies used their knowledge of the tea industry—bolstered by government affirmation of that knowledge—to shape plantation labor policy for laborers on the plantation in the early twentieth century and, most specifically, prior to 1931. The managing agents and their company representatives had a considerable voice and power in shaping industrial policy and regulation through the first half of the twentieth century, even that pertaining to the working and living conditions of their South Asian labor force. At the turn of the twentieth century, the relevant legislation was primarily concerned with reducing risks and abuses toward laborers during recruitment and transport to the plantation and less about conditions once on the plantation. Company representatives sat on government committees to persuade the government to act in the companies' interests, and government officials came to the association meetings of the tea companies and planters for insight into the industry and to discuss opportunities for collaboration.[13] In the early decades of the twentieth century, this relationship and "trust" in the plantation knowledge of managing agents and company representatives resulted in favorable legislation for their companies in regard to taxation, labor recruitment, and labor management.

Early Company Influence in the South Asian Tea Industry

The British tea industry in South Asia began in the region of Assam in the mid-1830s, in response to the desire of the chartered East India Company (EIC) to retain monopolistic privileges over the lucrative trade in tea. At the time, most tea was sourced from China, and the EIC traded opium from their territories in exchange for the product—leading to what is known as the Opium Wars.[14] When, by government charter, the EIC was reduced to a governmental body on the shores of India, and their commercial monopoly on tea slated to end (1833), the EIC sought to find indigenous tea plants in India, to smuggle some tea plants from China, and to develop large-scale gardens for their growth. Eventually, they were successful, and Assam tea became a marketable product.[15] The Assam Company, a joint-stock company comprised of merchants based in London and Calcutta, took advantage of the EIC's land-leasing rates and quickly invested, setting the precedent for the presence of large companies in the industry. After an initial bust in the industry following a "tea mania" in which many small and independent investors were ruined, large multiproduct trading and agro-industrial companies began to invest with the assistance of managing agencies, considerably expanding tea cultivation in the region.[16]

Finlays, for example, provides a great case study for examining the way that managing agencies and tea companies entered the tea industry. Finlays was founded as a trading company in Glasgow in 1750 by James Finlay (1727–1790) with financial interests in cotton, jute, warehousing, textile mills, and shipping.[17] It traded mainly with East and South Asia and was not known to be connected with the transatlantic slave trade. Its branches in South Asia (Finlay, Muir & Co.) were opened in Calcutta in 1870 and in Colombo in 1893 to oversee their own business interests in the East and to act as a managing agency for several joint-stock companies in varied industries.

Finlays continued to expand its operations; in the 1880s, it traded in hemp, tobacco, rape-seed, linseed, saltpeter, sugar, poppy seed, castor oil, shellac, rice, silk, jute, hides, indigo, and ginger.[18] It also began to invest in tea plantations and manage them for other companies.[19] Finlays invested some £5 million in South Asian tea estates and by 1901 possessed 270,000 acres of land—with approximately 77,000 of those acres planted with tea—and had a 70,000-strong South Asian labor force working across the Indian and Ceylonese plantations of its own four "leviathan" tea companies.[20] At the turn of the century, these four—Consolidated Tea & Lands Co. of Edinburgh, Amalgamated Tea Estates Co. of Glasgow, Kanan Devan Hills Produce Co. of Glasgow, and Anglo-American Direct Tea Trading Co. of Edinburgh—were some of the largest tea companies in South Asia.[21]

While managing agents like Finlays facilitated the management of other companies by building international connections that enabled the transport and storage of commodities, as well as the expansion of markets for consumer goods, they also directed the management personnel of their own tea plantations. In concert with the board in Glasgow, the Finlays managing agents assigned European employees, often from Glasgow, to management positions on the plantations, where they usually began working as assistant managers. The agents arranged for the employees' salary and contracts (that usually required three to five years of work) and ensured employee compliance with company policy.[22] These agents, though located miles away from the plantations themselves, were also involved in the creation of networks for the recruitment of South Asian laborers to work on the tea estates.

Because these managing agencies and company representatives were involved in all aspects of the industry, they were often consulted by the government for their knowledge and expertise, which allowed them to influence the crafting of legislation. The tea plantations in India were classified as industrial sites and thus had many legal and structural similarities to jute mills and factories throughout India run by British companies and officials. However, when it came to labor, the tea plantations were often exempted from legislation protecting laborers working in industrial concerns. This was, in part, because the tea industry leaders argued that their plantations were also agricultural concerns—as Whitley's definition at the start of the chapter implies.

The Tea Industry at the End of the Nineteenth Century as Agricultural Enterprise: Exemptions and Consequences for the Labor Force

The association with agriculture in the early part of the twentieth century meant that the tea industry was effectively freed from industrial taxation until 1927, when the exact percentage of the tea industry (and plantations) determined to be industrial, and thus taxable, was set at forty percent.[23] The exemptions that the tea industry experienced in the first several decades of the twentieth century were a topic of concern by Indian nationalist groups and those who considered these exemptions to be further examples of the tea industry's privileges and ability to persuade the government through a "sly but influential movement . . . to secure for the tea industry its old time privileges at the expense of the public revenue."[24] When the Indian government attempted to implement the tax because the tea industry was not entirely agricultural, the planters were able to persuade the government to extend their exemptions, which was viewed by Indian nationalist journalists as another concession "to the selfish agitation set up by the Calcutta tea-planters" which, in their eyes, impeded the government's ability to create public utilities and infrastructure that would benefit the wider Indian population.[25]

A court case put forward in 1918 by the Killing Valley Tea Estate (under the agency of Finlays from 1908) challenged the British Government of India in the Calcutta High Courts about whether tea was primarily an agricultural enterprise or an industrial one—and therefore taxable.[26] Prior judgments had concluded that the income tax be levied against employees of the companies (assistant managers, clerks, doctors, etc.) as industrial workers, yet managers of the plantations were exempted because they were determined to be agricultural cultivators rather than industrialists.[27] The Killing Valley Tea Estate court case resulted in an inconclusive verdict that the tea industry was agricultural and industrial, and therefore, the determination of what was taxable would be based on what part of the tea enterprise was industrial. Tea planters continued to argue that the tea enterprise was indivisible and that the determination of what was agricultural and what was industrial was irrelevant.[28] Planters felt threatened by increased and levied taxes because in addition to the cost, it seemed to be an encroachment on management and control of the tea plantation through the attempt to bring the tea industry in line with other agro-industrial industries, like sugar and jute.[29] Tea planters felt that tea plantations were significantly distinct from these other industries and merited their own evaluations regarding taxation and legislation. The debate continued until 1927.

Interestingly, the conversation about whether the tea industry was agricultural or industrial—or both or neither—also shaped the conversation about the conditions, wages, recruitment, and welfare of the laborers on the estates. The tea plantations were initially exempted from the welfare legislation that directed occupational conditions in other industries, primarily because they were not considered to be full industrial sites. If planters gave on the issue of taxation, then some of the other legislation and policies regarding industrial concerns might apply.

As the British tea companies had been given tremendous power to govern themselves, the encroachment of welfare legislation and labor discussions into the plantation were considered a challenge to the planters' control over the plantation and to their knowledge of their workers' needs. Government intervention was seen as an external restraint of the manager or company's ability to directly regulate and resolve issues that might arise on the plantation. The companies wanted to retain their autonomy to be able to respond to the exigencies of the market and international events without considerable government restrictions.

The lack of early twentieth-century legislation that applied to the welfare of laborers once they arrived on the plantations indicated that industry legislation was primarily made to aid the growth of the industry and regulate the worst atrocities. At the turn of the century, the labor policies and associated legislation for the tea industry in India were almost exclusively related to efficient and safe recruitment. Yet, these "early legislative measures taken in connection with the recruitment of labour from distant places to the Assam tea gardens were more protective of planters than of labour."[30]

In the case of the Assam region—the region of India in the northeast with the largest number of laborers and plantations—the Assam Labour and Emigration Act of 1901 was implemented to prevent some of the abuses and high mortality rates in the recruitment and transportation of laborers that had occurred in the decades prior. The 1901 act was intended to ensure that laborers went to the tea estates willingly—meaning they were neither kidnapped nor coerced—and that they arrived in good health. However, it was also meant to limit the cost of recruitment for planters by increasing government regulation. Deregulation had led to a tripling of the cost of recruitment for laborers heading to Assam between the 1880s and 1890s.[31]

The 1901 legislation extended the power of the planters to privately arrest and detain laborers who had not fulfilled the terms of their contracts—a policy that carried over from earlier centuries and was common at slavery-based sugar and cotton plantations in Mauritius, the US South, and the Caribbean. This policy remained after the abolition of slavery in 1834 when Indian indentured workers were recruited to take up the work on plantations formerly based on slavery in various parts of the British empire. These traditions certainly had an impact on the 1901 legislation in India. It is clear, however, that planters did not find the 1901 act to be as effective as hoped; increased bureaucracy slowed the process of recruitment, wage rates set by the law were deemed too high, and the clause about private arrest seemed to make the Assam plantations undesirable to potential laborers.[32]

Earlier critical perspectives on labor recruitment and management for the Assam tea plantations in the nineteenth century decried the similarities that the plantations shared with slavery-based plantations in the Caribbean and the US South. To fill vacancies left after the abolition of the slave trade in British colonies, South Asian and East Asian indentured laborers were recruited and contracted for plantation work; they replaced many of the enslaved workers on plantations in the Caribbean and other parts of the British Empire. However, historians debate how much of a transition actually occurred in the early shift from enslaved to indentured or contract labor on the plantations; they highlight the continuities and nuances in forms of bonded or unfree labor.[33] Hugh Tinker and others have argued that the imperial global indentured system exemplified a "new form of slavery" that reinforced and continued preexisting aggressive policies and behaviors toward laborers.[34] These policies could include restrictions on the mobility of laborers once on the estate, contracts that held criminal clauses for nonfulfillment of work, and race-based recruitment strategies supported by a legal system favoring the authority of managers over laborers on the plantations. Historians of the South Asian tea industry locate that same logic to the early plantations in Assam where extra-legal authority, coercion in recruitment, and even the right to arrest were given to planters under legislation (and sometimes to the locals in the surrounding countryside). These characteristics exhibited similarities to the styles of management and recruitment of slave-based systems.[35] Other historians highlight how the indenture system and other postslavery labor recruitment systems were not static in practice but rather evolved over the late nineteenth century to fit growing international and regional standards and exigencies in the various regions of the British Empire where plantation labor was needed.[36] They emphasize elements of freedom and unfreedom, choice, movement, and the development of information networks among individuals and small groups that enabled varied experiences within the structural frameworks observed.[37]

However, the system put into place in Assam, even as late as the early twentieth century, sparked debates among contemporaries about factors of bondage, coercion, and limited mobility. Sir Henry J. S. Cotton (1845–1915), the chief commissioner of Assam from 1896 to 1902, for example, thought the initial proposals put forward in the aforementioned 1901 Assam Labour and Emigration Act were not enough to protect laborers, and his position was harshly challenged by tea industry representatives in several newspapers.[38] Although several other colonial officials also critiqued the anomalous legislation that had been put into effect in Assam in the twentieth century—particularly the preservation of the right to privately arrest laborers for not fulfilling the terms of their contract—opponents to this critique argued for the value of the plantation to laborers, namely that they provided an opportunity for laborers to escape famine or drought and even to flourish and accumulate wealth in land and cattle.[39]

The difficulty that companies in the region of Assam had in securing and keeping laborers in the late nineteenth century led to the development of structured recruitment legislation for Assam in 1901 that then influenced legislation and policy in other regions of India—with varying degrees of implementation. The government of Madras in the south of India passed legislation in 1903 (Planters' Labour Law) that mirrored aspects of the Assam act; most specifically the introduction of a penalty clause in labor contracts making it a crime for laborers to abscond.[40] This latter policy would remain in force until 1929.[41] Recruitment legislation took precedent over legislation governing laborer's welfare on arrival on the estates. Even as late as 1943, the *Report on an Enquiry into Conditions of Labour in Plantations in India* that was completed that year described a Workmen's Compensation Act (amended in 1933) as the only "protective labour legislation" created for plantation laborers at the time.[42] A general "lack of adequate knowledge on the part of workmen regarding their legal rights in claiming compensation" meant that laborers also did not always receive the compensation that they deserved.[43] The other types of labor legislation that were passed in the 1920s and 1930s also dealt with particular situations (like the Workmen's Compensation Act for accidents). These acts addressed the nonpayment of wages, the necessity of maternity benefits, and stipulations around emigration rather than provision for the everyday, lived experiences of laborers. The acts included the Trade Union Act of 1926, the Trades Disputes Act of 1928, the Maternity Benefits Bill of 1929, and the Payment of Wages Act of 193[6].[44] Despite the creation of labor enquiry committees and labor boards, more comprehensive welfare legislation would not be passed until the postindependence era.

The Assam Labour Board

In 1909, a representative of the Government of Eastern Bengal and Assam visited "all the principal recruiting districts in Bengal, Madras, the United Provinces of Agra and Oudh, and the Central Provinces" to "write a simple account of the various systems of obtaining labor and of the way in which they work[ed] in different parts of the country."[45] The report argued for a free recruitment system with greater regulation facilitated by garden sirdars who were officially linked to specific gardens—a policy that would favor large companies.[46] The recommendations of this report were realized in a 1915 amendment to the 1901 Assam Labour and Emigration Act. The British tea companies established a system of recruiting agencies for their plantations with licensed sirdars across more than thirty recruiting districts in India and formed another association dedicated to the purpose of directing this—the Tea Districts Labour Association (TDLA). The 1915 amendment withdrew from Assam the right to private arrest of laborers by planters (although it was still practiced, and laborers were often not told of their freedoms concerning the legislation), as well as created a supervisory labor board to address ongoing issues in recruitment.

The Assam Labour Board, a committee of the Assam government, was duly formed in 1915 as part of the 1915 amendment; it was created to supervise the recruitment and emigration for the region and to ensure compliance with established regulations on recruitment.[47] The chairman of this board was a government official, but all other members were representatives of the British tea industry: Eight of the sixteen members represented the ITA of Calcutta/London, four represented the Assam branch of the ITA, and three represented the Surma Valley branch of the ITA. The board was funded mostly by a tax levied against the tea planters based on their number of sirdars and laborers.[48] The board kept detailed records of the recruiting agents and agencies in the different recruiting districts of India, the numbers of sirdars associated with particular plantations that were recruiting under those agencies, the cash advances that were given to sirdars for their recruiting efforts, and the annual number of laborers who were recruited to Assam. It was meant to be a central bureau that supervised the "recruitment, engagement and emigration to labour districts of natives of India" through oversight of local agents recruiting in established districts across India and to serve as proof of strides made in the industry to address abuses in recruitment so that the board's constituents could gain access to more recruiting regions outside of its established network (like further south into the Madras Presidency).[49] The board hired consultants like company-employed doctors and medical officers—one example being a Dr. Forsyth employed by Finlays—"to visit the local and forwarding recruiting agencies [in the recruiting districts] and to report on the medical and sanitary arrangements and to make any suggestions for their improvements" to this end.[50] Despite being a government committee, this board relied heavily on company knowledge.

The board also acted as a gatekeeper for recruitment—preventing the formation of other recruiting agencies, particularly those of Indian planters, that were formed outside of the ITA and TDLA associational networks.[51] For example, in 1929, members of the TDLA and other approved recruiting agencies submitted 127 applications to obtain or renew licenses for local agents that would act in the TDLA's recruiting districts; all were recommended. At the time, there were forty-one local agencies recruiting laborers in the regions of Bengal, Bihar, and Orissa, the United Provinces, the Central Provinces, and Madras. However, a group of Indian planters applied to the Assam Labour Board that same year for a local agent's license "to establish a local agency at Khargpur" in West Bengal.[52] The board declined the request by citing recruitment legislation that indicated the planters had to be recognized as a constituent group before their application could be received. The Indian planters then formed an association called the Indian Planters' (Recruiting) Association, and the Assam Labour Board passed their application on to the government of Assam, which responded negatively: "It was against the accepted policy of the Government to authorise a number of petty associations to undertake recruiting operations, and unless Government were satisfied that the proposed Association was reasonably representative of the gardens in Assam which do not belong to the ITA, Government would be unable to issue an authorization under section 64 (2) of the Assam Labour and Emigration Act VI of 1901."[53] By the time of Whitley's report in 1931, the TDLA still had control over ninety-three percent of registration, recruitment, and transport measures for laborers coming to Assam. The report called for the abolition of the board because of the board's power and lack of adaptation and impartiality to the changes that were occurring in the industry: "We were informed that the Board discouraged attempts to form other recruiting organisations, and, while we recognise that an increase of competition in recruiting is fraught with danger, it is hardly possible to expect employers, who are not members of the Tea Districts Labour Association or who differ from its policy, to feel complete confidence in the impartiality of the Board as at present constituted."[54] The Assam Labour Board was finally abolished in 1933, in part, for this reason.

The Welfare of Tea Plantation Laborers after World War I

The creation of the Assam Labour Board in 1915 had occurred during World War I (1914–1918), when increases in production led to increased recruitment. Per capita consumption of tea in Britain increased dramatically in the years just before the war as wider sections of British society began to consume it, and the question as to whether it was a staple or luxury entered public and commercial debates.[55] During the war, tea from India and Ceylon was purchased by the British government's tea controller at a fixed-rate—forty percent of India's tea and twenty-seven percent of Ceylon's in 1917 increasing to sixty-six and fifty percent, respectively, in 1918.[56] Because of this guaranteed purchase, many tea plantations increased their production rates and recruited more laborers to work. The power of these companies in the development of recruitment policies in the first two decades of the twentieth century translated to similar power in pushing against government influence over wages and welfare policies on the plantations in the years after the war.

Despite a substantial increase in tea production in India during World War I, the tea was increasingly stockpiled in storage units in India and Ceylon, due to disrupted shipping routes, limited transportation options, and limited warehouse space in Britain.[57] Although there were attempts to increase regional (that is, within South Asia) tea consumption through promotional campaigns, there were still considerable stockpiles that flooded the British market with the return of more regular shipping options at the end of the war.[58] In response to the market saturation of tea, the associations of tea planters in South Asia (comprised largely of representatives from the tea companies) proposed an agreement among themselves to reduce tea production industry-wide for a set period. In 1920, for example, they recommended to their members that each reduce tea production to ninety percent of their average production for the preceding five-year period and impose an earlier deadline in the season for plucking tea for export.[59] Although not all participated, tea production was reduced by approximately 9.71 percent that year. This resulted in some losses for the larger companies with widespread holdings but had an overall beneficial effect on the profits of the industry in the years that followed. For example, the four subsidiary companies of Finlays together suffered a massive loss of £458,000 that year, but by the year 1923 had recovered and registered record profits totaling £1,751,000.[60] Several factors contributed to this dramatic increase, including the cultivation and sale of finer grades of tea due to more careful plucking and improved methods of processing the tea, and increased tea prices due to a decrease in supply facilitated—in part—by a severe, prolonged, widespread drought in the region in 1922.[61]

The agreed-upon reduction in output in 1920 by the tea companies' upper management, however advantageous to company profits in the years that followed, had an immediate adverse effect on the laborers who worked on the plantations. The wage structure of plantation workers over this period was piece rate, meaning that the payment of wages was for daily tasks (*hazirah*) completed and not for a day's work itself. Though a minimum wage was instituted in regional legislation for the industry (particularly in Assam), the piece rate system was used by companies to circumvent the legal requirements and to avoid having to approach the magistrate to lower a laborer's wage if the laborer was unwilling to work.[62] The minimum wage was conditional, yet according to planters, "the full rate of wages [were said to be] within easy reach of every one who [did] an ordinary day's labor."[63] Laborers received additional pay from completing tasks (*ticca*) beyond the daily quota. However, there were recorded court cases of discrepancies as to what the laborer completed in a day and what was actually recorded in the *hazirah* or *ticca* book.[64]

Therefore, a reduction in plucking and more careful plucking meant that there was increased unemployment and laborers had less opportunity to meet daily quotas to receive a full day's wage and even less possibility of gaining any extra (*ticca*) pay on the completion of extra work. Further, to reduce expenditure during periods of crisis, the companies argued that the supplements provided on the estates (housing, food subsidies, hospitals, and creches), counted as a significant part of their wages, even if the laborers did not take advantage of them. The percentage was never solidified, so as to allow flexibility in what was actually given in money wages, but the reduced or stagnated money wages (and increased unemployment) led to labor unrest.[65] An analysis of one of the largest mass exoduses from plantations of the period, the Chargola Valley exodus, involved 7,000 to 10,000 laborers walking off the gardens with the intention of returning to their villages of origin.[66] The principal complaints were based upon unmet expectations concerning wage increases needed to meet the higher cost of living after the war. The marked increase in labor protests caused the regional government of Assam (where many of the protests were located) to launch an enquiry into the practice of supplementing low wages with payment-in-kind welfare benefits.[67]

The 1921–1922 Assam Labour Enquiry Committee sought to determine the monetary value of the welfare services offered on the plantations so as to understand the full remuneration that laborers received and whether more should be converted to cash wages to meet what was inscribed in labor legislation and to "maintain the labourers in health and a reasonable degree of comfort."[68] They found that the total remuneration was reasonable, even if there was no actual amount noted. In 1921, the governor of Assam, Sir Nicholas Beatson Bell (1867–1936), proposed the idea of giving commission to laborers based on the profits of the plantation. Company representatives replied that it would be better instead to use the money to fund education and other social welfare benefits on the laborers' behalf.[69] This paternalistic response became part of company practice; plantations began to be articulated as places of relief where impoverished laborers could receive some payment and payment-in-kind in exchange for their labor. Use of this language around laborers' living conditions contributed to the idea that laborers should be grateful for what they did receive on the estates since their needs were being met.[70] The replacement of partial wages with welfare, food, or small plots of agricultural land however, tied laborers to the estates, as they could not save money to leave the estate.[71] Further, regional companies created agreements between themselves to further tie laborers to specific estates, like the Memorandum of Agreement in Connection with Enticement of Labour from Tea Gardens and Other Concerns in the Brahmaputra Valley and Surma Valley.[72]

The tea plantation managers also argued that the labor unrest was the result of the growth of communist, nationalist, and unionist activity among their plantation workforce, which they observed happening among laborers in some of South Asia's industrial factories.[73] They viewed labor protests as part of Mohandas K. Gandhi's noncooperation movement to reduce British economic and political power on the subcontinent. Gandhi himself indicated that he was not directly involved, yet he did criticize the industry and postulated that any commercial interest that was exploitative was in danger of disintegration.[74] Planters also believed that agitation would grow, not because of bad management but because labor resistance was becoming increasingly linked to larger political and social issues.[75] Regardless of the associations they made, the planters suspected that the protests that were occurring in the 1920s were a turning point toward more organized labor agitation in the industry—though unionization would still be long in coming. Because of this, they were quick to reevaluate and strategize about their stance on laborers' wages.[76]

The chairman of a branch of the ITA (a planters' association) argued for a united front to prevent further instances of unrest in the future.[77] The companies aimed to resolve contentions in the industry outside of the constraints of law by arranging wage fixing and nonpoaching agreements among themselves: "Local variations in wages [were] largely eliminated by 'wage agreements' among the planters' enforced throughout the districts, in both the north and south of India."[78] This ability to affect the production of tea and unify their position in the industry enabled the planters to articulate themselves as benefactors acting toward the benefit of the industry and of the laborers on the plantations: "By controlling production and other means, these associations [could] influence the labour policy of their members in regard to such matters as recruitment, wages, hours, and trade unions."[79] Further, their influence over legislation regarding wages and hours was strengthened by the argument that plantations were not just places of employment but also sites of relief.

The Tea Plantation as Site of Relief?

The idea of plantations as sites of relief, and payment-in-kind welfare as a partial replacement for wages, thrived on the conceit, reinforced and articulated by the government of India, that "more than half a million immigrants drawn from the very poorest classes of India [were] indebted to the industry for a much more liberal supply of food and clothing than they could ordinarily have expected to enjoy in their homes."[80] The recruitment of laborers to the tea plantations during and in the aftermath of drought or famine was a significant recruiting strategy for company recruiters, who were aware of the fluctuations in recruitment that occurred during periods of plenty and scarcity in heavily environmentally dependent agricultural regions. For example, a manager for a Finlays plantation in the Duars attributed the number of workers that he was able to recruit in the 1905 and 1906 growing seasons to the "local scarcity" then prevailing in the recruiting districts.[81]

The government was also partial to this idea of welfare relief. The chairman of the Assam Labour Board and Tea Commissioner of India in 1918, Lt. Col. W. M. Kennedy, spoke at a meeting of the ITA to this effect. He believed that the tea industry played a critical role in famine relief. The emigration to plantations seemed to provide a benefit to newly recruited laborers and to the government—which did not have to implement as many relief measures in the areas that fell within the tea industry's recruiting districts.[82] Plantations could take in whole families and were therefore better locations for famine-stricken populations to seek relief:

> The emigration is conferring a benefit not only upon the tea industry and upon the province of Assam, but in itself is also a measure of famine relief in the recruiting districts, and I am glad to say that this has been recognised by many of the District Officers. There is no doubt but that if it had not been for emigration to Assam, and also to other places, a very much larger measure of famine relief would have been necessary than has had to be undertaken.[83]

Consequently, planters argued that what was provided physically on the plantations for laborers was more than adequate and that wages could therefore be kept low or be further reduced because the plantations were also providing welfare services to the laborers. This association with relief and the policies of welfare on the estates resulted in the aforementioned conflicts in the 1920s and 1930s, as labor protests spread throughout the region of Assam. The main concerns of the laborers were linked to the plantations' policies of payment-in-kind—the partial replacement of wages with benefits like food rations and welfare services—and unmet expectations concerning money wage increases.

While the Assam Labour and Emigration Act of 1901 had required some provisions for laborers in terms of "health sanitation, housing and rice," later amendments left welfare provisions outside of the letter of the law. Therefore, companies and planters could vary widely as to what was offered to the laborers on their plantations, and the monetary value of said services was never fixed so as to allow flexibility when determining money wages in a given year—especially if there had been a crisis in the industry, drought, and so forth. The welfare benefits that affected everyday life on the plantations was up to the discretion of the plantation managers or the company through which they were employed. This is perhaps one of the reasons why the policy of payment-in-kind or partial wage replacement, with welfare benefits, became such a contentious issue in the same decades.

In addition to recruitment measures that tied laborers to specific plantations (like direct recruiting district-to-company plantation transportation, enhanced by the Assam Labour Board and the TDLA in response to the 1915 Assam Labour and Emigration act amendment), wage fixing agreements, payments-in-kind, and wage stagnation contributed to reduced freedom of movement for laborers and increased dependency on the plantation. Laborers could not accumulate much money to transition from the estates, since a significant portion of the pay was food or welfare services provided on the estate. In 1931, the Report of the Royal Commission on Labour indicated that these welfare provisions could include "free housing, medical facilities and firewood . . . free grazing for cattle and land cultivation . . . and in a few cases the issue of rice at concession rates."[84] However, the report concluded that more government intervention with health boards was needed to monitor and apply industry-wide regulations for drinking water, conservancy, sanitation, medical facilities, and housing standards. This kind of implementation and enforcement would be a long time coming. In 1946, the year prior to Indian independence, a government Labour Investigative Committee Report found that the tea plantations were still "practically immune from any legislative control as far as regulation of labour conditions in them [was] concerned."[85] The standardization of welfare policies in the industry would not occur until after Indian independence.

Conclusion

During the early twentieth century, representatives of tea companies and their planters' associations often sat on the governing board and bodies of the regions that they represented, playing the role of knowledge brokers to inform the crafting of industry policy and legislation, which was often unique to plantations as agro-industrial concerns. One prime example would be G. E. Rayner who worked as a manager of a tea plantation for Finlays from the early 1900s into the 1930s. While on leave back in the United Kingdom, he lost many of his laborers during the labor exodus in 1921, and in 1922, he visited the recruiting districts and successfully invited some laborers to return.[86] Rayner then served as a representative for Finlays on multiple committees of the Surma Valley Branch of the ITA (including the Chargola Longai district committee) with eventual election to chairman in 1935, attended the executive committee meetings of the TDLA and the Indian Tea Cess Committee, was nominated to a seat on the Assam Legislative Council in 1929, served on the Assam Labour Board until it was dissolved in March 1933 (on the executive committee circa

1928/1929), and was consulted as a witness concerning the tea plantations by the Whitley Commission.[87] According to Finlays managing agents, his "connection with the labour organisations" made him an asset to the company and a select representative for the company's interests.[88]

According to the International Labour Organization in 1938, which conducted reports on in India, "large-scale employers . . . [had] constantly been consulted by the Government of India and Local Governments in regard to labour policy" and laws that were being considered in the legislatures.[89] Betraying a long-term continuity, this powerful lobby had striking similarities to the influence of plantation owners and managers in the British Caribbean and Mauritius in the century before, who, through economic suasion, had encouraged the British government to introduce an indentured labor system that would support and stabilize their industries after the implementation of the Slavery Abolition Act in 1834. The power and role of economic and business powerhouses in influencing labor policies across shifts in government during the colonial period cannot be overstated. Across this period, these firms sought to ensure access to a stable, subordinate, and inexpensive labor force.

The associational bodies of these tea companies, like the ITA, also exerted pressure on the members within the group to agree to specific policies and standards that would be implemented across the industry—outside of direct government control. During periods of stress to the industry, tea associations in India were able to persuade their constituents to agree to protective measures, such as restrictions on production, even if they had adverse effects on the livelihood of laborers, such as unemployment or reduced wages. The conditions and wages of laborers were often negatively affected by company decisions in response to fluctuations in the international market. The belief that plantations were also sites of relief in addition to places of work contributed to the replacement of part of the money wages of laborers with welfare benefits meant to boost their standard of living—a policy against which laborers repeatedly protested. However, even in the face of labor protests, factors such as the relationships between the companies and the government, the exemptions given the industry, and the self-governing power of companies and their managing agents resulted in more unified practices and policies in the tea industry in the early twentieth century that favored these international companies and extended their influence into the postindependence period. As this example shows, policy makers' assent to industrial claims to privileged access to plantation knowledge amounted to a protective policy—not for plantation workers but for the companies that deployed their labor.

Notes

1. The research for this project was completed during doctoral studies at McGill University's Indian Ocean World Centre and was partially funded by the Province of Quebec Canada Doctoral Scholarship (Fonds de Recherche du Québec Société et Culture) and McGill University's McCall-McBain Fellowship Award, Graduate Mobility Award, Graduate Research Enhancement and Travel Award, and the McGill/University of Glasgow Research Travel Award. The writing and editing of this chapter were completed while I was a Mellon Just Transformations Initiative/Humanities in the World postdoctoral scholar at the Humanities Institute at Pennsylvania State University.

2. John Whitley, *Report of the Royal Commission on Labour in India* (Government of India Central Legislation Branch, 1931), 349.

3. Rana P. Behal, "Power Structure, Discipline, and Labour in Assam Tea Plantations under Colonial Rule," *International Review of Social History* 51, no. 14 (2006): 143.

4. D. V. Rege and the Labour Investigation Committee, *Report on an Enquiry into Conditions of Labour in Plantations in India* (Manager of Publications, 1946), 2. British Library, India Office Records, IOR V 1680.

5. See also the discussions of management knowledge in the chapters by Marta Macedo, Claudia Roesch, Theresa Ventura, and Gillian McGillivray in this volume.

6. Michael Aldous, "Avoiding Negligence and Profusion: The Failure of the Joint-Stock Form in the Anglo-Indian Tea Trade, 1840–1870," *Enterprise & Society* 16, no. 3 (2015): 654–658.

7. Maria Misra, *Business, Race and Politics in British India, c. 1850–1960* (Clarendon Press, 1999), 7–10, 188–190.

8. Misra, *Business, Race and Politics*, 23–25, 69.

9. Behal, "Power Structure, Discipline, and Labour," 147.

10. Rana P. Behal, *One Hundred Years of Servitude: Political Economy of Tea Plantations in Colonial Assam* (Tulika Books, 2014), 253. For other examples of state-funded knowledge production schemes, see the chapters by Ted McCormick, Jennifer R. Saracino, Moritz von Brescius, and Theresa Ventura in this volume.

11. Assam Labour Enquiry Committee, *Report of the Assam Labour Enquiry Committee, 1921–22* (Government Press Assam, 1922), 4–5. This committee declined to involve laborers in direct interviews on questions of remuneration and wage increases; Crispin Bates and Marina Carter, "Enslaved Lives, Enslaving

Labels: A New Approach to the Colonial Indian Labor Diaspora," in *New Routes for Diaspora Studies*, eds. Sukanya Banerjee et al. (Indiana University Press, 2012), 70.

12. Assam Labour Enquiry Committee, *Report of the Assam Labour Enquiry Committee, 1921–22*, 71.

13. Indian Tea Association, *Proceedings of the Thirty-Eighth Annual General Meeting of Members of the Association Held on the 13th March 1919* (Criterion Printing Works, 1919).

14. Solomon Bard, "Tea and Opium," *Journal of the Hong Kong Branch of the Royal Asiatic Society* 40 (2000), 1–19.

15. Jayeeta Sharma, *Empire's Garden: Assam and the Making of India* (Duke University Press, 2011), 31–32.

16. Andrew B. Liu, *Tea War: A History of Capitalism in China and India* (Yale University Press, 2020), 121; Misra, *Business, Race and Politics*, 21–24; Geoffrey Jones, *Merchants to Multinationals: British Trading Companies in the Nineteenth and Twentieth Centuries* (Oxford University Press, 2009); Behal, *One Hundred Years of Servitude*, 108–111.

17. Colm Brogan, *James Finlay & Company Limited: Manufacturers and East India Merchants, 1750–1950* (Jackson Son & Company, 1951); Records of James Finlay & Co Ltd, Textile Manufacturers, Tea Planters and Merchants, Glasgow, Scotland, 1789–2010, University of Glasgow Archives & Special Collections, GB248 UGD 091/1.

18. Administrative/Biographical History, Records of Finlay, Muir & Co, Calcutta, University of Glasgow Archives & Special Collections, James Finlay & Co Ltd collection, GB248 UGD 091/11.

19. Roger Jeffery, "Merchant Capital and the End of Empire: James Finlay, Merchant Adventurers," *Economic and Political Weekly* 17, no. 7 (1982): 241–248; Brogan, *James Finlay & Company Limited*; Records of James Finlay & Co Ltd, Textile Manufacturers, Tea Planters and Merchants, Glasgow, Scotland, 1789–2010, University of Glasgow Archives & Special Collections, GB248 UGD 091/1.

20. "A Few Dates, Facts and Figures in the History of James Finlay & Co., Limited," Finlays Magazine Historical File, II General Information, University of Glasgow Archives & Special Collections, James Finlay & Co Ltd collection, GB248 UGD 091/1/9/2/10; Liu, *Tea War*, 120, 126; W. M. Fraser, *The Recollections of a Tea Planter* (Tea and Rubber Mail, 1935), 178.

21. Roger Jeffery, "Merchant Capital," 241–243, 245–248.

22. Other newly contracted employees were sent to the cities to work in transport positions, as engineering assistants, and as clerks. Hired doctors worked in specific regions of India or Ceylon as itinerants providing medical oversight for a group of plantations.

23. Arnab Dey, *Tea Environments and Plantation Culture: Imperial Disarray in Eastern India* (Cambridge University Press, 2018), 68–73; Percival Griffiths, *The History of the Indian Tea Industry* (Weidenfeld & Nicolson, 1967), 559; University

of Glasgow Archives & Special Collections, James Finlay & Co Ltd collection, GB248 UGD 091/1/3/1/2, 43.

24. India Office Library Records, "Protest Against the Attempt Made by the European Tea-Planters to Be Relieved of the Export Duty on Tea," *Bombay Chronicle*, December 28, 1920. *Report on the Native Papers for the Week Ending 1st January 1921*, 3. India Office Library and Records, South Asia Open Archives; Indian Tea Association, *Proceedings of the Thirty-Eight Annual General Meeting*, 5–8, 105–143.

25. India Office Library and Records, *Young India* 14 (August 21, 1918). *Report on Native Papers for the Week ending 24th August 1918*, 13. India Office Library and Records, South Asia Open Archives.

26. Dey, *Tea Environments*, 68–71; Griffiths, *History of the Indian Tea Industry*, 559; University of Glasgow Archives & Special Collections, James Finlay & Co Ltd collection, GB248 UGD 091/1/3/1/2, 43.

27. Dey, *Tea Environments*, 62–63.

28. Dey, *Tea Environments*, 70.

29. Dey, *Tea Environments*, 75.

30. D. V. Rege and the Labour Investigation Committee, *Main Report* (Manager of Publications, 1946), 57.

31. Rana P. Behal and Prabhu P. Mohapatra, " 'Tea and Money Versus Human Life': The Rise and Fall of the Indenture System in the Assam Tea Plantations 1840–1908," *Journal of Peasant Studies* 19, no. 3–4 (1992): 153.

32. Assam Labour Enquiry Committee, *Proceedings of the Assam Labour Enquiry Committee in the Recruiting and Labour Districts* (Office of the Superintendent of Government Printing, India, 1906); Behal, "Power Structure, Discipline, and Labour," 166–167.

33. Oliver Tappe and Ulrike Lindner, "Introduction: Global Variants of Bonded Labour" in *Bonded Labour: Global and Comparative Perspectives (18th–21st Century)*, eds. Sabine Damir-Geilsdorf et al. (transcript: Bielefeld, 2016), 9–20.

34. Hugh Tinker, *A New System of Slavery; the Export of Indian Labour Overseas, 1830–1920* (Oxford University Press, 1974).

35. See Rana P. Behal and Prabhu P. Mohapatra, " 'Tea and Money Versus Human Life,' 142–172; Jayeeta Sharma, " 'Lazy' Natives, Coolie Labour, and the Assam Tea Industry," *Modern Asian Studies* 43, no. 6 (2009): 1287–1324; Elizabeth Kolsky, *Colonial Justice in British India: White Violence and the Rule of Law* (Cambridge University Press, 2010); Behal, *One Hundred Years of Servitude*.

36. Marina Carter, *Voices from Indenture: Experiences of Indian Migrants in the British Empire* (Leicester University Press, 1996); Crispin Bates, "Some Thoughts on the Representation and Misrepresentation of the Colonial South Asian Labour Diaspora," *South Asian Studies* 33, no. 1 (2017), 7–22; Brij V. Lal, *Chalo Jahaji: On a Journey Through Indenture in Fiji* (Australian National University E Press, 2012).

37. Yoshina Hurgobin and Subho Basu, "'Oceans Without Borders': Dialectics of Transcolonial Labor Migration from the Indian Ocean World to the Atlantic Ocean World," *International Labor and Working-Class History*, 87 (2015): 7–26; Nitin Varma, *Coolies of Capitalism* (De Gruyter, 2017); Gaiutra Bahadur, *Coolie Woman: The Odyssey of Indenture* (University of Chicago, 2014).

38. "The Assam Labour Question" *Amrita Bazar Patrika* 34, no. 294 (September 24, 1902). https://jstor.org/stable/saoa.crl.34593271.

39. Assam Labour Enquiry Committee, *Proceedings of the Assam Labour Enquiry Committee*, 203; "The Assam Labour Question," *Amrita Bazar Patrika.*

40. "The Madras Planters' Labour Bill," *Ceylon Observer*, Weekly Edition, December 24, 1902, 21; Barbara Evans, "Cultural Context and Contractual Relations: The Madras Planters' Labour Law and the Rise of the Plantation Maistri, 1904–1927," *Journal of the Royal Asiatic Society* 7, no. 1 (1997): 73–92.

41. Whitley, *Royal Commission on Labour in India*, 355.

42. Rege, *Report on an Enquiry*, 5.

43. International Labour Office (ILO; League of Nations), *Industrial Labour in India* (P. S. King & Son, 1938), 208. See also Theresa Ventura's chapter in this volume.

44. Misra, *Business, Race, and Politics*, 157. The Payment of Wages Act was made law in 1936, though proposed as a bill a few years earlier. It required regular, at least monthly, payment of wages to the laborer yet still allowed managers to reduce wages for specific reasons. The Factories Act of 1934 provided some protections to full-time factory workers in different industries across India, but tea plantations may have been exempted from this because their factories were considered seasonal or part-time factories.

45. J. F. Gruning, *Recruitment of Labour for Tea Gardens in Assam* (n.p., 1909), 1. California Digital Library.

46. Sirdars, maistries, and kanganies were intermediary recruiters and managers of a group of laborers under the leadership of the companies' plantation managers and assistant managers. They often had ties to the villages where they recruited laborers. For more, see Jan Breman, *Of Peasants, Migrants and Paupers: Rural Labour Circulation and Capitalist Production in West India* (Oxford University Press, 1985), 328; Crispin Bates and Marina Carter, "Sirdars as Intermediaries in Nineteenth-Century Indian Ocean Indentured Labour Migration," *Modern Asian Studies* 51, no. 2 (2017): 462–484.

47. Government of India Department of Commerce and Industry, *Legislative Department Proceedings Regarding the Assam Labour and Emigration (Amendment) Act, 1915 (Act VIII of 1915)*, National Archives of India; Assam Labour Board, Reports for 1922–23 to 1930–31, British Library, V/24/2298, Appendix A.

48. Whitley, *Royal Commission on Labour*, 360, 367.

49. Assam Labour and Emigration (Amendment) Act, March 25, 1915. https://www.casemine.com/act/in/5a979d954a93263ca60b70af; Government of

India Department of Commerce and Industry, *Legislative Department Proceedings Regarding the Assam Labour and Emigration (Amendment) Act, 1915 (Act VIII of 1915)*, National Archives of India.

50. Letters concerning Dr. C. E. P. Forsyth (5 November 1919–1 July 1920), University of Glasgow Archives & Special Collections, James Finlay & Co Ltd collection, Finlays Managers and Assistants Letterbooks for India and Ceylon, GB248 UGD 91/1/6/3/1/4, 805-808 (plus inserts).

51. Whitley, *Royal Commission on Labour*, 367, 373.

52. F. C. King, *Annual Report on the Working of the Assam Labour Board During the Year Ending the 30th June 1929*. Assam Labour Board Reports for 1922–23 to 1930–31 (Government of India, 1929), 1–2. British Library, V/24/2298.

53. J. G. Bourne, *Annual Report on the Working of the Assam Labour Board During the Year Ending the 30th June 1930*. Assam Labour Board Reports for 1922–23 to 1930–31 (Government of India, 1930), 1–2. British Library, V/24/2298.

54. Whitley, *Royal Commission on Labour*, 367, 373.

55. Erika Rappaport, *A Thirst for Empire: How Tea Shaped the Modern World* (Princeton University Press, 2017), 226–227, 238.

56. V. D. Wickizer, *Tea Under International Regulation* (Ford Research Institute, 1951), 59–60.

57. Griffiths, *History of the Indian Tea Industry*, 170–172.

58. Wickizer, *Tea Under International Regulation*, 59; Rappaport, *Thirst for Empire*, 227–228.

59. William Ukers, *All About Tea* (Tea and Coffee Trade Journal Company, 1935), 1: 172; Wickizer, *Tea Under International Regulation*, 60; "Restriction of Tea Output," *The Economist*, October 2, 1920, 504.

60. "A Few Dates, Facts and Figures," 6.

61. D. M. Forrest, *One Hundred Years of Ceylon Tea, 1867–1967* (Chatto and Windus, 1967), 217, referencing C. E. Elliott and W. J. Whitehead, *Tea Production in Ceylon*, 2nd ed. (Times of Ceylon, 1931); Hamza Varikoden et al., "Droughts of Indian Summer Monsoon Associated with El Niño and Non-El Niño Years," *International Journal of Climatology* 35, no. 8 (2015): 1917.

62. Assam Labour Enquiry Committee, *Proceedings of the Assam Labour Enquiry Committee*.

63. Assam Labour Enquiry Committee, *Report of the Assam Labour Enquiry Committee* (Office of the Superintendent of Government Printing, India, 1906), 142–143.

64. See Case 985 (Mijikijan Tea Estate) and Case 941 (Modopee Tea Estate) in Assam Labour Enquiry Committee, *Report of 1921–22* (Government Press Assam, 1922), 80.

65. Dey, *Tea Environments*, 187.

66. Kalyan K. Sircar, "Coolie Exodus from Assam's Chargola Valley, 1921: An Analytical Study," *Economic and Political Weekly* 22, no. 5 (1987): 185; Nitin Varma, *Coolies of Capitalism*, 210–211.

67. Assam Labour Enquiry Committee, *Report of the Assam Labour Enquiry Committee, 1921–22*, 1. Behal, "Power Structure, Discipline, and Labour," 168.

68. Assam Labour Enquiry Committee, *Report of the Assam Labour Enquiry Committee, 1921–22*, 1.

69. "Colonial Administrators and Post-Independence Leaders in India (1616–2000)," *Oxford Dictionary of National Biography*, September 22, 2005; "Governor to Curate," *The Times*, May 3, 1922, 10; Assam Labour Enquiry Committee, *Report of 1921–22*, 73–74.

70. "Labour Law in Madras," *The Pioneer* (Allahabad), March 13, 1903, 9.

71. Behal, *One Hundred Years of Servitude*, 122–123.

72. Assam Labour Enquiry Committee, *Report of the Assam Labour Enquiry Committee, 1921–22*, 141.

73. "In the Tea Garden: Criminal Agitators (Through the Associated Press)," *Times of India*, July 14, 1921, 8–9.

74. M. K. Gandhi, "The Assam Coolies," *Young India* 3, no. 23 (1921), reproduced in M. K. Gandhi, *Young India, 1919–1932* (Navajivan Publishing House, 1981): 179.

75. "Extract from Minutes of AGM of Surma Valley Branch, ITA," British Library, MSS EUR F. 174/975 (8/3/1922).

76. Sircar, "Coolie Exodus," 184, 188.

77. "Extract from Minutes of AGM of Surma Valley Branch, ITA," British Library, MSS EUR F. 174/975 (8/3/1922).

78. Behal, *One Hundred Years of Servitude*, 294–296; ILO, *Industrial Labour in India*, 246–247.

79. ILO, *Industrial Labour in India*, 121.

80. Assam Labour Enquiry Committee, *Report of the Assam Labour Enquiry Committee, 1906*, 2.

81. Assam Labour Enquiry Committee, *Proceedings of the Assam Labour Enquiry Committee*, 127–128.

82. Indian Tea Association, *Proceedings of the Thirty-Eighth Annual General Meeting*, x.

83. Indian Tea Association, *Proceedings of the Thirty-Eighth Annual General Meeting*, x.

84. Whitley, *Royal Commission on Labour*, 384.

85. Rege, *Main Report*, 58. There were some regulations in the state of Cochin.

86. Letters concerning G. E. Raynor, University of Glasgow Archives & Special Collections, James Finlay & Co Ltd collection, *Finlay's Managers and Assistants Letterbooks for India and Ceylon*, GB248 UGD 91/1/6/3/1/11, 69–78.

87. Letters concerning G. E. Raynor, GB248 UGD 91/1/6/3/1/16, 571–590, and UGD 91/1/6/3/1/21, 105–120 and 324–336; Whitley, *Royal Commission on Labour*, Appendix III, 547; F. C. King, "Annual Report on the Working of the Assam Labour Board During the Year Ending the 30th June 1928," Appendix A.

88. Letters concerning G. E. Raynor, GB248 UGD 91/1/6/3/1/21, 107.

89. ILO, *Industrial Labour in India*, 116.

Contributors

Moritz von Brescius is a historian of Europe and the world from the mid-nineteenth century to the present, focusing on political, economic, and environmental history, as well as science and empire studies in comparative and global perspective. He is a research professor leading a Swiss National Science Foundation consolidator grant at the University of Basel. He is author of *German Science in the Age of Empir*e (Cambridge University Press, 2019). His second book project focuses on international conflicts over resource security and the fraught control of supply chains for modern industrial production.

Ulrike Lindner is Professor of Modern History at the University of Cologne. She is a historian of comparative European colonialism. Among other topics, she has published on British and German colonialism in Africa, gender roles in colonial societies, knowledge transfers between colonial empires, and colonial social policy. Her books in English include *New Perspectives on the History of Gender and Empire* (Bloomsbury Academic, 2018, co-edited with Dörte Lerp) and *Bonded Labour* (Transcript, 2016, co-edited with Sabine Damir-Geilsdorf, Gesine Müller, Oliver Tappe, and Michael Zeuske).

Marta Macedo is a researcher at the Institute of Contemporary History, NOVA University of Lisbon. She works on the relation between technology, science, and colonial power. More specifically, she examines the circulation of plantation materials and knowledge in the South Atlantic, combining approaches from the history of science and technology, labor history, environmental history, and the history of capitalism. Recently she co-edited *Global Plantations in the Modern World* (Palgrave Macmillan, 2023, co-edited with Irene Peano and Colette Le Petitcorps).

Rebekah McCallum is an independent historian specializing in British business and regional labor policy and legislation in twentieth-century South Asia and the Indian Ocean world. She received her doctorate in history from McGill University in affiliation with the Indian Ocean World Centre. Her prior studies at University of Virginia, Oxford, and Princeton and postdoctoral work at Penn State have informed her further work on international business and cross-cultural activism around labor and rights in the twentieth century.

Ted McCormick is Isobel Haldane Professor of British History at the University of Pennsylvania. A historian of scientific, technological, and economic ideas and projects in early modern Britain, Ireland, and the colonial Atlantic, he is the author of *William Petty and the Ambitions of Political Arithmetic* (Oxford University Press, 2009) and *Human Empire: Mobility and Demographic Thought in the British Atlantic World, 1500–1800* (Cambridge University Press, 2022).

Gillian McGillivray is Professor of History at Glendon College, York University (Toronto). Her publications include *Blazing Cane: Sugar Communities, Class, and State-Formation in Cuba, 1868–1959* (Duke University Press, 2009) and *Sugar and Power in Brazil, 1880–1965* (Duke University Press, forthcoming). She co-edited *The Entangled Labor Histories of Brazil and the United States* (Lexington Books, 2022, co-edited with Fernando Teixeira da Silva, Alexandre Fortes. and Thomas D. Rogers) and co-authored (with Thomas D. Rogers) "Populism in the Circum-Caribbean, 1920–1940," in *Transformations of Populism in Europe and the Americas: History and Recent Tendencies* (Bloomsbury Academic, 2015).

Nicholas B. Miller is Associate Professor of History at Flagler College. A social and intellectual historian of Europe and the Pacific in the eighteenth and nineteenth centuries with an emphasis on population, education, and ideas of the household and the family, he is the author of *John Millar and the Scottish Enlightenment* (Voltaire Foundation, 2017) and *Cameralism and the Enlightenment* (Routledge, 2020, co-edited with Ere Nokkala). His research on Hawai'i has been published in venues including *Labor: Studies in Working-Class History* (2024); *Global Royal Families* (Oxford University Press, 2024); *Global Plantations in the Modern World* (Palgrave Macmillan, 2023); and *International History Review* (2020).

Claudia Roesch is a lecturer of history at the University of Konstanz. Her research interests include the history of knowledge, North American history, gender and the family, and migration history. Her current research project "Utopian Engineering" investigates the role of science and engineering in social reform projects in the nineteenth-century Atlantic world. Her most recent publication is "Owen and the Engineers: Cross-Fertilization between Engineering and Early Socialism in the Owenite Tradition," *Global Intellectual History* (2023).

Jennifer R. Saracino is Assistant Professor of Art History at the University of Arizona. She holds a joint PhD in art history and Latin American studies from Tulane University. Her work has appeared in the journals *Imago Mundi* and *Artl@s Bulletin* and the edited volumes *Mapping Nature across the Americas* (University of Chicago Press, 2021) and *Collective Creativity and Artistic Agency in Colonial Latin America* (University Press of Florida, 2023). She has received fellowships from the Huntington Library, Dumbarton Oaks, the Newberry Library, and John Carter Brown Library. She is the author of a forthcoming monograph about the Uppsala Map of Mexico-Tenochtitlan (c. 1540), under advanced contract with University of Texas Press.

Christina Skott is a Life Fellow and former Director of Studies in History at Magdalene College, Cambridge. Her publications have revolved around European interactions with and knowledge of Southeast Asia in the long eighteenth century, with a focus on natural history, anthropology and race. Her present research interests include colonial agriculture and environment in nineteenth-century Malaya.

Theresa Ventura is Associate Professor of History at Concordia University, Montréal. Her research is on the overlapping production of agricultural, medical, and environmental knowledge in the American colonial Philippines. Articles on the medicalization of food scarcity, land surveying and enclosure, and the fashioning of expertise can be found in *Philippine Studies*, *Agricultural History*, *History and Technology*, and the *Journal of the Gilded Age and Progressive Era*. She has also co-edited and contributed to an *Isis* focus section on volcanology (December 2024).

Index

Afong, Chuck, 100–101, 103, 104, 113n8
Africans, enslaved, 4, 6, 18, 31, 47, 111; in cooperative systems, 126, 130, 219
Aka tribe, 164
Akina, Goo Tet Chin, 104
ali'i, 13, 95–96, 98, 106, 109, 111
animals, treatment and use of, 125, 134, 193, 202
artistic production, Nahuatl, 59–60, 71
Asian entrepreneurs, 112
Assam (India), 146–164 *passim*, 167, 309; Forest Department, 167; labor protests, 318; plantations, 146, 147, 148, 158, 166, 310; wages, 315. *See also* Charduar Plantation
Assam Company, 179n101, 306
Assam Labour and Emigration Act, of 1901, 309, 318, 319, amendment of 1915, 319
Assam Labour Board, 311–313, 314, 317, 318
Assam Labour Enquiry Committee, 316
Assamese forests, as revered landscapes, 164
Audiencia, First, 67
Audiencia, Second, 69
Azancot, Jacob Levy, 230
Aztec, as imprecise term, 79n2

Bacon, Nathaniel, 188
Badianus Herbal, 59–65, 70–73, 75–79. *See also* botanical knowledge
Bandmann, Daniel E., 99, 105
Batu Kawan (island), 186, 187, 191, 194
Bayonet Constitution (Hawai'i), 107, 108
Belgian trajectory in Africa, 220, 221.
Bencoolen (Benkulu) trading post, 185
Berlin Conference, 1884–1885, 220–221
Boate, Gerard and Arnold, 45
borgăch. See *ficus elastica*
botanical gardens, 10, 19, 146–147, 149, 247, 253, 264
botanical knowledge, 8, 13, 63, 76, 194, 245, 263, 265
Botanical Station at Lagos, 155
botany, economic, 59, 60, 63, 65, 71, 78, 80n9, 153
Brierfield Plantation, 124–128, 137n2
Briggs, L. Vernon, 102, 104
Brown family, 187
Buitenzorg (Java), 16, 252, 253, 264
Bureaus of Prisons and Agriculture (Philippines), merging of, 254

Bush, John E., *106,* 108

Campos dos Goytacazes, 289, 290
capitalism, plantation, 89, 109, 146; racial, 3, 30, 31, 47, 123, 136
Cartwright, Alexander Joy, 99–100
Casement, Roger, 228
Castilla elastica, 156
Catholicism, 30, 33, 34–35, 40, 41–42, 45–47, 66, 76, 236
cattle ranching, 95, 96, 198, 199, 319
Cavalcanti, Lima, 291
Censuses, 13, 279
Centro de Fornecedores de Cana de Pernambuco. *See* Pernambuco Cane Supplier's Association
Chalmers, G. C., 109
Charduar Plantation (India), 145, 146, 154; as pioneering venture, 146, 161, 164, 165; as propagators of *Ficus elastica,* 147, 149, 160; as site for study of pests and diseases, 146, 158, *159*; decline of, 150–151, 159, 170–171, 172; experimentations at, 146, 147, 148, 155; global entanglements of, 151–160, 163, 167, 168; illegal tapping of rubber trees, 165; wages for tappers, 166, 167, 178n92; worker resistance at, 165, 166
Chargola Valley, exodus from, 315
Cherokee, 111
Chinese Exclusion Act, 109
Chinese labor. *See* labor, Chinese
Chinese labor brokers and planters, 6; 93, 187, 189, 190, 195–196, 202, 203, 204
chocolate. *See* cocoa
civil scientists, 246–248, 251, 252, 254, 256, 262, 264–265; definition of, 266n4
Civil Survey. *See* Survey, Civil
Civil War (American), 14, 97, 122, 123, 125, 128, 133, 135
Civil War (English), 35
coatequitl (labor system), 70–71
cocoa, as crop, 218, 219, 222, 224–225; as political endeavor, 218; "cropscapes," 219, 238n11; planting, harvesting and shipping, 224–236 *passim*; slow violence from on plantations, 221
coconut palm, 247
coconuts, 166, 186, 197, 245, 254, 264. *See also* copra
coffee, as crop in Cuba, 299n48; as crop in Malaya, 200, 204; as crop in São Tomé, 222, 223, 224, 227, 228
Cole, Major, 161
Colegio de Santa Cruz, 59, 61, 62, 63, 65, 72, 76, 77
Collor, Lindolfo, 290
colonato system. See *colonos*
colonialism, 218, 219, 221, 247, 252, 264
colonies, Atlantic world, 58, 68; British, 4–6, 13; Congo, 237; definitions of, 17; French, 226; ideal, 46; penal, 245–265 *passim;* Portuguese, 225, 230, 240n35
*colono*s (Cuba), compared to Brazilian counterparts, 285, 289–290, 295; distinctions among, 279, 283, 290; origins of workers, 283; protections for, 287, 289, 298n34; relationship to factory work, 279, 280, 282, 293; definition, 283, 289
Congo Free State, 220, 221, 222, 223, 227, 228, 231, 233
Congo, Belgium. *See* Mayombe
Connacht (Ireland), survey of, 36, 41, 42; transplantation int0, 30, 34, 35, 39–42

Copeland, Edwin, 246, 247, 256–260, 265
copra, 254, 266n2; as export commodity, 245, 246, 256, 258, 263, 264, 265; described, 255–256; production of, 260–262. *See also* coconuts
corregimiento, 61–62, 66–70, 78–79. *See also* encomienda
Cortés, Hernán, 67, 80n12
cotton, gin, 125, 129; plantations, 123; production, 127–128, 131, 135, 136, 141n53, 236–237, 250
Cotton, Sir Henry J. S., 310
County Kerry, 42, 43
Cromwell, Oliver, 30, 32
Cromwellian policy, 30, 32, 33, 34–35, 37, 39–40
Cuban American Sugar Company, 283
Cummins Ranch, 100
Cummins, John Adams Kuakini, 14, 87, *91,* 98. *See also* Waimānalo Plantation
Cummins, Thomas, 95

d'Ursel, Hippolyte, 232, 233
Davis Bend, 121, 122, 123, 125–128, 129, 131, 133, 137n2; as refugee camp, 122; multiple plantations at, 138n12; principles of management of, 123–124, 126, 130, 135, 136
Davis, Joseph Emory, 121–125, 128–136
de Fuenleal, Sebastián Ramírez, 61, 69
de Guzmán, Beltrán Nuño, 67, 68
de la Cruz, Martín, 62, 70
de Mendoza, Antonio, 59, 61, 63, 65, 69, 71, 77, 78, 79
de Mendoza, Francisco, 59, 63, 71
de Ovando, Fray Nicolás, 66
de Zumárraga, Juan, 61, 68
debt bondage, 4
Diderrich, Norbert, 233
Donadieu, Joseph, 188
Down Survey (1654–1658), 30, 32, 33–34, 41, 46–48
drought, 189, 195, 198–199, 288, 315
Dunstan, Wyndham R., 167–168

East India Company. *See* English East India Company
El Niño events, 198–199
elephants, as aids to labor, 193
encomienda, 57–61, 65–71, 77–78
English East India Company, 183, 186
entomology, 147, 158–160

fertilizers, 100, 194; chemical, 200, 212n103; guano, 194, 200
ficus elastica (rubber fig), 146, 147, 149, 151, *152,* 153–157, 161, 163–166, 169–172; pests, *159,* U.S. cultivation attempts, 159; vernacular knowledge of, 151, 152
fieldwork, definition of, 247. *See also* civil scientists
Finlay, James, 306
Finlays (trading company), 306–307, 308, 312, 314, 317, 319–320
Finsch, Otto, 103
firewood, 192, 197
Fisher, W. R., 154, 166
Floyer, Ernest A., 155
Force Publique (Congo), 221, 222, 228, 229, 233
Franciscans, 59, 61, 68, 70, 78
freedmen, 126, 127, 128
Fukien (China), 187
Funtumia elastica, 154, 156

Gibson, Walter Murray, 107
Gonsalves, Joaquin A., 88

Great Māhele (Hawai'i), 94
Gross Survey. *See* Survey, Gross
guano, 100, 194, 200
Guerra y Sánchez, Ramiro, 285, 287, 293, 294

Hanley, Thomas, 253, 256
Harris, John, 236
Hartlib, Samuel, 32, 34, 35, 37, 45, 46, 51n38
Hawai'i, 13–14, 92, 93–104; chants, see *mele;* homesteading in, 17–18; monarchy, 92, 106, 108–109. See also *ali'i; mele;* Waimānalo Plantation
Hawaiian Patriotic League, 109
herbals. See *Badianus Herbal*
Hevea brasiliensis (rubber tree), 145, 147, 151, 157
Ho'oulu Lāhui, 107
hoe digging (*changkoling*), 193
Hopkinson, Henry, 154
Horsman, Edward, 189
Hui Aloha 'Aina. *See* Hawaiian Patriotic League
Humphreys, John, 42–43, 44, 132
Hurricane Plantation. *See* Brierfield Plantation

Ibáñez, Francisco Feliciano, 278–279
Imperial Institute (London), 167, 168
indentured labor. *See* labor, indentured
Indian Immigration Ordinance, 192
Indian Tea Association (ITA), 304
Indonesia, 157, 170
insects, and rubber trees, 158–160
Institut Colonial International (ICI), 15–16
Institute for Sugar and Alcohol (IAA), 285, 291, 292–294. *See also* Lima Sobrino, Barbosa
International Banking Corporation (IBC), 262
International Labor Organization, 17
Ireland, plantation history in, 6, 13, 30–31, 32
irrigation, 125, 205
Irwin, William G., 109, 110

Jacques, Auguste, 217, 233, 235, 236
Java, 184, 190, 193, 194, 195, 199, 200, 201, 204, 252, 264

Kahalewai, Rebecca, 96
Kalākaua, King, 88, 89, 99, 107
Kedah, 194, 196; River, 186; Sultanate of, 184, 186
Kekalo, Mary Rose, 101
Kekelaokalani, Fanny, 106
Kew Gardens, 149, 153, 200
Killing Valley Tea Estate, 308
Knutsford, Lord, 154

labor, 4; African, 4, 6, 18, 111, 218, 222–223, 236; African-American, 124–136; Afro-Caribbean, 280–283; Afro-Cuban, 280–283; Afro-Brazilian, 287–289; Chinese, 92, 95, 99, 101–104, 109, 185–187, 190–194, 204, 206n9, 206n18; contract, 99, 103, 107, 221, 225; economics of, 193–194; European, 92, 101, 102; family model of, 250; for cane, 289; for cocoa, 236; for rubber, *152*, 165–166; German, 101; Hawaiian, 101–102, indentured, 4, 16, 17, 88, 92, 101–103, 105, 107, 185, 190, 191–192, 204, 256, 309, 310, 320; Indigenous, 57–79, 101–102, 147, 149, 152, 162–165, 167, 195, 203, 225, 249, 251, 256; Indian, 148–150, *152*, 165–166, 185, 191, 192, 304–321; Irish, 33–48; Javan,

190; Malay, 185–187, 190, 192, 196; Micronesian, 102; migration schemes, 101, 107, 109; legislation, 311; Philippine, 246–248, 250–251, 257–258, 264–265; Portuguese, 88, 101; racialized, 2, 3, 6, 7, 101, 102, 219. *See also* Payment of Wages Act of 1936
Lacourt, Victorien, 227–231
Lamao Botanical Garden and Reserve, 252–253, 254, 270n38
land tenure systems, Hawaiian, 94; Indigenous Mexico, 71, 76, 79
latifundio, 291, 292, 293
Laurent, Emile, 222–223
Le Montais Giffard, Walter, 110
Leopold II, 220–221
Léopoldville (Kinshasa), 228
libertos, 287–289, 299n49
Light, Francis, 186
Lima Sobrino, Barbosa, 285, 292, 293, 294, 300n60
Louwers, Octave, 233
Low, James, 187, 193, 194
Lushai, Hills, 161–162; people, 161–162

Madeira (Portugal), as source of plantation labor, 88
Makaïa-Vuabi (plantation), *235*
Malacca (Straits Settlement), 186, 188, 197, 198, 199
malaria, 248, 249
Malays, 186, 187, 190, 192, 195, 196, 207n28
Manihot glaziovii (Ceara rubber), 156
Mann, Gustav, 153–154
Mansiri River, 163
marriage, Hawaiʻi, 93, 95, 100
Marwari (kayas), 162, 167
Masui, Theodore
Mayombe (Africa), 217–218, 221–222, 231, *232,* 233, *234–235,* 236, 237
mele, 89–90
Merrill, Elmer D., 252, 253, 269n32
Merseberg, Elizabeth Kapeka, 96
meteorology and climate science, 157, 199
Mexico, 57, 58, 60, 61, 63, 68, 69, 71, 77, 79. *See also* Nahua
Micronesia. *See* migrants to Hawaii, from Micronesia
migrants, 92, 100, 102, 108
Mirrless, Tait, and Watson (firm), 99, 104
missionaries, Franciscan, 78; in Hawaiʻi, 93, 94, 107
Moloney, Sir Alfred, 154
Montgomery, Benjamin T., 122, 123, 125, 127, 128–130, 131–136
Montgomery, Isaiah, 122, 124
Montgomery, William Thornton, 122

Nahua, 547, 59, 60, 62, 65, 71, 75–79. See also *Badianus Herbal*
National Liberal Party (Hawaiʻi), 108
National Reform Party (Hawaiʻi), 108
New Harmony (Indiana), 121, 122, 124
New Lanark, 121, 124, 125, 135
nutmeg, 186, 196, 198

Office of Foreign Seed and Plant Introduction (OFSPI), 251, 252
Owen, Robert. *See* Owenism
Owenism, 121–125, 127–128, 130, 134, 135, 136, 137n4, 138n16

Papaliʻaiʻaina, Kaumakaokane, 95
Parker, Samuel, *91,* 96
Payment of Wages Act of 1936, 311, 234n44. *See also* labor, legislation
penal farms and prisons (Philippines), 245–246, 249, 253–255, 258,

penal farms and prisons (Philippines) *(continued)*
262–265; as spaces of labor control, 248
Perak (Malaysia), 190, 198, 204–205
Pernambuco (Brazil), cane farmers and workers, 287, 290, 292, 293
Pernambuco Cane Supplier's Association, 291–292
Penang Island, 183–184, 186–188, 190, 194, 196, 198, 199, 201
Penang Sugar Company, 185, 202, 205, 207n26
pepper, 186, 191, 195–196
Petty, William, 31–33, 34, 35–46
Philippine Bureau of Agriculture, 251, 252, 253, 254, 255, 262
Philippines, 245–247, 264; copra exports from, 258; ideal for coconut production, 245; oil refining in, 263; U.S. foothold in, 252. *See also* penal farms and colonies (Philippines)
Phoenix Guano Islands Company, 100
photography, in Hawai'i 88–89; role as important medium for documentation, 259
Pierce, W. Dwight, 159
plantation knowledge, defined and characterized, 2, 13, 14; development in 20th century, 15–16; global circulation of, 184; stakes of, 8–11
plantation science, defined and characterized, 10, 11; examples of, 146
plantation societies. *See* names of individual groups
Plantationocene, 10
plantations, across historical eras, 29; ambiguities inherent in, 90–91, 237; as experiments, 14, 15–16, 89, 91, 92, 95, 98–108, 111, 122–124, 126–128, 131–132, 134, 135–136, 138n16; as sites for discipline, 16, 98, 226; 233, 234, 253, 264; as sites for exploitation, 3, 4, 8, 18, 58–60, 65, 68, 110, 125, 150, 235; as sites for innovation, 8, 13, 31, 37, 201; as sites of knowledge production, 8–9, 19, 29, 60–61, 123, 135, 136, 160; as sites of racialized labor, 2–3, 6, 7, 8, 11, 17, 47, 101, 102, 103, 222–223, 258–259; as sites of welfare relief, 317–319; definitions of, 1, 2, 6, 7, 110, 111; early modern, 9, 10, 13, 29, 30, 31; soil quality of, 5, 109, 186–187, 193, 196–197, 200, 218, 254, 256, 280; working conditions on, 4, 16, 17, 124, 293, 303, 305, 316, 319, 320. *See also* labor; names of individual plantations; types of plantations by product and region
Pratt, Franklin Seaver, 99–100, 104
Protestantism, 30, 33, 35, 41, 45, 46
Province Wellesley (Seberang Perai), 183, 186, 209n64; end of sugar cultivation in, 184, 204, 205; global interest in, 187, 195, 203; local interactions, 185, 190; natural advantages of, 192; *rumah kechil* system, 191; use of fertilizers in, 194; use of technologies, 201–202; weather at, 198–199

Railroads used in plantation operations, 89, 90, 98, 104–105, 193, 217, 231, 233, 282, 295
Ramsden, Sir John William, 189
Rayner, G. E., 319
Reciprocity Treaty, Hawai'i-U.S., 96–97; Spanish-U.S., 275
"red rubber" scandal, 218
Reform Party (Hawai'i), 108
repartimiento, 67

Restoration, 30, 45, 48
Ribbentrop, Berthold, 166
rice, as crop, 104, 183, 189, 200, 201, 205
Richmond, Thomas, 253
Ridley, Henry N., 157
Rionda, Manuel, 280, 282, 286
Rithet, Robert Paterson, 109
Rose, Myron J., 101
Royaux, Louis Joseph, 235
rubber plants, 148, 156–157, 171, 221. *See also* individual species of latex-producing plants

San Miguel Estate, *255, 257, 259*
São Tomé plantation, 218, 219, 224, 225, 226, 228, 229, 230, 233, 236
Schlich, Wilhelm, 154
Scribner, Frank Lamson, 251–252, 254
"second slavery," 9
Seward, W. T., 110
Siemens Brothers, 168
slave trade, trans-Atlantic, 221, 223–224
Smith, Lewis, 42–44, 54n79
Société Anonyme d'Agriculture et de Plantations du Congo, 231. *See also* names of individual plantation societies
Spanish Crown, 57–59, 65, 66, 68, 69, 71, 77–78, 248, 251, 275
Stanley, Henry Morton, 220
Stebbing, E. P., 158–159
Stewart, M. L., 262
Strafford Survey. *See* Survey, Strafford
Straits Settlements, 186, 188, 192, 199, 200, 201, 204
Sugar Coordination Law, 1937 (Cuba), 293–294
sugar, and *colono* system, 275, 276, 282–283, 285, 286–287, 289, 295; and quotas, 277, 285, 293; cane farmers, 275–277, 279, 283, 285–287, 290–295; cane varieties, 194–195; diseases in cane, 195, 198, 199, 282; milling and manufacturing of, 185, 194, 200, 201, 202; production in Brazil, 275–278, 288, 290, 293–295; production in Cuba, 275–280, 283, 285–287, 291, 293; production in Hawai'i, 87–111 *passim*; production in Penang, 188, 192, 199, 202, 203, 204; raw, 200, 202
Sugar-cane Growing Statute, 1941 (Brazil), 292
Sultanate of Kedah, 184
Sumatra, 186–187, 192
supply chains, 38, 97, 304
Survey, Civil, 35, 36; Gross, 35, 36; Strafford, 36

Tapioca, 184, 190, 193, 197
Taxation, 71, 228, 229, 307, 308, 312
tea, 305–310, 312, 316, 317–321; as agricultural vs industrial enterprise, 308; legal verdicts, 308; production, 18, 303, 304, 314–315, 317; replaced by other crops, 166, 171. *See also* Indian Tea Association (ITA)
Tea Districts Labour Association (TDLA), 312, 313
Teochew (China), 187
Theobroma cacao. See cocoa
Tlatoani, 76
tobacco, 192, 200, 228
Toohy, D. J., 99, 105
trading posts and companies. *See* by individual name
T'Serclaes de Wommersom, Charles de, 217–218

Valeriano, Antonio, 77
Van Horne, William, 280
Vann, James, 111

Vargas, Getúlio, 285–286, 291–292
Virginia, plantation history in, 29–30, 126, 136. *See also* plantations, early modern
von Liebig, Justus, 200

Waieleele, 99
Waimānalo Plantation, 87–91, 97–107, 109–110
weapons, 222
White, John R., 250
Wilcox, Robert, 108
Withard, B. M., 104
Worcester, Dean Conant, 245–246, 252b 258–259, 261–263
Workman's Compensation Act. *See* labor, legislation
World War I, 16–17, 282
Worsley, Benjamin, 35–36, 37
Wray, Leonard, 188, 192, 193, 196, 201, 202, 203
Wright, Francis, 122

Xochimilco (Mexico), 69, 70–71